The Microfinance Revolution

Sustainable Finance for the Poor

© 2001 by the International Bank for Reconstruction and Development/THE WORLD BANK
1818 H Street, NW, Washington, D.C. 20433 USA

The findings, interpretations, and conclusions expressed in this book are entirely those of the author and should not be attributed in any manner to Open Society Institute or to the World Bank, its affiliated organizations, or members of its Board of Executive Directors or the countries they represent

Library of Congress Cataloging-in-Publication Data

Robinson, Marguerite S., 1935–
    The microfinance revolution: sustainable finance for the poor / Marguerite S. Robinson.
        p. cm.
    Includes bibliographical references.
    ISBN 0–8213–4524–9
        1. Microfinance—Developing countries. 2. Microfinance. 3. Financial institutions—Developing countries. 4. Poor—Developing countries. I. Title.

    HG178.33.D44 R63 2001
    332.2—dc21
                                                                            2001026146

Edited, designed, and laid out by Communications Development Incorporated, Washington, D.C. and San Francisco, California

The Microfinance Revolution

Sustainable Finance for the Poor

Lessons from Indonesia

The Emerging Industry

Marguerite S. Robinson

The World Bank, Washington, D.C.

Open Society Institute, New York

Praise for *The Microfinance Revolution*

"Dr. Robinson has written a magnificent work that provides a jolt of energy as well as wise guidance to the fledgling microfinance industry. This book will quickly become required reading for students and professionals in and around the microfinance industry, for donors and government agencies, and for investors. This is also the first book that, through thoughtful analysis, vivid images, and extensive research, will beckon commercial bankers and the rest of the 'real world' to sit up and take interest in microfinance. It will thus be a potent force in fusing the small scale, donor-driven microfinance of today with the formal financial systems of tomorrow—systems that will provide high-quality financial services on a permanent and ever increasing scale to millions of poor households around the world."

—*Elizabeth Littlefield, Chief Executive Officer, Consultative Group to Assist the Poorest; Director, World Bank; and former Managing Director, JP Morgan*

"*The Microfinance Revolution* is a magnificent contribution to the theory and practice of international development. It is a much-needed wake-up call for economists who have long pooh-poohed the potential of microfinance institutions for promoting savings and investment and alleviating poverty. Likewise, it will alert advocates of subsidized microfinance that the financial needs of the vast majority of the poor can be met by commercially based microlending."

—*David E. Bloom, Clarence James Gamble Professor of Economics and Demography, Harvard University*

"Marguerite Robinson has produced a major work that will unquestionably lie at the very center of microfinance literature for many years to come. Dr. Robinson is uniquely qualified, having spent many years living in tiny villages as an anthropologist, seeing informal finance as it happens, and having spent many years advising top policymakers on how to design effective financial services for the poor, most notably in Indonesia with Bank Rakyat Indonesia projects. Her account of the paradigm shift in microfinance is both exhaustively researched and provocative. She has a wonderful ear for stories; her book is full of marvelous phrases, excerpts, and anecdotes from the world of poor people's finance, in addition to being a wellspring of quantitative documentation for the trends about which she writes. Highly recommended!"

—*Robert Peck Christen, Senior Adviser, Consultative Group to Assist the Poorest; Academic Director, Microfinance Training Program, Naropa University, Boulder, Colorado*

"*The Microfinance Revolution* is an ambitious achievement that will be the definitive work on microfinance now and for some time to come. In clear, convincing, and often elegant language, Marguerite Robinson gives us the fruits of her deep experience and painstaking research. This book provides the most complete statement existing on how microfinance arose, how it works, and why it matters. *The Microfinance Revolution* views microfinance from the commercial or financial systems perspective. Robinson sets microfinance in its correct place as one important tool in the 'poverty alleviation toolbox.' In so doing she dispels the fuzzy myths surrounding the image of microfinance

as a panacea for poverty. Every microfinance professional will want a copy of this work as a comprehensive reference for the field. Every policymaker or donor will be remiss if he or she makes decisions about microfinance without first internalizing Dr. Robinson's messages."
—*Elisabeth Rhyne, Senior Vice President, ACCIÓN International; former Director, Office of Microenterprise Development, U.S. Agency for International Development; author,* Mainstreaming Microfinance: How Lending to the Poor Began, Grew and Came of Age in Bolivia

"*The Microfinance Revolution* is a tour de force remarkable both for the breadth of its vision and for the wealth of experience it captures. Dr. Robinson folds page after page of telling information about real people and their financial behavior, and about real institutions and their achievements, into a vigorously argued—and sometimes controversial—synthesis. Anyone interested in financial services for poor people should read it."
—*Richard Rosenberg, Senior Adviser, Consultative Group to Assist the Poorest*

"Marguerite Robinson's book succeeds admirably in presenting and analyzing the fundamentals of microlending and mobilizing savings among the poor. In distilling the essence of microfinance, Dr. Robinson demonstrates with extraordinary clarity that the application of commercial principles to microfinance ensures the long-lasting capacity of institutions to reach those previously excluded from financial services. This book combines the detailed, painstaking research of a noted scholar with the experiences of successful microfinance institutions around the globe, and provides a view of remarkable scope and exceptional weight. Dr. Robinson's work is not only an essential contribution to our current understanding of microfinance, but also a key resource for laying out the future of this field."
—*María Otero, President and Chief Executive Officer, ACCIÓN International*

"If you read *Finance at the Frontier,* published in 1991, you should read *The Microfinance Revolution,* published in 2001. If you did not read *Finance at the Frontier* and you seek an authoritative source about microfinance, you should still read *The Microfinance Revolution.*"
—*J.D. Von Pischke, President, Frontier Finance International; author,* Finance at the Frontier

"Marguerite Robinson has spent 20 years at the cutting edge of microfinance. In this book Marguerite gives us a history lesson and a guide on how to build commercial finance that fits the needs of the world's poor majority. Policymakers, finance leaders, and anyone who wants to join this revolution in banking must read this book."
—*Nancy M. Barry, President, Women's World Banking*

"In the past five years the enormous promise of access to capital as an effective tool for the world's poor has erupted into the world's consciousness. But the facts have often come intertwined with myth and legend, until oft-repeated misinformation threatens today to debase the accomplishments of truth. In this fog Marguerite Robinson's book, *The Microfinance Revolution,* arrives as a beacon. In it she combines her exten-

sive first-hand experience, gained initially in Asia and then around the world, with the intellectual rigor of the first-rate scholar she also is. The result is a rare, comprehensive look at microfinance that is long on analysis and short on sound bites. By asking the right questions and seeking the tough answers around the globe, she expands our understanding even though we in the field might from time to time squirm in our seats. In the process she has presented all of us who are seriously committed to the field—practitioners, policymakers, academics, public servants, and most of all, the poor of the world—a wonderful gift of intellect and expertise."
—*Michael Chu, Chair, Capital Markets; former President and Chief Executive Office, ACCIÓN International; former Chairman of the Board, BancoSol*

"This book tells a long overdue story—that of commercial microfinance institutions. It highlights the world's most efficient rural microfinance institution, Bank Rakyat Indonesia's microbanking system. Marguerite Robinson provides extensive analysis of the remarkable traits that have made microbanking at BRI an unprecedented success, detailing its policies, creative mode of operations and incentives for clients and staff, and training programs. This program has achieved massive outreach to millions of low-income clients, providing clients with both savings and credit services. All this has been accomplished in the past decade without subsidies; in fact, it is a highly profitable operation. BRI's path-breaking achievements have often been overshadowed by other, overpublicized programs. *The Microfinance Revolution* is a timely publication that clearly demonstrates the tremendous potential embedded in well-designed microfinance programs."
—*Jacob Yaron, Senior Rural Finance Adviser, World Bank; author,* Successful Rural Financial Institutions

"For more than 20 years Marguerite Robinson has been at the forefront of the 'microfinance revolution' she documents so lucidly and persuasively in this book. She was deeply involved in the transformation and development of Bank Rakyat Indonesia's microbanking (unit *desa*) system, now the largest microfinance institution in the world with more than 20 million clients. This book brings together the author's wealth of practice-based wisdom and draws on her experience of working with institutions all over the world. It is a valuable, important, and necessary addition to the library of anyone seriously interested in microfinance."
—*Graham A. N. Wright, Programme Director, MicroSave-Africa; author,* Microfinance Systems

"Marguerite Robinson has written a wonderful book. Its declared aim is to make the case for large-scale commercial microfinance, a cause that Dr. Robinson champions with passion, logic, and plentiful examples from her years of experience. But in the process she sheds light on a host of important and contentious issues in microfinance, and the outcome is a work that will enormously enrich the debates it is bound to engender."
—*Stuart Rutherford, Chairman, SafeSave; author,* The Poor and Their Money

This book is dedicated to all those who have led the microfinance revolution around the world.

I add a special, personal dedication to those in Indonesia who developed large, financially self-sufficient microfinance institutions. For the first time in history, they made commercial microbanking available on a large scale to low-income people.

Ali Wardhana
Sugianto, in memoriam
Kamardy Arief
I Gusti Made Oka
Sri Adnyani Oka

About the author

Marguerite S. Robinson is a social anthropologist and internationally recognized expert on microfinance. She received her B.A. and Ph.D. from Harvard University and served as professor of anthropology and dean of the College of Arts and Sciences at Brandeis University before joining the Harvard Institute for International Development, where she worked from 1978–2000. She has worked extensively in rural areas and among the urban poor in India, Sri Lanka, and Indonesia—where she served for many years as an adviser to the Ministry of Finance and to Bank Rakyat Indonesia. She has also worked in Latin American and Africa, advising governments, banks, and donors, and is the author of many papers and books on development and microfinance.

Contents

Tables

Figures

Boxes

Foreword

Occasionally one meets someone with deep expertise in her chosen field. But rarely does one meet such a person who can also explain her views with equal ease to both other experts in the field and to other interested parties without prior knowledge of the field, such as government policymakers, central bank governors, or even members of the general public. Marguerite Robinson is such a person, having acquired deep knowledge of microfinance over some 20 years. She has worked primarily in Indonesia, advising the government and helping to create Bank Rakyat Indonesia's unit *desa* system, one of the world's most successful microfinance programs. But Dr. Robinson has also provided her expertise to policymakers and directors of microfinance institutions in many other countries, including Bolivia, China, India, Kenya, Tanzania, and Vietnam—to name just a few.

Dr. Robinson came to microfinance with a rich academic and professional background as an anthropologist, having spent many years in villages in India, Indonesia, and Sri Lanka. She describes herself as a financial anthropologist, given her unique credentials to understand both people—particularly poor people in remote villages or urban slums not normally served by financial institutions—and financial markets, and how the two interact. Few people have come to microfinance with such tools of the trade, and Dr. Robinson has honed those tools with long stints in Indonesia and other countries studying, observing, researching, teaching, writing, and practicing microfinance.

Now Dr. Robinson has bundled all that knowledge, and the result is a seminal work on microfinance that offers readers a richness and depth about the field that have long been needed. This long overdue book, *The Microfinance Revolution,* consists of three volumes. The first focuses on the paradigm shift in mi-

This seminal work offers readers a richness and depth on microfinance that have long been needed

crofinance, the second concentrates on microfinance in Indonesia, and the third (written with Peter J. Fidler) looks at the global experience with microfinance and documents the move to commercially viable microfinance.

The microfinance field is not short on information. There are scores of case studies on microfinance institutions; technical, financial, and practical guides to the field; and wonderful reports on savings, interest rates, client desertion and delinquency, supervision, audit, appraisal, planning, and management information systems for microfinance institutions. There are also works on the impact of microfinance on poverty and some selective works on theory. We have all the bits and pieces, but no one has really seamed it all together. No one has provided an overview of how the industry has developed and where it is headed. And no one has provided an overarching theory that supports these views—until now. Marguerite Robinson does all that and more. The third volume, *The Emerging Industry,* provides a global view on microfinance in developing countries (excluding the transition economies of Central and Eastern Europe and the former Soviet Union, which Dr. Robinson decided not to cover due to her lack of experience in the region). That volume also explores theory and the evolution of thinking on this subject.

This book contains wonderful anecdotal richness supported by a wealth of facts, figures, tables, notes, and citations

This book also contains wonderful anecdotal richness on a variety of microfinance themes: on microfinance institutions, on the voices of microfinance clients, on savings, and on moneylenders, as well as a unique assessment of Indonesia that makes up the second volume, *Lessons from Indonesia.* This rich anecdotal material is supported by a wealth of facts, figures, tables, notes, and citations reflecting Dr. Robinson's academic rigor, a rigor that has rarely been brought to this field.

The book's detail and richness are spun into a fine web supporting the author's basic thesis—that a fundamental shift is occurring in microfinance, inexorably pushing the industry to focus on commercially viable microfinance. This thesis and a detailed explanation supporting it are the main subject of the first volume, *Sustainable Finance for the Poor.* Only by making this shift, says Dr. Robinson, can microfinance fill the "absurd gap" between the demand for and supply of microfinance services. That gap is huge: at least 80 percent of the 900 million households in low- and lower-middle-income countries do not have access to formal financial services.

Most microfinance institutions are nongovernmental organizations (NGOs), often providing an array of social services. They focus on microfinance as a social intervention or a poverty alleviation tool. They see a dilemma between achieving commercial viability and serving the poor. For the most part they are not viable financial institutions and do not mobilize domestic savings or raise commercial funds. And they are largely dependent on donors to subsidize their operations. Yet the microfinance industry barely scratches the surface of its market potential, and the industry as currently structured cannot meet this need.

But increasingly, as spelled out in this book, commercially viable microfinance institutions are being established as banks or nonbank financial institutions. They operate from a financial systems perspective, and they see microfinance as filling an important niche in the financial system by providing financial services—for profit—to the working poor. The only way to close the absurd gap between demand and supply in microfinance is for microfinance institutions to mobilize savings, to raise capital commercially, and to service clients through extensive branch networks. This is increasingly the case in Latin America, as illustrated by the book's analysis of Bolivia's BancoSol. It is also true for a few large microfinance institutions in Asia, such as Bangladesh's Association for Social Advancement. Bank Rakyat Indonesia's unit desa system best illustrates the benefits of long-term adherence to commercial principles of microfinance, which is why this case is an important contribution of this book.

Let me try to sum up what this work offers to readers:

- A detailed overview of the development of microfinance over the past 20 years.
- A global view of microfinance in the developing world.
- A thesis on the future path of microfinance.
- A coherent theory about microfinance—why it works when so many other development interventions fail.
- Exquisite detail on a number of important microfinance topics—such as informal moneylending and savings.
- An important study of Indonesia, with detailed analysis of Bank Rakyat Indonesia.
- Brief studies of many other microfinance institutions in Africa, Asia, and Latin America.

This book reflects Marguerite Robinson's longstanding experience in microfinance. Readers will quickly understand that Dr. Robinson is one of the few people with deep knowledge in her chosen field—as well as the ability to convey that knowledge simply and clearly to a broad range of interested readers.

The author's basic thesis is that a fundamental shift is occurring in microfinance, inexorably pushing the industry to focus on commercially viable microfinance

Ira W. Lieberman
Former Chief Executive Officer,
  Consultative Group to Assist the Poorest, 1995–99
Senior Manager, World Bank

Introduction

We in Indonesia have a special, longstanding interest in the emerging microfinance revolution, which has made it possible for large numbers of low-income people to access institutional financial services—often for the first time. Financial services that are widely available in rural areas and in low-income urban neighborhoods help the poor improve their financial security, allow them to take advantage of business opportunities, and facilitate the growth of their enterprises. In Indonesia sustainable microfinance in the formal sector began in 1970 with the opening of Bank Dagang Bali (BDB), a private bank in Bali, and attained nationwide coverage with the 1984 restructuring of the unit *desa,* or local banking, system of the state-owned Bank Rakyat Indonesia (BRI).

BRI's unit desa system is now the largest financially self-sufficient provider of sustainable microfinance in the developing world. Indonesia's approach to microfinance—making it profitable, and so widely available—helped the country reduce the incidence of poverty from about 40 percent of the population in the mid-1970s to about 11 percent in 1996. In 1997, when the East Asian economic crisis began and poverty in Indonesia started to rise, BRI's microfinance system helped poor people who had lost their jobs finance informal sector enterprises. It also gave them secure and convenient deposit facilities—especially important to poor people in times of crisis.

Hindsight is, as we all know, a powerful analytical tool. In reviewing the restructuring of BRI's microbanking system, one can identify a number of components that might better have been done differently. In the 1970s, for example, BRI opened more than 3,500 village units to channel subsidized government credit to rice farmers through BIMAS, the credit component of Indonesia's massive

We in Indonesia have a special, longstanding interest in the emerging microfinance revolution

rice intensification program. As it turned out, the rice intensification program was highly successful, but its credit component was not. The long-term results of BIMAS were similar to those found in many developing countries. The subsidized loans, being at below-market interest rates and so in demand by wealthier farmers, often did not reach poor farmers. Moreover, arrears and losses were high. The program was phased out in 1985. Meanwhile, BRI's unit desa system also tried to mobilize savings. However, since the government required that banks lend at 12 percent and pay 15 percent on most deposits, there was a negative incentive for the banks to mobilize savings—and the incentive structure worked well!

During the 1970s and 1980s rural borrowers who qualified for loans larger than those available at the unit desas also had the option of obtaining subsidized government credit through bank branches in district capitals. The Small Investment Loan Program, known as KIK, and the Small Permanent Working Capital Loan Program, known as KMKP, provided loans of up to 15 million rupiah ($36,145 in 1975 and $13,333 in 1985). But these programs also resulted in high arrears and large losses to both the banks and the government, and were eventually phased out.

By the early 1980s we began to realize that year after year, the subsidies and arrears of BIMAS, KIK, and KMKP were large, the programs were inefficient, and the loans generally did not reach the intended borrowers. In brief, our approach to local finance was ineffective and unsustainable. Not only were our subsidized credit programs not driving rural development, they were actually slowing it down! Having recognized the severe deficiencies of these programs, we decided in 1983 to begin a new program for rural finance based on principles of commercial finance.

But in 1983, when the Indonesian government began to implement a variety of financial reforms, we did not have good models or examples—or even approximate ones—from other, similarly positioned countries. In many ways Indonesia was a pioneer in implementing financial reforms, and the reform of the unit desa system is a prime example. When we decided to transform it into a commercial microbanking system, we could find no example of a financial institution in any developing country that provided microfinance profitably on a large scale.

The development of commercial microbanking in BRI's unit desas can best be understood in the context of the broad set of economic reforms implemented by the Indonesian government. On the whole these reforms reflected a consistent intent to achieve three basic objectives:

- To move toward a predominantly market-based financial system.
- To provide effective protection, as needed, so that the general public could benefit from the services offered by the financial system.
- To build a financial system that would support the stable, healthy growth of the national economy.

To move effectively toward achieving these aims, in 1983 we began to introduce a series of far-reaching finance, tax, trade, and investment reforms.

The oil boom of the mid-1970s through the mid-1980s had been a mixed blessing for Indonesia. One economist, writing about oil-exporting countries, concluded that the boom left most economies no better off than they would have been if oil prices had stayed at 1972 levels in real terms. But unlike most oil exporters, Indonesia capitalized on its windfall oil revenues. Even when we had ample oil revenues, we looked ahead to days when we might not be so fortunate.

A critical element of Indonesia's development strategy has been to stimulate rural development, rural incomes, and rural employment. Thus in the 1970s a large share of our oil wealth was invested in agriculture—especially irrigation and new rice technologies—and in infrastructure, education, and health. Much of this investment was in rural areas, where about 80 percent of the population lived in the mid-1970s. This investment helped ensure that agriculture and other rural industries would continue to support rural income growth and create employment—an essential part of the foundation for our economic growth since the mid-1980s.

It is important to understand that this was not "trickle down" growth. Our approach to economic growth incorporates some of the poorest groups in the economy. Our food supply, especially rice, depends on the increasing productivity of small farmers—supported by the government's massive rural investment. Our export drive is based on the growth of firms that create jobs for low-skilled workers. Some of the country's largest industries—including construction, transportation, retail trade, and other services—employ large numbers of unskilled workers, especially in the informal sector. These service sectors are quick to respond to rapid growth in other sectors of the economy.

As the incomes of poor people rose, their demand for banking services increased. The reform of BRI's microbanking system was undertaken in order to bring about a major increase in the availability of financial services—initially for the rural population and later for low-income urban residents as well. Decisions to provide microbanking services delivered at the subdistrict level throughout the country, to pay positive real interest rates for savings, and to charge loan rates sufficient to cover all costs and to earn a reasonable profit for the bank were consistent with our overall reform agenda.

Financial reforms were extended to rural areas with the government's first major financial deregulation package, issued in 1983. That deregulation abolished credit ceilings and permitted banks to set their own interest rates on most loans and deposits. This made possible the transformation of BRI's unit desa system from a channeling agent for targeted, subsidized government loans to a profitable financial intermediary providing small loans and deposit services to clients in rural areas throughout Indonesia. In 1989 BRI extended its microbanking services to urban areas as well.

When making the decision to reform the unit desas, we asked ourselves three questions. First, would there be local demand for credit at the interest rates needed for BRI to cover all its costs and earn a profit? We studied the demand for small loans in different areas and found it to be very large. Poor borrowers were

A 1983 deregulation made possible the transformation of BRI's unit desa system from a channeling agent for targeted, subsidized government loans to a profitable financial intermediary

paying much higher interest rates to local moneylenders, and it seemed that they would generally welcome the rates that BRI would charge.

Second, would people place their savings in BRI's village units? We conducted studies in many parts of the country and found huge demand for savings services if the deposit instruments and services were designed to meet the needs of poor savers.

Third, with an eye on the government budget, we asked how long it would take for the restructured microbanking system to break even and begin to make a profit. Under the assumptions we used, we predicted that the system, which began in 1984, would break even in two years—which it did in just under two years. And it has been profitable every year since.

Our approach to reforming BRI was market-based: in BRI's thousands of local microbanking units, performance-based cash awards and other incentives motivate staff to act as bankers. Unit personnel also required training to change their behavior. Most important, unit staff had to learn about the markets they served. Responsibility for loan decisions had to be delegated from branch offices to village units, while regional offices had to de-emphasize their control-minded approach and become more oriented toward promotion. In a large, complex institution like BRI, these changes took careful planning and implementation. The restructuring of BRI's unit desa system was a major institutional reform—and it succeeded. As a result savers have a secure outlet for their funds, on which they generally earn positive real returns, while borrowers with productive uses for small loans have access to credit on commercial terms.

The BRI reforms have enjoyed remarkable success. The unit desa system has a single loan product, KUPEDES, that offers loans of 25,000–25,000,000 rupiah ($3–$3,406 in 1999) for any productive purpose. Most KUPEDES loans carry an effective annual interest rate of about 32 percent if payments are made on time. Savings instruments offer a choice between different combinations of liquidity and returns—enabling depositors to combine the products in ways that best meet their needs.

Unit desa deposits, a highly stable source of funds, finance all KUPEDES loans. The system has been profitable since 1986 and without subsidy since 1987. Contrary to much international experience with rural finance, KUPEDES has had very high repayment rates. In Indonesia we have found that a less regulated economy, with widespread access to institutional finance at the local level, can open new opportunities to people previously excluded from full participation in the country's economic growth.

But in 1997 a severe financial and economic crisis developed that affected all East Asian economies, from Thailand to Japan and the Republic of Korea. Indonesia's currency fell from 2,450 rupiah per U.S. dollar in June 1997, just before the crisis began, to about 17,000 at its weakest point in 1998. The rupiah then recovered to levels of 7,000–8,000 in the fourth quarter of 1998. At the end of 1999 there were 7,430 rupiah to the U.S. dollar. Indonesia's average annual inflation for 1998 was 57.6 percent—a sharp contrast to the 1980s, when annual inflation had stayed below 10 percent. GDP, which had grown by more than 7 percent a year

The BRI reforms have enjoyed remarkable success. The system has been profitable since 1986 and without subsidy since 1987

for over a decade, grew just 4.9 percent in 1997 and fell 13.7 percent in 1998. But in 1999 inflation dropped to 20.5 percent, while GDP rose to 0.2 percent.

The economic meltdown that hit Indonesia—and one can hardly describe it differently—had multiple causes. Some were self-inflicted; others were external. Among the external events I would list the sharp decline in the world oil price, a decline in prices for other primary product exports, and a serious drought in 1997. But to explain the severity of Indonesia's economic crisis relative to that of our neighbors, we have to look at internal weaknesses. Let me highlight two.

First, our financial institutions were encouraged to fund risky, unprofitable ventures. Government officials could and did direct loans to favored firms and activities. Loans were rarely subjected to even the most rudimentary economic and financial analysis. Second, the involvement of well-connected parties in many economic activities led to a problem of moral hazard: in the presence of a perceived guarantee, implicit or explicit, there is little incentive to avoid risky behavior. In addition, actions by the government and the central bank suggested that Indonesian banks would be protected from failure. Our foreign exchange regime also encouraged risky behavior that, after the depreciation of the rupiah, resulted in unmanageable debt that effectively bankrupted a substantial portion of our corporations.

At this writing more than two years have passed since Indonesia's crisis began. While it may be too optimistic to say that the crisis has passed, much has been accomplished, and there is general consensus on what needs to be done to get our economy back on track. With assistance from the International Monetary Fund, World Bank, Asian Development Bank, and others, an economic reform program was introduced in 1998. Structural reforms are under way. Safety net policies to protect the poor have been given high priority. The weaknesses in the financial system have been clearly identified, a bank restructuring program is in process, and the legal and supervisory framework for the banking sector is being strengthened. Emphasis is being placed on making our capital markets more transparent and better regulated. Many other reforms are also in process.

Numerous policy measures must still be implemented, but my prediction is that the crisis will pass and growth will resume. In the 1980s and 1990s the rapidly growing Asian economies created a base of human and physical infrastructure, and that base remains intact. It is on this base that we will eventually be able to resume rapid growth.

While it has been important to identify our weaknesses in order to rebuild the Indonesian economy, it is also important to identify the institutions that remained strong throughout the crisis and to understand the reasons for their strength and stability. One of those institutions is related to the subject of this book: commercial, sustainable microfinance.

In sharp contrast to the Indonesian banking sector generally, commercial microbanking at BRI's unit desa system continued its wide outreach, high repayment rate, and profitability throughout 1997–99. The system remained stable and profitable throughout the crisis. Deposits in the unit desas more than

The economic meltdown that hit Indonesia in 1997—and one can hardly describe it differently—had multiple causes. Some were self-inflicted; others were external

doubled in rupiah terms, from 7.7 trillion rupiah ($3.2 billion) in June 1997 (the month before the crisis began) to 17.1 trillion rupiah ($2.3 billion) at the end of 1999. The number of savings accounts increased from 17.0 million in June 1997 to 24.2 million at the end of 1999.

KUPEDES lending has remained stable. In June 1997 there was 4.3 trillion rupiah outstanding ($1.75 billion) in 2.5 million KUPEDES loans. By the end of 1999 the outstanding loan balance was 6.0 trillion rupiah ($802 million) in 2.5 million loans. The repayment rate, 98 percent in June 1997, was also 98 percent in December 1999. In 1998, the worst year for the Indonesian economy in the past three decades, pretax unit desa profits were 714 billion rupiah ($89 million), while the pretax return on assets for the unit desa system was 4.9 percent. In 1999 pretax profits were 1.2 trillion rupiah ($160 million) and the pretax return on assets was 6.1 percent.

BRI's microbanking system emphasizes understanding local markets and meeting the demand for financial services from low-income households and enterprises. It provides products and services designed to be appropriate for this market segment. We now know that the unit desas are so robust that they have withstood an extraordinary national economic and financial crisis. This strength in microbanking has helped to mitigate the effects of the crisis on the poor and to improve the foundations for future economic development.

The creation of BRI's unit desa system cannot be separated from Dr. Marguerite S. Robinson. She actively participated in developing the unit desas into what is now a strong, viable microbanking system that provides financial services to low-income people in rural and urban areas throughout Indonesia. To ensure that the system would function effectively for local communities—consisting largely of small farmers and microentrepreneurs—Dr. Robinson visited many unit desas and the villages they served. She coordinated research teams that surveyed the income flows and savings habits of local people, studied their need for capital and their demand for financial services, and assessed opportunities for investment in the community. The studies covered villages in Java, Sumatra, Kalimantan, Sulawesi, and other Indonesian islands, and resulted in ongoing recommendations to the Ministry of Finance and the BRI about unit desa instruments and services that would be appropriate for local demand.

When decisions were made to add new savings and loan products and services in the unit desa system, to open new units, or to expand unit desa operations to urban neighborhoods, Dr. Robinson advised BRI, assisting with staff training and advising on the management and supervision of unit operations. She has often returned to the units to learn whether they function properly and to advise BRI on the development of its microbanking system.

BRI's unit desa system has made great progress since 1984, rapidly becoming a financial institution capable of contributing to rural development and rural employment. It has also expanded to serve low-income urban areas. At the same time, the unit desas have a considerable way to go—and like many newly developed financial institutions, they face problems of institutional development.

In sharp contrast to the Indonesian banking sector generally, commercial microbanking at BRI continued its wide outreach, high repayment rate, and profitability throughout the crisis

Dr. Robinson deserves credit for her active role in creating the unit desas, not only at the initial stages of their restructuring but also during the entire period of their subsequent development. This book reflects her deep insight and thorough knowledge of BRI's unit desas.

During the 1990s BRI's unit desa system received nearly 1,000 international visitors from more than 30 countries. The bank has had to create a separate office to serve the many international visitors to the unit desas. A number of the visitors have also visited Bank Dagang Bali, well-known as the earliest bank to institute commercial microfinance, as well as some of Indonesia's other financial institutions that provide services at the village level on a commercial basis, such as the Badan Kredit Desas (Village Credit Organizations) of Java and Madura.

Many developing countries in Asia, Africa, and Latin America are at different stages of learning about and implementing institutional commercial microfinance. This book documents Indonesia's experience with sustainable microfinance, explores the spread of commercial financial services to low-income people in other countries, and analyzes the ideas that underlie both.

Indonesia, which has played a leading role in the Non-Aligned Movement, is active in transferring technology and sharing experiences that lead to economic growth, equity, and stability in the developing world. We are especially pleased that our approach to sustainable microbanking—which has provided poor people in Indonesia with new opportunities for economic growth and financial security—is useful for the development of microfinance in other developing countries.

We are especially pleased that our approach to sustainable microbanking is useful for other developing countries

Ali Wardhana
Minister of Finance, Government of Indonesia, 1968–83
Coordinating Minister for Economics, Finance, and
 Industry, Government of Indonesia, 1983–88
Economic Adviser, Government of Indonesia, 1988–

Preface

When I began life as a social anthropologist in the 1960s, carrying out field work in remote areas of developing countries in Asia, outsiders rarely visited the villages where I lived. Those who did come, other than the occasional scientist, were missionaries of various religions. Over the years I noticed that the few outsiders I encountered in the field were increasingly less likely to be missionaries—and more likely to be bankers. This gradual change was my first introduction to the then-embryonic microfinance revolution.

The bankers who began showing up in small villages on their bicycles, motorcycles, or jeeps in the 1960s and 1970s were usually employees of local branches of state-owned banks. They came along with the green revolution. Their mission, as assigned by their governments and assorted international donors, was to find trustworthy villagers to whom they could provide credit. This, it was thought, would both help feed the population and increase rural economic growth.

The bankers and the missionaries, who shared much of the same client pool, were curiously alike in some ways. Usually outsiders to the local community, both tended to discover in the villages their own preconceptions, rather than the local realities and dynamics (a problem to which, of course, anthropologists are not immune!). But many cared about helping poor people increase their incomes and improve their lives, and some were quite successful. They came with powerful ideas, found others already present, and often became catalysts for the cross-fertilization of thought and sometimes for the introduction of social and economic reforms.

I watched from villages in different countries and continents as, over the decades, the balance switched from outsiders bringing religion to outsiders bringing finance. Of course, those who lived in the villages already had both. As an

Over the years I noticed that the few outsiders I encountered in villages were less likely to be missionaries—and more likely to be bankers

ancient Indian proverb has it, a village can be formed wherever there come together "a river, a priest, and a moneylender."

During this period the idea took root in many countries that financial services should and could be made widely accessible to low-income people through the formal financial sector. The aims at first were usually to increase food production, improve rural development, and decrease rural poverty. Later the effort spread to low-income urban neighborhoods as well. Financial services are, of course, not a panacea for poverty alleviation. Other strategies are needed simultaneously, especially for very poor people who need food and employment before they can make use of financial services. Still, it became clear that finance delivered at the local level through the formal sector could have far-reaching effects on social and economic development and on poverty reduction.

During the 1970s and 1980s a few people from a variety of backgrounds—agriculture, anthropology, banking, business, economics, government service, law, public policy, religion, social work—began, in scattered locations, to learn the dynamics of local financial markets in developing countries and to consider whether and how financial institutions could operate viably in these markets. The word microfinance had not yet been coined. Work focused on what was then called rural finance, agricultural credit, nonfarm credit, cooperative credit, rural savings, microenterprise finance, and others.

The successful development of large-scale microfinance was too complex for the tools of any one discipline

The successful development of large-scale microfinance—savings and credit services for economically active low-income people in different occupations—was too complex for the tools of any one discipline. But gradually a financial systems approach developed that joined principles of commercial finance with the growing knowledge of the demand for financial services among poor people in developing countries. What resulted was a model for financing the economically active poor through profitable financial institutions.

The Emergence of the Microfinance Revolution

The emerging microfinance revolution—the large-scale provision of small loans and deposit services to low-income people by secure, conveniently located, competing commercial financial institutions—has generated the processes needed to democratize capital. (I first heard the term microfinance revolution used by María Otero and Elisabeth Rhyne in 1993.) Appropriately designed financial products and services enable many poor people to expand and diversify their economic activities, increase their incomes, and improve their self-confidence. Financial institutions knowledgeable about microfinance can become profitable and self-sustaining while achieving wide client outreach. Governments and donors no longer need to provide ongoing credit subsidies; they also need not cover the losses of state banks providing credit subsidies. Over the past 20 years these characteristics of the microfinance revolution have been demonstrated in widely differing country environments.

In the beginning, however, most of the bankers—and the economists, policy analysts, policymakers, and international donors—got it wrong. (Some still do.) The approach local bankers took when visiting villages in the 1960s and 1970s generally did not work. The bankers' actions were based on government policies rooted in economic theories that were uninformed by the realities of how local markets operate. Why many of these theories were wrong, and how the resulting development mistakes occurred, are documented and analyzed throughout the book. But this book is not a diatribe by an anthropologist against economists and bankers—far from it. At least they addressed the problem of finance for the poor. Anthropologists in villages, who often knew a lot about how local markets worked, tended to ignore the policy issues related to the poverty we so carefully studied.

The primary problem was that banks were using government or donor funds to provide subsidized credit, an approach that continues in many countries today. Because subsidized programs are constrained by their budgets, relatively few borrowers can be served. Often these are local elites with the influence to obtain rationed loans at below-market interest rates. The poor generally do without credit or borrow from informal sources. But for reasons analyzed in chapter 6, the interest rates of informal commercial moneylenders, and the total costs of such loans, are often so high that they preclude or severely limit the growth of the borrower's enterprise—or in some cases threaten its existence. In addition, most low-income households in most developing countries do not have access to secure, convenient savings services.

Donor-funded nongovernmental organizations (NGOs) were among the first to identify the vast, unmet demand for microcredit in developing countries, to develop methodologies for delivering and recovering small loans, and to begin credit programs for the poor. While many of these programs failed, some reached the poor and recovered their loans. But typically even successful programs were severely capital constrained. Unregulated and unable to access substantial amounts of commercial finance, they could normally meet only a tiny fraction of microcredit demand in the regions they served. They also usually did not provide voluntary savings services.

The best known of the early microcredit models is the poverty lending approach pioneered at Bangladesh's Grameen Bank and elsewhere. That approach first made the world aware that poor people can be good credit risks. In some cases it has enabled wide outreach to poor borrowers, especially in Bangladesh. But the poverty lending approach has required large amounts of continuing subsidies and has not proven a globally affordable model. And as its name implies, poverty lending does not meet poor people's demand for savings services. A different solution is required to meet the massive global demand for small loans and savings services. Thus this book is not about the poverty lending approach to microcredit, although the topic is discussed in the first and third volumes. It is about commercial microfinance.

Many institutions and many people were responsible for the innovative, wide-ranging contributions on which the new commercial microfinance paradigm was built. Starting in the 1970s, scattered institutions in different parts of the

In the beginning most of the bankers—and the economists, policy analysts, policymakers, and international donors—got it wrong

world began to develop commercial microfinance programs. Though the programs differed, the underlying principles were similar. Gradually, a paradigm shift took place—from the delivery of government- or donor-subsidized credit to the development of sustainable financial intermediaries that capture local savings, access commercial finance, and lend these funds to low-income borrowers at interest rates that enable full cost recovery and institutional self-sufficiency.

The microfinance revolution developed in the 1980s (before it had a name) and came of age in the 1990s. It occurred when the many advances of previous decades in market knowledge, lending methods, and savings mobilization were combined with a commercial approach to financial intermediation for low-income people, making financially sustainable formal sector microfinance possible. This breakthrough—which also required the development of organizational structures and management resources capable of delivering microfinance services profitably throughout an entire country—first occurred in Indonesia in the 1980s and then in Bolivia in the mid-1990s.

Commercial microfinance is now found in many countries, where it is at different stages of development. In its most advanced form, in banks and other formal financial institutions, all microloans are fully financed by savings, commercial debt, for-profit investment, and retained earnings (in a variety of forms and combinations). As a result all savers and all creditworthy borrowers can be served, repeat borrowers can be accommodated as they expand their enterprises and qualify for larger loans, and many economically active poor people can be helped out of poverty. Industry standards for commercial microfinance began to develop in the 1990s. And in some countries intense competition has erupted among commercial financial institutions aiming to attract the business of poor clients.

Nevertheless, in most developing countries the formal financial sector still does not serve microfinance clients. The traditional view—that it is neither important nor profitable for institutions to provide commercial financial services to low-income people—is still widely held. The microfinance revolution is still emerging. But it is probably irreversible: because there is massive unmet demand for microfinance, because it has been proven that this demand can be met profitably on a large scale, and because information about the profitability of financing the economically active poor has begun to be widely disseminated.

Microfinance in the developed world is beyond the scope of this book. But many low-income people in industrial countries lack access to financial services, also with pervasive negative effects on society and the economy. Rich countries could learn many lessons on sustainable microfinance from developing countries.

A number of people have asked whether, because this book is in three volumes, it is intended to be a reference book. While to some extent it can be used for reference, the book was not written primarily for that purpose. Rather, it is an analytical narrative on why and how capital is becoming democratized on a global scale for the first time in history. The reason the book is in three volumes is that it concerns a major revolution of our times.

Gradually, a paradigm shift took place— from the delivery of government- or donor- subsidized credit to the development of sustainable financial intermediaries

A reader who wants to learn about a particular microfinance institution—such as Bangladesh's Association for Social Advancement, Bolivia's BancoSol, or Mexico's Compartamos—can find these institutions in the indexes of these volumes and read about them. But the approach is not encyclopedic. The aim is not a comprehensive summary of the institution, but an emphasis on its contributions (and in some cases lack thereof) to the microfinance revolution.

Finance for the poor is a topic on which many opinions are held, usually passionately. This book will undoubtedly be controversial, as is intended. But microfinance is unusual. As in any emerging industry, debates are endemic. But in microfinance these debates are among people who work every day to increase the employment opportunities, incomes, and self-confidence of the poor. These are debates among good people. In presenting new data and analyses and in reexamining long-held assumptions and conclusions, this book aims at stimulating constructive dialogue—in ways that will help financial institutions meet the demand for microfinance sustainably and soon.

What Is an Anthropologist Doing in Banking?

During my first decade as an anthropologist, I conducted the kinds of research I was taught at Harvard and Cambridge universities: studying the people of different societies and recording, comparing, analyzing, writing, and teaching about their cultures and social structures. While the education I received was well suited for its multiple purposes, there was little in it to prepare me for the fact that most of the people I would study would be poor—and in some cases starving, abused, and in bonded servitude.

As part of extended field work in a very underdeveloped rural area in India, I had long conversations with many bonded laborers, members of "untouchable" castes, and others among the desperately poor and disenfranchised. Once after a long discussion, I rose to leave a small group from whom I had been learning about their social and economic activities and their political environment. We had been sitting on the mud floor of a small, crowded, windowless house that provided only minimal protection from the driving rain of the monsoon.

One of the men with whom I had been talking said to me, "We are pleased that you are interested in us, that you visit our houses, and that you sit and talk with us. We try to tell you whatever you want to know. But we would like to ask you a question. There is something that we cannot understand. We are sitting here in the mud because this is all that we have. Can you not see that we are cold and wet, and that we are poor and have nothing? But you are educated and wealthy. Why do you want only to sit here and learn about our customs? Why do you not also use your knowledge and resources to help us to have better lives and to improve our customs?"

He was right. Since then, while continuing my anthropological research, I have worked on the social and economic development of the poor people in

Finance for the poor is a topic on which many opinions are held, usually passionately. This book will undoubtedly be controversial, as is intended

the societies I try to understand. Since 1979 I have worked simultaneously as an anthropologist and as a policy adviser to governments and financial institutions.

As an anthropologist working on microfinance, I analyze local markets and their wider networks, the economic activities of their participants, and the nature and extent of the demand for financial services. My knowledge of local financial markets comes largely from those who participate in them: people of varying ages and both genders employed in a variety of occupations, from different social, economic, religious, and political backgrounds. My anthropological training stands me in good stead here. I try to learn from whom, and at what cost, they obtain credit; how their credit options are linked with transactions in other markets; in what forms and for what purposes they save; and what they like and dislike about their current methods of borrowing and saving.

In the process it becomes possible to learn how informal credit markets, government interventions, and bank programs work at the local level. The vested interests that might oppose the development of institutional commercial microfinance in particular regions can be identified, and attention can be given to how such interests can be challenged, circumvented, or co-opted. It then becomes feasible to design financial instruments and services appropriate for the social, political, and economic environment in general, and for the varied types of local demand in particular. As a policy adviser on microfinance, my role has been to learn the country's policy goals and its constraints, to provide information to decisionmakers about their country's microfinance demand and its relevance to development more broadly, and to suggest strategies to achieve policy objectives, drawing on lessons from the country's financial markets and from international best practices in commercial microfinance.

This book focuses on how the demand for microfinance can be met on a global scale

Plan of the Book

This book focuses on how the demand for microfinance can be met on a global scale. It documents the contributions of institutions and of people who have led the development of commercial finance for the poor, and it analyzes the principles on which the microfinance revolution is based. The book's intended audience is diverse, including those with interests directly related to microfinance, such as policymakers and other government officials, microfinance practitioners, social scientists, economists, bankers, and donors; those with more general interests in social and economic development and in the fundamentals of poverty reduction; and those drawn to difficult problems that can be solved only through an interdisciplinary approach.

But this book is limited in a number of ways. Among these, no attempt is made to cover all the many types of financial institutions that provide some form of finance to the poor; emphasis is placed instead on the lessons from leading commercial microfinance providers. Second, it was not possible to cover all regions. For example, Eastern Europe, which has seen important growth in microfinance since the breakup of the Soviet Union, is largely omitted from the discussion here. My impression is that microfinance in former centrally planned economies is somewhat different from microfinance in most developing countries, but I am not knowledgeable enough about transition economies to include them in the discussion. Third, this is not a "how to" book for microfinance institutions on specifics such as operations, business planning, or financial analysis—though aspects of these topics are discussed, and references are provided to excellent sources on these subjects.

Fourth, important as the topic is for poverty reduction and human rights, this book does not focus on gender issues. Many microcredit institutions have targeted poor women as clients and, as demonstrated in chapter 3 and elsewhere in the book, there is little doubt that this approach has helped women and their families increase their incomes and self-confidence. But this book is about large-scale sustainable microfinance for all economically active poor people, women and men.

Fifth, except for what clients of microfinance institutions tell us in their own words, this book does not focus on the impact of microfinance on clients' households or enterprises. Money is fungible, and the use of small loans and savings is difficult to track accurately. Most impact studies on microfinance have deep methodological flaws, although breakthroughs are beginning and better knowledge of the impact of financial services on the lives of the poor can be expected in coming decades.

Finally, except in the second volume—which provides extensive discussion on the development of microbanking in Indonesia—it has not been possible to provide the historical, macroeconomic, political, legal, and regulatory backgrounds for the development of microfinance institutions in the many countries discussed.

Because of these and other areas not discussed or covered in only a limited way, I have called attention throughout the book to relevant works by microfinance practitioners, bankers, financial analysts, economists, and others that will be helpful to readers pursuing in more depth specific components and analyses of the growing microfinance industry. Despite the book's omissions, I believe it tells a critical story—one that is little known outside the microfinance industry. Writing this book brought to mind Charles Kindleberger's statement, "My thesis does not rest on small differences in quantities—or so I believe" (Kindleberger 1996 [1978], p. 5).

There are difficulties in writing about a revolution in process. New ideas and practices spawn others. Realities change. Thus the emphasis here is on the principles and processes of the microfinance revolution. This book will soon be outdated as a current description of the state of microfinance—but not, it is hoped, as an analysis of the development and meaning of the microfinance revolution.

The first volume: sustainable finance for the poor

The book's first volume, which considers the shift from subsidized microcredit to commercial microfinance, has two parts. Part 1 (chapters 1–3), "The Paradigm Shift in Microfinance," explores the reasons for the massive gap between

The first volume considers the shift from subsidized microcredit to commercial microfinance

the low level of commercial microfinance generally available from financial institutions and the extensive worldwide demand for such services among the poor.

Chapter 1 explores the differences between the poverty lending approach to finance for the poor and the financial systems approach. The poverty lending approach emphasizes lending to the poorest of the poor, while the financial systems approach focuses on lending to the creditworthy among the economically active poor—people with the ability to use small loans and the willingness to repay them—and on voluntary savings mobilization.

In this context a poverty alleviation toolbox is introduced. The tools include food, employment, financial services, education, health care, infrastructure, and the like. Credit is a powerful tool that is used effectively when it is made available to the creditworthy among the economically active poor. But other tools are required for the extremely poor, who have prior needs such as food, shelter, medicine, training, and employment.

The focus then turns to the recent shift in microfinance from government- and donor-subsidized credit delivery programs to financially self-sufficient institutions providing commercial microfinance. The link between institutional self-sufficiency and large-scale outreach to low-income clients is examined; large-scale outreach is shown to depend on institutional self-sufficiency for long-term viability.

Chapter 2 introduces the emerging paradigm shift, considers how and why it is occurring, and discusses the implications of sustainable microfinance for social and economic development. In chapter 3 the focus shifts from institutions to clients. Clients of microfinance programs in different countries provide their views on the role that financial services have played in their economic activities, income growth, and household development. The voices of these clients show that microfinance helps them expand and diversify their enterprises, increase their incomes, raise their living standards and those of their families, and gain self-confidence. Their statements indicate strong underlying commonalities in microfinance demand across countries, economies, and institutions.

Part 2 (chapters 4–7), "Theories of Local Finance: A Critique," reviews the theoretical background of microfinance. Four main streams of literature are analyzed. Chapter 4 considers supply-leading finance theory, its resulting subsidized credit programs, and the criticisms of this approach that have filled the literature for more than 20 years. Chapter 5 examines the imperfect information paradigm and considers asymmetric information and moral hazard as these concepts have been applied to rural credit markets. The literature on informal commercial credit markets and market interlinkages is reviewed in chapter 6, while that on the role of savings in microfinance is explored in chapter 7.

These chapters share a common thread. They examine a variety of theories and models that, when applied to microfinance markets, have impeded the development of formal sector commercial microfinance. The theorists' intentions were not to create obstacles to financing the poor, but that was often the

Large-scale outreach is shown to depend on institutional self-sufficiency for long-term viability

result. The theories are contrasted with the ways real microfinance markets work, and suggestions are offered for improving the theoretical framework for microfinance.

The second volume: lessons from Indonesia

Indonesia's exceptional accomplishments in microfinance are documented and analyzed in volume 2, which forms part 3 of the book ("The Indonesian Experience," chapters 8–15). In one sense the Indonesian experience takes up a disproportionate amount of space in this book, partly because it is the example that I know best. But the choice of Indonesia for detailed examination, and particularly the long case study of Bank Rakyat Indonesia's (BRI's) microbanking system, can be justified on other grounds.

Indonesia is home to what is, to the best of my knowledge, the world's oldest commercial microfinance institution—the Badan Kredit Desas (BKDs), which began in 1896. It is also home to Bank Dagang Bali (BDB), a private bank that opened in 1970 and is thought to be the world's oldest licensed, full-service commercial bank providing continuous, profitable microfinance services on a substantial scale. And it is home to the world's largest fully self-sufficient microfinance system: the microbanking division of BRI, which has operated profitably on a nationwide scale, without subsidy, since 1987.

In addition, it was possible to discuss here only one institution at considerable length and detail, and BRI's microbanking system is much less well known internationally than some microfinance institutions in other countries that have been written about extensively.

Emphasis is placed on the reasons the microfinance revolution emerged on a large scale in Indonesia, on the ways this occurred, and on the lessons for other countries. Chapters 8 and 9 present material on Indonesia's history, economy, and society (chapter 8) and on its rural development and rural financial markets (chapter 9). These chapters provide the background for understanding why commercial microfinance developed in Indonesia nationwide, turning on its head the conventional wisdom of the time.

Chapter 10 examines the history and performance of BDB. Chapters 11–15 document and analyze the remarkable restructuring of BRI's nationwide local banking system from a government-subsidized credit program with high arrears and substantial losses during 1970–83 to a profitable, unsubsidized microbanking system beginning in 1984.

The Indonesian section of the book, which was first written in early 1997, provides detailed material through 1996. It documents and analyzes the history of Indonesia's commercial microbanking over more than 25 years, a period when the country achieved unprecedented economic growth and massive social and economic development. But in mid-1997 Indonesia was hit by its biggest economic, financial, and political crisis in three decades. The crisis that began in mid-1997 affected Southeast Asia and some East Asian countries, causing steep currency devaluations, plunging stocks, widespread bank failures and corporate bankruptcies, loss of foreign investment, rising inflation, growing unem-

The second volume documents and analyzes Indonesia's exceptional accomplishments in microfinance

ployment, and increasing poverty throughout much of the region. For reasons discussed in chapter 8, Indonesia was hit hardest by the crisis.

Given both the deadlines for this book and the importance of the post-1996 Indonesian material, certain compromises were adopted in writing part 3. Chapter 8 was revised to provide an introduction to Indonesia through 2000, and chapter 9 was updated with post-1996 material on rural finance. Chapters 10–14 analyze microbanking in Indonesia through 1996. But chapter 15, which concludes part 3, updates the microbanking material through 2000 and compares the 2000 results with those of 1996.

Nearly everyone in Indonesia was affected by the crisis. Despite massive efforts by the government—aided by international agencies—to provide food, employment, and social safety nets, many low-income households faced very difficult times. Their purchasing power shrank substantially, many workers were laid off as businesses closed or were retrenched, bank savings declined sharply in value, and some who had emerged from poverty slipped back under the poverty line.

Of crucial importance for this book is that as all this occurred and while the country's financial system collapsed, Indonesia's commercial microbanks remained stable. They continued to serve millions of low-income households without any major interruption. In general these institutions saw the amount of rupiah savings and the number of savings accounts increase considerably, loans held steady, repayments continued to be high, and the microbanks remained profitable.

Thus the Indonesian crisis offers some basic lessons about the importance of microfinance to low-income households, and about the extraordinary stability that sustainable microfinance institutions can maintain in a highly unstable environment. Thus part 3 demonstrates how BRI's microbanking system was transformed from a loss-making rural credit program to the world's largest sustainable microfinance system—and how it has continued to attain profitability and wide outreach through good times and bad.

The third volume: the emerging industry

The book's third volume, in two parts, analyzes the emerging microfinance industry, suggests a microfinance model for 2025, and discusses policy issues likely to be important for the microfinance industry over the next 25 years.

Part 4, "Microfinance in Developing Countries: A Global View" (chapters 16–20), written with Peter J. Fidler, analyzes the history and performance of selected institutions that have played key roles in the microfinance revolution—village banks, credit unions and cooperatives, NGOs, banks created by NGOs, commercial banks, central banks and bank superintendencies, microfinance networks, international organizations and donors, and others. Its focus is on the creation and rapid spread of underlying principles and best practices of the new paradigm in varied institutional and country contexts in Asia, Latin America, and Africa, and on the further dissemination of these principles and practices.

The microfinance revolution can be said to have reached a region when competitive institutions in the formal financial sector provide appropriately designed small loans and savings services (and in some cases other products as well),

The Indonesian crisis offers some basic lessons about the extraordinary stability that sustainable microfinance institutions can maintain in a highly unstable environment

serve low-income clients efficiently, and price their products to cover all costs and risks—and when together these institutions provide financial services to a large share of the country's low-income households and enterprises.

Chapter 16 offers a brief introduction to the history of microfinance as it developed in multiple regions. The contributions to microfinance made by non-bank financial institutions such as village banks, credit unions, and cooperatives—as well as the limitations of most of these institutions—are the focus of chapter 17. NGOs, along with regulated financial funds and companies (some of which are recent creations of NGOs that decided to expand microfinance outreach), are considered in chapter 18. The role of banks in microfinance is discussed in chapter 19, which highlights both the historical reluctance of most banks to enter microfinance and their growing interest in the market today. A few banks are selected for detailed discussion because of their special relevance for the development of the microfinance industry.

Chapter 20 explores the roles played in the development of commercial microfinance by governments and international organizations, including international NGOs, foundations, networks, and donors. Emphasis is placed on three kinds of microfinance activities: information dissemination, banking laws and regulation and supervision of institutions providing microfinance, and capacity-building initiatives that concentrate on tools, training of managers and staff, and institutional development. This chapter also focuses on the crucial partnerships being forged between governments and many kinds of organizations. Thus the discussion concerns the roles played in microfinance by central banks, a donor consortium, multilateral and bilateral donors, an equity fund, an NGO, a non-profit charitable organization, a private microfinance rating company, a practitioner network, a training program, and an Internet list.

Part 5, "The Twenty-first Century: Democratizing Capital" (chapters 21–22), analyzes the status of the microfinance revolution at the turn of the century and projects advances in the democratization of capital by 2025.

A new model of institutional commercial microfinance is developed in chapter 21. Unlike earlier models also analyzed there, the commercial microfinance model assumes an arena in which competing formal sector institutions act as intermediaries, providing commercial loans and savings services to the economically active poor. In this model profitable microfinance institutions that are publicly regulated and supervised hold a sizable share of the microcredit market and a large share of the microsavings market. Organizational structures are streamlined for efficiency. Loan sizes are limited but savings, in any amount over a tiny minimum, are collected from the public—providing ample funding for loans and making savings mobilization cost-effective. Depending on the institution, loan portfolios are also financed by commercial debt and investment. The model emphasizes horizontal links between formal and informal sectors in the same locality, as well as vertical links between local financial markets and actors in regional, national, and international arenas.

The chapter ends with some thoughts on the microfinance industry in 2025. It projects a rapid advance in the market share of microcredit provided by reg-

The third volume analyzes the emerging microfinance industry and suggests a microfinance model for 2025

ulated formal institutions, along with a substantial decline in the market share of informal moneylenders. This shift implies a much larger number of formal sector borrowers in 2025 relative to 2001, but not necessarily a major decrease in the number of moneylenders or their clients. As commercial microfinance develops into a competitive industry with funds to finance loans coming from capital markets, investments, and savings, the formal sector will lend more funds to far more microfinance clients. A substantial increase in the market share of microsavings is also envisaged for formal sector microfinance institutions.

The book concludes, in chapter 22, with a discussion of policy issues that are likely to be crucial for microfinance over the next 25 years. The focus is on the kinds of policy decisions that will probably engage governments, banks, non-bank financial institutions, donors, and others. The policy choices for the various players are explored.

There are many routes to large-scale, sustainable microfinance. Banks may enter the market. NGOs may become regulated, for-profit institutions. Village banks may become linked with formal sector financial institutions. And some credit unions and cooperatives may decide to focus on microfinance. But the focus here is on the basics that underlie the microfinance revolution and are common to all large-scale, profitable microfinance institutions. A macroeconomic and policy environment that permits commercial financing and pricing enables institutional profitability and self-sufficiency. Institutional sustainability allows financial services to be made widely available to the economically active poor over the long term. Profitability engenders competition, which increases efficiency—improving the services available to low-income clients and lowering the costs they pay for them.

What does all this mean for the poor people who become clients of these institutions? This is best explained by the clients themselves. A customer of Indonesia's Bank Dagang Bali for more than 20 years put it this way:

> I grew up poor and without education. I learned, though, that I could improve myself, and that the bank would help me. The president of Bank Dagang Bali is a great man. Why do I say that? Not because he is a bank president; there are many bank presidents. Because he knew that poor people fear banks, and he taught us not to be afraid. BDB taught us something important that we never knew before. BDB taught us that the bank is not a king, the bank is a servant.

"The bank is not a king, the bank is a servant."
—A customer of Indonesia's Bank Dagang Bali

Acknowledgments

During the years that I have been learning about microfinance, I have become greatly indebted to many people. This book draws on the help, insights, and guidance of many people in many parts of the world. It is not possible to mention all of them here, but I want to thank those who have helped in especially important ways.

First, I must record my debt to the thousands of men and women in villages and low-income urban neighborhoods of developing countries who have answered my questions and taught me about their enterprises, their finances, and their lives. Most were poor in economic terms but rich in terms of wisdom and social responsibility. My knowledge of microfinance is largely derived from them.

Microfinance made an impression on me at an early age. My late father, Philip Van Doren Stern, wrote a story called *The Greatest Gift* that was made into a movie titled *It's a Wonderful Life*. The film, which I saw many times while growing up, is about the owner (played by Jimmy Stewart) of a small-town building and loan institution who fights the local establishment to provide financial services to the town's working poor. The movie's message seems to have sunk deep into my subconscious to emerge many years later.

I first learned directly about the power of formal sector finance for the social and economic development of low-income people from the late Burra Venkatappiah, who served at different times as deputy governor of the Reserve Bank of India (India's central bank) and chairman of the State Bank of India. As the driving force behind the famous 1954 All India Rural Credit Survey, he played a major role in the first nationwide study of rural credit and its relation to economic and social development. The study found that government and cooperative credit together reached only about 6 percent of rural borrowers—mostly large farmers. As a result major changes were recommended in rural credit policy, laying the foundations for the country's long-term interest in providing finance to low-income borrowers. Much later the novelist Aubrey Menon, while being interviewed by the press, was asked what he considered the most important book written in India since independence. He replied: "The 1954 All India Rural Credit Survey." I am much indebted to Burra Venkatappiah and his family for sharing with me their wisdom and their hospitality for a very long time.

Among his many far-reaching contributions to the Indonesian economy, Professor Ali Wardhana—minister of finance from 1968–83, coordinating minister for economics, finance, and industry from 1983–88, and economic adviser to the government since 1988—was primarily responsible for creating Indonesia's commercial microbanking system, the world's first large-scale system of sustainable microfinance. Ali Wardhana first played a crucial role in the economic reforms that resulted in extensive rural development in the 1970s and 1980s—and in the consequent emergence of millions of potential bank clients. He led the country's widespread financial reforms that began in 1983; among their results was a policy and regulatory environment in which commercial microbanking could be born and sustained. He then arranged the establishment of Bank Rakyat Indonesia's (BRI's) nationwide commercial microbanking system, and he has watched over and guided its development ever since. Thus his introduction to this book is especially relevant. As Stephen Grenville, now deputy director of the Reserve Bank of Australia, said in 1994: "Not only was Pak Ali present at the creation of the Indonesian financial sector as we know it, but he was midwife at its birth and its guardian as it grew up." I am deeply indebted to Pak Ali both for the privilege of having worked for him for so many years and for all that I have learned from him. I am also much indebted to Ibu Nani Gandabrata for her many years of assistance and kindness; through her example she has taught me much.

I would like to express my gratitude to Drs. Radius Prawiro, for whom I worked when he was Indonesia's minister of finance (1983–88) and coordinating minister for the economy (1988–93), and who supported the development of microfinance in Indonesia throughout his long career in the cabinet.

For many years I have been fortunate to have served as an adviser to BRI and to have had the opportunity to observe closely the development of its microbanking system. To the thousands of BRI managers and staff—from the board of commissioners, president-director, and board of directors to the staff of the local bank units with whom I have interacted since 1979—I am indebted in a special way. They set the example for the development of sustainable microfinance on a nationwide scale. I have learned much from their achievements, as well as from the goals, strategies, tactics, and methods that lie behind BRI's success in microfinance. Kamardy Arief, former president-director of BRI (1983–92), provided long-term, active, committed leadership for the transformation of BRI's approach to banking for the poor. Djokosanto Moeljono has been president-director since 1994, and it was during his term that BRI's microbanking system emerged as a model of technology transfer among developing countries.

A special acknowledgment must be made to the late Sugianto, BRI's managing director who was responsible for its unit *desa* (microbanking) system from the inception of its commercial approach to microfinance in 1984 until his sudden death in 1998. After the financial deregulation of 1983 made it possible, Sugianto (who like many Indonesians used only one name) managed the transition of the unit desa system from a network of banking units with high arrears, high losses, low savings, and low staff morale to the world's largest self-sufficient microbanking system. Sugianto once said to me, "You can succeed in microfinance only if you love it." He did both. The unit desas now provide financial services profitably to millions of poor people throughout the country, continuing even throughout the financial and economic crisis that began in 1997. I am much indebted to Sugianto for all that I learned from him for nearly two decades, and for his careful reading and helpful comments on chapters 1–14 of this book. His successor, Rustam Dachlan, who has managed the unit desas successfully at a time of great difficulty in Indonesia, has continued BRI's interest in the effort made in this book to document the development of BRI's microbanking system.

From 1979–83 I coordinated with Donald R. Snodgrass the Development Program Implementation Studies (DPIS), an interdisciplinary study of Indonesian development programs conducted by the Harvard Institute for International Development (HIID) for the Indonesian Ministry of Finance. I had the privilege of coordinating the four-year DPIS study on Indonesia's rice intensification program, which resulted in recommendations to change the network of rural banks created to channel subsidized credit to rice farmers into a system of commercial financial intermediation. Many of the DPIS recommendations were accepted by the government and implemented by BRI. I am much indebted to the many people with whom I worked on that study.

I am also grateful to the Center for Policy and Implementation Studies (CPIS) in Jakarta, the Indonesian foundation that grew out of the DPIS project, and to the many people with whom I worked there. As coordinator of the CPIS local banking group, which provided assistance to BRI from 1983–90, I learned much from Ismah Afwan, Hilman Akil, Kwan Hwie Liong, R. J. Moermanto, Ilyas Saad, L. Hudi Sartono, Bambang Soelaksono, Sudarno Sumarto, and others.

The CPIS also studied urban informal sector labor in Indonesia, and those studies helped me understand the demand for microfinance among the urban poor. From 1986–92 I served as coordinator of the CPIS informal sector group and worked closely with a number of CPIS research staff. Those whose work has been especially relevant to the issues considered here are Akhmadi, Sri Budiyati, Reno Dewina, Leni Dharmawan, Inca Juanita, the late Iman Juwono, Dewi Meiyani, Isono Sadoko, Kamala Chandrakirana (Nana) Soedjatmoko, and Darwina Wismoyo, in addition to others from the CPIS mentioned above. I would also like to express my appreciation to Reitje Koentjoro for her long, continuing, kind assistance.

The research on which the Indonesian sections of the book are based was supported primarily by Indonesia's Ministry of Finance. The Ministry of Finance and the coordinating minister for economy, finance, and industry provided long-term support and provided me with extensive information on rural development, banking, and government policy. My work with BRI was also supported by BRI, the U.S. Agency for International Development (USAID), and the World Bank. All this generous support is acknowledged with gratitude.

Much of what I have learned about successful microfinance has been garnered from years of discussions with I Gusti Made Oka, president-director of Bank Dagang Bali (BDB), and his wife Sri Adnyani Oka, and through observation of their bank's operations. Putu Indra Suryatmaja provided extensive help explaining and helping me to document BDB's activities and performance. Kadek Edy Setiawan provided help with BDB's financial data. Chapter 10, on BDB's development, is based primarily on research that I carried out in 1994, supported by USAID through its GEMINI Project (administered by Development Alternatives Inc. of Bethesda, Maryland) and by Calmeadow of Toronto. I am much indebted to all who helped me understand BDB's remarkable and pioneering role in microfinance.

From 1996–98 I served as coordinator of HIID's advisory project for BRI's International Visitors Program, funded by an agreement between BRI and USAID. I am indebted to BRI, USAID's Office of Microenterprise Development, the USAID mission in Jakarta, and those at BRI with whom I worked on this project: Soeseno As, Andi Ascarya, Widjojo Koesoemo, Siti Sundari Nasution, Tini Purwaningsih, Andrina Rivai, Iman Sarosa, and Jarot Eko Winarno. This work broadened my perspective on the aspects of commercial microbanking developed at BRI that are applicable—directly or indirectly—to institutions in other countries.

I learned much about microfinance from my work in the mid-1990s with the Reserve Bank of India, especially from R. V. Gupta, then deputy governor, and Y. S. P. Thorat, then additional chief general manager. This work was funded by USAID through its India mission, its Office of Microenterprise Development, and the GEMINI Project; this support is gratefully acknowledged.

On numerous trips to Bolivia I gained important information about microfinance institutions and their clients from Francisco (Pancho) Otero, Hermann Krutzfeldt, Maria-Elena Querejazu, and the many others with whom I have worked at BancoSol; from Eduardo Bazoberry and others at PRODEM; from Sergio Prudencio, with whom I worked at both institutions; and from managers and staff of other Bolivian microfinance institutions. My Bolivian work was supported partly by BancoSol and partly by USAID through its Bolivian mission and the GEMINI Project.

Albert Kimanthi Mutua, C. Aleke-Dondo, and others with whom I worked at the Kenya Rural Enterprise Programme (K-REP) shared with me their extensive experience on microfinance and related institutional and policy issues. My work there was supported by the Ford Foundation. Jaime Aristotle Alip, Dolores Torres, and others with whom I am now working at the CARD Bank (the Philippines) have helped me understand the opportunities, constraints, and internal dynamics of NGO-created banks committed to financing microloans with voluntary savings. This work is being supported by Women's World Banking.

Work with the Bank for the Poor in Vietnam, sponsored by the Consultative Group to Assist the Poorest, World Bank, and United Nations Development Programme; with the Bangladesh Ministry of Finance and Bangladesh Bank, supported by the United Nations Educational, Scientific, and Cultural Organization; and with the Bank of Tanzania, supported by the bank and the World Bank, has provided important insights on how governments view the introduction of commercial microfinance. Work with financial institutions and government bodies in the Philippines and South Africa, funded by USAID; in East Africa, funded by the U.K. Department for International Development; and in China, funded by the Consultative Group to Assist the Poorest and the United Nations Development Programme, have broadened my perspective in this area. The support of these organizations is gratefully acknowledged.

As a consultant to the U.S. Comptroller of the Currency on its effort to encourage bank use by people in the United States who are not participating in the formal financial sector, I had an opportunity to learn about the role of microfinance in industrial countries. I am grateful to Constance E. Dunham for making this possible, and for encouraging an ongoing comparison of lessons about financing the poor in both environments.

Calmeadow, Ohio State University's development finance Internet discussion forum, the Microfinance Training Program (first at the Economics Institute and now at Naropa University in Boulder, Colorado), the Private Sector Initiatives Corporation (known as MicroRate), USAID's Office of Microenterprise Development, and Women's World Banking have provided assistance in various ways during the writing of this book, broadening my understanding of microfinance issues.

I am especially indebted to Irene Arias-Hofman, Carlos Castello, Gregory C. Chen, Michael Chu, Michael Goldberg, Jennifer Isern, Elisabeth H. Rhyne, Laura O. Robinson, Richard Rosenberg, Stuart Rutherford, Donald R. Snodgrass, and Jacob Yaron. Each read all or substantial parts of the manuscript and provided comments, corrections, criticisms, and improvements. I am also much indebted to Christopher P. A. Bennett, David E. Bloom, Robert Peck Christen, James J. Fox, Mohini Malhotra, Joyita Mukherjee, and María Otero, who contributed to this book in many ways. My understanding of microfinance has been informed by the knowledge of these friends and colleagues, and enriched by their help.

I would like to express my appreciation to many others who have contributed to my thinking about the role of microfinance in social and economic development. They include Dale W Adams, Nancy M. Barry, Lynn Bennett, Lakshmi Reddy Bloom, John R. Bowen, Ernst A. Brugger, Barbara Calvin, Anita Campion, Catherine Mansell Carstens, Martha Alter Chen, Md. Shafiqual Haque Choudhury, Craig Churchill, Monique Cohen, David C. Cole, Martin

Connell, Hernando de Soto, Deborah Drake, Cheng Enjieng, Todd Farrington, S. Malcolm Gillis, Claudio Gonzalez-Vega, Turabul Panjatan Hassan, Brigit Helms, Richard M. Hook, Don E. Johnston Jr., James R. Kern, Nathan Keyfitz, Klaas Kuiper, Dharma Kumar, Johan Leestemaker, Patricia Markovitch, Jonathan Morduch, Julia Paxton, Sayeeda Rahman, Ashok Rai, N.V. Raja Reddy, the late Michael Roemer, Leo Schmit, Chiranjib Sen, Parker M. Shipton, Michael Simpson, Stephen Smith, Joseph J. Stern, the late Ann Dunham Sutoro, C. Peter Timmer, Norman T. Uphoff, Marzuki Usman, R. C. G. Varley, Robert C. Vogel, J. D. Von Pischke, and Damian von Stauffenberg.

ACCIÓN International, the *MicroBanking Bulletin,* and the MicroFinance Network provided information on countless occasions and steered me in many right directions. Scores of people contributed information and insights that were used in writing chapter 3 ("Voices of the Clients") and chapters 17–20 (which analyze the development of microfinance in institutions around the world). The assistance of all is most gratefully acknowledged.

Carol Grotrian, Mary Ruggiero, and Flora Segundo provided extensive assistance in the preparation of the manuscript, and Jonathan Ramljak provided exceptional help in overseeing its production. Jessica Roberts helped in multiple ways and prepared the bibliography and the glossary with much care and uncommon dedication. I am much indebted to all.

Peter J. Fidler provided superb research assistance on all aspects of this book and co-wrote part 4. He has been invaluable in the effort to understand, untangle, clarify, document, and analyze the many issues discussed here, and I am much indebted to him.

This book and its author owe an enormous debt to Ira W. Lieberman. He supported the book from the start and played an extraordinary and continuing role in arranging for its financing, editing, and publication—even as the book grew from one to three volumes. The help, encouragement, and support I have received from him is exceptional, and it is acknowledged with much gratitude.

The book has received funding and support from the Consultative Group to Assist the Poorest, Ford Foundation, HIID, Open Society Institute, and World Bank. All this support is acknowledged with much appreciation.

I am particularly grateful to have had Communications Development Incorporated as my editors. Paul Holtz and Bruce Ross-Larson provided superb editing at every stage, and I have learned a lot from both of them. I am also indebted to Terrence Fischer, Daphne Levitas, and Jessica Moore, who coordinated production, and to Garrett Cruce and Megan Klose, who laid out the chapters, all with Communications Development. Deborah E. Patton compiled the index.

I would also like to thank the publishers of the book, the World Bank and Open Society Institute. Paola Scalabrin of the World Bank's Office of the Publisher served as project manager for the publication of the three volumes and played a crucial role throughout. I am indebted to her for help on a wide variety of matters.

The three volumes of this book, especially the second one, are based primarily on work carried out for many years at HIID, and they draw on a number of my earlier papers written at HIID. I am indebted to HIID for its support of my work generally, and for its support for the writing of these volumes.

Members of my family have contributed to this book in a variety of ways, both direct and indirect, and I am most grateful for their help: Allan R. Robinson, Sarah P. Robinson, Perrine Robinson-Geller, Laura O. Robinson, Salvatore A. d'Agostino, Eric B. Geller, and Peter Rosendorff.

Once when I was at the Jakarta airport, about to leave for Boston, the immigration officer challenged my embarkation card. "It says here you are an anthropologist," he said. "It also says you work for the Ministry of Finance. Which is it? It cannot be both!" It took some time to explain that both were correct. As an anthropologist who has been given the opportunity to serve as a policy adviser to finance ministries, central banks, and a variety of banks and other financial institutions in many parts of the world, I have been especially fortunate, and am most grateful.

Part  1

The Paradigm Shift in Microfinance

Large-scale sustainable microfinance can be achieved only with a financial systems approach

The microfinance revolution is the process—recently begun, but under way in many developing countries—through which financial services for the economically active poor are implemented on a large scale by multiple, competing, financially self-sufficient institutions. Part 1 of this book (chapters 1–3) explores the historic reasons for the "absurd" gap between supply and demand in microfinance and discusses the rapid rise of the commercial microfinance revolution over the past several decades.

Chapter 1 defines microfinance and its clients and shows the reasons that the provision of small savings and credit services matters to poor people and to social and economic development more broadly. Comparison is made of the two main approaches to financing the poor: the poverty lending approach, which promotes donor-funded credit for the poor, especially the poorest of the poor; and the financial systems approach, which advocates commercial microfinance for the economically active poor and other, subsidized and charitable nonfinancial methods of reducing poverty and creating jobs for the extremely poor. The primary goal of the two approaches to microfinance is similar—widespread financial services for the poor. The debate is on the means. However, the choice of means can limit the goals that can be reached. Large-scale sustainable microfinance can be achieved only with a financial systems approach.

Chapter 2 analyzes the paradigm shift that is in progress in microfinance: from government- or donor-subsidized credit delivery systems to self-sufficient institutions providing commercial finance. For the first time in history, commercial institutions operating in the formal financial sector have begun to meet the enormous demand for small loans and savings services profitably. The meaning of institutional sustainability in this context is discussed. The microbanking division of Bank Rakyat Indonesia (BRI) and Bolivia's BancoSol, both leaders in the microfinance revolution, are examined from the point of view of what it means to be a financially self-sufficient microfinance institution. Both banks provide wide outreach to low-income clients commercially, and both have been consistently profitable. BRI finances its loan portfolio with locally mobilized savings; BancoSol finances its loans with savings, commercial debt, and for-profit investment. The relationship between sustainability and outreach in both is emphasized.

In chapter 3 the focus shifts to the clients of microfinance institutions. Savers and borrowers in microfinance programs from different countries give their views on the financial services they use and on the roles these services have played in their economic and household activities. Five questions are asked. Do poor people understand microfinance products and services, and do they know how to use

For the first time in history, formal sector financial institutions have begun to meet microfinance demand profitably

them? Can microfinance help the economically active poor expand and diversify their enterprises and increase their incomes? Can access to financial services enhance the quality of life of the clients of microfinance institutions? Can access to microfinance help the economically active poor in times of severe household difficulty? And can successful microfinance institutions promote the self-confidence of their clients? The voices of the clients heard in this chapter provide strong indication that the answers to all these question are yes. But these clients are among the small minority of the economically active poor who have access to microfinance institutions. Most of the developing world does not yet have the opportunities for microfinance that helped these clients build their enterprises, increase their incomes, care for their families, and gain in self-confidence.

① | Supply and Demand in Microfinance

This chapter explores the reasons for the "absurd gap" between supply and demand in microfinance.[1] Among the economically active poor of the developing world, there is strong demand for small-scale commercial financial services—for both credit and savings. Where available, these and other financial services help low-income people improve household and enterprise management, increase productivity, smooth income flows and consumption costs, enlarge and diversify their microbusinesses, and increase their incomes. But the demand for commercial microfinance is rarely met by the formal financial sector. One reason is that the demand is generally not perceived. Another is that many actors in the formal sector believe, wrongly, that microfinance cannot be profitable for banking institutions.

What matters to microfinance clients is the access and cost of financial services. Many poor people are served by informal moneylenders, who generally provide easy access to credit but at high cost, charging poor borrowers nominal monthly effective interest rates that typically range from about 10 percent to more than 100 percent—many times the monthly effective rates of sustainable financial institutions, which are usually 2–5 percent. Even when real (inflation adjusted) interest rates are used and borrowers' transaction costs are included, it is normally far less expensive to borrow from a commercial microfinance institution than from a local moneylender. Commercial microfinance institutions can also offer much-in-demand savings services that provide savers with security, liquidity, and returns, a combination not generally available in the informal sector.

Some poor people are served by government- or donor-financed nonbank financial institutions such as nongovernmental organizations (NGOs) and village banks. But most of these organizations are capital constrained and can meet only a tiny fraction of the demand for credit. While such institutions provide credit at relatively low cost, access to credit by borrowers is limited. Access to voluntary savings facilities is poor or nonexistent at many of these institutions.

Other households are served by state-owned formal financial institutions that provide government- and donor-financed subsidized credit. But the below-market subsidies are often siphoned off by local elites and so may not reach the poor. In addition, many such institutions have high arrears and large losses. Access by the poor tends to be low; despite the subsidies, the costs of borrowing may be high because of widespread inefficiency and corruption.

Microfinance in the 1990s was marked by a major debate between two leading views on how to fill the absurd gap in microfinance: the *financial systems* approach and the *poverty lending* approach. Both approaches share the goal of making financial services available to poor people throughout the world. But the poverty lending approach focuses on reducing poverty through credit and other services provided by institutions that are funded by donor and government subsidies and other concessional funds. A primary goal is to reach the poor, especially the poorest of the poor, with credit. Except for mandatory savings required as a condition of receiving a loan, savings is not normally a significant part of the poverty lending approach to microfinance. Often the poor cannot save in such an institution unless

It is normally far less expensive to borrow from a commercial microfinance institution than from a local moneylender

they also borrow from it. As indicated by the term poverty lending, the emphasis is on microcredit, not microfinance.

Many institutions using the poverty lending approach provide microcredit to poor borrowers at low cost. But these institutions are typically not sustainable, primarily because their interest rates on loans are too low for full cost recovery. In addition, they do not meet the demand among the poor for voluntary savings services.

In contrast, the financial systems approach focuses on commercial financial intermediation among poor borrowers and savers; its emphasis is on institutional self-sufficiency. With worldwide unmet demand for microcredit estimated in the hundreds of millions of people and characterized by requests from creditworthy borrowers for continuing access to loans of gradually increasing size, government and donor funds cannot possibly finance microcredit on a global scale. But within the past several decades fully sustainable commercial microfinance intermediaries have emerged. These intermediaries provide loans and voluntary savings services to the economically active poor, and they offer easy access at reasonable cost. Their loan portfolios are financed by savings, commercial debt, and for-profit investment in varying combinations. These institutions are the subject of this book for two reasons: they have been able to attain wide outreach profitably, and they represent a globally affordable model.

Commercial microfinance is not appropriate, however, for extremely poor people who are badly malnourished, ill, and without skills or employment opportunities. Starving borrowers will use their loans to buy food for themselves or their children. Such people do not need debt. They need food, shelter, medicines, skill training, and employment—for which government and donor subsidies and charitable contributions are appropriate. For these people, microfinance is the next step—after they are able to work.

Bank Rakyat Indonesia's microbanking system and Bolivia's BancoSol are introduced here as leading examples of profitable microfinance institutions. Their records show that commercial financial institutions can attain nationwide outreach among the economically active poor, providing microfinance extensively and profitably. In this context the relationship between institutional self-sufficiency and the scale of outreach to low-income borrowers and savers is examined; over time the breadth of outreach is shown to depend on the self-sufficiency of the institution.

Government and donor funds cannot possibly finance microcredit on a global scale

Just as new agricultural technologies spawned the green revolution in the 1970s and 1980s, new financial technologies are producing the microfinance revolution in the 1990s.
—Berenbach and Churchill 1997, p. 1

About 90 percent of the people in developing countries lack access to financial services from institutions, either for credit or for savings.[2] Among them, of course, are nearly all the poor of the developing world. While not all the poor can make use of microfinance, there remains a massive gap between the low level of commercial microfinance available from financial institutions and the extensive worldwide demand for such financial services among low-income people.

What Is Microfinance?

Microfinance refers to small-scale financial services—primarily credit and savings—provided to people who farm or fish or herd; who operate small enterprises or microenterprises where goods are produced, recycled, repaired, or sold; who provide services; who work for wages or commissions; who gain income from renting out small amounts of land, vehicles, draft animals, or machinery and tools; and to other individuals and groups at the local levels of developing countries, both rural and urban. Many such households have multiple sources of income.[3]

Savings services allow savers to store excess liquidity for future use and to obtain returns on their investments. Credit services enable the use of anticipated income for current investment or consumption. Overall, microfinance services can help low-income people reduce risk, improve management, raise productivity, obtain higher returns on investments, increase their incomes, and improve the quality of their lives and those of their dependents.

Such services are rarely accessible through the formal financial sector, however. Credit is widely available from informal commercial moneylenders but typically, as will be documented, at very high cost to the borrowers—especially poor borrowers. Banks generally assume that providing small loans and deposit services would be unprofitable. It is widely believed—wrongly, as will be demonstrated—that the cost of delivering small-scale financial services at the local level is too high for nonsubsidized institutions and that the informal financial market satisfies demand. NGOs and other nonbank financial institutions have led the way in developing appropriate credit methodologies for low-income borrowers. But with few exceptions, these institutions are able to operate only on a very small scale.

The problem is exacerbated by the limited influence of the poor people who require microfinance. They are usually unable to inform formal markets about their creditworthiness or about their demand for savings services and loans. Accordingly, services are not provided. Those who hold the power do not understand the demand; those who understand the demand do not hold the power.

About 90 percent of the people in developing countries lack access to financial services from institutions

There are differences among countries and regions in the availability of microfinance services and in the level of unmet demand for these services. There are also differences in demand among small businesses, microenterprises, farmers, laborers, low-income salaried employees, and others. Common to nearly all parts of the developing world, however, is a lack of commercial microfinance institutions—a shortcoming that unnecessarily limits the options and lowers the financial security of poor people throughout the world.

But this pattern is changing. The *microfinance revolution* is emerging in many countries around the world. As it is used here, this term refers to the large-scale, profitable provision of microfinance services—small savings and loans—to economically active poor people by sustainable financial institutions.[4] These services are provided by competing institutions at the local level—near the homes and workplaces of the clients—in both rural and urban areas. Financial services delivered at the local level refer to those provided to people living in villages and other types of rural settlements and to people living in low-income neighborhoods in semiurban or urban areas. *Large scale* as used here means coverage by multiple institutions of millions of clients; or, for small countries or middle- and high-income countries with low demand, outreach to a significant portion of the microfinance market. *Profitability* means covering all costs and risks without subsidy and returning a profit to the institution.

In aggregate, commercial microfinance institutions can provide outreach to a significant segment of their country's poor households. In a few countries this has already occurred; in others it is at various stages of progress. This book is about the microfinance revolution—the principles on which it is based, the dynamics of its processes, the speed of its progress, and its role in economic and social development.

Those who hold the power do not understand the demand; those who understand the demand do not hold the power

Estimating the Demand for Microfinance

The microfinance revolution is best understood in the context of the population and income levels of developing countries, and of estimates of unmet global demand for formal sector commercial financial services.

According to the World Bank's *World Development Report 1999/2000: Entering the 21st Century,* in 1998 about 1.2 billion people—24 percent of the population in developing and transition economies—lived on less than $1 a day.[5] In 1999, 4.5 billion people, or 75 percent of the world's population, lived in low- and lower-middle-income economies. Of these, 2.4 billion were from low-income economies with an average annual GNP per capita of $410, while 2.1 billion lived in lower-middle-income economies with an average annual GNP per capita of $1,200 (World Bank, *World Development Report 2000/2001: Attacking Poverty*).

The following are crude but conservative assumptions:

- Some 80 percent of the world's 4.5 billion people living in low- and lower-middle-income economies do not have access to formal sector financial services. (It is probably more accurate to say 90 percent, but these are conservative estimates.)

- Among these 3.6 billion people, the average household size is five people (720 million households).
- Half of these households (360 million) account for the unmet demand for commercial savings or credit services from financial institutions.[6]

The average productivity of these households could be increased substantially with access to appropriate institutional savings and credit services delivered locally. Because the benefits of financial services would also extend to the dependents of microfinance clients, the economic activities and the quality of life of more than 1.8 billion people could be improved by providing them with local access to formal commercial microfinance.

This is not a scale that can be reached by government- or donor-funded institutions.[7] Microfinance demand can be met on a global scale only through the provision of financial services by self-sufficient institutions.

Most of the demand for microfinance comes from households and enterprises operating in the unregulated, informal sector of the economy. Yet there is "no clear-cut division between a 'formal' and an 'informal' sector … the complex reality could be better described as a continuum with sliding transitions" (Weiss 1988, p. 61). Thus in the labor markets of developing countries, some microenterprises combine informal and formal characteristics, and some move back and forth between the two sectors.

Still, a number of features generally associated in aggregate with informal enterprises tend to be absent from formal enterprises. These include scarcity of capital, family ownership, small-scale operations, nonlegal status, lack of security of business location, operation in unregulated markets, relatively easy entry into markets, labor-intensive production modes, nonformal education and low skill levels, irregular work hours, small inventories, use of indigenous resources, and domestic sales of products, often to end users. But the informal sector is far from homogeneous. It includes people who collect and recycle cigarette butts and people who subcontract for large industrial concerns—and many others in between (such as petty traders, carpenters, brickmakers, recyclers of paper and metal, shoemakers, and tailors).

The formal financial sector has generally been self-deterred from financing informal enterprises by characteristics typically associated with such businesses, including the nonlegal status of enterprises, the frequent lack of an authorized business location, the unavailability of standard forms of collateral, the small size of transactions (and associated high cost per transaction), and the perceived riskiness of such businesses.

The full magnitude of the demand for microfinance has begun to be understood only recently. During the second half of the 20th century credit for agriculture has generally been accorded high priority, if usually in misguided ways. But the huge demand for finance from self-employed microentrepreneurs has typically been ignored by the formal financial sector. Until the 1980s the presence of in-

Microfinance demand can be met on a global scale only through the provision of financial services by self-sufficient institutions

formal microenterprises—street vendors, home workshops, market stalls, providers of informal transportation services—was generally perceived by policymakers and economists to be a result of economic dysfunction. Microenterprises were thought of as little more than an indicator that the structure and growth rate of the formal economy were inadequate to absorb the national labor force, and so were perceived as a disguised form of unemployment.[8]

Given this perspective, the typical response on the part of governments was to focus on improving the management of the formal economy, thereby increasing its absorptive capacity. This approach, it was thought, would enable low-income and unemployed people to become integrated into the formal sector. Since the "problem" of informal microenterprises was seen as one that would be resolved through better macroeconomic performance, there was no reason to focus on the contributions of this sector to the economy or to improve the environment in which it operated—including increasing access to formal financial services (Webster and Fidler 1996).

The result was that the huge informal sector in many countries remained essentially invisible—in government plans and budgets, in economists' models, in bankers' portfolios, and in national policies.[9] In fact, the most visible government policies on the informal sector tended to aim at repressing or eliminating the sector (making it even more invisible) by removing microentrepreneurs from the streets, by sending urban informal laborers back to their villages—which they had usually left because of lack of employment opportunities, or by turning some into formal sector workers.

Yet microenterprises provide an income stream for poor entrepreneurs. They create employment. They recycle and repair goods that would otherwise become waste. And they provide cheap food, clothing, and transportation to poor people—including those at the lower levels of the formal sector—who would not otherwise be able to live on their salaries. Microentrepreneurs accomplish all of this despite severe obstacles, since they typically lack capital, skills, legal status, and business security. But they generally have strong survival skills: shrewd business sense, long experience of hard work, knowledge of their markets, extensive informal support and communication networks, and a fundamental understanding of flexibility as the key to microenterprise survival.

Since the mid-1980s many developing countries have improved their macroeconomic management. Simultaneously, however, their informal sector populations have typically grown larger. On the one hand, failing state enterprises were closed or retrenched and governments tightened spending. On the other hand, demand for the low-cost goods and services produced by the informal sector increased as agricultural technologies and policies changed and rural incomes increased. The growth of the already large informal sector was a predictable, rational response to structural adjustment. In this context policymakers in some countries reexamined their approach to informal enterprises, viewing them not as a problem for the economy for the short and medium term but rather as an important solution to crucial aspects of current problems that are caused by poverty and multiplied by massive rural-urban migration.

The growth of the already large informal sector was a predictable, rational response to structural adjustment

It was under these conditions, in the 1980s, that attention began to be paid to improving the legality, security, and financing of informal enterprises. If the formal economy cannot absorb the labor force, then why not help the informal enterprises that provide employment—at least to the extent of removing the obstacles they face? If microentrepreneurs did not have to face routine removal from their business locations, confiscation of their goods, constant demands for bribes, detention, and other forms of harassment, they would be more likely to invest in their enterprises—which could then raise incomes and increase employment.

The growing interest in commercial microfinance is related to the recent recognition on the part of some policymakers that the informal sector is very large, it is here for the foreseeable future, it provides employment and contributes to the economy, and its performance can be improved with the removal of legal and financial obstacles. Thus increasing microenterprise access to financial services—both credit and savings—has become a priority for many governments and donors. With this has come awareness that the demand for commercial microfinance is far larger than was previously understood.

Informal Commercial Moneylenders and Their Interest Rates

Financial institutions that provide commercial microfinance help poor people manage enterprise growth and diversification and raise their household incomes. Yet informal commercial lenders—local traders, employers, and landlords, commodity wholesalers, pawnbrokers, and moneylenders of various types—provide loans to the poor in many developing countries. Why, then, are formal commercial loans so crucial for social and economic development? Why fix a system that seems to work?

Many bankers, economists, and government officials assume that the informal commercial credit market works efficiently, satisfies demand, and helps the poor. A common view is that "widespread use of informal finance suggests that it is well suited to most rural conditions" (Von Pischke, Adams, and Donald 1983, p. 8). "Most informal lenders provide valuable financial services at a reasonable cost to borrowers" (Gonzalez-Vega 1993, p. 23).

> The role and strength of informal finance agents in small-scale rural economies . . . and their importance to low-income households should not be underestimated . . . The informal sector allows low income people access to services . . . at a relatively low cost. *It can do so because the informal sector is the natural environment for rural people* [emphasis added].
> —Bouman 1989, pp. 8–9

From a development perspective, therefore, there has been no broadly recognized, compelling reason to afford high priority to establishing self-

Increasing microenterprise access to financial services—both credit and savings—has become a priority for many governments and donors

Bank Rakyat Indonesia's (BRI) microbanking system offers a loan product, known as Kredit Umum Pedesaan (KUPEDES), that has typically charged prompt payers a nominal flat monthly interest rate of 1.5 percent on the original loan balance for most loans. (This is equivalent to about a 2.8 percent effective monthly rate on the declining loan balance.) KUPEDES loans vary in size from 25,000 to 25 million rupiah. These rupiah amounts were equivalent to about $11 to $10,693 at the end of 1996; because of the subsequent decline of the value of the rupiah against the dollar, they were equivalent to about $3 to $3,400 at the end of 1999.

Many of BRI's microbanking borrowers had previously borrowed from local moneylenders, usually as part of interlinked transactions in which the borrower was also a commodity supplier, employee, or tenant of the lender. Below, four BRI microbanking customers compare the nominal interest rates they paid at BRI to the rates they paid to moneylenders before receiving their BRI loans and discuss their use of credit. The loans reported below were taken between 1992 and 1996, when the average annual inflation rate in Indonesia ranged from 7.6 to 9.6 percent. In 1998, when average annual inflation was 57.6 percent, the KUPEDES flat monthly interest rate was raised to 2.2 percent a month (about a 45 percent annual effective rate for prompt payers on most loans). In September 1999 the flat monthly rate was lowered to its original 1.5 percent.

- *RM operates a microenterprise in which he constructs and sells stoves made from scrap metal.* He first came to his local BRI unit in South Sulawesi in 1994, after obtaining information about its services from the head of his village. RM works out of his home and has trained three of his sons to help him with the business. He said that before he came to BRI, whenever he needed money he took loans from informal lenders in his neighborhood. But he could obtain only one-week loans at 100 percent interest for the week (equivalent to an effective monthly interest rate of 1,939 percent; see chapter 6 and table 6.1 for discussion and for the method of calculating the monthly effective interest rates given in this box). His first BRI loan, provided at the standard 2.8 percent effective monthly interest rate, was an 18-month loan for 600,000 rupiah ($273); the loan was taken in 1994 for working capital to develop his business. In 1996 he borrowed 1.5 million rupiah ($629) in his third KUPEDES loan. RM said that in the three years that he had been borrowing from BRI, his sales and profits had almost doubled. By 1996 he had begun renovating his house with the profits earned from his business.

- *AC has been selling bean sprouts in a local market in Central Java since the mid-1970s.* Her husband is a rice farmer. In 1995 AC received a 200,000 rupiah ($87) unsecured loan for 12 months from her local BRI unit. AC said that this was the first time she had ever borrowed from an institution. After repaying her first loan, she received a second loan for the same amount. Previously, AC had purchased bean sprouts daily on credit from her supplier (who was also the cultivator). To purchase on credit, she paid him a daily commission that ranged from 5 to 10 percent of the loan (equivalent to an effective monthly interest rate ranging from 332 to 1,645 percent).

- *NP, who lives in Central Java, has been making and selling bean curd since the mid-1980s.* Initially she worked for an aunt who also makes bean curd, but in 1994 NP moved her operations to the back of her parents' house. Her father and her husband help her with the business. When she began her business, NP often borrowed money for working capital from a neighborhood moneylender. But the maximum she was permitted to borrow was 100,000 rupiah ($45), and the interest she had to pay was calculated on "five-six" terms for a two-month period. Thus she borrowed 100,000 rupiah and returned 120,000 rupiah two months later (equivalent to an effective monthly

Box   **1.1**   **(continued)**

interest rate of 10 percent). When later in 1994 she needed additional working capital
to expand production, her father suggested that they take a loan from the local BRI
unit, located less than 1 kilometer from their home. NP took out a 750,000 rupiah
KUPEDES loan ($340). By 1996 she had received her third KUPEDES loan for 1.3 mil-
lion rupiah ($546), which she used to purchase a wood-heated steam furnace for proc-
essing bean curd.

- *JR and TR, husband and wife, have operated a small shop out of their home in Yogyakarta for more than 15 years; they sell vegetables, rice, snacks, tea, sugar, and other
  basic foods.* In 1992 JR started a second enterprise, a furniture trading business that
  is also operated out of their home. In 1994 he borrowed 200,000 rupiah ($97) for 12
  months from the local BRI unit. After repaying the loan, he received a second 12-
  month loan for 500,000 rupiah ($237). The loans are used for both businesses. JR con-
  trasted the BRI flat interest rate of 1.5 percent a month (2.8 percent in effective
  terms) with the interest charged for the one-month loans he had taken from a local
  moneylender before he started borrowing from BRI. The loans from the moneylender
  had to be repaid in daily installments, with a 50 percent flat interest rate for the month
  (equivalent to an effective monthly interest rate of 132 percent).

Note: These were the only BRI clients whose loans from informal commercial moneylenders were
discussed in the sources below. The range of interest rates is consistent with that provided by many
poor Indonesians with whom I talked during the 1980s and 1990s.
Source: BRI 1996a, pp. 5, 6, and 8; 1997b, p. 7.

sufficient microfinance institutions. Why make changes for people living in
their natural environments? The answer is that rural environments can har-
bor huge income disparities and extensive economic, legal, and gender in-
equalities and injustices. There is nothing "natural" about this.

While it is true that informal commercial moneylenders provide important financial services to the poor, they typically charge very high interest rates
to low-income borrowers in developing countries. The reasons for the high interest rates have been hotly debated, but the evidence for the high rates is unmistakable. While the transaction costs of obtaining a loan are normally higher
for a borrower who obtains credit from a commercial microfinance institution
than from an informal moneylender, the difference in interest rates is often so
large that the total cost to the borrower is much lower at the institution (see
chapter 6).

Box 1.1 compares the nominal interest rate charged by the microbanking—or unit *desa* division—of Bank Rakyat Indonesia (BRI) with the nominal interest rates that four BRI unit desa borrowers reported paying previously
to informal commercial moneylenders. Both the BRI loans and the loans from
moneylenders were taken during 1992–96, when annual average inflation rates
in Indonesia ranged from 7.6–9.6 percent. For purposes of comparison, the
moneylenders' rates—which had been stated in various forms by the different lenders—have been converted to monthly effective interest rates. As can
be seen in the box, these interest rates ranged widely, but all were much high-

er than the unit desas' monthly effective rate, which for most loans was 2.8 percent for prompt payers.[10] Three of the four borrowers paid enormously higher rates to the moneylenders: JR and TR (example 4) paid 47 times the BRI rate, AC (example 2) paid from 119–588 times the BRI rate, and RM (example 1) paid 693 times the BRI rate.

In addition to the high interest rates, the moneylenders' loan terms were not suitable for the borrowers' needs. RM and JR and TR wanted 12–18-month working capital loans, but RM could obtain only a one-week loan, and JR and TR only a one-month loan, from their moneylenders. NP (example 3) wanted to borrow several hundred dollars, but the moneylender would only loan her $45.

The range of interest rates shown in box 1.1 is common elsewhere as well.[11] The reasons for the high interest rates of moneylenders in many developing countries are analyzed in chapter 6, where extensive documentation of the rates charged is provided.

Each moneylender tends to have a range of interest rates that he or she charges to different customers. Poor borrowers are usually charged the higher rates for two main reasons: because poor borrowers have few other options and low bargaining power, and because for lenders the transaction costs for making small loans are essentially the same as for large loans. If the interest rates were the same, small loans would be less profitable. In some cases there is also a third reason: moneylenders may consider poor borrowers risky and so add a premium to cover the extra risk. In my experience, however, this factor is generally considered less important than the other two. Outside of risks that borrowers may face because of collective shock in the region—drought, hyperinflation, war—moneylenders normally do not lend to poor borrowers who pose high risks.

Informal credit from moneylenders is often provided in the context of interlinked transactions; the borrower is also the lender's commodity supplier, employee, tenant, or sharecropper, for example. In such situations the lenders have good information about the borrowers and a variety of methods for ensuring loan repayment.

Moneylenders typically calculate interest rates on a flat rate basis—that is, on the original loan balance. This is in contrast to most standard banks, where the effective interest rate is used, calculated on the (declining) outstanding loan balance.[12] Converting moneylenders' stated rates to effective monthly interest rates enables comparison with the rates of commercial microfinance institutions. In general, moneylenders' rates tend to be much higher than those of commercial microfinance institutions. In many parts of the developing world informal commercial lenders typically charge nominal effective interest rates of 10 percent to more than 100 percent a month, while sustainable microfinance institutions usually charge nominal effective rates between 2 and 5 percent a month. Moreover, some moneylenders charge even higher rates, especially to poor borrowers.

Nominal interest rates for small one-day loans can range from 5 percent to more than 20 percent, and many such borrowers continue to borrow on the same terms, day after day. AC (case 2 in box 1.1) is an example. The nominal interest rate she paid ranged from 5–10 percent a day. But these rates are

Informal commerical lenders typically charge nominal effective interest rates of 10 percent to more than 100 percent a month

equivalent to monthly effective rates of 332–1,645 percent (see table 6.1 for the method of conversion). In parts of Latin America and Asia *five-six* terms are especially common. A borrower receives, for example, a loan of $10 in the morning and repays $12 at the end of the day—a 20 percent interest rate for a one-day loan. This can represent a monthly effective interest rate of more than 20,000 percent (see example 1 in table 6.1). In some cases high interest rates are accompanied by below-market prices or wages as part of the interlinked transactions the lenders maintain with the same borrowers in other markets.

In some, usually better-developed areas, however, nominal effective monthly interest rates in the informal sector are lower, in the range of 3–15 percent (see U Tun Wai 1977, 1980; Chandavarkar 1987; Fernando 1988; Bouman 1989; Von Pischke 1991; and Mosley 1996). It is unlikely, though, that many poor people obtain loans at these rates (Siamwalla and others 1993).

In assessing the cost of credit to borrowers, transaction costs must also be considered. These are the costs that borrowers incur in obtaining loans, such as paying for transportation, producing certified records, absorbing the opportunity cost of time spent traveling and waiting, paying fees and bribes, and the like. Low-income borrowers often report that their transaction costs in borrowing from informal moneylenders are quite low. So too, profitable institutions providing commercial microfinance keep procedures simple and quick, locations convenient, and staff trained and motivated to be efficient and helpful to clients. In such institutions borrowers' transaction costs are moderate—if still typically higher than their transaction costs in borrowing from moneylenders.

Because of the large difference in interest rates, however, low-income clients of commercial microfinance institutions typically have a much lower total cost of credit than those who borrow from moneylenders. The crucial point here is that the poor pay unnecessarily high interest rates for credit because commercial microfinance institutions do not yet exist in most areas of the developing world.

Sustainable microfinance institutions usually charge nominal effective interest rates of 2 to 5 percent a month

The Economically Active Poor and the Extremely Poor

Poverty comes in many forms and causes multiple harms. The poor may suffer from lack of food and water, unemployment or underemployment, disease, abuse, homelessness, degradation, and disenfranchisement. The results among those affected often include physical, mental, and emotional disability, limited skills and education, low self-esteem and lack of self-confidence, and fear, resentment, aggression, and truncated vision. Some individuals break out of poverty. Some societies have social safety nets that prevent the poor from reaching destitution. Impoverished refugees face special problems. The effects of poverty combine in different ways and in varying degrees, affecting the poor differently depending on the society and the individual.

While all such people are poor by the standards of the wider society, there are substantial differences among them. Those who are severely food-deficit, bonded laborers whose full-time work pays only the interest on their loans, and displaced refugees are different from poor people who have some land, employment, or a microbusiness—except that in many cases the latter were once the former. Sometimes it works the other way around. At any level of poverty, however, women and some minorities tend to be the poorest, with girls typically the most deprived. Overall, as Nobel Prize winner Amartya Sen (1999, p. 71) has observed, "poverty must be seen as the deprivation of basic capabilities rather than merely as low incomes."

Though there are multiple degrees and kinds of poverty, here we distinguish only between the extremely poor and the economically active poor. The World Bank defines extreme poverty as living on less than 75 cents a day; about two-thirds of the people defined as poor by the $1 a day standard are classified as extremely poor (World Bank, *World Development Report 1990: Poverty*).

People living in extreme poverty exist below the minimum subsistence level; they include those who are unemployed or severely underemployed, as well as those whose work is so poorly remunerated that their purchasing power does not permit the minimum caloric intake required to overcome malnutrition. Also included are people who live in regions severely deprived of resources; those who are too young, too old, or too disabled to work; those who for reasons of environment, ethnic identity, politics, gender, and the like have little or no employment opportunities—and who have no earning assets or household members to support them; and those who are escaping from natural or humanmade catastrophes.[13]

As Henry Mayhew put it in 1861, people who "cannot work" include those who are incapacitated from want of power—the old, the young, the ill, the insane, and the untaught; those who are incapacitated from want of means (having no tools, clothes, "stock money," materials, or workplace); and those who are incapacitated from want of employment (because of a business glut or stagnation, a change in fashion, the introduction of machinery, or the seasonality of the work).[14] These categories are still relevant for identifying the extremely poor in many developing countries.

The term *economically active poor,* in contrast, is used in a general sense to refer to those among the poor who have some form of employment and who are not severely food-deficit or destitute. The contrast made here between the economically active poor and the extremely poor is similar but not identical to distinctions that have been made between the poor and the core poor. Thus Hulme and Mosley (1996, vol. 1, p. 132) define the minimum economic threshold that separates the core poor from the poor as "the existence [among the poor] of a reliable income, freedom from pressing debt, sufficient health to avoid incapacitating illness, freedom from imminent contingencies and sufficient resources (such as savings, non-essential convertible assets and social entitlements) to cope with problems when they arise."

My experience in developing countries, however, has been that many of the economically active poor, sometimes even the better off among them, do not fit this set of criteria. Therefore, as defined here, the economically active poor include people who have achieved some but not necessarily all of these benchmarks, who have marketable skills or control over earning assets—and who are or could become creditworthy borrowers and savers in commercial

As Amartya Sen has observed, "poverty must be seen as the deprivation of basic capabilities rather than merely as low incomes"

financial institutions. This definition includes Hulme and Mosley's poor as well as some of their core poor.

The distinction between the extremely poor and the economically active poor is not precise. Households move from one category to the other over time. People with skills may not find employment. The issue may be further complicated by gender, because women may not be permitted to learn marketable skills or to leave their homes. Even within a single household, women may be poorer and more malnourished than men.

In addition, some people who work full time remain in extreme poverty because they are held in various forms of labor bondage under which they are not compensated for their work beyond the food they require to carry out the work (see chapter 6). The term economically active poor as used here implies not only work but also its compensation.

Poverty contains many anomalies. Imprecise as they are, however, the two general categories of the economically active poor and the extremely poor can be usefully distinguished in the planning and implementation of effective strategies for overcoming poverty. The delineation of an official poverty line, defined by consumption or by a basket of goods, can be a useful tool for governments and donors in making policy decisions and in planning long-term development strategies. But the poverty line concept is not directly relevant for microfinance. Savers are commonly found on both sides of the official line, and many borrowers below the line are creditworthy, while many above the line are not.

In commercial microfinance the critical distinctions among the poor are those that differentiate the economically active poor from the extremely poor, and the poor who participate in a cash economy from those who do not (some pastoralists, subsistence agriculturalists, and hunters and gatherers). There is also a crucial distinction between creditworthy and noncreditworthy borrowers.

On the savings side, people with incomes that provide for their most minimal needs often save in small amounts in whatever forms are appropriate for their purposes and conveniently available. The demand among even the lowest levels of the economically active poor for secure, convenient, and appropriately designed financial savings services is well documented from many parts of the world. Such facilities are often more in demand among the poor than are credit services.

While the extremely poor may not be directly affected by commercial microfinance, they can benefit indirectly from its development. Thus microfinance helps to create employment; some of the extremely poor may find jobs if kin and neighbors among the economically active poor have access to commercial financial services. And if commercial microfinance is made locally available, the very poor who become employed will eventually be able to make use of its services.

Savings facilities are often more in demand among the poor than credit services

A Poverty Alleviation Toolbox

Alleviating poverty requires many tools, including food, shelter, employment, health and family planning services, financial services, education, infrastructure, markets, and communication. The key to reducing poverty is knowing how to use these tools.

Credit is a powerful tool that is used effectively when it is made available to the creditworthy among the economically active poor participating in at least a partial cash economy—people with the ability to use loans and the willingness to repay them. But other tools are required for the very poor who have prior needs, such as food, shelter, medicine, skills training, and employment.

It is sometimes forgotten—although generally not by borrowers—that another word for credit is debt. When loans are provided to the very poor, the borrowers may not be able to use the loans effectively because they lack opportunities for profitable self-employment, and because the risks involved in using the credit may be unacceptably high (see Hulme and Mosley 1996, vol. 1, ch. 5). For example, extremely poor households living in small, isolated communities in areas that lack basic infrastructure and markets may be unable to use credit in any way that would enable them to repay loan principal and interest.

Placing in debt those who are too poor to use credit effectively helps neither borrowers nor lenders. Food-deficit borrowers without opportunities to use credit or to market their output may have no choice but to eat their loans.[15] This can, in turn, lead to humiliation and the diminishing of an already low level of self-confidence. Lenders to the extremely poor also face difficulties because low repayment rates caused by borrowers who cannot repay prevent the development of sustainable financial institutions.

The poorest of the poor should not be the responsibility of the financial sector. The food, employment, and other basic requirements needed to overcome desperate poverty are appropriately financed by government and donor subsidies and grants. These tools are properly the responsibility of ministries of health, labor, social welfare, and others, as well as of donor agencies and private charities.

But credit subsidies to the economically active poor—who could make good use of commercial credit—prevent them from having widespread access to available loans because subsidized loans are usually rationed. In addition, this approach uses scarce donor and government funds that would be better spent on other forms of poverty alleviation. The use of tools in these ways—providing credit to the extremely poor and credit subsidies to the economically active poor—is like trying to build a house by using a saw to hammer the nails and a screwdriver to cut the boards.

A schematic diagram of a poverty alleviation toolbox, with an emphasis on its financial component, is shown in figure 1.1. The first column in the figure shows three income levels: lower-middle income, the economically active poor, and the extremely poor. No attempt is made to define these income categories because both the absolute scale and the relative proportions of the three categories vary considerably by country and region. In general, the extremely poor are those living on less than 75 cents a day, while the economically active poor have sufficient employment and income to meet basic nutrition, housing, and health needs. As shown in chapter 3, the economically active poor

Providing credit to the extremely poor and credit subsidies to the economically active poor is like trying to build a house by using a saw to hammer the nails and a screwdriver to cut the boards

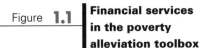

Figure **1.1** | **Financial services in the poverty alleviation toolbox**

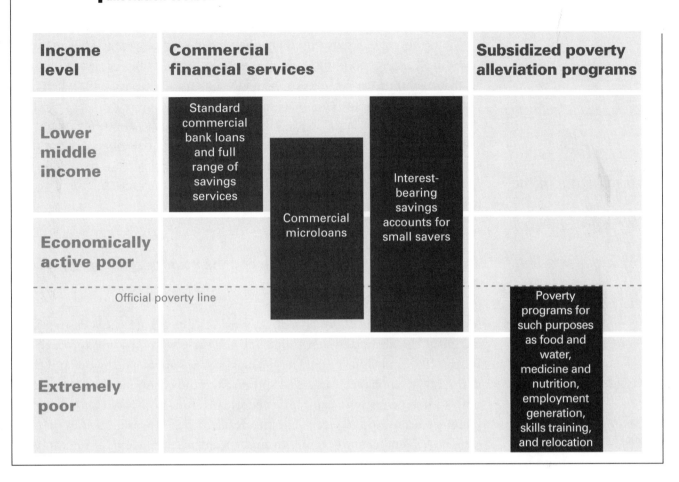

category is broad, ranging from households just barely above extreme poverty to those about to enter the lower-middle-income group. The lower-middle-income category is also a broad one. Although there is wide variation, such households typically have a relatively reliable income; higher standards of health, nutrition, housing, and education; a selection of consumer durables; and some forms of investment. Both economically active poor and lower-middle-income households tend to have some savings and, where possible, to emphasize nutrition, health, housing, and children's education. The amounts and degrees generally depend on their income levels and on the availability of these services.

The second column in figure 1.1 shows the financial services that are typically suitable for the different income levels. Commercial microcredit is appropriate both for many lower-middle-income households and for most of the economically active poor, including some below the official poverty line. Microsavings services reach even the lowest levels of the economically active poor, some well below the poverty line.

The third column in figure 1.1 shows nonfinancial poverty alleviation tools that are appropriate for those below the poverty line and essential for the extremely poor. The tools shown in the third column are funded by direct subsidies and grants;

their purpose is to provide the very poor with immediate necessities. In addition, broader tools such as education, health, and family planning (as well as the development of infrastructure, wastelands, markets, industries, communications, and the like) benefit the larger population—often, though not always, including the poor.

Some households start extremely poor and gain employment. They may then open small savings accounts. Some households with savings accounts then add small loans. Some start with loans and add voluntary savings accounts when these become available. Some clients are able to expand and diversify their enterprises and to qualify for larger loans. When permitted by the institution, many microbanking clients save continuously and borrow only occasionally. Over time, some qualify to become clients of standard commercial banks. The people represented in figure 1.1 whose demand is suitable for commercial microfinance inhabit most of the households of the developing world.

The Financial Systems Approach and the Poverty Lending Approach: A Fork in the Road

Microfinance in the 1990s was marked by a major debate between two leading views: the financial systems approach and the poverty lending approach

Microfinance in the 1990s was marked by a major debate between two leading views: the financial systems approach and the poverty lending approach (see Rhyne 1998 and Gulli 1998). The financial systems approach, the one presented in this book, emphasizes large-scale outreach to the economically active poor—both to borrowers who can repay microloans from household and enterprise income streams, and to savers. The financial systems approach focuses on institutional self-sufficiency because, given the scale of the demand for microfinance worldwide, this is the only possible means to meet widespread client demand for convenient, appropriate financial services.

The poverty lending approach concentrates on reducing poverty through credit, often provided together with complementary services such as skills training and the teaching of literacy and numeracy, health, nutrition, family planning, and the like. Under this approach donor- and government-funded credit is provided to poor borrowers, typically at below-market interest rates. The goal is to reach the poor, especially the extremely poor—the poorest of the poor—with credit to help overcome poverty and gain empowerment. Except for mandatory savings required as a condition of receiving a loan, the mobilization of local savings is normally not a significant part of the poverty lending approach to microfinance.

Bangladesh's Grameen Bank and some of its replicators in other countries represent leading examples of the poverty lending approach. The microbanking division of Bank Rakyat Indonesia (BRI), BancoSol in Bolivia, and the Association for Social Advancement (ASA) in Bangladesh are at the forefront of the financial systems approach.[16]

In a discussion about the debate between the two views, Elisabeth Rhyne (1998, p. 6) points out, *"everyone involved in microfinance shares a basic goal: to provide credit and savings services to thousands or millions of poor people in a sustainable way.* Everyone wants to reach the poor, and everyone believes sustainability is important" (box 1.2). Rhyne is right that the debate is about the means, not the goals. But the means can limit the goals that can be achieved. Thousands of clients can be served through either method. But serving millions of clients on a long-term basis in multiple, competing institutions requires a financial systems approach.

Rhyne goes on to say that "it became clear that the poverty/sustainability debate is ultimately about whether to subsidize interest rates" (p. 7). She comments further that *"there is in fact only one objective—outreach. [Institutional] sustainability is but the means to achieve it"* (p. 7).

Substantial contributions to the development of institutional microfinance have been made through both approaches. Some institutions using the poverty lending approach to microcredit have successfully reached poor people with donor- and government-subsidized credit services. These institutions have helped their borrowers develop their enterprises and increase their incomes, and they have had high repayment rates. But the literature on both microfinance and rural finance is filled with examples showing that most institutions that provide subsidized credit fail (see chapter 4). And even successful institutions following the poverty lending approach, in aggregate, can meet only a small portion of the demand for microfinance.

In contrast, formal sector commercial microfinance has proven itself able to make financial services—both credit and savings—available to low-income clients on a large scale, and to do so profitably. Institutions such as BRI and BancoSol have demonstrated that broad outreach to economically active poor clients can be achieved without ongoing subsidies.

As a global solution to meeting microfinance demand, the two views on microfinance—and the means they advocate—are not equal. Governments and donors cannot finance the hundreds of millions of people who constitute present unmet demand for microcredit services. In addition, the poverty lending approach, as indicated by its name, does not attempt to meet the vast demand among the poor for voluntary savings services.

The rest of this book is about the financial systems approach to microfinance. Before moving on, let me specify where and why I disagree with advocates of poverty lending. I agree with many of their views on poverty, both its causes and its solutions. I share their goal of providing financial services to poor people through sustainable institutions. I admire their commitment to eradicating poverty. And I recognize their important contributions to the development of methodologies for microcredit. But the tools of the poverty lending approach are poorly suited for building microfinance on a global scale. Resources for developing microfinance are limited, and donors and governments must choose among options if microfinance services are to be made available to all who can use them. In these choices are very large stakes.

Michael Chu, a former Wall Street financial specialist in the use of capital markets for company acquisitions, became a leader of the financial systems approach to microfinance. While president of ACCIÓN International, Chu (1998a, p. 2) described his view of the future of microfinance:

Institutions such as BRI and BancoSol have demonstrated that broad outreach to economically active poor clients can be achieved without ongoing subsidies

Box **1.2** **Excerpts from Elisabeth Rhyne's**
"The Yin and Yang of Microfinance:
Reaching the Poor and Sustainability"

In microfinance today the split continues between those in the "poverty" camp and those in the "sustainability" camp . . . Let us begin by noting that *everyone involved in microfinance shares a basic goal: to provide credit and savings services to thousands or millions of poor people in a sustainable way.* Everyone wants to reach the poor, and everyone believes sustainability is important . . . One of the fundamental poverty/sustainability questions is whether services can be delivered at a cost that is affordable to clients. Answering this question requires looking carefully at the cost structures and delivery methodologies of microfinance institutions, especially those claiming that their outreach to the very poor is the reason they are not becoming fully sustainable. Such institutions bear the cost of proving they are as efficient and low-cost in their operations as it is technically possible to be. If they are not efficient, their subsidies support those inefficient operations, and concern for the poor, however earnest, can also become an excuse to avoid difficult improvements.

The cost of a strategy of serving exclusively the very poor can be contrasted empirically against the cost of serving the same clients through a broad-based program . . . Once it is evident that a program is using the most efficient methods possible, the question turns to affordability for clients. The Maximizing Outreach study [Christen, Rhyne, and Vogel 1995] found that the most financially viable programs differed from their less viable peers in their willingness to set interest rates at levels that would fully recover costs. These programs chose to be financially viable, while other programs that held interest rates down chose to remain subsidy dependent. Although they may not have admitted it, these programs were subsidizing interest rates to clients.

The realization that pricing was such a direct determinant of viability led to other clarifications. *It became clear that the poverty/sustainability debate is ultimately about whether to subsidize interest rates.* Those who let go of sustainability in the name of reaching the poor are saying, in effect, that the poor cannot fully pay for their borrowing. If the poverty/sustainability debate were discussed in this way, it would be much more transparent. It would move away from the question of being "for the poor" or "against the poor" to the question of whether or not the poor need subsidized interest rates . . . It is possible to determine whether clients can afford to pay full cost interest rates by charging such rates and seeing whether client demand decreases. Little or no documentation of microfinance programs reports that increasing rates has significantly altered client demand for their loan products.

In [the] 1995 [study] we found microfinance programs that were sustainable at every level of clientele. More importantly, we found that for well-performing institutions there was no correlation between the poverty level of clients (as measured imperfectly by loan size) and the financial viability of the institution . . . *Even in relatively unfavorable settings these institutions had developed service delivery methods so tailored to their clientele and so efficient that clients could afford to pay the full cost of the services, making the institutions financially viable.*

Poverty and sustainability [are] the yin and yang of microfinance. They are two sides of a whole, each incomplete without the other. This view emphasizes that reaching the poor and sustainability are in large measure complementary, and particularly that sustainability serves outreach. Only by achieving a high degree of sustainability have microfinance programs gained access to the funding they need over time to serve significant numbers of their poverty-level clients. This image reveals that *there is in fact only one objective—outreach. Sustainability is but the means to achieve it.* Sustainability is in no way an end in itself; it is only valued for what it brings to the clients of microfinance. This is a point on which the "poverty camp" frequently misstates the motives of the "sustainability camp." It would do wonders for the state of the debate if the poverty camp more readily acknowledged that the sustainability camp valued sustainability only as a tool.

Box **1.2**

(continued)

However, at this point some underlying differences in perspective surface about the role of government, donors, and the private sector. *The sustainability camp views the private sector as the future home of microfinance, while those in the poverty camp seem wary of allowing that future to be dominated by commercial, for-profit operators. They foresee donor and government involvement in microfinance for an extended period of time.* Faced with a choice between donors, governments, and the private sector, they seem more comfortable keeping microfinance attached to donors and governments, perhaps because they trust donors and governments to have some ongoing concern with the poor. They also fear that for-profit operators will ignore the poorest clients.

In contrast, the sustainability group argues that any future which continues dependence on donors and governments is a future in which few microfinance clients will be served. Donors and governments, both notably prone to fads, are unlikely to continue subsidizing microfinance indefinitely and are not generous enough to do so on a major scale. This group believes that the only way to assure access by the poor to financial services is to ensure that the private sector finds it profitable to provide such services. Only the private sector has plenty of resources and will stick with a moneymaking activity even if it is not in fashion.

Source: Rhyne 1998, pp. 6–8.

Microfinance today stands at the threshold of its next major stage, the connection with the capital markets . . . The reason why the connection with capital markets is a watershed lies in the fact that, if accomplished, it will make the outreach of microfinance to date . . . a mere prologue for what will come. The millions reached today will increase a hundredfold. This is nothing short of changing *the very nature of banking,* from servicing the top 25 or 30 percent (at the most) of the population of the developing world to meeting the demand of the rest. It is the reclaiming of finance for society at large—the true democratization of capital.

In contrast, a microcredit summit held in Washington, D.C., in 1997 developed a charter stating that "credit is more than business. Just like food, credit is a human right." A commitment was made "to ensure that 100 million of the world's poorest families, especially the women of those families, receive credit for self employment and other financial and business services by the year 2005" (Muhammad Yunus, in a speech to the Microcredit Summit, February 1997). This aim is to be met through a campaign that seeks to raise $21.6 billion.[17]

A second microcredit summit was held in New York in 1998. But these were microcredit summits, not microfinance summits; the distinction is crucial.[18] The summit views are well intentioned. But if large-scale poverty alleviation is their goal, the billions of dollars earmarked for microcredit loan portfolios could be spent much more effectively. Five issues can be highlighted:

- *Food is a universal need; credit is not.* Not all poor people want or need debt. Some cannot make use of it within reasonable risk limits, and some cannot repay it. Credit is important—but for many of the poorest, other poverty alleviation tools are more needed and more effective.

- *If credit were a human right, the poverty lending approach would not enable the right to be widely exercised.* The first reason is that there are an estimated 500 million people operating microbusinesses and small businesses (CGAP 1998f, p. 1). There are many poor people in other occupations as well. Thus the scale is well beyond the reach of donor and government funding. The second is that a one-time microloan carries little development impact. Low-income people throughout the developing world need continued access to credit and savings services, with the option of gradually increasing the size of their loans as borrowers become qualified through repayment records and enterprise performance. While $21.6 billion is a lot of money for microfinance by the standards of donors and governments, it represents just a small part of the funds required to finance potential worldwide microcredit demand on an ongoing basis.

- *From the point of view of poverty alleviation, the funds collected for financing microcredit portfolios in developing countries could be better used in other ways.* Worldwide demand for microfinance would be met sooner if the funds allocated for direct financing of loan portfolios were used instead for the development of selected financial institutions committed to developing large-scale commercial microfinance services. Building sustainable institutions—by funding equity, technical assistance, information systems, management and staff training, and the like—allows donors to maximize the outreach of their scarce funds. This is because self-sufficient commercial microfinance institutions (unlike donor-funded microcredit programs) can leverage substantial additional funds for their portfolios by mobilizing public savings, accessing commercial debt, or attracting for-profit investment. In addition, it would be more effective to use donated funds to provide the extremely poor with food, water, medicines, training, and employment rather than to put them in debt before they are financially able.

- *For many of the world's poorest people, appropriately designed voluntary savings services are a more important and appropriate development instrument than credit.* Formal savings services with appropriate products are especially important for poor savers because options for nonformal financial savings at the local level may offer security or returns, but normally not both. In addition, restrictions may be placed on liquidity. The poor are sometimes so desperate for a safe place to store their savings that they even pay collectors to hold their deposits safely, thus realizing a negative return on their savings (see chapter 7).[19] However, institutions following the poverty lending approach tend not to focus on mobilizing voluntary savings, but on securing subsidized funds from governments and donors to finance their portfolios. The result of this choice is that the demand for savings services is not met, and savings that could finance the loan portfolios are not mobilized.

- *Where are the institutions qualified to handle the microcredit summit's projected massive increase in the volume of lending—from the summit's estimated 8 million borrowers in 1997 to 100 million borrowers in 2005?* Nearly all microcredit programs today are in small, unregulated, unsupervised institutions. Microfinance best practices tell us that an institution should increase its portfolio gradually, that it should charge high enough interest rates on loans to ensure that all costs and risks are covered, that it should provision realistically for loan arrears and defaults, and that it should maintain internationally accepted accounting standards. Very few microcredit programs meet these standards. In addition, many suffer from uncertain ownership structures, poor governance, and lack of accountability. A rapidly expanding loan portfolio would carry substantial risks for most of today's microfinance institutions. Neither small microcredit programs nor the few large microfinance institutions in operation are equipped to handle the large and immediate increase in microloans expected under the summit program. This is especially the case for institutions charging subsidized interest rates, because their operating cost budgets may not be large enough to provide for needed high-quality financial management and internal supervision, adequate staff training and incentives, appropriate information systems, and so on. Thus the priority should be to establish a sequence, emphasizing the building of institutions and the development of commercial microfinance first, then following with rapid but safe expansion of the microloan portfolio.

Overall, the poverty lending approach poses a deep dilemma for governments, microfinance institutions, donors, and others. This is because microfinance has reached a fork in the road. The microfinance revolution, based largely on the financial systems approach, and the poverty lending agenda, based largely on eradicating poverty through credit, have begun to move in different directions. In one sense the roads heading out from the fork are complementary. Both lead to assistance for the poor, though in different ways. But donors and governments supporting microfinance have scarce resources, and they must choose how best to use them.

The poverty lending approach uses subsidies primarily to fund loan portfolios. The financial systems approach uses subsidies primarily to disseminate lessons from the best practices of fully sustainable microfinance systems and to finance the development of financially self-sufficient microfinance institutions. These institutions then finance their microloan portfolios commercially, enabling them to multiply outreach by leveraging additional capital. One road leads toward donor-dependent microcredit institutions that cannot meet the demand for credit and do not meet the demand for savings services. The other leads to self-sufficient financial intermediaries and large-scale microfinance outreach. This book is about the latter.

Financially self-sufficient institutions finance their microloan portfolios commercially, enabling them to multiply outreach by leveraging additional capital

Financially Self-sufficient Microfinance Institutions

Sustainable microfinance is carried out by commercial institutions that deliver financial services to the economically active poor at interest rates that enable the institutions to cover all costs (including the commercial cost of funds) and risks, and to generate a profit. Such institutions include banks and, in some countries, savings and credit cooperatives, credit unions, and other nonbank financial organizations.

The term *commercial microfinance institution* refers here both to institutions that provide microfinance to the public (such as banks) and those that serve only their members (such as credit unions). It refers to institutions that finance their loan portfolios from locally mobilized savings, those that access commercial debt and for-profit investment, and those that use retained earnings to finance their lending. The term also includes institutions that provide only microfinance, as well as those that offer microfinance as part of a wider set of financial services.

Commercial microfinance institutions are differentiated from informal commercial lenders who lend money for profit (often as part of interlinked transactions with borrowers), from subsidized formal microcredit (in which a regulated institution such as a state-owned bank channels government or donor funds to borrowers at subsidized interest rates), and from unregulated institutions such as NGOs (which onlend subsidized donor or government funds to their borrowers).

Commercial microcredit provided by financial institutions is not new. It was common in parts of Europe in the 19th century and was sometimes exported to countries under colonial rule. Thus Indonesia's oldest institutions providing commercial microcredit profitably—the Badan Kredit Desas (BKDs), or village-owned credit organizations on the islands of Java and Madura, now a special category of secondary banks, were begun by the Dutch in the late 1890s. While not developed specifically as microfinance institutions, the BKDs provide microcredit and voluntary savings services to large numbers of poor clients.

Financial institutions that mobilize the savings of the poor are also not new. In Colombia, for example, the Banco Caja Social began mobilizing savings from poor households in 1911. What is new—begun by the Bank Dagang Bali in Indonesia in 1970—is financially self-sufficient formal financial intermediaries providing small loans and voluntary savings services profitably to the economically active poor.

The microfinance revolution is a commercial revolution, based on new financial technology and greatly accelerated by the information revolution that developed concurrently. It began in the 1970s, developed in the 1980s, and took off in the 1990s. The profitable provision of small loans was made possible by the lending methodologies, pricing, products, and services that were designed specifically for microcredit clients during the 1970s and 1980s. In Indonesia the new lending methods were joined with the widespread mobilization of voluntary microsavings in the 1980s; in Bolivia they were combined with access to commercial debt and investment in the 1990s. These combinations enabled

The microfinance revolution has been greatly accelerated by the information revolution that developed concurrently

institutional profitability and long-term viability, making possible large-scale formal-sector financial outreach to low-income segments of the population.

Information on these breakthroughs spread widely through rapidly expanding forms of communication, and institutions in a variety of countries began experimenting with commercial microfinance during the 1990s. Other advances followed. It became possible to deepen outreach by reducing the denomination of financial services and serving even poorer clients, while maintaining institutional profitability and self-sufficiency. ASA in Bangladesh and Compartamos in Mexico, discussed in chapter 18, provide good illustrations of this process. By the late 1990s in a few countries, the result was—for the first time in history—competition among commercial microfinance institutions for the business of low-income clients.

From the point of view of borrowers, the crucial words in microcredit are access and cost. Subsidized loan programs typically have limited capital and do not provide low-income households with wide access to credit.[20] Informal commercial moneylenders, in aggregate, provide wide access to credit, but generally at very high cost to borrowers.

From the perspective of savers, the key words are security, convenience, liquidity, confidentiality, access to credit, good service, and returns. Indigenous forms of saving—in gold, animals, raw materials, cash held in the home, grain or other agricultural commodities, rotating savings and credit associations (ROSCAs), savings collectors, and the like—normally do not provide this combination of characteristics (see chapters 7 and 13).

In contrast to informal commercial moneylenders and informal savings methods, formal institutions providing commercial microfinance can make financial services—both credit and savings—widely available at a cost that enables both the profitability of the financial institutions and the growth and diversification of their clients' enterprises.

For savers, the key words are security, convenience, liquidity, confidentiality, access to credit, good service, and returns

Providing credit and savings services profitably

Microcredit methods designed for individuals and those designed for groups have both proven effective; these can also be combined in the same institution. For both kinds of microloans, however, commercial microfinance institutions must charge interest rates that are significantly higher than the normal lending rates of the country's standard commercial banks. Operating costs are typically several times those of the banking industry standard in the same country. There are a number of reasons. Microfinance institutions are necessarily labor intensive. They must maintain and staff many small, widely dispersed outlets that are conveniently located for clients. Infrastructure and communications in the areas serviced are often rudimentary. And it is more costly to process many small loans and savings accounts than a smaller number of larger ones.

In the microfinance arena, discussion of 'market rates' and 'subsidized rates' tends to be confused. The term 'market rate' should mean a rate that arises from the interplay of supply and demand *in some defined range of transactions* . . . Market rate is used to refer to the rate at which commercial banks and their conventional customers conduct deposit and loan transactions. Loan interest rates are called 'subsidized' or 'unsubsidized' depending on whether they cover the full cost of providing the loan. Costs of providing microloans are higher, as a percentage of loan amount, than costs of conventional bank loans. Thus a market rate (as defined here) is likely to be a "subsidized rate" if it is applied to microloans.

—Christen 1997a, p. 18; see also Rosenberg 1996

Savings services for the poor remain forgotten in many countries—not only in rural areas but also in low-income urban neighborhoods

Delivering microfinance services at many small, scattered locations is considerably more expensive than providing clients with services for larger loans and deposits in centrally located urban banks. Still, the interest rates on microloans charged by profitable financial institutions—even though they are higher than standard bank rates—are highly attractive to low-income borrowers in many developing countries because they represent a small fraction of the rates normally charged to such borrowers in the informal commercial market.

Politicians, journalists, social workers, and the general public often have a difficult time understanding why interest rates on microloans need to be higher than those on larger loans. This is, after all, somewhat counterintuitive. Often mistakenly perceived as discrimination against the poor, the issue of commercial microcredit interest rates can be highly controversial. Institutions and governments that want to introduce commercial microfinance into the formal financial sector must be well informed about the reasons that interest rates permitting full cost recovery are important for the clients, the institution, and the economy—and must hone their political skills.

Unlike most informal moneylenders, subsidized credit programs, and NGOs that provide microcredit, many commercial microfinance institutions also offer voluntary savings services that are designed to be suitable for small savers.[21] As will be demonstrated, these services are greatly in demand. But in many countries they are unavailable. In 1984 savings was called "the forgotten half of rural finance" (Vogel 1984b, p. 248). More than 15 years later, savings services for the poor remain forgotten in many countries—not only in rural areas but also in low-income urban neighborhoods.[22]

However, commercial microfinance institutions provide savings and credit services to a wide range of the poor. Credit can be made available to the poorest borrower with the ability and willingness to repay a small loan (say, $10) at the interest rates required for institutional self-sufficiency, up to the largest borrower whose loan requirement is still too small to be met by standard commercial banks at a conveniently located branch. Savings products are designed to be appropriate for the demand of low-income households, required opening balances are low, and a very low minimum balance is required.

Commercial microcredit is provided to borrowers who have experience in a particular type of enterprise and who, it is believed, can and will repay the loan and the interest on time. A major role of credit officers is to distinguish between credit applicants who do not operate an efficient enterprise, who are unlikely to be able to repay the loan, for whom the loan terms are inappropriate, and so on, from applicants who are creditworthy. Thus, in one sense, commercial microcredit is exclusive in its approach.

Microsavings, on the other hand, is inclusive. More of the economically active poor generally want to save than want to borrow at a given time. Such savers will take advantage of savings facilities in secure, conveniently located formal institutions if the kinds of products and services that meet their demand are made available to them. And with careful pricing, commercial financial institutions can accommodate nearly all microsavers. In addition, a commercial microfinance institution that serves the public mobilizes deposits from anyone—rich or poor—who lives or works nearby and wants to save in the institution's local branch. This approach makes it possible to serve poor savers cost-effectively while making available increased funds for microlending (see chapters 7 and 13).

In another sense, however, formal-sector credit and savings are both inclusive services. Profitable microfinance institutions can provide financial services at a moderate cost to far more of the economically active poor than can any alternative provider. Such institutions can reach large numbers of low-income households who would otherwise be excluded from available, affordable microfinance services. And "there is overwhelming empirical evidence that huge numbers of poor borrowers can indeed pay interest rates at a level high enough to support MFI [microfinance institution] sustainability" (Rosenberg 1996, box 1.3).

There are many types of successful microcredit and microsavings programs. But only financially self-sufficient commercial microfinance institutions can meet the demand for microfinance on a global scale.

Reaching scale

The defining characteristic of the microfinance revolution is its large-scale outreach in the provision of financial services to low-income clients—a scale that is made possible by regulated, self-sufficient financial intermediaries.[23] This does not mean that other types of microfinance programs are not valuable or that other kinds of institutions have not contributed to the development of the microfinance revolution; they are and they have. But the future of most microfinance is in profitable financial intermediaries operating within their countries' formal financial sectors. Still few in number, such institutions nevertheless serve large numbers of clients and represent the frontier of the microfinance industry.

> The microfinance industry embraces several thousand organizations offering microcredit and other financial services to poor clients. Almost all of these institutions are concerned with poverty alleviation, but relatively few of them are fundamentally committed to long-term financial sustainability and exponential growth.

Profitable microfinance institutions can provide financial services at a moderate cost to far more of the economically active poor than can any alternative provider

1. CAN Microborrowers Pay High Interest Rates?

There is overwhelming empirical evidence that huge numbers of poor borrowers can indeed pay interest rates at a level high enough to support MFI [microfinance institution] sustainability.

- Informal credit markets already exist in most poor communities. One typically finds lower-income borrowers taking and repaying repeated informal loans at interest rates much higher than any formal MFI would charge.[1]
- MFIs charging very high interest rates almost always find that demand far outstrips their ability to supply it. Most of their customers repay their loans, and return repeatedly for new loans: this pattern demonstrates the customers' conviction that the loans allow them to earn more than the interest that they have to pay. This phenomenon does not appear to be restricted to particular regions or countries.
- For the past ten years, the author of this paper has been asking in conferences, courses, and (more recently) Internet newsgroups whether anyone present has ever heard of a microfinance program that ran into trouble by driving away clients with interest rates that were too high. No one has yet pointed to a single example. This remarkable piece of data does not indicate that there is no limit to the interest rates that the microcredit market can bear; but it does suggest that the limit is probably considerably higher than what even the more aggressive MFIs are presently charging.

Thus, there is abundant proof that poor people's tiny businesses can often pay interest rates that would strangle a larger business. Still, this proposition strikes many as confusingly counterintuitive. There are several approaches to making it more intelligible.

Let us begin with the case of a Bolivian woman who sells merchandise from a blanket that she spreads every day on a street in La Paz. Her sales, and thus her income, are directly proportional to the time she is sitting on the street, offering her goods. Because of her shortage of working capital, she spends two hours of each ten-hour workday traveling to purchase supplies from her wholesaler, whose warehouse is outside the city. These two hours produce no sales or income for her. If a working capital loan allows her to buy inventory for three days at a time instead of one, she can save eight hours in travel time each six-day week. This translates into a 17% increase in selling time, and thus in her sales, every week. If the amount of the working capital loan is double her daily sales, and her gross profit is 25% of sales, then she could afford to pay 40% a month on the loan and still come out slightly ahead. A loan from an MFI at, say, 5% per month would be immensely advantageous to her . . .

Another useful perspective on this issue emerges when we look at microborrowers' interest costs in the context of their overall income and expense. Castello, Stearns, and Christen [1991] report such an analysis on a sample of MFI borrowers in Chile, Colombia, and the Dominican Republic. These borrowers were paying relatively high effective interest rates, averaging 6.3% per month. But these interest payments made up a tiny fraction of their overall costs, ranging from 0.4% to 3.4%.[2]

This kind of analysis makes it easier to understand the oft-repeated assertion that for poor entrepreneurs, access to finance tends to be a much more important issue than the cost of that finance.

2. SHOULD Micro-Finance Institutions Charge High Interest Rates?

The preceding section reviewed the ample evidence that many poor people can pay, and therefore MFIs can charge, rates of interest that are much higher than the rates that commercial banks charge to their usual customers. Moreover, it attempted to explain why this result is not particularly surprising. But given that MFIs can charge such rates, the question remains whether they should. Most MFIs are lodged in grant-funded non-governmental

Box   **1.3**

(continued)

organizations whose overarching objective is helping the poor, not maximizing profits. And while many poor entrepreneurs can pay high interest rates, it is also clear that some cannot, and are thus excluded from programs that insist on charging interest high enough to cover all costs.

Some people treat this question as if it comes down to a value judgment: which do you care more about—poor people or profits (. . . or financial systems . . . or neoliberal ideology). To avoid any such confusion, let's assume that the only objective we care about is maximizing benefit to poor people. From this perspective, the argument for high interest rates is straightforward. In most countries, donor funding is a limited quantity that will never be capable of reaching more than a tiny fraction of those poor households who could benefit from quality financial services.[3] We can hope to reach most of those households only if MFIs can mobilize relatively large amounts of commercial finance at market rates. They cannot do this unless they charge interest rates that cover the costs laid out in the first section of this note (see Rosenberg 1996).

1. The highest MFI interest rate observed by the author was a monthly effective rate of 10.1% charged by a village banking program in Mexico during a period when inflation hit 52% a year. Various studies report rural moneylender rates in Mexico as high as 25–30% per month during periods of much lower inflation.
2. "Exposing Interest Rates: Their True Significance for Microentrepreneurs and Credit Programs," AC-CIÓN International 1991, p. 12ff.
3. In Bolivia, for instance, it is estimated that US$300 million in micro-finance assets would be required to saturate the feasible micro-finance market. In ten years of unusual intense activity in this area, donors have managed to provide only about $20 million.

Source: Rosenberg 1996.

Most MFIs [microfinance institutions] would *like* to be large and sustainable; but it is a much smaller group which understands the full price of such sustainability and is willing and able to pay it. MFIs without this profound commitment to sustainability may often be doing excellent work, but they do not represent the cutting edge of the microfinance industry.

—*MicroBanking Bulletin* 1998, p. 40

Components of the microfinance revolution emerged, slowly and sporadically in many countries, with each institution in relative isolation from the others. Generated by a mix of public and private sector involvement, the revolution gained momentum in the 1980s and 1990s, galvanized in part by the large-scale successes beginning in Indonesia in the 1980s and in Bolivia in the 1990s.

Indonesia has played a special role in the microfinance revolution because it was the first country where the following pieces of the puzzle were put together on a national scale:

- A loan methodology and savings services suitable for microfinance clients.
- Staff training and incentives that encourage in-depth knowledge of the microfinance market.
- High loan repayment rates.

- Pricing based on full cost recovery and returning a profit to the institution.
- Management and organizational systems with the capacity to deliver financial services efficiently to low-income people throughout a large country.
- Continuing institutional profitability without subsidy.
- Widespread outreach among the economically active poor.

More than a hundred institutions are developing sustainable microfinance programs, and the number is steadily increasing

At the microbanking division of BRI, a large state-owned commercial bank, local savings are mobilized and lent out profitably in small loans in both rural and urban areas throughout the country. BRI's microbanking division, which began its commercial approach to microfinance in 1984, reaches millions of clients. It has been profitable each year since 1986 and independent of subsidy since 1987. In December 1999 the division had $802 million in 2.5 million outstanding loans, $2.3 billion in 24.1 million savings accounts, and a long-term repayment rate of 98 percent.[24] The 1999 record of BRI's microbanking division was achieved in a year when Indonesia was just beginning to emerge from the most serious economic downturn of any country in recent history (see chapters 8 and 15). There are also smaller financial institutions in Indonesia with a similar orientation; in that country, the world's fourth most populous, a substantial part of the large demand for microfinance, for both credit and savings, is met by profitable institutions that do not require ongoing subsidies from donors or from the government. These institutions have proven extremely stable, even in time of severe national crisis.

In Bolivia the microfinance revolution emerged in the 1990s. Large-scale commercial microcredit is provided there by BancoSol, a privately owned bank for microentrepreneurs, and by a number of competitors following hotly on BancoSol's heels (and profits). By 1997 BancoSol, financed by a combination of domestic and international commercial debt and investment and locally mobilized voluntary savings, provided loans profitably to more than one quarter of Bolivia's bank clients.

Overall, the 1990s saw massive efforts to spread best practices in microfinance, to develop standards for the infant industry, and to bring to the attention of policymakers the potential contributions that formal commercial microfinance institutions could make to their countries and their economies. More than a hundred institutions in many parts of the world are developing sustainable microfinance programs, and the number is steadily increasing.

The revolution is still emerging, however, and commercial institutions providing microfinance remain relatively rare. Instead, in many countries funds provided for microcredit by governments and donors continue to be misdirected into large subsidized credit programs. This leaves most of the economically active poor without access to credit for working capital or investment, except at high cost from informal moneylenders. It also leaves them without access to savings services that provide security, liquidity, and returns.

In many parts of the developing world, microfinance continues to be perceived by the formal financial sector as unimportant for the economy, unprofitable for financial institutions, and unnecessary for the poor. We will show that all these views are wrong: that institutional commercial microfinance is of major importance for the economy, that it can be profitable for the financial institution, and that it is a necessary component of large-scale poverty reduction.

Why Has the Demand for Institutional Commercial Microfinance Not Been Met?

Nearly every economist I meet asks the same question: if formal sector microfinance is profitable, and if there is high demand, why has the demand not been met? The primary answer is the lack of appropriate and efficient financial technology and the lack of information that prevailed until recently. Moneylenders the world over know that microfinance is profitable. It is no accident that the first formal commercial bank to provide extensive commercial microfinance, Bank Dagang Bali, was founded by a couple with long experience in informal markets and moneylending. Yet accurate information about the dynamics and interactions of local markets reaches most bankers, economists, and policymakers rarely if at all. It is not yet widely understood that commercial microfinance can be profitable in an institutional setting. And until the 1970s and 1980s, little was known about lending methods and savings products and services appropriate for poor clients. The microfinance revolution awaited the pioneering methodological efforts of Bank Dagang Bali, India's Self-Employed Women's Association (SEWA), the Grameen Bank, BRI's unit desa system, Bolivia's Fundación para la Promoción y Desarrollo de la Microempresa (PRODEM), the NGO that created BancoSol, and many others discussed in later chapters.

Other reasons that most of the demand for microfinance remains unmet include the generally limited interest in microfinance among policymakers and managers of financial institutions (international and corporate banking are considered "sexy" postings—microfinance is not), prohibitive government regulations (especially with regard to ceilings on loan interest rates), lack of basic infrastructure, and sparsely settled populations. The first two of these reasons will become less important as more information on the profitability of microfinance becomes widely available; the third will decrease with development. The last remains unsolved; it is not cost-effective for institutions to provide commercial microfinance in areas of very low population density. Many loans can be disbursed and collected at central locations on market days, but this method does not provide an adequate level of service for savers. But this problem is likely to be solved through collaboration between technology and microfinance experts.

Still, lack of reliable information is the main reason for most of the unmet demand for formal sector commercial microfinance today. The formal financial sector has been poorly advised from many quarters, including people who:

If formal sector microfinance is profitable, and if there is high demand, why has the demand not been met?

- Advise that formal institutions cannot provide microfinance profitably because of the high transaction costs the institution would have to bear.
- Warn of high institutional risk because of asymmetric information, moral hazard, and the adverse selection of borrowers (chapter 5).
- Assert that institutions cannot compete successfully with the informal commercial credit market.
- Believe that institutional commercial microfinance is not a development priority because informal commercial lenders meet the credit demand of low-income households and are generally beneficial to the poor.
- Think that low-income people are uneducated and backward, and so unable to participate in the formal financial sector.
- Assume that low-income people cannot afford commercial loans and so require government- or donor-funded credit subsidies (thereby insuring that demand remains unmet).
- Believe that most rural economies in developing countries do not generate a sufficient volume of business to be attractive to formal financial institutions.

The main reason for the vast unmet demand for institutional microfinance is the paucity of reliable information that reaches the formal financial sector

All this advice, discussed in part 2, has served for decades to slow the learning curve of the formal financial sector about the profitability of microfinance. The conventional wisdom—that microfinance is not suited to the commercial formal financial sector—is still widely believed within many governments, banks, and donor agencies. This, in turn, leads to the kinds of government supervision and regulation that, when enforced, do not permit the development of sustainable microfinance institutions. It also contributes to the dearth of high-level, skilled managers willing to commit themselves to the development of commercial microfinance.

During the 1990s, however, information about commercial microfinance expanded exponentially. The leaders of the microfinance revolution—microfinance institutions; central banks, finance ministries, and bank superintendencies; foundations and networks; donor agencies; and others—have begun to be effective, both individually and collectively, in making the principles and practices of sustainable microfinance known in countries around the world. The approach promoted is one of adaptation, not of replication; commercial microfinance does not advocate clones or replicators. Rather, the process emphasizes the underlying principles of the commercial approach, selects and uses indigenous practices, adapts experiences from other countries to the local context, and encourages local innovations.

The 1990s will likely be seen as a watershed period in the development of commercial microfinance. The decade has been marked by expanding international and regional communication about aspects of commercial microfinance; growing attention to crucial issues of regulation, supervision, and governance; increasing visits of policymakers and microfinance practitioners to leading microfinance institutions; the founding of microfinance training programs and practitioner networks; the introduction of Internet discussion groups and Websites;

the early development of industry standards and the birth of rating agencies; and a shift in focus by some donors from direct financing of microloan portfolios to allocation of their scarce resources to institution building for selected commercial microfinance institutions and to dissemination of information about best practices in sustainable microfinance.

The recent and rapid spread of information about the viability of commercial microfinance is having major effects on microfinance planning in numerous countries. Advice to policymakers has been changing rapidly. The microfinance revolution has benefited greatly from its emergence in history at the same time as the information revolution.

Why Does Meeting the Demand for Institutional Commercial Microfinance Matter?

Why does it matter if the economically active poor have access to institutional microfinance—to commercial credit and savings services? Microfinance matters for two reasons. First, it provides the financial services that many need to expand and diversify their economic activities, to increase their incomes,[25] and to improve their lives. As shown in chapter 3, the first things that many poor families do when their income rises is improve their nutrition and send their children to school. Microfinance plays an important, if not yet well recognized, role in promoting education and health and in decreasing child labor.

Second, microfinance matters because it has proven a powerful method of building the self-confidence of the poor. Commercial microfinance institutions deliver more to the poor than savings services and loans: they provide a demonstration of trust in their clients. The self-confidence on the part of clients that often develops from such trust is at least as essential for the development of their enterprises as the loan and deposit facilities provided. The subsequent growth and diversification of the enterprises, in turn, build continuing and increased self-confidence for their proprietors.

Access to financial services

Credit. Formal sector commercial credit services provide microloans offering a range of amounts, maturities, and repayment terms. These services enable low-income people to better manage the growth and diversification of their enterprises. At the lower end, commercial microfinance programs can provide loans of less than $10, while the higher end varies considerably from several hundred dollars to more than $10,000. An incremental approach to loan size permits borrowers to start with small loans and to increase the size of their loans gradually as they qualify for larger loans.

A woman who sells food in a market stall in La Paz, Bolivia, told me about her successive loans from BancoSol. Her loan at the time of the discussion in 1993 was for four months, with an annual effective rate of interest of 55 percent; the (inflation adjusted) real interest rate was 46 percent.

During the 1990s information about commercial microfinance expanded exponentially

The first things that many poor families do when their income rises is improve their nutrition and send their children to school

This is my fourth loan from BancoSol. With my first loan [of about $50] I was able to get a little better price from the wholesale food sellers because I could buy more supplies at one time. But there was not much difference in my income. When I took out my second loan I could bargain with the wholesalers for a better price because I could buy a greater amount at one time. I could see the increase in my income. By the third loan I could begin to buy more types of food items, and the number of my customers grew. Now with the fourth loan [of about $250] I have a larger stall, a number of different products for sale, and many new customers. Now my customers respect me because I am a big market woman, and my family is happy because we have a higher income.

When borrowers with good repayment records have reached the loan ceiling of a commercial microfinance institution, they are often eligible for standard loans from commercial banks. By this time such borrowers may qualify for the bank's minimum loan size, have gained access to the collateral needed, and be able to handle the formalities required by the bank. Because of their good repayment records, even standard commercial banks may consider such borrowers to be desirable clients.

Savings services. Throughout the world and across many cultures and economies, the economically active poor—even the poorest of them—save in multiple forms and for a variety of purposes. They save for household emergencies because they know that in most cases they will have few other options at such times. They save to manage irregular income streams, for social and religious obligations, and for long-term investment opportunities such as housing construction or children's education. They save in a variety of nonfinancial forms. Many, however, will save in financial form if suitable institutions and instruments are available.

Appropriately designed voluntary microsavings services delivered by financial institutions at the local level are much in demand because they permit poor people to store permanent, seasonal, or temporary excess liquidity safely for future use and to increase income through returns on savings. The widespread provision of secure, convenient microsavings services is a much-underestimated tool in the poverty alleviation toolbox. As noted, for the poorest among the economically active poor, savings services are often more important than credit.

The value of voluntary savings services can be best explained by poor savers themselves. A couple who lives in the Dhaka slums of Bangladesh and saves in SafeSave, a cooperative institution (see chapter 17), provide a good example of the demand for savings services among the lowest levels of the economically active poor. The conversation below took place in 1997 in Dhaka among the couple, a SafeSave representative, and a foreign visitor. The couple's income is derived from their work of breaking bricks into small pieces to be used as construction materials—for which they receive a daily wage.[26]

Visitor:	How much do you need to live on each day— for the five of you in the household?
Husband:	We need 50 taka ($1.11).
Visitor:	How much do you earn in your work breaking bricks?
Husband:	Usually about 35 taka ($0.78).
Visitor:	But in your passbook it says you save 5 taka ($0.11) most days! How can you do that? Why?
Wife:	What do you mean?
SafeSave representative:	He means if you need 50 taka a day but you get only 35, then how do you manage?
Wife:	We go hungry. What else could we do? What does he say we should do?
SafeSave representative:	But he wants to know why you save.
Husband:	For our future. Everyone needs to think about their future. Don't we have a daughter and two grandchildren?

Building the self-confidence of the poor

By showing respect to customers and indicating confidence in their enterprises, microfinance institutions help to set the example that many poor households are well regarded and worthy of trust. This role is especially important in societies where certain segments of the population—whether because of ethnic origin, gender, religion, occupation, or other characteristics—are systemically subjugated by those who are locally dominant. Because financial services help the poor expand their economic activities and increase their income and assets, their self-confidence grows simultaneously. Illustrations are given in chapter 3.

Because financial services help the poor expand their economic activities and increase their income and assets, their self-confidence grows simultaneously

A poor, illiterate man in India provides a good example of how such self-confidence can develop. LG, a member of a tribal group in central India, participated in a development program initiated by a large landowner of the area, a leader in social and economic development (see Robinson 1980 and Pingle and von Furer-Haimendorf 1998). The landowner experimented with new uses of wastelands, knowing that badlands are the kind of land to which the poor have the best chance of gaining access. Conducting tests in his home area of Adilabad, Andhra Pradesh, in the 1960s, he found that with hand watering of mango grafts the roots can reach the subsoil moisture within a few years. Thus mango trees could be cultivated on the dry and barren lands found in that area. The landowner then developed a mango orchard project in which the participants were either poor members of the tribal groups of the region or low-caste people.[27]

The participants in the project already had, or were provided, wasteland plots with very dry, sandy soil. They were shown how to plant, water, and care for the mango grafts. In 1970 each participant took a $25 an acre loan for cultivation expenses from the local branch of a state-owned bank. LG planted his three acres of sandy soil with mango grafts, and he and the members of his household hand watered these during the summer months. This type of mango tree does not bear fruit for the first five years, and it bears only little in the sixth year. But LG's trees began to produce income in 1976. Between 1975 and 1984 his average household income rose from about $140 to about $780. During this period average annual inflation was in the single digits.

The mango income caused significant changes in the lives of all the participants, and mango cultivation by the poor spread widely in the area. After 10 years of income from the orchards, nearly all the original participants had improved their nutritional standards and their housing. In addition, most had accomplished some or all of the following: purchased or improved land, constructed wells or houses, installed electricity, purchased pumpsets, and repaid old debts to moneylenders. Some had started sending their children to school.[28] Without exception, the bank loans taken for mango cultivation were fully repaid.

I visited the participants each year for nearly 20 years to learn how their incomes and their lives were changing. After they had been receiving mango income for 10 years, as well as income from other activities that had been started with mango profits, I asked each of the participants a question: "Of the economic development in your household since 1976, the year when you first gained income from mango cultivation, how much of the results do you think come from your own efforts, and how much do you think come from the will of God?" LG replied:

> Before the mango scheme, I had a little dryland, but nothing grew unless there was rain. God controls the rain, so everything was up to Him. With the mango scheme, things changed. I got a loan from the bank and planted mango grafts. It was difficult in the beginning because there was no income from the trees [during the first five years], and still I had to work very hard. I had to water and care for the trees and also work as a daily laborer whenever work was available. But when the mangoes began to bear, I had income every year. I could repay my loan easily. Then I was able to dig a well, and now I have water year round. Now that I have water I can run my own farm. God has much to do; He is very busy running the universe. He does not need to take care of my farm anymore. Now I do that myself.

Microfinance matters because it increases the options and the self-confidence of poor households by helping them to expand their enterprises and add others, to decrease risks, to smooth consumption, to obtain higher returns on investment, to improve management and increase their productivity and incomes, to store their excess liquidity safely and obtain returns on their savings, to escape or decrease exploitation by the locally powerful, and to conduct their businesses with dignity. The quality of their lives improves. Children are sent to school, and child labor decreases. And housing and health improve. In addition, the economically active poor who are able to expand their economic activities often create jobs for others; among those who gain employment in this way are some of the extremely poor.

"God has much to do; He is very busy running the universe. He does not need to take care of my farm anymore. Now I do that myself"

Commercial microfinance institutions can become profitable and viable over the long term. Governments benefit because they do not need to provide credit subsidies or cover the losses of subsidized credit programs—and because the resulting savings can be used as needed for direct poverty alleviation programs for the extremely poor. Economies benefit from the increased production, from the new resources made available for investment, and from improvement in equity. Further, large-scale sustainable microfinance helps create an enabling environment for the growth of political participation and of democracy.

Notes

1. The "absurd gap" is a phrase used by Michael Chu, then president of ACCIÓN International, at a conference on Building Healthy Financial Institutions for the Poor, sponsored by the U.S. Agency for International Development and held in Washington, D.C., on 27 September 1994. ACCIÓN is a U.S.-based nonprofit organization that works with a large network of microfinance organizations in Latin America and the United States.

2. For estimates of people in developing countries without access to institutional financial services, see Rosenberg (1994) and Christen, Rhyne, and Vogel (1995, p. 9), which states that "in most countries (possible exceptions include Bangladesh and Indonesia), [microfinance] programs have not yet succeeded in reaching the majority of poor households; market penetration by microfinance programs seldom exceeds 5 percent; most countries have yet to reach 1 percent." This statement appears to refer primarily to credit; in some countries, especially in Asia, a higher percentage of poor households has access to savings services. In many countries, however, most of the poor have little or no access to institutional savings services or credit. Estimating that there are about 500 million people who operate small businesses and microbusinesses, CGAP (1998f, p. 1) comments that "despite the growing number of microfinance institutions operating today (some estimates put the number at 3,000), back of the envelope calculations indicate that they reach less than 2 percent of entrepreneurs." The September 2000 issue of the *MicroBanking Bulletin* (issue 5) reports on 65 fully financially sustainable microfinance institutions, which probably represent a large portion of those currently in existence. IDB (1995) estimates that less than 5 percent of enterprises in Latin America have access to credit from formal institutions. The extent of the world's population lacking access to financial services was highlighted by Jean-Francois Rischard, then vice-president of Finance and Private Sector Development at the World Bank, in an address to a workshop on The Efficient Promotion of Small Enterprises, organized by the Fundación para el Desarrollo Sostenible (FUNDES) in Interlaken, Switzerland, on 18 September 1993.

3. Some analysts have restricted microfinance to narrower definitions. Thus the term is often used to refer to those who work in the informal sector of the economy. While most microfinance serves the informal sector, the definition used here is broader and includes financial services to poor employees of the formal sector as well. Such employees can, in fact, be poorer than those in the informal sector. For example, a 1987–88 study of 500 urban informal sector workers (pedicab drivers, scavengers recycling waste materials, and peddlers selling food or garments) in Jakarta, Indonesia, found that the average daily income of those surveyed was higher than the salaries of most of Jakarta's formal sector employees (as reported by the Indonesian Bureau of Statistics). Additional household income was not considered in either case (CPIS

Large-scale sustainable microfinance helps create an enabling environment for the growth of political participation and of democracy

1988a). Other uses of the term *microfinance* sometimes have the effect of restricting its meaning to specifics, such as village lending programs or group lending methodologies. However, microfinance is used here to refer generally to all types of financial services provided to low-income households and enterprises.

4. The criteria of institutional sustainability and scale of outreach were used by Yaron (1992b) in developing a framework for comparative analysis of microfinance programs; these criteria were further developed by Christen, Rhyne, and Vogel (1995). Full sustainability or self-sufficiency means that revenues cover all nonfinancial costs, all financial costs without subsidy and risk, and that the institution returns a profit. Most microfinance institutions are not fully self-sufficient. But those that are drive the microfinance revolution because large-scale outreach depends on institutional sustainability. See chapter 2 for definitions and discussion of institutional sustainability and self-sufficiency.

5. See *World Development Report 2000/2001,* chapter 1, for the method used to calculate the $1 a day poverty line.

6. Christen, Rhyne, and Vogel (1995, pp. 8–9) estimate that "potential clients for microenterprise finance institutions may number between 100 and 200 million." In arriving at this estimate, the authors exclude all those with incomes of more than $1 a day, as well as wage laborers and small farmers. Here, however, we estimate presently unmet demand for microfinance for all the economically active poor.

7. "Even the roughest calculations of potential market size reveal a need for microfinance assets far in excess of donor funding available for the purpose" (Rosenberg 1994, p. 2).

8. Another, older explanation for the neglect of the informal sector came from the financial dualism model, a colonial heritage. Financial dualism holds that the formal financial sector coexists with informal financial markets, the sectors operating with little or no interaction. In this model the formal financial sector, primarily urban, serves the regulated, institutionalized, and monetized sector of the economy, while the informal market, primarily rural, meets what are believed to be the more limited needs of the traditional nonmonetized subsistence economy. See Germidis, Kessler, and Meghir (1991, ch. 1) for an overview of financial dualism; see chapter 11 of this book for a discussion of this concept in the history of the Indonesian economy; and see chapter 21 for an analysis of rural credit and microfinance models, including the financial dualism model.

9. Keith Hart (1986, pp. 845–46) put it this way: "The 'formal' economy is the epitome of whatever passes for regularity in our contemporary understanding . . . The 'informal' economy is anything which is not entailed directly in these definitions of reality. . . From the standpoint of high civilization, whatever it cannot control or comprehend is 'informal'—that is irregular, unpredictable, unstable, even invisible. Of course the people whose activities appear in this light believe that they have social forms." Japan, however, has been a notable exception to the general rule of ignoring the informal sector. The informal economy has been, in various ways, explicitly and visibly incorporated into Japanese economic planning since the Meiji Restoration of 1868 (see Rosovsky and Ohkawa 1961 and Ohkawa and Rosovsky 1965).

10. For most loans the unit desas' stated monthly interest rate for prompt payers was 1.5 percent calculated on a "flat" basis on the original (not the declining) loan balance. For purposes of comparison, the flat rate was converted here and in box 1.1 to a monthly effective interest rate. See chapters 12 and 15 for further discussion of unit desa interest rates.

11. For examples of interest rates in these ranges, see Reserve Bank of India (1954b); Nisbet (1967); Ladman (1971); Bottomley (1983 [1975]); Mundle (1976); Tun Wai (1977, 1980); Kamble (1979); Marla (1981); Adams and Graham (1981); Singh (1983

[1968]); Wilmington (1983 [1955]); Roth (1983); Chandavarkar (1987); Hossain (1988); Robinson (1988); Bouman (1989); Varian (1989); Von Pischke (1991); Germidis, Kessler, and Meghir (1991); Chen (1991); Floro and Yotopoulos (1991); Aleem (1993); Braverman and Guasch (1993); Siamwalla and others (1993); Ghate and others (1993); and Carstens (1995). For a classic study, see Darling (1978 [1925]). In Indonesia, based on the findings of the Development Program Implementation Studies (DPIS) and Center for Policy and Implementation Studies (CPIS) field research from 1979–90, people interviewed in many areas reported that the nominal interest rates they paid to informal commercial lenders for loans with maturities of one month or more ranged from about 10 percent to more than 80 percent (expressed here as effective monthly rates), with low-income borrowers reporting the higher rates. Rates for small one-day loans varied from about 5–25 percent; rates for one-week loans paid at the end of the week ranged from about 20 percent to more than 100 percent (CPIS unpublished field data). Similar rates for Indonesian moneylenders have been reported by BRI during the 1990s as well (BRI 1997b, 1998b).

12. When comparing the stated interest rates of informal commercial lenders with those of standard commercial banks, it is important to bear in mind that different methods of computing and collecting interest can produce large differences in the effective cost of the loan to the borrower. For example, the total interest on a one-year loan of $120 payable in 12 equal monthly installments at an interest rate of 10 percent a month computed against the declining principal balance totals $91.34; the effective cost to the borrower is the same as the stated rate, 10 percent a month. By contrast, if the 10 percent stated interest on this loan is computed against the original loan amount, ignoring the fact that the borrower is reducing the principal over the life of the loan, the borrower will pay total interest of $144; the effective interest rate for this loan, assuming 12 equal monthly payments, is about 15 percent a month. Other practices that inflate the effective monthly cost above the stated rate include collecting interest at the beginning of the loan, charging a loan fee, and requiring daily or weekly repayment (which raise the effective monthly cost by more frequent compounding). (See Rosenberg 1996 for a discussion of microcredit interest rates and how these are calculated.)

13. See the World Bank's *World Development Report 2000/2001: Attacking Poverty* for an extensive discussion of the nature and causes of poverty.

14. Mayhew's (1968 [1861], vol. 4, pp. 22–23) classic four-volume study of poverty in 19th century London remains the most comprehensive source on different kinds of poverty, shown from the point of view of the poor themselves. Mayhew divides the population of Great Britain into four categories: those who will work, those who cannot work, those who will not work (vagrants, beggars, criminals), and those who need not work. In the terminology used here, the extremely poor would include many in Mayhew's second category and some in his third category. Access to formal sector commercial microfinance could help the economically active poor in his first category and some of those in his second category.

15. For example, the state-owned Vietnam Bank for the Poor, a highly subsidized institution created in 1996, requires that loan funds be allocated starting with the poorest household in the village. While this regulation is not always followed, the principle is that the poorest of the poor have priority in receiving credit. In China subsidized programs in some financial institutions provide credit to severely food-deficit borrowers who live in remote mountainous areas, lacking basic infrastructure. In both cases many of the debtors thus created have no opportunity to use the credit productively and cannot repay their loans.

16. See Von Pischke (1998) for a recent history and analysis of the financial systems approach to microfinance.

17. The campaign, known as Countdown 2005, is directed by Sam Daley-Harris, president of RESULTS International and the RESULTS Educational Fund. The

summit organizers arrived at $21.6 billion by assuming that 8 million very poor families are already receiving microcredit, leaving 92 million for whom credit is to be provided by 2005 (88 million in developing countries and 4 million in developed countries); and that $200 a family is required in developing countries (of which $150 is to be provided for loan funds and $50 for training and institutional costs) and $1,000 a family is required in developed countries (half for loan funds and half for institutional development costs). It is assumed that in total, $17.6 billion is needed for institutions in developing countries and $4 billion for institutions in developed countries.

18. Some advocates of the financial systems approach suggested that the name of the first summit be changed from the Microcredit Summit to the Microfinance Summit; this suggestion was not accepted by the summit organizers.

19. See Rutherford (2000, pp. 13–17). In an example from Vijayawada, India, analyzed there, poor savers pay fees to a collector who holds their savings. "The annual percentage rate (APR) is about 30 percent. In other words, the client is 'earning' interest at *minus* 30 percent APR" (p. 15). I also met savings collectors while conducting field work in central India in the 1970s and 1980s. Savings collectors serving the poor for a fee have been reported in numerous other developing countries as well (see chapter 7).

20. This holds true whether the institution onlends the subsidized funds that it has received to its borrowers at subsidized interest rates or at interest rates that enable full cost recovery. While institutions that pursue full cost recovery can become more financially viable than institutions that lend at subsidized interest rates, both types of institutions are limited in their outreach if they rely on donor- or government-subsidized funds to finance their loan portfolios.

21. The term *voluntary savings* refers to noncompulsory deposits made by the client by choice. In contrast, some financial institutions require the borrower to deposit a percentage of her loan; this is termed "forced" or compulsory savings. Usually the borrower cannot withdraw the savings until the loan is repaid, and the result is an increase in the effective interest rate on the loan. Many institutions require continued borrowing as a condition of continued membership; this has the added effect of requiring a client to borrow in order to save (see Rutherford 1998).

22. In some countries, however, financial institutions serving low-income clients are effective in mobilizing savings but not in making loans; see chapter 7.

23. There are a few exceptions in countries with weak banking systems and strong microfinance institutions, most notably Bangladesh. There, for example, the Association for Social Advancement (ASA) provides large-scale credit and some voluntary savings services while remaining an NGO.

24. As measured by BRI's long-term loss ratio (2.06 percent on 31 December 1999), which measures the cumulative amount that has come due and is unpaid since the opening of the unit, relative to the total that has come due. See chapter 12 for a discussion of the loan loss ratios used by BRI's microbanking division.

25. "Financial services help people meet their household and business goals. Despite the apparent simplicity of their activities, microentrepreneurs and self-employed people make a complex, ongoing series of financial decisions and must be sophisticated managers of their financial affairs. Their many financial decisions include how to allocate income from a business between household and business expenses; how much to save, when, and in what form; how much and when to invest and in what; how to balance between short-term consumption and long-term goals; how to protect themselves against the many risks they face; and how to position themselves to take advantage of business opportunities. These decisions are crucial and are more likely to lead to success if supported by good financial services" (Christen, Rhyne, and Vogel 1995, p. 5).

26. This exchange was contributed by Stuart Rutherford, SafeSave, Bangladesh.

27. N. V. Raja Reddy initiated and developed the mango scheme, which was later expanded to other horticultural activities and other areas.

28. At first only a few boys were sent to school. My suggestions that they also send their girls to school were rejected: "We want our girls at home, not in school." Four years after the participants began receiving income from their mango trees, a few girls began to attend school. When I asked the parents what had made them change their minds, I was told, "the boys are demanding educated wives."

2

Shifting the Microfinance Paradigm: From Subsidized Credit Delivery to Commercial Financial Services

This chapter considers the emerging shift from the old paradigm of subsidized credit delivery to the new paradigm of sustainable commercial microfinance. The focus is on how and why this shift occurred, and on its implications for microfinance worldwide.

In the old paradigm loan portfolios are subsidy dependent, limiting the number of borrowers who can be served. Microfinance institutions that operate with subsidized loan portfolios cannot achieve wide outreach in both lending and savings operations because their lending interest rates are too low to cover the costs and risks of large-scale financial intermediation. Thus four models are typically found in association with subsidized credit:

- Institutions that provide microcredit but are not permitted to mobilize savings from the public (most institutions that are not regulated and publicly supervised).
- Institutions that do well in lending but poorly in mobilizing savings (such as Bangladesh's Grameen Bank).
- Institutions that do well in savings but poorly in lending (India's Regional Rural Banks and China's Rural Credit Cooperatives).
- Institutions that fail in both (most microfinance institutions that provide subsidized credit and are permitted to raise public savings, particularly state-owned banks).

Microfinance institutions that provide both large-scale savings and credit profitably are found only outside the subsidized credit model.[1] Thus, in sharp contrast to the old paradigm, the new paradigm operates through a fifth model: commercial financial institutions that can attain wide outreach sustainably. Credit is financed by savings and through access to commercial financial markets. Many institutions are in various stages of transition between the old and the new paradigms.

The microbanking division of Bank Rakyat Indonesia (BRI) and Bolivia's BancoSol are examined here in more detail. BRI reaches about a quarter of the households of the world's fourth most populous country and has done so profitably, without subsidy, for over a decade. Moreover, it continued to do so in the late 1990s, in the midst of the country's largest economic, political, and financial crisis in 30 years. BancoSol serves nearly a third of all clients in the Bolivian banking system, and in 1997 it became the most profitable bank in Bolivia. These institutions and others following the financial systems approach to microfinance have achieved a major breakthrough. They have been among the first to realize that the large-scale provision of microfinance to the economically active poor, sustainable over time, can be attained only in financially self-sufficient commercial institutions in the regulated financial sector.

Providing microfinance is more expensive than providing standard banking services to larger clients, however. As a result self-sufficient microfinance institutions must charge higher interest rates on loans than those charged by the banking industry in the same country. Yet in a number of countries microcredit borrowers have

The new paradigm operates through a fifth model: commercial financial institutions that can attain wide outreach sustainably

shown that they will pay the costs that enable the financing institution to achieve full cost recovery and to earn a profit—if the products and services offered to them are appropriate for their needs.

The chapter begins with a brief introduction to local financial markets, indicating some of the relationships between formal and informal finance and providing a background for the discussion that follows. The main focus, however, is on the paradigm shift and on the development of the financial systems approach that underpins the new microfinance paradigm. To highlight the emphasis on outreach to poor borrowers and savers that is the hallmark of the microfinance revolution, the performance of BRI's microbanking division is compared with a group of 140 nongovernmental organizations (NGOs), a group of 18,822 credit unions, and the Grameen Bank. These comparisons show clearly the power of commercial microfinance.

Commercial microfinance is a globally affordable model

The chapter concludes that the emerging microfinance revolution is based on substantial evidence that microfinance can be profitable; that because it is profitable, it can attain wide outreach to poor clients; and that commercial microfinance is a globally affordable model.

The microfinance revolution is based on a new paradigm, components of which developed slowly and sporadically in different parts of the world before 1980. The 1980s proved that commercial microfinance institutions could profitably serve the economically active poor and could attain wide outreach. The 1990s saw an emphasis on developing microfinance as an industry. At the start of the new millennium, commercial microfinance is beginning an exponential expansion because of the spread of information about the extent of microfinance markets and the profitability of microfinance institutions that has been made possible by the information revolution. And because microfinance institutions have begun to mobilize public savings and access capital markets, they have realized that they need not remain capital constrained. The ability to leverage capital has created the potential for greatly increased outreach to low-income people in many parts of the world.

Financial Markets in Developing Countries

In rural areas and low-income urban neighborhoods of developing countries, local financial markets typically include a mix of formal, semiformal, and informal components (see Germidis, Kessler, and Meghir 1991). These components are most usefully represented by a continuum. At one end of the continuum, the formal financial sector covers a wide variety of institutions ranging from the central bank and treasury administration to banks and post office savings systems, and in some countries includes regulated credit unions, cooperatives, pawnshops, finance companies, and other nonbank financial institutions. The formal sector includes various kinds of banks (commercial, development, specialized, regional, cooperative), insurance companies, social security schemes, pension funds, and in some countries, capital markets. The formal sector is largely urban based and organized primarily to supply the financial needs of the modern sector.

Nonbank financial institutions such as pawnshops, small-scale finance companies, cooperatives, and credit unions occupy positions on the formal-informal continuum that vary by country and sometimes even by region, as well as over time.[2]

A wide variety of semiformal financial organizations occupies the middle ranges of the continuum. These organizations are unlicensed and generally unsupervised; nevertheless, they may operate under particular laws and regulations. In many countries private finance companies accept deposits from the public at large, but may be limited in the types of deposit accounts they are permitted to offer. Specialists, such as consumer lenders, may limit their activities to particular forms of credit. Some organizations, such as NGOs, provide microcredit but are usually not permitted to mobilize voluntary savings from the public. Some credit cooperatives, credit unions, and diverse forms of credit societies that are considered semiformal in their countries provide their members with facilities for both savings and loans. Store-linked consumer credit programs pro-

Large-scale microfinance, sustainable over time, can be attained only in financially self-sufficient commercial institutions in the regulated financial sector

vide installment credits. Like pawnshops and finance companies, they typically provide credit to a wide range of clients—including the poor—quickly, easily, and at high interest rates.

At the other end of the continuum, informal financial markets serve multiple sectors, financing households and enterprises in a wide range of income levels and geographic areas. Characterized in general by personal relationships, individual operators, ease of access, simple procedures, rapid transactions, and flexible loan terms and amounts, informal financial markets are ubiquitous. Most such markets can be considered to have three main components, with many variants in each. First, there are local organizations such as rotating savings and credit associations (ROSCAs) in which members both save and borrow, regular (nonrotating) savings and credit associations (RESCAs) in which all members save but all do not necessarily borrow (Bouman 1989, pp. 52–53),[3] mutual aid societies, both general and specific (such as burial societies), self-help organizations, and the like.

Individual informal commercial moneylenders are also widely found in developing countries, although they are more prevalent in some countries (such as India) than others (such as China). There are many types of informal moneylenders, including pawnbrokers, professional moneylenders, commodity wholesalers, shopkeepers, traders, employers, and landlords. There are also savings collectors who collect and hold the savings of poor people for a fee.

Finally, there are relatives, friends, and neighbors from whom those in need can borrow, although primarily for emergencies or special purposes rather than for ongoing working capital needs. Each borrower or household forms an ego-centered network with its own pool of potential lenders and borrowers. Even two members of the same household may have different, although usually overlapping, networks of this type. In this situation lenders tend to provide small loans at no or low interest, but they may expect nonfinancial obligations in return for the credit. They may also expect future loans from borrowers.

Informal financial markets are uncontrolled and unregulated by the formal sector. It has long been recognized, however, that these markets are not unorganized. Thus within the informal commercial market, financial channels, information flows, and market shares of lenders form part of the local political economy. Informal financial markets coexist with the formal financial sector, interacting with the formal sector in numerous ways—especially, although not exclusively, at the local level. Some informal lenders are financed through the formal financial sector, and some operate through semiformal organizations such as cooperatives and NGOs.

At all levels of the formal-informal continuum, there may be parallel and black markets in operation.[4] Most parallel markets are illegal (black) markets—for example, markets in drugs or currency. Some parallel markets, however, are legal, such as the curb market in domestic credit, which has been encouraged in Taiwan, China (Roemer and Jones 1991, p. 5).

Interactions among financial markets occur vertically as well as horizontally: national, regional, and local arenas are often linked through financial net-

Informal financial markets are uncontrolled and unregulated by the formal sector. But it has long been recognized that these markets are not unorganized

works in which formal finance is blended with and incorporated into informal, parallel, and black markets. Informal networks can be illustrated by arbitrage in the informal credit market, parallel networks by bank finance for production of commodities that are sold in parallel markets, and black markets by the use of a combination of formal and informal channels to deliver payment from urban drug dealers to their rural suppliers.

Recent literature on local markets demonstrates a variety of complex interactions among different markets beyond the price and income interactions traditionally incorporated in economic theory. For example, transactions involving credit linkages with trade, land, and labor have been explored extensively (see chapter 6 for discussion and references). Different local situations, of course, provide different kinds of market interlinkages. Growth in one market can affect the operations of others through effects on information, contracts, production decisions, and so on.

Market interactions can reduce information costs and risks within particular markets. As shown by Hoff, Braverman, and Stiglitz (1993), this can occur in various ways. For example, an increase in activity in goods markets generates interlinked trade-credit contracts that can serve as a substitute for collateral, expanding the credit market. Similarly, the diversification of production reduces the covariance of risk and seasonality of credit demands, increasing possibilities for financial intermediation.

Thus in competitive markets, interlinked transactions may reduce risk, expand financial intermediation, and contribute to economic development at the local level.[5] But the opposite can occur in markets characterized by monopoly and monopsony where land, credit, labor, and commodities markets converge in the person of the landlord-cultivator-employer-moneylender-trader (see Bell 1993; Robinson 1988; and the references cited in chapter 6). In some cases local monopolies are buttressed by subsidies provided by the formal sector to these multifaceted local elites.

This book does not attempt to cover all aspects of financial markets in developing countries, or even all suppliers of finance to low-income borrowers. Volumes 2 and 3 provide examples of formal and semiformal financial organizations that have contributed to the microfinance revolution: village banks, NGOs, credit unions, and other forms of nonbank financial institutions, as well as different types of banks. But these are considered from the point of view of the institution's role in the development of commercial microfinance, not as part of an effort to examine the range of financial organizations that operate in local financial markets.

The same approach is taken with informal financial markets. Thus rotating savings and loan associations, mutual aid societies, self-help groups, and the like are mentioned only briefly—not because they are not important in microfinance (they are) but because they have not been leading players in the development of large-scale sustainable microfinance.

In contrast, informal commercial moneylenders are considered at some length. They are the subject of chapter 6, and their roles in microfinance are discussed

National, regional, and local arenas are often linked through financial networks in which formal finance is blended into informal, parallel, and black markets

in other chapters as well. The decision to emphasize the analysis of moneylenders was made for four reasons:

- In aggregate, moneylenders are large-scale providers of credit to low-income borrowers.
- The interest rates that moneylenders charge to poor borrowers are typically far larger than the rates that profitable microfinance institutions charge. While the transaction costs to borrowers are generally lower in borrowing from moneylenders than from even efficient microfinance institutions, the difference is comparatively small. Thus many borrowers pay unnecessarily high costs for loans from moneylenders because of the lack of available commercial microfinance institutions—a development issue of crucial importance.
- One of the reasons that banks have chosen not to enter microfinance markets commercially is that they believe (incorrectly, as will be shown) that they cannot compete successfully with moneylenders, who are thought to have much better information about local borrowers than banks could obtain cost-effectively.
- Having spent much time living in villages of developing countries over more than 30 years, I have had the opportunity to learn not only about the operations of various kinds of moneylenders, but also about how they obtain information; how they make decisions about interlinked transactions, borrower selection, and use of capital; how they keep records; and how they collect loans (see Robinson 1988).

Banks can serve microfinance markets profitably and on a large scale. But most banks do not yet know this

Knowledge of informal commercial moneylenders is important for the microfinance revolution. First, moneylenders know the market well, and many of their methods have been studied and adapted by commercial microfinance institutions (Christen 1989). Second, moneylenders are constrained by their local political economies in ways that banks are not. As will be discussed in chapters 5, 6, and 21, banks can gain wider access to reliable information about borrowers than can moneylenders who serve the same area. Banks can serve microfinance markets profitably and on a large scale. But most banks do not yet know this.

Development of the Financial Systems Approach to Microfinance

A few scattered, early pioneers—such as the Badan Kredit Desa (BKD) village banks and the Bank Dagang Bali (BDB) in Indonesia, the Self-Employed Women's Association (SEWA) Women's Cooperative Bank in India, the early ACCIÓN affiliates in Latin America, and various NGOs, credit unions, and cooperatives in a variety of countries—led the way in developing the financial systems approach to microfinance. During the 1970s these institutions developed lending methodologies suitable for low-income clients in both rural and urban areas, and demonstrated that microcredit provided at interest rates that enable full cost recovery could be delivered with high repayment (see volumes 2 and 3). In addition, by then some commercial banks, especially in parts of Asia, had gained decades of experience in mobilizing large amounts of savings from the rural poor.

Most banks, however, tended to avoid microcredit, except for government or donor-funded subsidized credit programs. The few exceptions included BDB, which began in 1970 (see chapter 10), and SEWA Bank, which opened in 1974 (see chapter 19). Members of SEWA, a trade union of vendors, artisans, agricultural laborers, and other poor women, formed the bank to meet their members' credit needs. Both BDB and SEWA operated from the start without subsidies, emphasized voluntary savings as well as loans, set interest rates to cover all costs and risks, and developed early models of sustainable microfinance intermediaries.

The growth of commercial microfinance institutions, however, is largely a product of the past 20 years. Before that, large, poorly designed subsidized rural credit programs dominated the institutional approach to microfinance in developing countries. Beginning in the 1950s and proliferating in the 1960s and 1970s, these programs were usually accompanied by high loan defaults, high losses, and a general inability to reach poor rural households. This pattern still holds in many countries.

Microfinance in the 1980s: Going to scale

By the 1980s, however, numerous institutions in many parts of the developing world were providing microcredit and recovering their loans. The Grameen Bank's group lending methodology, part of the paradigm shift in microfinance, became widely adopted by institutions in many parts of the world. In addition, an increasing number of institutions began mobilizing voluntary savings from low-income savers. In the 1980s BRI developed the first large-scale sustainable microbanking system operating without subsidy.

This was the general context in which the financial systems approach was developed. It joined the principles of commercial finance with the growing knowledge of the microfinance market and made the adaptations to the financial technology that were necessary to create institutional commercial microfinance.

The new paradigm refers to the concepts and methods that have been developed to enable financial institutions to provide microfinance services without ongoing subsidy. These include methodologies for both individual and group lending, new financial products suitable for poor borrowers and savers, interest rate spreads that permit institutional profits, innovative operating methods and information systems, widely dispersed small service outlets, specialized staff training and incentives, the financing of loan portfolios from locally mobilized savings and from commercial debt and investment, and others.

Many institutions in numerous countries have provided inputs into the new paradigm. However, they often make use of some aspects of commercial finance, but not others. This approach can result from the institution's particular circumstances—for example, NGOs may not be permitted to mobilize voluntary savings, while governments or donors may set limits on NGOs' interest rates for loans. In other cases, however, institutions choose to adopt some aspects of

In the 1980s BRI developed the first large-scale sustainable microbanking system operating without subsidy

the financial systems approach and not others. Thus not all institutional contributors to the paradigm shift have chosen to become sustainable institutions, limiting their participation in the microfinance revolution.

Some institutions, however, have shown that they can provide small loans and savings services profitably on a large scale. They receive no continuing subsidies,[6] are commercially funded and fully sustainable, can attain wide outreach to clients, and are viable for the long term.

The 1980s represented a turning point in the history of microfinance; by the end of that decade the paradigm shift was well under way. Both the Grameen Bank and BRI showed that microfinance institutions could reach more than 1 million borrowers with very high repayment rates. By the end of the decade BRI had also shown that its microbanking system could service more than 6 million savings accounts and could operate its entire microbanking system without subsidy. An increasing number of institutions had then entered the microfinance market. Meanwhile, "most of the programs created in the 1960s and 1970s for microlending disappeared due to dismal repayment rates, corruption, and heavy subsidization, leading to a 'grant mentality' among clients" (Paxton 1996, p. 9). A 1995 worldwide survey of 206 microfinance institutions that had opened in or before 1992 found that only 7 percent had been in operation before 1960; 48 percent had been founded between 1980 and 1989.[7]

In the 1980s it became clear for the first time that microfinance could provide large-scale outreach profitably. It was in the 1990s that microfinance began to develop as an industry.

Microfinance in the 1990s: Developing the industry

The 1990s saw accelerated growth in the number of microfinance institutions created and an increased emphasis on reaching scale. In Bolivia, BancoSol pioneered the access of microfinance institutions to domestic and international financial markets and to for-profit investors. Internationally, a microfinance industry began to develop. Attention was given to developing appropriate regulation and supervision for formal sector microfinance institutions. Regulated nonbank microfinance intermediaries were developed in some countries. Rating agencies for microfinance institutions began operation. Channels for disseminating information about best practices in commercial microfinance proliferated. Teaching programs on commercial microfinance were instituted, drawing participants from around the world. And worldwide networks of microfinance practitioners were formed (see chapter 20).

By the late 1990s commercial microfinance was no longer limited to a small group of scattered institutions. It was an industry—a fledgling industry, but a rapidly growing one. In this context the development of BRI's microbanking system and of BancoSol are of particular interest, both because of the scale on which they conduct continuously profitable operations and because of their leadership roles in the development of the commercial microfinance industry.

Sustainable microfinance on a national scale depends on institutional governance, management, and organization as well as on products, pricing, and

In the 1980s it became clear that microfinance could provide large-scale outreach profitably. In the 1990s microfinance began to develop as an industry

knowledge of the market. These banks were the first of the self-sufficient microfinance institutions to develop the management, organizational structures, information systems, staff training systems, and internal supervision and control that, along with their commitment to full cost recovery and institutional self-sufficiency, enabled them to provide microfinance profitably on a large scale. Their success has spawned both imitation and competition within their own countries and adaptation and extension of their methods by institutions in other developing countries.

In Bolivia and Indonesia about a third of households are clients of self-sufficient microfinance institutions as savers, borrowers, or both. In Bangladesh too, nearly a third of all households are clients of microfinance institutions, including 524 credit-providing NGOs that report their data to the Credit and Development Forum (CDF), the Grameen Bank, and the banking sector (see Credit and Development Forum 1999). The difference is that most of the Bangladesh institutions, including most of the large ones, depend—to varying degrees—on donor and government subsidies. If the subsidies were to decrease significantly, as has already happened in some cases, the microfinance activities of many of these institutions could be at risk.

Large-scale microfinance is a business for which many current microfinance institutions are unsuited

Large-scale microfinance is a business for which many current microfinance institutions are unsuited. In addition, some potentially sustainable microfinance institutions have chosen to remain small, and some that are large have chosen to remain dependent on subsidies.

Those leading the microfinance revolution are commercial microfinance intermediaries; foresighted government agencies, such as some central banks, bank superintendencies, and ministries of finance; and a variety of organizations with specific interest and expertise in finance for the poor (see chapters 17–20). In addition, some donor agencies have provided strong support for the shift from donor-driven microcredit programs to self-sufficient microfinance institutions, and have initiated and coordinated the dissemination of best practices in microfinance on regional and global scales (see chapters 20 and 22).

BRI's unit *desa* system and BancoSol are discussed later in this chapter. First, however, we turn to a discussion of what institutional sustainability means and how it is defined.

Institutional Sustainability

The authors of a 1995 study by the U.S. Agency for International Development (USAID) of sustainability in 11 microfinance institutions in Asia, Africa, and Latin America developed a framework for evaluating the self-sufficiency of microfinance programs.[8] This section is drawn from that study, and the definitions of institutional self-sufficiency developed there are used throughout this book.

The study found that microfinance services can be sustainably delivered in a wide variety of economic, political, and geographic environments, and that among the various macroeconomic conditions considered, the only ones that are prohibitive for microfinance institutions are hyperinflation and interest rate controls.

The institutions examined were selected as a sample of the best-performing microfinance programs in developing countries. The analysis was based on 1993 data adjusted for subsidies, inflation, and provision for loan losses so that the institutions could be compared with one another, and with the private sector, on a fully commercial basis.[9] The 11 microfinance programs were found to be located along a sustainability continuum ranging from one new institution in which revenues did not yet cover operating costs to institutions that were fully self-sufficient without subsidy.

A 1995 USAID study found that microfinance services can be sustainably delivered in a wide variety of economic, political, and geographic environments

Levels of sustainability

For purposes of comparative analysis, the USAID study divided the continuum into three categories of sustainability:

- Institutions in which revenues from interest and fees do not cover operating costs.
- Institutions in which revenues cover operating costs but do not cover the commercial costs of loanable funds.
- Fully self-sufficient institutions that cover all costs and risks and generate a profit.

Most of the world's microfinance programs belong in the first category. These are credit programs financed by grants or low-interest loans from donors or governments, and they are heavily dependent on subsidies. Among this group the spread between the lending interest rate and the cost of funds is too low to cover operating costs. An institution may unable to cover its operating costs because interest rates on loans to borrowers are too low, because loan losses are high, because loan volumes are too low, or because of inefficiency—or because of a combination of these factors. Over time many such programs exhaust their funds and end their operations, leaving their clients with expectations that cannot be fulfilled. Of course, some programs in the first category are in a transitional stage either because they are new or because they are undergoing a period of planned expansion. One of the institutions studied, Niger's Bankin Raya Karara (BRK)—then a three-year-old NGO—was placed in this category.

The second category, represented by a wide band on the continuum, refers to programs in which fees and interest charges cover nonfinancial costs.[10] But these programs still depend on subsidies to varying degrees for the cost of loanable funds. As a result basic problems remain. Financial institutions that are subsidized by governments and donors are often prevented by government regulation from mobilizing voluntary savings from the public, or have little incentive to do so because they receive continuing injections of low-cost funds. Financial institutions funded by low-interest loans or grants typically do not mobilize substantial voluntary savings; since they cannot raise significant equity, they also cannot leverage much commercial investment or access substantial commercial debt. Based on adjusted 1993 data, institutions in the second category were represented in the USAID study by Bangladesh's Grameen Bank and by four NGOs: the Dominican Republic's Asociación Dominicana para el Desarrollo de la Mujer (ADOPEM), Senegal's Agence de Crédit pour l'Enterprise Privée (ACEP), Costa Rica's Fundación Integral Campesino (FINCA), and the Kenya Rural Enterprise Programme (K-REP).

Among the institutions in the third category, however, revenues cover both nonfinancial and financial costs calculated on a commercial basis. Interest rates include inflation premiums. Such institutions are profitable without subsidy, and a return on equity can be expected that is equivalent to returns that can be obtained in the private sector generally. Institutions at this level may mobilize savings from the public and may be able to leverage domestic or international commercial investment (using the institution's equity to obtain additional capital from commercial investors). The ability to leverage funds is of major importance for institutions providing commercial microfinance, as it helps maximize the scale and depth of microfinance coverage.

Based on adjusted 1993 data, BRI's unit desa system; the Badan Kredit Desa (BKD), or village credit organizations of Java and Madura (Indonesia); the Lembaga Perkreditan Desa (LPD) of Bali (Indonesia), village-owned financial institutions supervised by the provincial government of Bali; and BancoSol (Bolivia) were classified by the study as being fully self-sufficient—that is, institutions in the third category.[11]

Entering the formal financial sector: scale and depth of outreach

Most microcredit programs are run by small organizations that do not collect voluntary savings. Such institutions are usually unregulated and not subject to public supervision. But to move toward large, commercially funded microcredit portfolios and to mobilize voluntary savings, a microfinance institution aiming at large-scale outreach now normally enters the regulated formal financial sector.[12]

Such institutions are regulated and supervised, although in different ways, depending on the type of institution and on the capacity of the country's authorities to regulate and supervise institutions providing large numbers of small loans and savings accounts with low balances. Industry standards are being developed, and many microfinance programs are undergoing transformations from one institutional form to another. Some NGOs that are at or close to full self-sufficiency are applying for licenses to become banks or regulated nonbank financial intermediaries in order to increase scale. Other NGOs that are already at scale are held back from becoming regulated institutions by country regulations or political issues. But a growing number of microfinance institutions are seeking to become part of the regulated formal financial sector in order to increase the scale of their operations. Simultaneously, some banks are moving into the microfinance market. Where they are hampered by regulations that prevent or inhibit commercial microfinance, some are seeking regulatory changes.

A growing number of microfinance institutions are seeking to become part of the regulated formal financial sector in order to increase the scale of their operations

Large-scale outreach

depends on access to

commercial sources of

finance, which

in turn depends

on institutional

sustainability

Large-scale outreach depends on access to commercial sources of finance which in turn depends on institutional sustainability. Rhyne and Rosenberg (1998, p. 11) draw the bottom line succinctly: *"every decision to settle for less than full financial viability is of necessity a decision to reduce the number of people who will gain access to financial services in favor of giving a larger benefit to a smaller number."*

As the emphasis on sustainability and scale increases, does the depth of outreach—reaching poorer clients—decrease? The February 2000 *MicroBanking Bulletin* (MBB) database incorporates financial results from 104 microfinance institutions; of these, 60 are fully financially sustainable. For reasons of confidentiality, MBB data are not published by institution, but only by peer groups (see chapter 16). However, this is still the best database in the industry. Of particular interest is the finding that on average the 58 older, more experienced microfinance institutions (those above six years in age) are 102 percent financially self-sufficient.[13] This compares with 86 percent for institutions that are three to six years old and 69 percent for those in operation less than three years. The average loan balance as a percentage of GNP per capita is 81 percent in the institutions that are less than three years old, while it is 59 percent in those that are three to six years old and 55 percent in those more than six years old. Although amount of loan balance as a percentage of GNP per capita is commonly used as a proxy for depth of poverty (because it is widely available), this is an imperfect proxy. Nevertheless, these findings suggest that mature microfinance institutions can both reach financial sustainability and deepen outreach to the poor.[14] These results, if they continue to hold, can have far-reaching implications for the future progress of the microfinance revolution.

Pioneers in Large-scale Commercial Microfinance

BRI's microbanking system in Indonesia and BancoSol of Bolivia are introduced here as among the most advanced examples of the microfinance revolution. They are discussed further in later chapters.[15] Many of the other institutions that have played crucial roles in developing commercial microfinance are discussed in chapter 10 and part 4.

Microbanking at Bank Rakyat Indonesia

BRI, a century-old state-owned commercial bank, has traditionally held a special assignment from the government to provide banking services to the rural areas of Indonesia, with particular emphasis on agricultural credit.[16] The bank also serves almost all market segments in the banking industry, including micro, small, medium-size, and large businesses, and both individual and corporate clients.[17] This book does not cover the development of BRI in its entirety; it concerns only BRI's unit desa system—the microbanking division that has made the bank internationally known for its provision of financial services to low-income people.[18] Because of its unit desas, which provide small loans and savings services in both urban and rural areas, BRI serves more clients than any other bank in Indonesia.

Development of the unit desa (microbanking) system. In the early 1970s BRI developed its microbanking system to provide subsidized government credit to rice farmers through BIMAS,[19] the credit component of Indonesia's massive effort to reach national rice self-sufficiency—a goal first achieved in 1985. About 3,600 unit desas were established nationwide at the subdistrict level; these local bank outlets functioned primarily as channeling agents for BIMAS and other subsidized rural lending programs.

Although in its early years BIMAS helped farmers learn the new high-yielding technologies of rice cultivation then being introduced, the long-term results were similar to those in many other developing countries. The program's low-interest loans tended to reach the local elites who had the influence to obtain them. Low-income people typically did without credit or borrowed on the informal commercial market at much higher interest rates. And the program experienced high arrears and losses. The credit component was not among the forces driving the success of the rice intensification program (see chapter 11 for discussion and analysis of the reasons for the failure of the BIMAS program at BRI).

Savings accounts were offered in the unit banks beginning in the mid-1970s. But annual interest rates, set by the government at 12 percent for loans and 15 percent for most deposits, discouraged BRI's units from undertaking active savings mobilization. Losses mounted, and by 1983 the unit desa system had reached a point at which it would either have to be closed or converted into a fundamentally different system.

In June 1983 the first of a series of major financial reforms was announced: government banks would now be permitted to set their own interest rates on most loans and deposits. Among its other purposes, this deregulation provided an enabling environment for the transformation of BRI's local banking system. After the June 1983 reform, the government decided that the subsidized unit desas would be converted into a sustainable system of commercial banking at the local level, and that a program of general purpose credit at commercial interest rates would be implemented through the unit desa system. After an initial period, the loan program would be financed by locally mobilized savings.

In early 1984 BRI began its new program of general purpose credit, called Kredit Umum Pedesaan (KUPEDES),[20] offered throughout its unit desa network. Individual loans were made available to creditworthy rural borrowers for all productive purposes. The nominal monthly interest on loans was set at a flat rate of 1.5 percent on the original loan balance; this is equivalent to about a 32 percent annual effective interest rate for a one-year loan with 12 monthly installments, if all payments are made on time. Average annual inflation was 10.4 percent in 1984 and remained below 10 percent between 1985 and 1997; it rose sharply in 1998 during the Indonesian crisis (table 2.1).

During 1984–85 new savings instruments for the unit desas were designed and tested, and by 1986 a package of savings instruments was introduced that provided, for the first time at the local level, the much-in-demand combination of security, convenience, liquidity, confidentiality, good service, and returns. Creditworthy savers had access to loans, and potential borrowers could build their credit ratings with savings. The savings instruments, along with the

Annual interest rates, set by the government at 12 percent for loans and 15 percent for most deposits, discouraged BRI's units from active savings mobilization

| Table 2.1 | Exchange rates, inflation rates, and consumer price indexes in Indonesia, 1970–99 | | |

Year	Year-end exchange rate (rupiah per $1)[a]	Average annual inflation rate (percent)[b]	Consumer price index (1990 = 100)
1970	378	12.3	9.1
1971	415	4.4	9.5
1972	415	6.3	10.1
1973	415	31.7	13.3
1974	415	40.6	18.7
1975	415	19.3	22.3
1976	415	19.7	26.7
1977	415	10.9	29.6
1978	625	8.4	32.1
1979	627	16.2	37.3
1980	627	18.0	44.0
1981	644	12.3	49.4
1982	693	9.5	54.1
1983	994	11.8	60.5
1984	1,074	10.4	66.8
1985	1,125	4.5	69.8
1986	1,641	6.2	74.1
1987	1,650	9.2	80.9
1988	1,731	8.0	87.4
1989	1,797	6.4	93.0
1990	1,901	7.5	100.0
1991	1,992	9.4	109.4
1992	2,062	7.6	117.7
1993	2,110	9.6	129.0
1994	2,200	8.5	140.0
1995	2,308	9.4	153.1
1996	2,383	8.0	165.4
1997	4,650	6.7	176.5
1998	8,025	57.6	278.2
1999	7,430	20.5	335.6

a. Throughout this book, end-of-period exchange rates are used unless otherwise specified.
b. Annual change in the consumer price index.
Source: IMF, Financial Statistics Yearbook 1998 and 1999 and International Financial Statistics 1999.

KUPEDES credit program, were offered in the unit desas in rural areas throughout the country. The spread between loan and deposit interest rates was set to cover all estimated costs, financial and nonfinancial, and to generate a profit.[21] In 1989 the unit desa system was extended to low-income urban areas as well.

Table **2.2** | **Performance indicators for BRI's unit desas, 1984–96**

Indicator	1984	1985	1986	1987	1988	1989	1990	1991	1992	1993	1994	1995	1996
Loans													
Number of outstanding													
loans (millions)	0.6	1.0	1.2	1.3	1.4	1.6	1.9	1.8	1.8	1.9	2.1	2.3	2.5
Value of outstanding loans													
(millions of U.S. dollars)	103	204	204	260	313	471	727	731	799	928	1,117	1,383	1,710
Average outstanding loan													
balance (U.S. dollars)	171.1	204.0	170.0	200.0	223.6	294.4	382.6	406.1	443.9	488.4	531.9	601.3	684.0
Outstanding ratio of													
loans to savings (percent)	2.64	2.72	1.91	1.49	1.10	0.88	0.82	0.57	0.48	0.45	0.47	0.53	0.57
Long-term loss ratio													
(percent)[a]	1.0	1.7	2.2	2.6	3.2	2.9	2.6	3.3	3.3	3.1	2.6	2.3	2.2
Portfolio status (percent)[b]	0.5	2.1	4.5	5.8	7.4	5.4	4.1	8.5	9.1	6.5	4.5	3.5	3.6
Savings													
Number of savings													
accounts (millions)	—	—	—	4.2	5.0	6.3	7.3	8.6	10.0	11.4	13.1	14.5	16.1
Value of savings													
(millions of U.S. dollars)	39	75	107	174	285	534	892	1,275	1,648	2,050	2,378	2,606	2,976
Profitability [c]													
Profit or loss													
(millions of U.S. dollars)	–23	–1	6	14	18	21	34	33	41	66	121	174	177
Return on assets (percent)	—	—	—	—	—	—	3.0	2.7	2.6	3.3	5.1	6.5	5.7
Share of units													
profitable (percent)	13.6	48.3	72.5	80.6	80.9	79.2	89.1	84.0	85.9	89.3	93.7	95.7	94.9

— Not available.
a. Measures the cumulative amount due but unpaid since the opening of the unit relative to the total amount due.
b. Measures the aggregate amount of overdue principal installments relative to the total principal outstanding.
c. Pretax data.
Source: BRI unit desa monthly reports, 1984–96.

Performance of the microbanking division, 1984–96. The unit desa system has performed extremely well since 1984 (table 2.2 and figures 2.1 and 2.2). Between 1984 and 1996 the system extended about $11.1 billion[22] in 18.5 million KUPEDES loans. KUPEDES loans were available from about $11 to about $10,685; at the end of 1996 the average loan balance was $687 (64 percent of GNP per capita).

The system broke even in just two years and has been profitable since 1986 and independent of subsidy since 1987. The 1996 return on assets for BRI's microbanking division was 5.7 percent before tax. The banking industry average in Indonesia for return on assets (after tax) was 1.5 percent in the same year. But Indonesia's banking industry has long failed to provision properly for loan losses. In contrast, since 1984 BRI's unit desa system has adhered to conservative international accounting standards

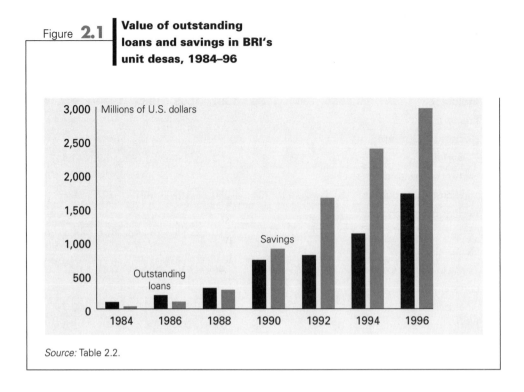

Figure **2.1** | Value of outstanding loans and savings in BRI's unit desas, 1984–96

Source: Table 2.2.

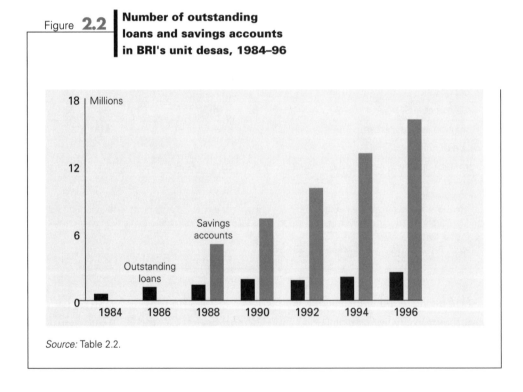

Figure **2.2** | Number of outstanding loans and savings accounts in BRI's unit desas, 1984–96

Source: Table 2.2.

and has made appropriate provision for doubtful loans. Hence the real gap between the average return on assets of the Indonesian banking industry and that of the unit desas, adjusted for tax payments, was significantly larger than the figures above suggest.

From the early 1970s until the financial deregulation of June 1983, the unit desa system had mobilized deposits of only about $18 million. This small amount was widely assumed within the government and the formal financial sector to result from a lack of local demand for financial services, an absence of "bank-mindedness," and a mistrust of banks among Indonesia's rural population. These assumptions were wrong.

At the end of 1996 the unit desa system held locally mobilized deposits of $3 billion in 16.1 million deposit accounts (see table 2.2). The Simpanan Pedesaan (SIMPEDES) and Simpanan Kota (SIMASKOT) instruments, which have relatively low interest rates but permit an unlimited number of withdrawals and provide lotteries, together accounted for 76 percent of the value of unit desa deposits and for 71 percent of the number of unit desa savings accounts.[23] Because the new instruments and services were designed with an extensive knowledge of local financial markets (acquired by selected BRI staff through intensive training and field work in 1984–85), the savings instruments—introduced nationwide in 1986—were immediately in demand, and have been so continuously. Unit desa deposits, a highly stable source of funds, finance all KUPEDES loans. The average account size, including all types of unit desa savings and deposits accounts, was $185 at the end of 1996 (17 percent of GNP per capita).

A 1996 report by the World Bank's Operations Evaluation Department (OED) states the reasons for the success of BRI's unit desas as follows:

> The program succeeded because the banks loaned at market rates,[24] used income to finance their operations, kept operating costs low and devised appropriate savings instruments to attract depositors. By mobilizing rural savings ... [the unit desa system] was not only provided...with a stable source of funds, it also kept financial savings in rural areas, thus helping development growth in the countryside. Other reasons for success included: the simplicity of loan designs, which enabled the banks to keep costs down; effective management at the unit level, backed by close supervision and monitoring by the center; and appropriate staff training and performance incentives.
>
> —*World Bank News,* 4 April 1996, p. 6[25]

However, BRI's highly successful unit desas represent only one division in a large bank that has had serious problems in other divisions.

> The vast [unit desa] profits have been used to cross-subsidize [other divisions that serve] wealthier clients. In fact, even as the [unit desa] system succeeded, the rest of the bank continued to suffer from low recovery rates. This issue is of the utmost importance, because the enormous size of the cross subsidy results in regressive income distribution; year after year small-scale entrepreneurs subsidize their more affluent countrymen. The rural lending scheme's very success may have reduced the pressure on the parent bank to achieve an equivalent level of self sufficiency ... It is clearly time to review these arrangements in light of their substantial

BRI's unit desa system broke even in just two years and has been profitable since 1986 and independent of subsidy since 1987

economic costs to the country and their perverse effect on poverty reduction objectives.

—Yaron, McDonald, and Charitonenko 1998, p. 167

This problem began to be addressed during the Indonesian crisis (see chapter 15).

Performance of the microbanking division, 1997–99. The severe economic, financial, and political crisis that began in mid-1997 showed BRI's microbanking system to be one of the most stable institutions in the country (see chapter 8 for discussion of the Indonesian crisis and chapter 15 for unit desa performance during the crisis). There were no runs on the unit desas; in rupiah terms, savings more than doubled during the crisis (table 2.3). Outstanding loans held steady, and repayment rates continued to be extremely high.[26]

The exchange rate changed dramatically between 1997 and 1999—from 2,450 rupiah to 1 U.S. dollar at the end of June 1997 (just before the crisis began) to 14,900 rupiah to $1 at the end of June 1998. The rupiah recovered to 8,025 to the U.S. dollar by the end of 1998 and to 7,430 by the end of 1999. However, the consumer price index showed a lower rate of change (see table 2.1). Table 2.3 should be read with this in mind. Most of the unit desas' borrowers and savers are not associated with direct import or export operations. Therefore, the changes in the CPI are a better indicator of their real purchasing power than the changes in the exchange rate (see chapter 15).

In April 1998 nominal flat monthly interest rates on KUPEDES loans—which in 1995 had been reduced for prompt payers from 1.5 percent on all loans to a range of flat monthly rates between 1.2 and 1.5 percent depending on loan size—were returned to the original 1.5 percent flat rate a month for prompt payers on all loans (about a 32 percent annual effective rate for a 12-month loan with monthly installments). The effective rate was raised to 45 percent in September 1998; subsequently it was reduced in steps to the pre-crisis rate of 32 percent. The average loan balance, which had been $687 at the end of 1996, was $324 at the end of 1999.

Partly because of substantial increases in interest rates paid on rupiah deposits as a result of the crisis, and partly because people removed their savings from failing banks and deposited them at BRI units (which are considered relatively secure), the rupiah amount of savings held at the units more than doubled between the end of 1996 and the end of 1999: from 7.1 trillion rupiah ($3 billion) to 17.1 trillion rupiah ($2.3 billion). The average account size, including all types of savings and deposit accounts, increased in rupiah terms, though it decreased substantially in dollar terms. The average account size, which was 439,188 rupiah ($185) at the end of 1996, was 703,969 rupiah ($95) at the end of 1999.

By the end of 1999 there were 24.2 million savings accounts with a total of 17.1 trillion rupiah ($2.3 billion; see table 2.3). In 1996 annual interest rates for savings accounts ranged from 0–14.5 percent; fixed deposits ranged up to 16 percent. In contrast, during 1997 and 1998 annual interest rates fluctuated widely, reaching a tem-

The severe economic, financial, and political crisis that began in mid-1997 showed BRI's microbanking system to be one of the most stable institutions in Indonesia

Table **2.3**

**Performance indicators
for BRI's unit desas, 1996–99**

(millions except where otherwise indicated)

Indicator	1996	1997	1998	1999
Loans				
Number of loans disbursed				
(cumulative from 1984)	18.5	20.4	22.1	24.0
Value of loans disbursed				
(cumulative from 1984)[a]				
Rupiah (current)	22,378,500	27,430,400	32,309,100	39,034,000
Rupiah (constant 1996)	30,160,200	34,894,300	37,794,900	41,109,300
U.S. dollars (current)	11,138	12,875	13,362	14,218
Number of outstanding loans	2.5	2.6	2.5	2.5
Value of outstanding loans[b]				
Rupiah (current)	4,076,200	4,685,400	4,696,800	5,956,500
Year-end exchange rate				
(rupiah to US$1)	2,383	4,650	8,025	7,430
U.S. dollars (current)	1,710	1,008	585	802
Long-term loss ratio				
(percent)[c]	2.15	2.17	2.13	2.06
Savings				
Number of savings accounts	16.1	18.1	21.7	24.2
Value of savings				
Rupiah (current)	7,091,690	8,836,510	16,146,020	17,061,390
U.S. dollars (current)	2,976	1,900	2,012	2,296
Pretax profit				
Rupiah (current)	422,877	417,035	713,676	1,190,331
U.S. dollars (current)	177	90	89	160
Return on assets (percent)[d]	5.7	4.7	4.9	6.1

a. Cumulative loan disbursements (since 1984) in U.S. dollars were calculated by dividing each year's disbursements in rupiah by the same year's (monthly average) exchange rate. The sum of the yearly disbursements in dollars equals the cumulative dollar disbursements. Changes in the consumer price index may better reflect changes in the purchasing power of balances and flows of the unit desas' financial statements, because BRI clients are seldom engaged in direct export and import. Because the exchange rate moved sharply in a very short period (from 2,450 in June 1997 to 4,650 in December 1997 to 14,900 in June 1998), monthly average exchange rates (instead of year-end exchange rates) were used to calculate the annual average exchange rate.
b. Calculated using year-end exchange rates.
c. Measures the cumulative amount due but unpaid since the opening of the unit relative to the total amount due.
d. Measures adjusted net income before tax divided by average adjusted assets.
Source: BRI unit desa monthly reports, 1996–99. This table was prepared with the help of Jacob Yaron, whose advice is gratefully acknowledged.

porary high of 22 percent on some savings accounts and 60 percent on some fixed deposits. By the end of 1999 fixed deposit rates were down to 11–12 percent, and interest rates for SIMPEDES and SIMASKOT ranged from 0–11 percent.

Pretax unit profits, which had been 423 billion rupiah ($177 million) in 1996, dropped to 417 billion rupiah ($90 million) in 1997—the rupiah decrease was largely because of a reserve requirement imposed by the central bank in 1997. Calculated on the same basis as 1996 profits, however, 1997 unit profits would have been 477 billion rupiah ($103 million). In rupiah terms, unit profits were 714 billion rupiah ($89 million) for 1998, and 1.2 trillion rupiah ($160 million) for 1999. Pretax returns on average assets, which had been 5.7 percent in 1996, dropped to 4.7 percent in 1997 and 4.9 percent in 1998, and then rose again to 6.1 percent in 1999.

As a result of the Indonesian crisis, unit desa clients saw a sharp drop in their purchasing power, a general increase in unemployment and underemployment, and continuing risk and uncertainty. Yet in rupiah terms, unit savings grew significantly in both number and value during those years, while loans remained stable, repayments stayed high, and profits increased.

These are strong indicators that unit desa borrowers value highly their credit ratings and want to retain their options to reborrow in a time of crisis. Moreover, unit desa savers have proliferated and savings have grown, partly because of higher interest rates (also available in other banks) but primarily because savers trust BRI units and like their products, services, and convenience.

The crisis has thus far had a relatively small effect on the unit desa system. In part this is because clients do not borrow in foreign-denominated loans; the units are engaged solely in financial intermediation within Indonesia. The unit desas serve clients whose enterprises are mostly within the domestic economy, and BRI's microbanking portfolio was of excellent quality and high liquidity before the crisis. In part also the effects of the crisis on the unit desas have been limited because of the excellent services provided by the units and the trust that their clients place in them.

But like most other banks in the country, BRI as an institution was badly hit by the crisis (Yaron, Benjamin, and Charitonenko 1998). In 1998 corporate banking at BRI, as at Indonesia's other banks, involved large foreign exchange losses and high loan arrears and defaults. As part of an overall restructuring of banks that followed the crisis, the government developed a plan for BRI to concentrate on its retail and microbanking activities; this is discussed further in chapter 15. Leading to BRI's microbanking strengths (and its original mandate to provide banking services in rural areas), this important change was still in the planning stage when this book went to press.

The Badan Kredit Desa. In addition to its own unit desa microbanking system, BRI supervises and in some cases provides commercial loans to capitalize the village-owned credit organizations of Java and Madura (Badan Kredit Desa, or BKD). At the end of 1998 there were 4,806 BKDs in operation, serving about 800,000 clients. The BKDs and BRI's unit desas together provide a two-tiered system, with the BRI units located at the subdistrict level, serving the surrounding villages, while the BKDs reach deeper into their respective villages.

Each BKD provides small commercial loans within its village. Most BKDs are open one morning a week; they are capitalized by savings, retained earn-

During the crisis the unit desas' return on average assets dropped only from 6 percent in 1996 to 5 percent in 1997 and 1998; it rose again to 6 percent in 1999

ings, and commercial loans from BRI. BKD loans to village borrowers are for short terms, often for three months; payments are usually made weekly. Compulsory savings range from 8–10 percent of the loan. Effective monthly interest rates on loans, set by the various local governments, are higher than the rates charged by the unit desas. The BKD system, which has been profitable for decades, is discussed further in chapters 14 and 15. Like the unit desas, the BKDs continued to be profitable during the crisis years (BRI 1998a, p. 9).

Outreach and profitability. A combination of wide coverage and institutional self-sufficiency has made Indonesia a world center of sustainable microfinance. Even in the midst of the country's worst financial crisis in 30 years, BRI's state-owned unit desa system and the BKDs (village banks) continued to be stable and profitable, as did Bank Dagang Bali (a private bank). All use the financial systems approach to microfinance, and all have remained profitable throughout the crisis.

All these institutions have had frequent visits in recent years from hundreds of delegations representing governments, central banks, commercial banks, NGOs providing microcredit, and international donors and foundations from around the world.[27] The visitors represent many institutions that are at various stages of learning about the commercial institutional approach to microfinance and adapting this approach to conditions in their own countries. They have started to adapt lessons from successful institutions, to invent complementary strategies, to expand the models, and to exchange information across international borders. Indonesia has played an important role in this process.

BancoSol

Bolivia's Banco Solidario—translated as the Bank for Solidarity (groups)—known as BancoSol, was the first bank in Latin America built expressly to provide financial services for microenterprises profitably on a national scale. The bank was created by the Fundación para la Promoción y Desarollo de la Microempresa (PRODEM), an NGO that provides commercial credit to microentrepreneurs.[28]

PRODEM was founded in 1986 by ACCIÓN International, a U.S.-based NGO operating in Latin America, and by a group of Bolivian business leaders. Funding was provided by USAID, the Bolivian Social Emergency Fund, the Calmeadow Foundation, and other donors; by international and Bolivian foundations; and by the Bolivian private sector. PRODEM became highly successful in delivering and recovering microcredit provided at interest rates that allowed full cost recovery.

However, being a donor-funded NGO, PRODEM remained capital constrained. Studies of PRODEM's activities indicated that its credit program met less than 2 percent of estimated microenterprise demand (Glosser 1994). As an NGO, however, PRODEM was legally restricted from collecting savings from the public or borrowing from the central bank. To gain access to other sources of funds, increase the volume of lending, and provide full financial services to microentrepreneurs, PRODEM's board of directors decided to open a private commercial bank that would serve microenter-

BancoSol was the first bank in Latin America built expressly to provide commercial financial services for microenterprises on a national scale

Table **2.4** | **Performance indicators for BancoSol, 1992–99**

Indicator	1992	1993	1994	1995	1996	1997	1998	1999
Number of active borrowers	27,174	79,012	61,255	63,336	71,745	76,216	81,555	73,073
Value of outstanding loan portfolio (millions of U.S. dollars)	8.8	24.8	33.2	36.7	47.4	63.1	74.0	82.3
Loans past due over 30 days as share of outstanding loan portfolio (percent)	3.2	2.9	5.1	3.1	2.6	2.1	2.6	5.6 [a]
Return on average assets (percent)	–3.7	0.7	1.9	1.3	2.3	3.4	4.2	0.7 [b]
Return on equity (percent)	–8.5	4.3	13.3	8.5	14.9	23.7	28.9	5.1 [b]

a. Data are from ACCIÓN International.
b. Adjusted data from MicroRate.
Source: BancoSol reports, 1992–2000.

Table **2.5** | **Sources of funding for BancoSol, 1994–98**

	1994		1996		1998	
	Amount		**Amount**		**Amount**	
	(millions of	**Share**	(millions of	**Share**	(millions of	**Share**
Instrument	U.S. dollars)	(percent)	U.S. dollars)	(percent)	U.S. dollars)	(percent)
Capital markets[a]	31.0	85	38.6	78	53.8	74
Certificates of deposit of less than $50,000	3.4	9	6.3	13	10.4	14
Savings accounts	2.2	6	4.7	9	8.5	12
Total	36.6	100	49.6	100	72.7	100

a. Includes interbank loans, credit lines, and bonds.
Source: ACCIÓN International data.

prises. In exchange for an 18 percent share in BancoSol equity,[29] PRODEM's loan portfolio ($4.7 million)[30] and staff were transferred to the new bank.[31]

BancoSol opened in early 1992 with four branches. The new bank disbursed $21.7 million that year in small, short-term loans to low-income borrowers. In 1998 BancoSol disbursed $135.9 million to Bolivian microentrepreneurs. The nominal monthly effective interest rate for BancoSol loans made in bolivianos in 1998 was 3.75–4.0 percent; for loans made in U.S. dollars it was 2.0–2.5 percent.

At the end of 1998 BancoSol had 81,555 active clients and an outstanding loan portfolio of $74 million (table 2.4 and figure 2.3). Portfolio at risk was 4.5 percent on a one-day past-due basis; it was 2.6 percent when defined using

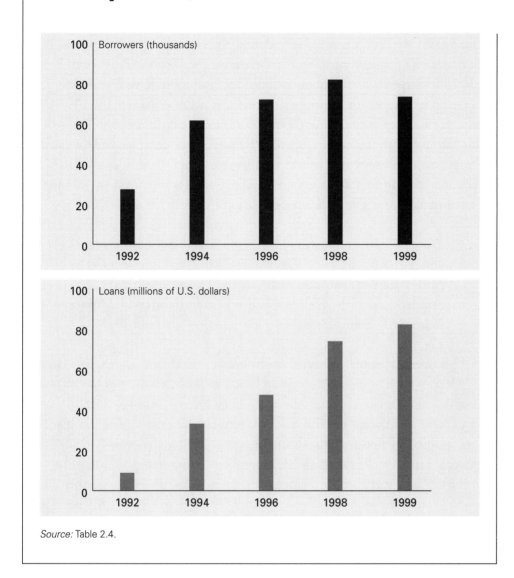

Figure **2.3** | Number of active borrowers and value of loan portfolio at BancoSol, 1992–99

Borrowers (thousands)

Loans (millions of U.S. dollars)

Source: Table 2.4.

BancoSol is the first bank to have gained access to significant capital from international investment firms based partly on the security of loans to microenterprises

late payments of 30 days or more.[32] The number of BancoSol branches grew from 4 in 1992 to 40 in 1998. Total funding increased from $36.6 million in 1994 to $72.7 million at the end of 1998—an increase of 99 percent. At the end of 1998, 74 percent of the bank's funding came from capital markets (table 2.5). The value of BancoSol's savings accounts, although still relatively low, showed the highest growth rate among the various funding sources.

BancoSol (like BRI's unit desas) became financially sustainable less than two years after it opened. USAID's study of 11 microfinance programs lists BancoSol as profitable and self-sufficient in 1993, calculated on a commercial basis (Christen, Rhyne, and Vogel 1995, p. 26).

In 1998 BancoSol reported net profits of 19.3 million bolivianos ($3.5 million), a return on average assets of 4.2 percent, and a return on equity of 28.9 percent. BancoSol is the first bank to have gained access to significant capital from international investment firms based partly on the security of loans to microenterprises—shoemakers, food vendors, carpenters, tailors, and others (Otero 1997). It was also the most profitable bank in Bolivia in 1997 and 1998; it had the highest portfolio quality of any bank in Bolivia and was also the most solvent bank in the country (Chu 1998b). By 1997 BancoSol served more than one-quarter of the clients of the Bolivian banking system and about 15 percent of the clients of the country's entire financial system—including nonbank financial institutions as well as banks.

Given its interest in attaining substantially larger outreach, the PRODEM board of directors made the right decision in creating BancoSol. Donors and foundations first provided funding for PRODEM and then backed the creation of BancoSol, a strategy that others are now learning. Most important, the Bolivian microfinance market has become increasingly competitive since BancoSol opened in 1992. As *The Wall Street Journal* (15 July 1997) reported:

> The real measure of its success is that BancoSol has spawned a slew of competitors . . . Ten Bolivian financial institutions that started out with backing from U.S. and European aid givers have decided to get out of the subsidized credit business and follow BancoSol's example.

The overall contributions to microfinance made by BancoSol—and by PRODEM—reach far beyond their clients. BancoSol has shown that regulated, financially self-sufficient microfinance institutions can access international commercial markets and can remove funding as a constraint to microfinance growth. The fact that Bolivian commercial banks and other financial institutions have followed BancoSol's lead represents a major milestone in the development of commercial microfinance.

By 1999 competition for microcredit clients among Bolivian commercial microfinance institutions, joined by consumer lending companies that decided to enter the microfinance market because of its demonstrated profitability, reached a point of frenzy. Borrowers were provided multiple loans, and virtually all Bolivian microfinance institutions found themselves with overindebted borrowers and growing arrears. (Some consumer lenders provided loans to borrowers on the basis of the fact that they already had loans from BancoSol.) In 1999 the number of BancoSol borrowers fell, its portfolio at risk rose, and its returns dropped sharply—although the institution remained profitable (see table 2.4). All of Bolivia's microfinance institutions had similar problems in 1999, and BancoSol performed comparatively well. On 26 October 2000 Damian von Stauffenberg, president of MicroRate (a private microfinance rating company that assesses many Latin American institutions, including BancoSol), contributed the following to Ohio State's Development Finance lists:

> In Bolivia . . . a recession hit just as consumer finance agencies piled into the microfinance market, leaving many of their clients over-indebted. When sales contracted, microentrepreneurs naturally used easily available consumer credit to meet their debt service payments. They very soon found themselves in a hopeless debt

"The real measure of its success is that BancoSol has spawned a slew of competitors." By 1999 the competition reached a point of frenzy

spiral ...The Bolivian microfinance institutions MicroRate tracks (BancoSol, [Los] Andes, and FIE) emerged from this mess relatively unscathed. Microentrepreneurs defaulted on consumer lenders but they kept paying the microfinance institutions.

Commercial microfinance first developed into a competitive industry in Bolivia in 1999, with all the attendant pains found in any emerging industry. But the current competition in Bolivia (and elsewhere in Latin America) is one of the clearest hallmarks of the microfinance revolution (see chapters 18 and 19).

Like BRI, BancoSol receives constant flows of visitors from around the world and participates actively in disseminating best practices of sustainable microfinance. Both BRI and BancoSol have played significant roles in expanding their countries' financial systems and in leading the microfinance revolution. Yet Bolivia and Indonesia are vastly different in their history, culture, population, economy, religion, politics, and geography, and in other ways as well. One is a sparsely populated, landlocked country; the other is the world's fourth most populous nation located on its largest archipelago. While there are some prerequisites for the success of sustainable microfinance—political will, absence of hyperinflation and of sustained catastrophic events, and certain regulatory and supervisory conditions—there is increasing evidence that commercial microfinance can operate successfully in very different country environments.

The Old Paradigm: Subsidized Credit Delivery

The new microfinance paradigm is emerging, but the old one remains entrenched in many places. There are also numerous institutions at various stages of transition. In addition, in some countries (Vietnam is a good example) new microcredit programs built on old paradigm principles have recently been established. These programs already face the same problems that have been found for decades in similar programs in other countries. Old and new here refer to concepts, not necessarily to the historical development of microfinance programs in actual time and space.

The old paradigm—derived from theories of supply-leading finance—and the widespread subsidized credit programs that evolved from these theories, emerged in response to conditions after World War II. Governments of the many newly developed nations placed high priorities on economic development, and especially on increasing food cultivation. Foreign donors held mandates for substantial investment in developing country agriculture. In this context, supply-leading finance theorists asserted that most farmers would need more capital than they could save and that they could not pay the full cost of the credit they would need for the inputs required to cultivate the new high-yielding varieties of rice and wheat that marked the green revolution of the 1960s and 1970s. As a result government- and donor-subsidized credit programs proliferated rapidly in developing countries throughout the world.

Old and new here refer to concepts, not necessarily to the historical development of microfinance programs in actual time and space

But supply-leading finance did not take into account the social and political realities of life in rural areas of developing countries or the financial dynamics of their rural markets. Large-scale subsidized credit programs led to massive problems: the programs often did not reach low-income farmers, repayment was frequently low, and losses were high. In addition, because the loans are subsidized and therefore rationed, they encourage corruption and often reach better-off rather than poorer villagers. The old paradigm is discussed further in chapters 4 and 11, as are the difficulties that result from this approach.

In developing countries the large-scale mobilization of voluntary savings and the operation of subsidized microcredit programs can both be found, but not together. Under the subsidized credit model, financial institutions, whether savings-driven or credit-driven, have not and cannot provide microfinance— credit *and* savings services—on a large scale.

The large-scale mobilization of voluntary savings and the operation of subsidized microcredit programs can both be found— but not together

Even the best of the institutions that operate with subsidized loan portfolios are effective either in capturing savings or in providing microloans with wide outreach. They cannot afford to be effective in both because their lending interest rates are too low to cover the costs and risks involved in the practice of large-scale sustainable microfinance. Microfinance can attain wide outreach sustainably only outside the subsidized credit model—in self-sufficient commercial institutions.

As discussed in chapter 7, there are four microfinance models often associated with subsidized credit programs. In the first, institutions provide microcredit but are not permitted to mobilize savings from the public because they are not regulated and publicly supervised; most microcredit institutions fall in this category. In the second, institutions perform well in lending but poorly in mobilizing savings. The third is the reverse: institutions are successful in savings but fail in lending. It is characteristic of the transitional state of microfinance that many such institutions incorporate aspects of both the old and the new paradigms. The fourth model consists of institutions that fail in both savings and lending; there are many examples throughout the world—especially in state-owned agricultural banks and in development banks generally.

Heavily subsidized microcredit programs "require frequent injections of fresh funds. If these injections are not forthcoming, the program will quickly consume its capital in financing routine operational costs . . . Studies indicate this has happened hundreds, perhaps thousands of times" (Christen, Rhyne, and Vogel 1995, p. 10). This applies to all except the third model, which has a different problem—high loan losses put at risk the savings of the poor.

Another characteristic of the old paradigm that is found in examples of all the models discussed above is the direct linkage of credit with borrower training programs. The underlying belief is that to use their credit properly, the poor need training—in skill development, business, literacy, finance, agriculture, and so on. But two problems can arise when training is linked directly to credit programs. First, institutional sustainability is hindered because training costs are rarely covered by revenues. Second, the training provided is often not considered valuable by the trainees.

The issue is not the value of training in general. Many kinds of training— in literacy, health, family planning, skill development, and the like—can be extremely important tools for alleviating poverty. The issue is the linking of credit and training.

The economically active poor tend to know their businesses and to understand their financial needs better than the institutional staff who train them. General training programs that can reach large numbers of people at low cost are typically inappropriate for the heterogeneous needs of microfinance clients. Trainers often have little understanding of the dynamics of the informal economy and the local markets in which the borrowers operate, or of clients' enterprises and options. Borrower training of this kind not only comes at a high cost to the institution, hindering its efforts toward self-sufficiency, but is often considered to be of little value by borrowers (Adams and Von Pischke 1992, p. 1466). It can also be costly for borrowers, who must add opportunity and transaction costs to the interest costs of the loan.

Anther option is specialized training programs covering particular skills. But these programs tend to reach only a small number of people and to be costly for the financial institution. The experience of the Kenya Rural Enterprise Programme (K-REP) in linking training with credit is instructive:

> It ... became obvious that the 'integrated' method of developing microenterprises, which combined traditional methods of making loans with intensive entrepreneur training and technical assistance, had limited impact on the beneficiaries, was costly, and could be sustained or expanded only through grant funding.
> —Mutua 1994, p. 268

While there are a few exceptions (the Bangladesh Rural Advancement Committee, or BRAC, is a notable example), institutions providing both social services and microfinance have typically shown themselves to be inept at financial management. Lacking a focus on financial viability, they have often been unwilling or unable to manage loan delinquency, and generally have not achieved financial self-sufficiency.

The New Paradigm: Sustainable Commercial Microfinance

The new paradigm emphasizes the idea that, given enabling macroeconomic, political, legal, regulatory, and demographic conditions, commercial institutions can be developed to provide financial intermediation for the economically active poor and can deliver services at the local level profitably, sustainably, without subsidy, and with wide coverage. Examples of institutions successfully grappling with constraints created by macroeconomic, political, legal, and other conditions are provided in volumes 2 and 3. The prerequisites for commercial microfinance are discussed in chapter 22. Also emphasized throughout is that commercial microfinance is a complement to, not a substitute for, government and donor poverty alleviation and employment generation programs for the extremely poor.

The economically active poor tend to know their businesses and to understand their financial needs better than the institutional staff who train them

Among sustainable microfinance programs, there is a considerable variety of institutional types and sizes, organizational structures, loan methodologies, funding sources, corporate cultures, and other features. For example, BRI, Bank Dagang Bali (BDB), and the BKDs provide individual loans; BancoSol provides loans to small, self-formed groups. Loan portfolios are financed primarily by locally mobilized savings at BRI and BDB, by commercial debt and locally mobilized savings at BancoSol, and by retained earnings, savings, and commercial debt at the BKDs. BancoSol and BDB are privately owned, BRI is state owned, and the BKDs are owned by their villages. All are regulated and publicly supervised, though in different ways.

There are many routes to large-scale sustainable microfinance. But there are also fundamental characteristics that underlie all fully self-sufficient commercial microfinance institutions. One is that they understand their clients' businesses and financial needs, which are in some important respects different from those of conventional bank clients. Thus, Rutherford shows that the poor use both savings and loans to acquire the lump sums they often need for such purposes as emergencies, social and religious obligations (puberty ceremonies, marriages, funerals), and investments in their enterprises (Rutherford 2000; see also Rutherford and others 1999). In this context he analyzes three ways that poor people commonly exchange small savings for lump sums. Two are asset-based: the sale of assets that one owns or expects to own (as with advance sales of crops) and the mortgage and pawning of assets—converting assets into cash and then reversing the process. But poor people have few assets, and these methods are typically inadequate for their lump sum needs.

Except for the extremely poor, however, most poor people have a flow of savings, even though it may be small or irregular. The third and most common method, therefore, is to swap savings for lump sums. To obtain funds to cope with emergencies or to take advantage of investment opportunities, poor people swap one large sum at one time for a series of much smaller sums spread out over time. This can be accomplished in several ways (figure 2.4):

- Saving up: a series of savings made now is exchanged for a lump sum in the future.
- Saving down: a lump sum taken now in the form of a loan is exchanged for future savings (used for repayment installments).
- Saving through: a continuous stream of savings that is converted when a lump sum is required. If the amount needed is larger than the savings, the saver also takes a loan, using both to create the lump sum needed, then repays the loan from future savings.

These patterns are found in a wide variety of social and economic environments around the world, as is illustrated in chapter 3 and in other parts of this book.

Common elements of sustainable microfinance institutions

The common elements shared by self-sufficient institutions can be broadly grouped into five categories: knowledge of the commercial microfinance business and its clients,

Figure **2.4** | **Swapping small savings for lump sum savings**

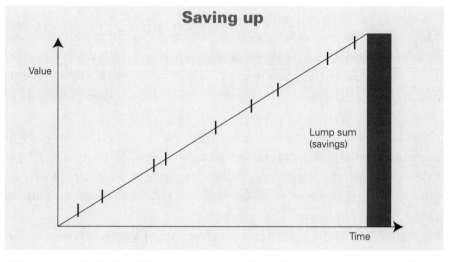

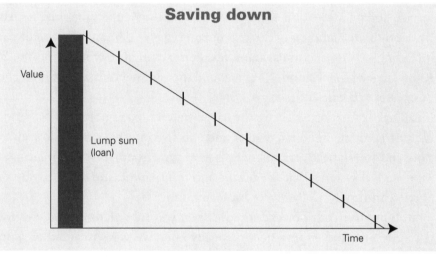

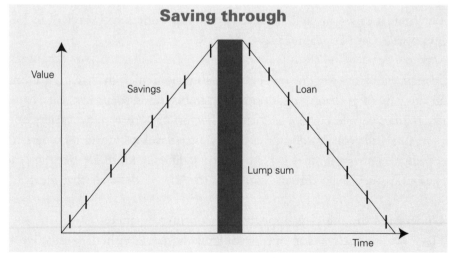

Source: Adapted from Rutherford 2000.

characteristics of institutional ownership, priorities in organization and management, development of human resources, and corporate philosophy. Many of the shared elements are found in other kinds of microfinance programs as well, but they are common in aggregate to sustainable microfinance institutions operating on a large scale.

Knowledge of the commercial microfinance business and its clients. Self-sufficient microfinance institutions with large-scale outreach know the business of providing financial services to low-income people. Their owners, boards, managers, and staff have among them a wide range of business knowledge and skills, including:

- Knowledge of the economics, politics, legal and social structures and practices, and natural environments of the areas served.
- Familiarity with the relevant policies and regulations of national and regional governments, and, where possible, well-developed channels of communication with the concerned policymakers.
- Understanding of the operations and dynamics of local markets, both formal and informal, in a variety of sectors, including agriculture, small industry, trade, service, and finance—and of the activities of these markets in wider networks.
- In-depth understanding of the extent and types of demand for microfinance, including savings accounts, loans, transfers, payment facilities, and the like.
- Knowledge of the institution's clients and their households, and of their clients' businesses and rates of return.
- Financial expertise, including the capacity to manage portfolio risk and liquidity; to provide frequent, regular, and effective internal supervision and controls; and to establish and maintain accounting, reporting, and management information systems that are simple and transparent, and that provide managers with timely, well-selected information.
- The ability to treat poor clients consistently as valued, respected customers.
- Awareness of, and experience in, locally effective ways to avoid pressure to direct credit to politically selected individuals or enterprises.
- Public relations skills and the ability to sell products and services in locally appropriate and appealing ways.

Institutional ownership. The owners of self-sufficient microfinance institutions are a curious mix of governments, donors and foundations, social investors, bankers, banks, businesspeople, current or former directors of NGOs, and a variety of others. The mix will probably change as the industry develops. Current owners, however, bring to a new industry long experience of different kinds. Despite their varied backgrounds, they share certain characteristics. Among these are that they:

- Understand the business opportunities of microfinance.
- Have defined the mission of their organization, established an effective governance structure, and appointed a governing board whose members are committed to profitable microfinance with wide outreach, and who work together with reasonable mutual cooperation.

The owners of self-sufficient microfinance institutions are a curious mix of governments, donors, banks, businesspeople, NGOs, and others. The mix will probably change as the industry develops

- Act as commercial shareholders.
- Mandate the setting of interest rates and fees that fully cover all (nonsubsidized) financial costs, operating costs, and risks, and that enable institutional profitability.
- Are active, committed, and accountable for the financial health of the organization.
- Have the capacity to access additional capital as needed.
- Help the institution to avoid or overcome bureaucratic and political hurdles.

Organization and management. While their organizational structures may be quite different, profitable commercial microfinance organizations operating at a large scale share a number of features. For example, their branches and other low-level outlets are treated as profit centers, everyone connected with the institution is held accountable for his or her performance, and responsibility is decentralized. Strong emphasis is placed on effective supervision, internal controls, and internal audit. Staff training, performance-based staff incentives, and human resource development are given high priority. And there is an appropriate, effective, well-understood, and well-operating management information system.

Managers of sustainable microfinance institutions are committed to the profitable delivery of microfinance services to large numbers of low-income clients. But their institutions are also mindful of the fact that regulated commercial microfinance is a new industry with substantial new industry risks, and that industry standards are at an early stage of development. Managers of such institutions must learn to pilot some difficult waters.

On the one hand, microfinance is different in many ways from standard commercial banking. The managing director of a microfinance division in a full-service commercial bank may be in a division where the board, the chief executive officer, and others among the managing directors do not know the microfinance business. The board or the chief executive officer may be unwilling to allocate necessary resources for microfinance or to make exceptions to bank rules, such as agreeing to the relatively high operating costs required for profitable microfinance, waiving collateral requirements for small loans or accepting nontraditional forms of collateral that are appropriate for poor borrowers, or allowing the use of a cash accounting system rather than the accrual accounting method. Managing the microfinance division of a full-service commercial bank can be a difficult job because most banks do not yet consider microfinance to be "real" finance. Managers and staff tend to consider an appointment to a microfinance division as a punishment posting—which in some banks it is.

On the other hand, formal microfinance is also different from unregulated microfinance. In the case of a regulated microfinance institution created by an unregulated NGO and owned wholly or substantially by the NGO, the owners may know the microfinance market well. But they may not be financially competent to supervise a regulated financial intermediary or qualified to hire or supervise its managers. There may also be conflicts of interest between the interests of the NGO and those of the regulated microfinance institution it owns (see chapter 18).

Most banks do not yet consider microfinance to be "real" finance. Appointment to a microfinance division is often considered a punishment posting

Managers of commercial microfinance institutions must develop good working relationships with regulatory and supervisory authorities, who may or may not understand the goals and methods of commercial microfinance. In addition, microfinance managers often need to explain to politicians, journalists, and others why their institutions are not engaged in charity work. Microfinance institutions that have achieved self-sufficiency and wide outreach have done so by overcoming these and other difficulties. Especially in this early, transitional stage of the industry, successful managers of profitable microfinance institutions are rather like tightrope walkers. In addition to the factors already mentioned, good managers ensure that their institutions have:

Institutions that decide to enter the microfinance market must decide at the beginning to commit high-level management resources on a long-term basis

- Effective asset-liability management.
- Products and services that are in demand by low-income households and enterprises, and that are priced for institutional sustainability and client affordability.
- High loan repayment rates.
- Monthly profit and loss statements and balance sheets issued for each outlet providing financial services.
- Effective cash management.
- Well-designed and well-implemented systems of staff recruitment, evaluation, promotion, and incentives.
- Service locations and opening hours that are convenient for clients.
- High-quality supervision, internal control, and internal audit.
- Appropriate management information systems and staff that are qualified in their use.
- Suitable security systems.

This is not an institutional wish list; this is what managers of profitable, sustainable microfinance organizations do. It is for this reason that institutions that decide to enter the microfinance market must decide at the beginning that they will commit high-level management resources to the effort on a long-term basis.

Development of human resources. Microfinance is a business that is necessarily labor intensive, and profitable commercial institutions accord high priority to human resource development. In particular, successful microfinance institutions have:

- Developed a management career track with positions that are considered desirable within the institution.
- Established effective recruiting methods for entry-level positions that result in the hiring of staff who are respectful of, and helpful to, low-income clients, and who are efficient in their jobs.
- Established promotion tracks, career paths, and appropriate compensation packages for staff at all levels of the organization.
- Developed management and staff training programs that are specifically designed for microfinance. Such programs include training in assessing the creditworthiness of different types of microenterprises, in recognizing creditworthy

borrower groups, in estimating the expected rate of return of a client's enterprise, in talking with poor clients and putting them at ease, in locating potential savers and mobilizing their savings, in preparing profit and loss statements for individual outlets, and in managing and supervising outlets and branches.

- Developed a culture of accountability.
- Provided attractive staff incentives that are based on performance indicators such as the profitability and outreach of each branch or other outlet.
- Combined responsibility, accountability, training, and incentives so that a staff member is given responsibility for a task, held accountable for carrying it out effectively, provided the training to be able to do so, and rewarded for doing the job well.

Corporate philosophy. Sustainable microfinance institutions have corporate cultures that vary somewhat depending on the country and culture, the institutional type, and so on. Nevertheless, the basic philosophy is much the same in all these institutions. Success in commercial microfinance is based on trust, incentives, commitment, simplicity, and standardization, along with service, transparency, flexibility, accountability, profitability, training of staff, and knowledge of the local market. Moreover, as Sugianto, BRI's long-time managing director responsible for its microbanking system, said, "You can succeed in microfinance only if you love it." Every successful microfinance institution that I am familiar with qualifies on this criterion as well as on the others.

As Sugianto, BRI's long-time managing director responsible for its microbanking system, said, "You can succeed in microfinance only if you love it"

Basic operating principles

Loan repayment is very high in fully sustainable microfinance programs. But this is a relatively new phenomenon in institutional microfinance. Before new microloan methods were developed in the 1970s and 1980s, loan repayment was often poor in microcredit institutions—as it still is in many institutions that continue to provide subsidized credit to targeted borrowers.

> High delinquency rates in credit programs for the poor were often blamed on the weather, poor market infrastructure, economic recession, deficient business practices, or clients' misallocation of loan funds into consumption activities, rather than on the credit instruments themselves. Modern microenterprise credit programs debunked these explanations by demonstrating that *repayment depends fundamentally on factors within the control of the lending institution,* such as reliability and quality of loan service, communication of clear repayment expectations, administrative efficiency, and the development of a close, almost personal, relationship with clients. [emphasis added]
> —Christen 1997a, p. 16

Profitable microfinance institutions have learned much about lending from moneylenders (Christen 1989, 1997a). They have adapted for their own use many

Loan products

- Standardization with flexibility is key. Within standardized loan programs, loan purposes, maturities, and amounts are customized to meet borrowers' needs.
- Credit and savings products are designed and priced together, with a spread that enables institutional profitability.
- Loans are offered to any creditworthy borrower for any viable business or household investment purpose; they are not limited to any sector, commodity, or group.
- Loans are made to individuals or to self-formed small groups whose members guarantee one another's loans.
- New borrowers start with small loans; larger loans are provided as borrowers prove both willingness and capacity to repay.
- Most loans are for working capital, with relatively short terms (typically two months to two years) and frequent payment installments (weekly, biweekly, or monthly); borrowers repay both principal and interest in their installments.
- Loans are made only to ongoing enterprises or people experienced in their work; a track record of good business performance is required.
- Borrower training, other than orientation to the loan program, is not required to receive a loan.

Loan approval and disbursement

- Staff are trained to evaluate the character of borrowers, the capacity of their enterprises to generate sufficient income to repay loans, and, in group loan programs, the cohesion of groups and their capacity to repay.
- Loan amounts are based on assessments of borrowers' repayment abilities from their current income flows, not from estimates of possible returns from use of the loans.
- Loan applications are simple, and most credit decisions are made quickly at the lowest-level outlet—for example, within a week for new borrowers and one or two days for repeat borrowers.
- Borrower transaction costs are relatively low because forms and procedures are simple, loan disbursements are timely, and repeat visits to the institution to obtain a loan are usually unnecessary.

Loan collection policies and procedures

- Where regulations and circumstances permit, lending institutions bear the full credit risk and so are motivated to develop effective loan collection systems.
- The same local staff who approve and make loans are responsible for collecting them.
- Credit officers do not monitor borrowers' businesses or the use of loans unless borrowers are in arrears, thus enabling each officer to serve more clients.
- Borrowers are informed that if they maintain a good repayment record and if their enterprises remain creditworthy, they will be permitted to reborrow. Larger loans, up to the institution's maximum, can be approved for borrowers with good repayment records who qualify for them.
- Borrowers who do not repay are not permitted to borrow again (however, there may be rare exceptions in which loans are rescheduled because of a visible catastrophic event).
- Borrowers can be offered incentives (such as interest rebates) for prompt payment.
- Borrowers who miss a payment are visited by a staff member immediately (the next working day). Borrowers in arrears are repeatedly followed up on.
- Late payments are recorded promptly. When a loan payment is one day late, the entire outstanding balance of the loan should be shown as delinquent. Not all sustainable institutions use this method, but they typically at least show the payment as overdue one week after its due date.

Box **21**

(continued)

Loan portfolio management
- Loan accounting and reporting are simple and transparent; management information systems are simple but designed to permit frequent, regular, and accurate assessments of the performance of each borrower, officer, outlet, and branch, as well as of the overall institution.
- Loan loss reserves and provisions are adequate and regularly reviewed; bad debt is written off based on standardized aging criteria established by the governing board of the institution (although collection efforts continue).
- Delinquency measurement and management are accorded high priority by the institution's governing board which sets policies and procedures and reviews them regularly. Managers focus on effective implementation of procedures for timely repayment of loans.
- Outlets that make loans are regularly and carefully supervised, on at least a weekly basis, by specially trained personnel from the next highest level in the financial institution. Outlets are also supervised by higher-level personnel as necessary.
- Estimates of the demand for loans are routinely and carefully made at every level of the microfinance organization.
- Asset-liability management is carried out on a frequent, regular basis and given high priority.
- Loan portfolios are diversified with regard to enterprise type and, where possible, region.

Note: For detailed discussion of the operations of sustainable financial institutions, see Christen 1997a and Ledgerwood 1999.

of the techniques of moneylenders—especially character-based lending methods that rely more on the borrower's demonstrated willingness to repay the loan than on loan guarantees or project feasibility assessments. New borrowers begin with small loans and move up to larger loans as they demonstrate their capacity to repay and their willingness to do so.

On the one hand, commercial microfinance institutions have learned from the methods of moneylenders how to lend to small borrowers and to recover their loans. On the other, they have used their own advantages—scale, savings mobilization, financial intermediation, political neutrality, institutional professionalism, and financial focus (unlike moneylenders, they are not engaged in multiple interlinked transactions with their borrowers)—to undercut the moneylenders' interest rates by a large margin (see chapter 6).

In successful microfinance programs, borrowers repay partly because of the institution's loan methodology (which emphasizes simplicity, efficiency, and quality of service), partly because of peer group and other social pressures, partly because of repayment incentives, and partly because of the collection activities of the institution's staff—but mainly to keep open the options of reborrowing on what they consider advantageous terms. Because profitable commercial institutions can usually mobilize local savings or leverage capital as needed, borrowers understand that their ability to reborrow is based on their own performance, not on external factors. This contributes substantially to the institution's loan repayment rate.

On the deposit side, assuming that regulation and public supervision are appropriate, that hyperinflation and sustained political turmoil are absent,

Because profitable commercial institutions are usually not capital constrained, borrowers understand that their ability to reborrow is based on their own performance, not on external factors

- Staff are taught that the poor do not need to be trained or taught discipline in order to save—because most of them already save in a variety of forms. Instead, emphasis is placed on designing instruments appropriate for microsavers and on training the staff (not the savers).
- Savings are mobilized from people who live or work near the institution's outlet. This permits the institution to meet local demand for savings services; collect small savings from the poor since the bigger accounts of larger savers raise the average account size, making it cost-effective for the institution to mobilize savings from all levels of the public; and use savings from all sources to finance an expanding microloan portfolio.
- Loans and savings accounts are designed, priced, and managed together.
- Long-range institutional planning is based on the likelihood that at a given time more clients will demand appropriate savings services than will demand microloans. However, unmet demand for savings services varies widely in different countries and regions; institutions plan their services in relation to the local context.
- Savings instruments are for voluntary savings only; no compulsory savings are required. If financial guarantees (compensating balances) are required for loans, or if a contractual savings and loan product is offered that requires accumulation of a certain amount of savings before the first loan is offered, the deposit requirement for the loan is kept separate from the savings instruments offered by the institution. Savings instruments are available to borrowers and nonborrowers alike—it is not necessary to borrow in order to save. And it is not necessary to save in order to borrow.
- The mobilization of voluntary public savings requires both effective public supervision and high-quality, regular internal supervision and audit.
- The institution consistently provides good security, quick and friendly service, and effective cash management. Given normal expectations of withdrawals, sufficient cash is on hand during opening hours to permit savers to withdraw when they come in, according to the terms of the deposit instruments they hold.
- Several savings and deposit instruments with different ratios of liquidity and returns are offered; opening and minimum balances are set low on savings accounts. Savers are encouraged to select an account or a combination of accounts that meets their needs.
- Interest rates on fixed deposit accounts are set at or near the rates of the nearest standard commercial banks. Interest rates on most liquid savings accounts held at conveniently located local outlets can be significantly lower than the rates for similar accounts in banks located at district or provincial levels. In addition, interest rates for savings accounts can be tiered by account size (with lower rates for smaller account balances) to maintain a sufficient spread between loan interest rates and the cost of mobilizing savings. For most small savers, security, convenience, liquidity, and service are usually more important than returns.
- Staff are trained to identify potential savers. They visit them, explain the available instruments and services, and help them open accounts appropriate for their needs. Staff maintain ongoing relations with their clients and develop information networks through which they locate potential savers.
- Savings and deposit accounts are kept confidential.
- In addition to household savings, deposits are collected from local institutional and association funds (for example, from government and private corporate offices, schools, religious institutions, professional associations, and local organizations such as women's, sports, religious, and neighborhood groups).

Box **2.2**

(continued)

- Special arrangements may be made by particular branches to collect savings on pay-day from local employees in their offices, factories, businesses, schools, or other places of work.
- In regions with high social stability and low crime, mobile savings teams can visit clients regularly at their homes and places of work.
- Locally appropriate public relations activities are emphasized. These include educating the public about the services provided and about how these can help in managing business and household activities. Promotional incentives may be offered, such as lotteries in which free lottery numbers are distributed to savers according to the amount of savings they hold in the institution.

On the credit side, the institution must trust the borrowers. On the deposit side, the clients must trust the institution

and that the area is not very sparsely populated or destitute, voluntary savings can probably be mobilized cost-effectively at the local level. Local savings mobilization can work well when staff treat clients helpfully; when savings products are offered that meet clients' needs for security, convenience, liquidity, confidentiality, and returns; and when institutions have good internal supervision and effective management information and cash management systems.

Microfinance outlets that have excess liquidity deposit funds with their institution and receive interest; outlets with insufficient funds for their portfolios borrow from the institution and pay interest. Financial intermediation, with such a transfer price mechanism, permits demand to be met from large numbers of savers and creditworthy borrowers, regardless of the loan-to-deposit ratio of the particular outlet or branch.

Basic operating principles for loans and savings mobilization in sustainable commercial microfinance programs are summarized more specifically in boxes 2.1 and 2.2. Underlying both types of efforts are concepts of trust and mutual advantage. On the credit side, the institution must trust the borrowers. On the deposit side, the clients must trust the institution. Incentives may be provided to borrowers for timely repayment. Borrowers with good repayment records maintain an ongoing option to reborrow in the future. Savers are provided a secure, convenient place to store their excess liquidity, they have the option to withdraw their savings whenever they wish, and above a small minimum their savings earn returns. In the best microfinance programs, clients gain through increased income and greater self-confidence, and they repay in institutional loyalty. The institution gains in profits, reputation, and long-term viability.

Crucial points in the emerging paradigm shift are shown in box 2.3; figures 2.5 and 2.6 show the old and new approaches. As can be seen there, it is the new paradigm that leads to financially sustainable microfinance institutions with high levels of outreach.

Policy issues

- The demand for microcredit among the economically active poor is far too large to be met by government and donor funding.
- Microfinance demand can be met worldwide only through a substantial increase in the number of profitable, sustainable institutions providing commercial financial services to low-income clients.
- Successful institutional commercial microfinance can be carried out in widely different environments—with the probable exception of those characterized by hyperinflation, recurring warfare or civil strife, or very low population density (or moderately low population density combined with severely deficient infrastructure).
- Regulatory authorities must provide an enabling environment if institutional commercial microfinance is to succeed. This includes allowing banks and other relevant financial institutions to set their own interest rates and select their own customers, removing regulatory obstacles to commercial microfinance, and providing effective supervision. Examples of regulatory obstacles include inappropriate regulations for unsecured loans, capital requirements, salary structure requirements, reporting requirements, and branch office specifications. But such obstacles generally represent insurmountable difficulties only when they are enforced; in practice they are often ignored or waived.
- Donors supporting the growth of commercial microfinance assist through capacity-building initiatives for selected institutions and by developing microfinance tools: diagnostic tools for evaluating financial performance, management information systems that can provide reliable information on such matters as portfolio quality and staff performance, handbooks for business planning and financial modeling, and tools for external auditors of microfinance institutions (chapter 20).

Institutional issues

- The owners of a self-sufficient microfinance institution operating on a large scale, or one aiming to do so, must be committed to profitable microfinance. To attain wide outreach to low-income customers, the owners have to establish an effective governance structure that establishes and maintains the mission of the organization, oversees its management, and regularly evaluates its profitability and the breadth and depth of client coverage.
- Where microfinance is offered by a division of a commercial bank, the bank's owners and managers must understand that microfinance is a different business from the bank's other activities. For example, microfinance requires staff, products, pricing, staff training, and reporting systems that are considerably different from their counterparts in conventional commercial banking.
- Commercial institutional microfinance necessarily has higher operating costs than the operating costs of the banking industry in the same country. This is because it is more expensive to provide small loans and deposit services to many clients in small bank units in numerous, widespread locations than it is to provide larger loans and collect bigger deposits in standard bank branches.
- Profitable commercial microfinance requires interest rates or fees on loans that are high enough for the institution to return a profit after covering general business risk, the full commercial cost of funds, all operating expenses, and appropriate loan loss provisions.
- Voluntary savings instruments that are well designed for the market and offered in secure, convenient locations are required to meet the widespread demand for savings services.
- Demand for microloans can be met by sustainable institutions that finance their loan portfolios from various mixes of locally mobilized savings, commercial debt and other financial instruments, for-profit investments, and retained earnings.

Box **2.3**

(continued)

- Startup subsidies may be provided by governments, donors, foundations, and the like for purposes such as initial equity, staff training, buildings, technical assistance, and management information systems. Such subsidies must be for institutional development, not for operating expenses. The crucial point is that it is institutions, not borrowers, that are being subsidized; subsidies have to be designed and implemented so that institutional dependence is not created.
- Standardization of a small number of simple, carefully designed and tested products and delivery systems is essential for long-term institutional viability on a large scale.
- Simple, transparent accounting and reporting systems with regularly issued profit and loss statements and balance sheets are required for each outlet, as are the frequent and regular supervision of each outlet.
- Requirements for responsibility and accountability are coupled with high-quality specialized management and staff training and with performance-based monetary and other incentives.

Results
- Commercial institutions can make credit widely accessible to the economically active poor at much lower cost than such borrowers typically pay on the informal credit market.
- Commercial institutions providing savings instruments and services appropriate for the microfinance market offer low-income clients a secure, convenient place to store excess liquidity and to obtain returns on their deposits. This is frequently the financial service most essential for this group—and one that is often not otherwise available to them.
- The self-confidence of low-income clients of institutions providing commercial microfinance is frequently improved because the clients are treated as valued customers of a formal sector institution.
- Meeting microfinance demand and building sustainable financial institutions are mutually reinforcing goals.
- When well implemented, commercial microfinance programs can be both socially and economically profitable.

Meeting the Demand for Microfinance

The microfinance revolution is rooted in the new paradigm. Its emphasis is on the self-sufficiency of multiple, competing institutions as the only route to meeting microfinance demand. As an illustration of the commercial approach, client outreach at BRI's microbanking system is compared below with the outreach of microfinance institutions of other types. These are the largest reliable databases that could be found for such comparison. The BRI data have been selected to match the years for which data for the other institutions are available.

Tables 2.6–2.8 and figures 2.7–2.12 compare the outreach of BRI's unit desa system of commercial financial intermediation with:

- A World Bank survey of 140 NGOs in developing countries in 1995 (Paxton 1996).[33]
- The 1997 *Statistical Report* of the World Council of Credit Unions (WOCCU), which provides 1996 data about its members. Used here are the data reported

Assumptions about the poor on which the old paradigm was built

Creditworthiness

- The poor cannot afford and will not be able to repay credit at commercial rates.
- Loans need to be targeted to specific activities.
- Borrowers need to be monitored to make sure loans are being used for the activities for which the funds were lent.

Willingness and capacity to save

- The poor generally cannot afford to save.
- Those who save prefer nonfinancial forms.
- The poor do not trust banks and formal institutions.

Need for technical assistance

- Credit will be of little productive use to the poor unless it is complemented with financial or business training that teaches the recipients how to maximize use of the loan.

Policies and practices adopted under the old paradigm

Targeted, supply-led subsidized credit programs are provided to assist the poor.

Pattern 1: Voluntary savings services are not provided or are not effective; the savings cannot finance the loan portfolio.
Pattern 2: Voluntary savings services are provided but lending is poor; defaults and losses are high. The institution tends either to deposit or invest the savings; little microcredit is provided.

Training programs in finance or business are required for those who want institutional loans. Additional training programs in literacy, health, and skills may be required.

Results of the old paradigm

- Often there are high rates of arrears and heavy losses.
- Subsidized loans encourage corruption.
- Loans often reach elites instead of targeted poor "beneficiaries."

- Subsidized credit tends to discourage institutional savings mobilization due to the low or negative spread between interest rates on savings and on loans.
- Lack of voluntary savings inhibits institutional sustainability.
- Where voluntary savings is successful, lending tends to be ineffective because the spread is too low to implement both sustainably.
- High loan losses may put at risk the savings of poor clients.

- The cost of providing auxiliary services decreases the possibility of institutional sustainability.
- The technical assistance comes at a high cost, and is often reported to be of little value to borrowers.

Assumptions on which the new paradigm is based

Demand for credit

- Extensive demand exists for microcredit at rates that commercial providers need to charge to achieve full cost recovery.
- The economically active poor are capable of repaying loans at commercial rates when loan terms are appropriate and borrowers have a reason to preserve their relationship with the institution.

Demand for savings services

- Massive demand exists for institutional voluntary savings among the poor.
- The poor do not need to be taught to save; they already save in a variety of forms.
- In a stable economy with adequate infrastructure, other forms of savings will often be inferior to financial savings.
- The institution needs to learn in what forms and for what purposes the poor save, and to design instruments that meet the demand better than the savers can do by themselves.
- A mature, sustainable microfinance intermediary is likely to have more savings accounts than loans.

Sustainability

- The demand for institutional microfinance can be met only by sustainable institutions. There are not enough donor and government funds to meet worldwide demand for microcredit, while global demand for savings services remains very large.
- In a sustainable microfinance system the spread between loan interest rates and the cost of funds will be higher than in the banking industry for the country, because the costs are higher.
- Sustainability does not require large expenditures from government or donors. Instead it requires an enabling macroeconomic, political, legal, and regulatory environment.

Policies and practices adopted under the new paradigm

Microloans are priced at levels that enable institutions to cover all costs and return a profit. Short-term working capital loans with simple procedures and built-in repayment incentives are emphasized.

Voluntary savings instruments provide security, convenience, liquidity, confidentiality, and returns. The spread between interest on loans and the cost of funds is set to enable institutional sustainability.

Governments and donors are increasingly concerned with providing an enabling environment and disseminating information about best practices in commercial microfinance, rather than with funding the ongoing loan portfolios of particular institutions.

Results of the new paradigm: Financially sustainable institutions with high microfinance outreach

Table 2.6 — **Outreach: BRI's unit desa system compared with 140 NGOs in developing countries, 1995**

System	Number of institutions	Number of outstanding loans	Value of outstanding loans (millions of U.S. dollars)	Number of savings accounts	Value of savings (millions of U.S. dollars)
Unit desas	1	2,263,767	1,383	14,482,763	2,606
East Asian NGOs	17	78,642	25.7	103,734	15.1
South Asian NGOs	18	200,821	51.1	305,791	25.3
African NGOs	40	292,048	103.6	82,769	4.0
Latin American and Caribbean NGOs	65	324,903	101.1	44,868	13.6
Total NGOs in East Asia, South					
Asia, Africa, and Latin America	140	896,414	281.5	537,162	58.0
Share of combined unit desa					
and NGO totals (percent)					
Unit desas		71.6	83.1	96.4	97.8
NGOs		28.4	16.9	3.6	2.2

Note: Seven South Asian and three East Asian NGOs included in the 1995 Sustainable Banking with the Poor survey were omitted because of incomplete data.
Source: BRI unit desa monthly reports, 1995; World Bank 1997a, b, c, d, and e.

for 18,822 credit unions in Latin America, Africa, and the developing countries of Asia (including 1,400 credit unions in Indonesia).
- Data for 1995 from Bangladesh's Grameen Bank (the latest year for which comprehensive published data and analysis of financial performance could be found).[34]

The NGOs and the Grameen Bank, recipients of grants or concessional loans from governments or donors, emphasize microcredit; their deposits are wholly or primarily from compulsory savings.[35] BRI's unit desas and the credit unions engage in financial intermediation—the credit unions typically among their members, and BRI among the public. These institutions serve different purposes in different countries and economies, and they are not easily comparable. The tables provided here are not intended to compare the quality of the institutions; their purpose is to show that providing commercial microfinance to the public enables a larger outreach to borrowers and savers than other microfinance approaches.

Table 2.6 and figures 2.7 and 2.8 show that in 1995 the 140 NGOs surveyed had in aggregate 17 percent of the total value of the combined unit desa and NGO loans that year, and 28 percent of the total number of loans outstanding. On the savings side, the NGOs had only 4 percent of the number of deposit accounts and 2 percent of the value of the deposits in the unit desa system.[36]

These findings would have been somewhat different if other NGOs had been selected for the sample. For example, Bangladesh has three of

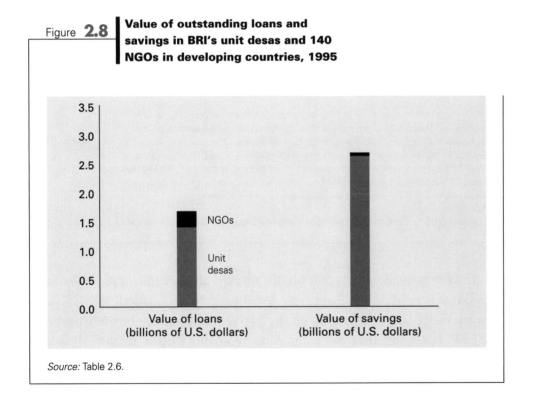

Figure **2.7** | Number of outstanding loans and savings accounts in BRI's unit desas and 140 NGOs in developing countries, 1995

NGOs
Unit desas

Number of loans
(millions)

Number of savings
accounts (millions)

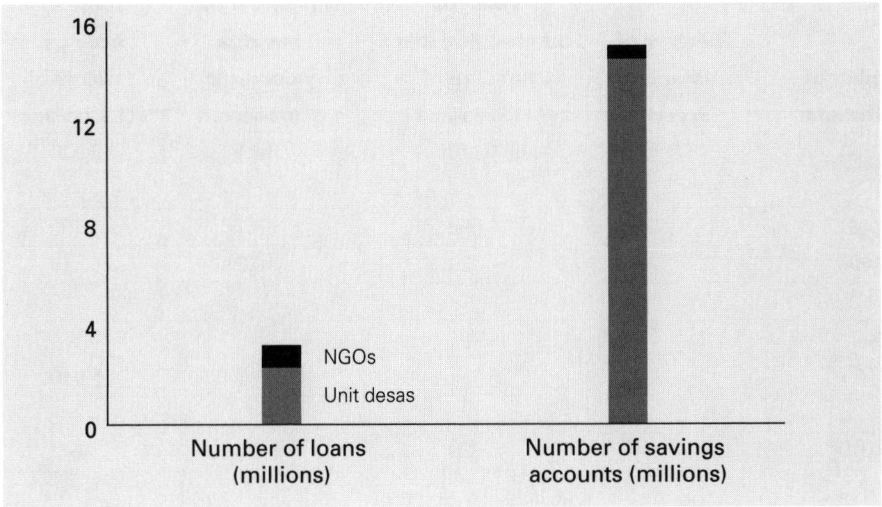

Source: Table 2.6.

Figure **2.8** | Value of outstanding loans and savings in BRI's unit desas and 140 NGOs in developing countries, 1995

NGOs

Unit
desas

Value of loans
(billions of U.S. dollars)

Value of savings
(billions of U.S. dollars)

Source: Table 2.6.

the world's largest NGOs providing microfinance: the Bangladesh Rural Advancement Committee (BRAC), Proshika, and the Association for Social Advancement (ASA). BRAC, the largest of these—with nearly 1 million current borrowers in 1995—was included in the survey but the other two were not.

Table **2.7**

Outreach: BRI's unit desa system compared with 18,822 credit unions in developing countries, 1996

System	Number of institutions	Number of outstanding loans	Value of outstanding loans (millions of U.S. dollars)	Number of savings accounts[a] (millions)	Value of savings (millions of U.S. dollars)
Unit desas	1	2,499,197	1,710	16.1	2,976
Credit unions reported for					
developing Asia[b]	11,481	—	4,592	3.1	1,780
In Indonesia	1,400	—	23	0.3	18
Credit unions reported					
for Latin America and					
the Caribbean[c]	2,322	—	5,887	6.3	5,540
Credit unions reported					
for Africa[d]	5,019	—	289	2.5	481[e]
Total credit unions reported					
for developing Asia and for Latin					
America and the Caribbean					
and Africa	18,822	—	10,768	11.9	7,801
Share of combined unit desa					
and credit union totals (percent)					
Unit desas			13.7	57.5	27.6
Credit unions			86.3	42.5	72.4

— Not available.

a. The number of credit union members is used as a proxy for the number of savers because all members are also savers.

b. Bangladesh, Indonesia, Philippines, Sri Lanka, and Thailand. Data are not available for other developing countries in Asia.

c. Antigua and Barbuda, Argentina, Bahamas, Barbados, Belize, Bermuda, Bolivia, Brazil, Cayman Islands, Chile, Colombia, Costa Rica, Dominica, Ecuador, El Salvador, Grenada, Guatemala, Guyana, Honduras, Jamaica, Mexico, Montserrat, Netherland-Antilles, Nicaragua, Panama, Paraguay, Peru, St. Christopher and Nevis, St. Lucia, St. Vincent and the Grenadines, Suriname, Tortola, Trinidad and Tobago, Uruguay, and Venezuela.

d. Benin, Botswana, Burkina Faso, Cameroon, Côte d'Ivoire, Ethiopia, the Gambia, Ghana, Kenya, Lesotho, Liberia, Malawi, Mauritius, Namibia, Rwanda, Senegal, Seychelles, Sierra Leone, South Africa, Tanzania, Togo, Uganda, and Zimbabwe.

e. Data for Lesotho and South Africa are not available.

Source: BRI unit desa monthly reports, 1996; World Council of Credit Unions, 1997 *Statistical Report* (on 1996 performance).

But the general finding that NGOs are typically not microcredit providers of scale still holds. Data from June 1999 for 524 Bangladesh NGOs show that the three largest had most of the NGO microfinance business and that the 524 NGOs together had a significantly smaller outreach than BRI's unit desa system (*Credit and Development Forum Statistics,* vol. 8, June 1999). In aggregate, BRAC, Proshika, and ASA accounted for 60 percent of the microfinance members of the 524 NGOs; they also had 62 percent of the NGOs' outstanding loan balances ($327.0 million) and 64 percent of their savings ($122.1 million).

The next comparison is with the 18,882 credit unions in Latin America, Africa, and the developing countries of Asia for which data are available (table 2.7 and figures 2.9 and 2.10).[37] While the credit unions had 72 per-

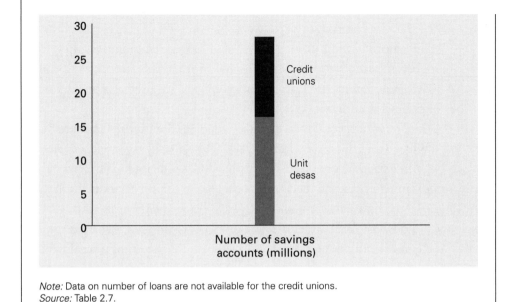

Figure **2.9** | Number of savings accounts in BRI's unit desas and 18,822 credit unions in developing countries, 1996

Number of savings
accounts (millions)

Note: Data on number of loans are not available for the credit unions.
Source: Table 2.7.

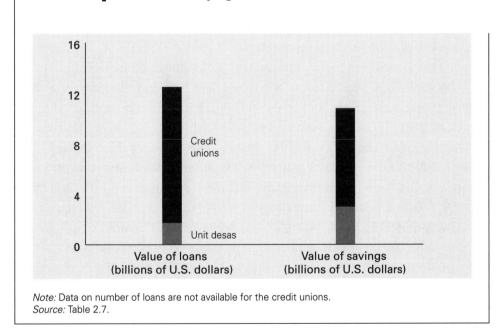

Figure **2.10** | Value of outstanding loans and savings in BRI's unit desas and 18,822 credit unions in developing countries, 1996

Note: Data on number of loans are not available for the credit unions.
Source: Table 2.7.

cent of the aggregated savings of the unit desas and the credit unions in 1996, the unit desas had 58 percent of the savings accounts. Thus the unit desas had smaller savings accounts on average than the credit unions. The average savings account balance at the units was $185,[38] compared with $656 at the credit unions. The WOCCU *Statistical Report* does not provide the number of credit union borrowers, but it is likely that the same pattern prevails since credit unions tend to lend mainly to middle-class salaried borrowers (see chapter 17).

In considering the institutional outreach shown in table 2.7, it should be remembered that the comparison is between one division of one bank and nearly 19,000 credit unions. Credit unions vary greatly in size of membership—from fewer than 100 members to many thousands of members. Because all members have savings accounts, the number of members was used as a proxy for the number of savings accounts.

In the third example, BRI's unit desas are compared with the Grameen Bank for 1995 (table 2.8 and figures 2.11 and 2.12). These are the two giants of microfinance, both in Asia; they are discussed further in later chapters. This is a particularly important comparison because, with regard to microcredit, both have contributed to the new paradigm and both have reached large scale. But BRI has developed a model for large-scale microfinance that is profitable without subsidy, while Grameen has not yet demonstrated a sustainable system of microfinance.

Compulsory savings as a condition for obtaining a loan and the collection of voluntary savings reflect two completely different philosophies

Both institutions began their current microbanking activities in the mid-1980s, and by the end of 1995 the number of active borrowers was roughly comparable at 2.1 million for Grameen and 2.3 million for BRI's unit desas. Although their credit methods are different (Grameen uses a group lending methodology, while BRI provides individual loans), both banks provide small loans delivered locally. In 1995 the value of outstanding loans was $289 million at Grameen and $1.4 billion at BRI's unit desas. Grameen, however, provides both financial and social services to its members, while BRI's unit desas provide financial services to the public.

In 1995 Bangladesh had a population of 120 million and Indonesia, 194 million. Per capita GNP was $240 in Bangladesh and $990 in Indonesia. Annual average inflation for 1995 was 5.8 percent in Bangladesh and 9.4 percent in Indonesia.

Both banks serve low-income borrowers, although Grameen reaches the poorest borrowers directly, while BRI reaches them primarily through the BKDs. Bangladesh is a much poorer country than Indonesia, and the average 1995 loan balance at Grameen ($140) was considerably smaller than at BRI's units desas ($601). Most Grameen borrowers are poorer, on an absolute scale, than are most borrowers of BRI's microbanking system. Moreover, BRI's units, which are not capital constrained, provide qualifying repeat borrowers with loans of increasing size up to higher absolute amounts than does Grameen. But the average loan balance as a percentage of GNP per capita was strikingly similar in the two banks: 58 percent for Grameen and 61 percent for BRI's unit desas. In addition, in 1995 the 4,806 BKDs supervised by BRI had an average loan balance of $51 (5.2 percent of GNP per capita).

At the end of 1995 the Grameen Bank, which collects mandatory savings from borrowers as a condition of obtaining a loan, had $133 million in savings, with an average account size of $65. BRI's unit desas—which do not have compulsory savings and instead collect voluntary savings from the public—had $2.6 billion in savings. The average size of all types of accounts at the unit desas

Table **2.8**	Outreach and sustainability: BRI's unit desa system compared with Bangladesh's Grameen Bank, 1995

Indicator	Unit desas	Grameen Bank
Number of branches	3,512	1,056
Number of staff	17,174	12,268
Annual effective interest rate for loans (percent)	26–33	20 [a]
Real effective interest rate for loans (percent)[b]	15.6–22.0	13.4
Average outstanding loan balance (U.S. dollars)	601	140
Average loan balance as a share of GNP per capita (percent)	61	58
Number of outstanding loans (millions)	2.3	2.1
Value of outstanding loans (millions of U.S. dollars)	1,383	289
Arrears as a share of the total loan portfolio[c]		
One month after due date	3.5	
One year after due date		3.6 [d]
Value of savings (millions of U.S. dollars)	2,606	133.3 [e]
Number of savings accounts (millions)	14.5	2.1
Average savings account (U.S. dollars)	180	65
Total savings as a share of outstanding loans (percent)	188	46.1
Return on assets (percent)	6.5	0.14 [f]
Memorandum items		
Country population (millions)	194.0	119.8
Country GNP per capita (U.S. dollars)	990	240
Country average annual inflation (percent)	9.4	5.8

Note: All data are 1995 end-year figures.
a. The reported annual effective interest rate does not include the implicit effect of Grameen's compulsory savings; if included, this would raise the Grameen interest rate. BRI's unit desas do not have compulsory savings. They do, however, have a prompt payment incentive of 0.5 percent a month (returned to the borrower at the end of six months or at the end of the loan period, whichever is shorter) if all payments are made in full and on time. If these payments were included in the calculation of the unit desa interest rate for loans, the rate would be higher.
b. [(1 + effective interest rate) / (1 + inflation rate) − 1].
c. Grameen's reported arrears rate does not conform to any standard international definition. It includes only amounts overdue after at least one year. In contrast, BRI's unit desas classify an unpaid installment as overdue one week after its due date.
d. After 1995 Grameen's repayment rate declined sharply. In 1996 Grameen's arrears on loans overdue one year or more were 13.9 percent and on loans overdue two years or more, 3.8 percent. In 1997 arrears overdue one year or more were 9.4 percent and those overdue two years or more, 6.8 percent. The most conservative of BRI's loan loss measures for the unit desas (portfolio status) was 3.6 percent in 1996 and 4.7 percent in 1997.
e. The data on the value of Grameen's savings are difficult to interpret. There are apparent discrepancies among the various recent sources, and the terms used are not always clearly defined. This figure is the best estimate available based on a comparison of multiple sources.
f. This return on assets was positive only because of the substantial subsidies that Grameen received. BRI's unit desas received no subsidy.
Source: World Bank 1996c, 1997f, and 1997g; Yaron, Benjamin, and Piprek 1997; Morduch 1998b; BRI unit desa monthly reports, 1995; Khandker, Khalily, and Khan 1995; Christen, Rhyne, and Vogel 1995.

was $180; however, a 1995 unit desa survey showed that 71 percent of the unit desa account balances in the survey were below $87.

Compulsory savings as a condition for obtaining a loan and the collection of voluntary savings reflect two completely different philosophies.[39] The former assumes that the poor must be taught to save and that they need to learn financial discipline. The latter assumes that the economically active poor already save in a variety of forms; what is required for effective savings mobi-

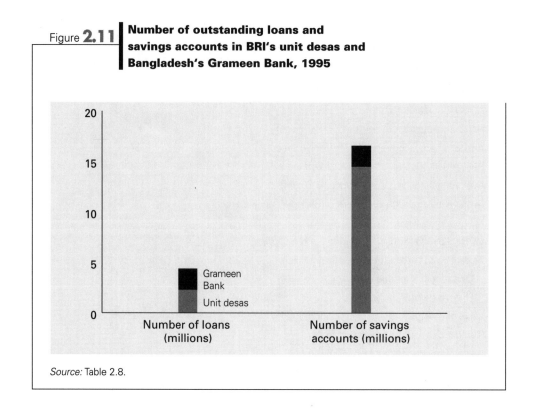

Figure **2.11** | **Number of outstanding loans and savings accounts in BRI's unit desas and Bangladesh's Grameen Bank, 1995**

Source: Table 2.8.

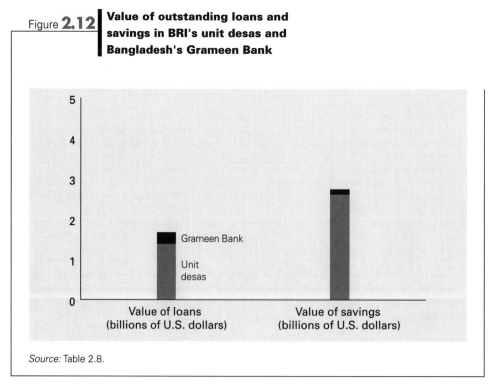

Figure **2.12** | **Value of outstanding loans and savings in BRI's unit desas and Bangladesh's Grameen Bank**

Source: Table 2.8.

lization is that the institution learns how to provide instruments and services that are appropriate for local demand. BRI's 6:1 ratio of savings accounts to loans, compared with Grameen's 1:1 ratio, highlights the difference between requiring compulsory savings from members and mobilizing voluntary savings from the public.

BRI's unit desas had a 6.5 percent before-tax return on assets in 1995. In contrast, Grameen's 1995 return on assets (0.14 percent) was positive only because of the substantial subsidies the bank received. Both results raise problems, although of very different kinds.

As noted, at BRI profits from the unit desas are used to subsidize other divisions of the bank that serve wealthier clients, resulting in regressive income redistribution. However, as part of the response to the financial and economic crisis in Indonesia during 1997–99, the government undertook a major bank restructuring effort. Part of the plan for restructuring BRI is for the bank to concentrate primarily on its micro and retail banking activities. If this change is implemented, it should enable BRI to review the pricing of its unit desa services, to further expand its service to the country's small and micro banking customers, and to end the cross-subsidies in lending interest rates, which benefit wealthy borrowers with poor repayment records at the expense of poor borrowers with high repayment records.

The problems at Grameen are of the opposite kind: the bank remains unprofitable and subsidy dependent (box 2.4).

> While the [Grameen] Bank reports profits that sum to $1.5 million between 1985 and 1996, the profits rest on $16.4 million of direct grants, $79.2 million of implicit subsidies via soft loans, $47.3 million of implicit subsidies through equity holdings, and at least $26.6 million in loan loss provisions that should have been made. Holding all else the same, the Grameen Bank would have to raise the nominal rate on general loans from 20 percent per year to 33 percent to get by without subsidies.
>
> —Morduch 1998b, p. i [40]

In 1995 BRI's unit desas had a 6.5 percent before-tax return on assets. Grameen's 0.1 percent return on assets was positive only because of the substantial subsidies the bank received

Grameen has reduced its subsidies from more than 20 cents per $1 in 1985 to about 8 cents in 1996. But "the bank still remains a fair distance from operational self sufficiency and the ability to get along without soft loans" (Morduch 1998b, p. 4).

The Grameen Bank has developed a program of social and financial services that has benefited many poor people in Bangladesh, especially poor women. Grameen, however, has chosen not to raise annual interest on loans above a nominal 20 percent effective rate. Globally, the problem remains that about 90 percent of the developing world's population does not have access to microfinance institutions—and Grameen does not yet offer a model that is widely affordable or that meets the needs of low-income savers.

In contrast, the commercial microfinance model is both adaptable and affordable. Grameen, BRI, and BancoSol have all been important contributors to the new paradigm. But the two basic differences between Grameen on the one hand and BRI and BancoSol on the other are that BRI and BancoSol have emphasized full cost recovery and commercial funding, hallmarks of the microfinance revolution.

The subsidy dependence index, developed by Jacob Yaron (1992a and 1992b), measures the percentage increase in the average yield obtained on the loan portfolio needed to compensate for the elimination of all subsidies in a financial institution. An index of 0 percent means that an institution is fully self-sufficient; an index of 100 percent indicates that a doubling of the average onlending interest rate is required to eliminate subsidies. Yaron (1992b) calculated the subsidy dependence index for Bank Rakyat Indonesia's (BRI's) unit desa system and for the Grameen Bank for 1989. At that time the unit desa system's index was –7.6 percent, "indicating that [the unit desas] did not depend on subsidies in 1989" (p. 58). In 1989 the Grameen Bank's index was 130 percent, indicating that "the average on-lending interest rate would have had to be increased by 130 percent (from 12 percent to 27.6 percent [a year]) to compensate for the full elimination of the subsidies received by [the Grameen Bank] in 1989" (p. 67).

In 1995 the subsidy dependence index for BRI's unit desa division was –44.5 percent, indicating that profits had grown substantially since 1989 (Yaron and Benjamin 1997, p. 42). While the unit desa system had startup subsidies, it has had no subsidy dependence since 1987 (Yaron and Benjamin 1997, p. 43). However, the large profits of the units have been used to cross-subsidize BRI's wealthier clients in the bank's other divisions, resulting in regressive income redistribution (Yaron, McDonald, and Charitonenko 1998). During the Indonesian financial and economic crisis that began in 1997, plans were made to restructure BRI to concentrate on retail and microbanking activities. If this plan is implemented, the regressive income distribution resulting from BRI's use of profits could be reversed.

Yaron, Benjamin, and Piprek (1997, p. 122) report that "the Grameen Bank [in 1994,] while still subsidy dependent, has markedly reduced its subsidy dependence over recent years." This decrease was largely due to several factors: the annual nominal effective interest rate on general loans was increased from 16 percent to the current 20 percent, the average loan size increased substantially (the average loan balance increased from $80 in 1989 to $140 in 1994), the cost of capital decreased significantly, and many Grameen branches matured and grew, spreading fixed costs over more clients. However, using data through 1997, Morduch (1998b, p. i) estimates that Grameen would have had to raise its nominal annual effective interest rate from 20 percent to 33 percent in 1998 in order to break even.

Both banks have attained wide outreach to borrowers. Bangladesh is poorer than Indonesia, and the depth of outreach to poor borrowers is greater at Grameen than at BRI's unit desas. However, BRI also supervises the Badan Kredit Desas (BKDs), which serve many poor clients in their own villages.

BRI's unit desas also serve millions of voluntary savers, including many who are among the lower levels of the economically active poor; all the loans in the unit desa system are financed by locally mobilized deposits. Grameen does not emphasize voluntary savings mobilization; it funds its portfolio through loans from the central bank; from government-guaranteed bond sales, and from loans and grants from foreign donors; these are provided at rates below the standard commercial lending rates in Bangladesh. BRI's unit desa system has been fully self-sufficient without subsidy since 1987; Grameen has not yet reached financial self-sufficiency (see chapter 19).

The Grameen Bank could become financially sustainable if it raised its interest rates on loans to cover fully all costs and risks, and if it maintained and expanded its loan portfolio with commercial funding.[41] BRI's microloans are financed entirely by its savings; BancoSol funds its loans from commercial debt, savings, and for-profit investment. Although permitted to mobilize voluntary savings, Grameen—which has been the continuous recipient of low-cost funds from donors and the Bangladesh government—has not undertaken significant savings mobilization from the public. Grameen is therefore in the anomalous (and essentially nonreplicable) position of having reached scale without sustainability.

Comparison of BRI's unit desas and the Grameen Bank raises a number of important policy issues for the global spread of microfinance. Given their large profits, should BRI's units reduce their lending interest rates further? Raise their savings rates? Deepen their coverage? Should Grameen raise its interest rate and become sustainable? Separate its social from its financial activities, financing the financial activities commercially? Adopt internationally accepted accounting standards? Mobilize savings from the public? These questions are explored further in volumes 2 and 3.

Governments, donors, banks and nonbank financial institutions are beginning to reexamine their priorities, policies, and strategies for microfinance. Some governments saddled with losses from old-paradigm subsidized credit programs have begun to rethink their policies and programs. Some banks have begun to see the opportunities for the formal financial sector afforded by the microfinance revolution. Some NGOs are moving toward the formal sector. And increasingly, donors that support microfinance are shifting away from financing loan portfolios and toward funding institutional development and information dissemination.

Poor people have begun to learn that institutions providing commercial microfinance can help them expand their enterprises and increase their incomes. Simultaneously, the formal financial sector has begun to realize that financing the poor can be both economically and socially profitable, and that microfinance is one of the largest potential markets in the world. This is the emerging microfinance revolution.

The formal financial sector has begun to realize that financing the poor can be both economically and socially profitable

Notes

1. A sixth model, not discussed here, refers to institutions (such as some savings banks and postal savings services) that provide savings facilities but do not offer credit (see chapter 7). Of these, some are financially sustainable, some are not.

2. For example: "Savings and credit cooperatives and credit unions have a different legal status from one country to another. In some cases, they may be full-fledged legal entities regulated by government and can thus be considered as part of the formal financial sector, as are co-operative banks in India. In other cases, they have what could be characterized as a more 'semiformal' status: in Zimbabwe, for example, there is no full, obligatory registration or regular supervision of co-operatives, but their rules of functioning are laid down by law. Finally, there are cases where the co-operative and credit union movements—even those which are government sponsored—are considered part of the informal sector, as in the Philippines. However, many, if not most of these organizations have accounts with banks where the collected savings are deposited, so that these funds are, in effect, introduced into formal financial channels" (Germidis, Kessler, and Meghir 1991, p. 81).

3. RESCAs are also known as ASCAs (accumulating savings and credit associations).

4. A parallel market has been defined as "a structure generated in response to government interventions that create a situation of excess supply or demand in a particular product or factor market" (Roemer and Jones 1991, p. 4).

5. For example, Bell and Srinivasan (1989a, p. 82) show that in commercialized areas of India important trade-credit interlinkages between farmers and urban traders and commission agents developed as a result of the increasing agricultural production made possible by green revolution technology. As they point out, these market linkages are not remnants of an old agrarian order but rather serve as mechanisms that permit urban financing of the increasing marketable agricultural surpluses.

6. When they began, BRI's microbanking system and Bolivia's BancoSol received subsidies for such purposes as initial equity, startup costs, and institutional development (for example, staff training and technical assistance), but their loan portfolios have not been subsidized. BRI has not been dependent on subsidies since 1987 (Yaron and Benjamin 1997, p. 43). Both BRI and BancoSol have been rated as fully self-sufficient (Christen, Rhyne, and Vogel 1995). BDB did not receive any startup subsidies and has been profitable without subsidy since it began in 1970.

7. Paxton (1996, p. 9). The survey, conducted by the Sustainable Banking for the Poor group at the World Bank, was limited to institutions that served at least 1,000 clients at the time of the survey.

8. Christen, Rhyne, and Vogel (1995); see also Christen (1997a) and *MicroBanking Bulletin* (1997, 1998, 1999, 2000a and b). For early development of this framework for classification, see Yaron (1992b) and Rosenberg (1994).

9. To allow comparison across the sample and to examine each institution from a fully commercial perspective, the approach "in effect places the statements on a fully commercial basis, as if the institutions were not subsidized, thus making the standard return-on-assets measure a valid reference for comparing the institutions against each other and against private sector standards" (Christen, Rhyne, and Vogel 1995, p. 16).

10. Nonfinancial costs include salaries and administrative costs, depreciation of fixed assets, and the cost of loan defaults; see Christen, Rhyne, and Vogel (1995, p. 10) for discussion.

11. Corposol in Colombia (formerly Actuar/Bogotá) was also classified as fully self-sufficient in the study. But after Corposol created Finansol, a commercial finance company, both institutions underwent severe difficulties. Corposol went bankrupt, and Finansol was recapitalized and renamed Finamérica; see chapter 18 for discussion.

12. There are some exceptions; the ways in which supervision and regulation of microfinance institutions are developing are discussed in chapter 20.

13. Financial self-sufficiency is defined as adjusted operating income divided by adjusted operating expense. See *MicroBanking Bulletin* (2000a) and chapter 16 for details. The averages of the MBB groups are calculated on the basis of the values between the 2nd and 99th percentiles.

14. The database and its findings are discussed further in chapter 16.

15. See chapters 11–15 for discussion of BRI's unit desa system; see chapter 19 for discussion of BancoSol.

16. For more details on the development of BRI's unit desa system, see *Development Program Implementation Studies Report No. 2* (1983); Robinson and Snodgrass (1987); Patten and Snodgrass (1987); Sugianto (1989, 1990a, 1990b); Robinson (1992a, 1992b, 1994a, 1994b, 1995a, 1995c, 1996, 1997a, 1997c, 1998a, 1998b); BRI (1996a, 1996b, 1997a, 1997b, 1998b); Boomgard and Angell (1990); Sutoro and Haryanto (1990); Patten and Rosengard (1991); Snodgrass and Patten (1991); Martokoesoemo (1993); Schmit (1991); Sugianto, Purnomo, and Robinson (1993); Gonzalez-Vega (1992); Boomgard and An-

gell (1994); Hook (1995); World Bank (1996b); Yaron, Benjamin, and Piprek (1997); Sugianto and Robinson (1998); Charitonenko, Patten and Yaron (1998); Yaron, Benjamin, and Charitonenko (1998); Charitonenko, Patten, and Yaron (1998); Institute for Development of Economics and Finance and BRI (1999); Maurer (1999); Patten, Rosengard and Johnston (1999); and Maurer (1999). For comparative studies that include BRI's unit desa system, see Yaron (1992a, 1992b); Otero and Rhyne (1994); Rhyne and Rotblatt (1994); Christen, Rhyne, and Vogel (1995); Chaves and Gonzalez-Vega (1996); Hulme and Mosley (1996); Yaron, Benjamin, and Piprek (1997); and Versluysen (1999).

17. In 1999, however, the Indonesian government made plans to restructure BRI to concentrate on retail and microbanking (see chapter 15).

18. BRI's units at the subdistrict level were originally called unit desas (village units); urban units (unit *kota*) were added in 1989. The term unit desa or unit bank has come to be used as a generic term for all of BRI's local units, both rural and urban.

19. Improved National BIMAS (an acronym for Bimbingan Massal, which means Mass Guidance) was begun during the 1970–71 wet season.

20. Kredit Umum Pedesaan is literally translated as General Rural Credit. But when unit desas were opened in urban areas in 1989, and KUPEDES began to be offered there as well, it began to be referred to as General Purpose Credit.

21. In the discussion of financial savings in this book, the terms savings and deposits are used synonymously, except where specified. The unit desas offer both passbook savings accounts and fixed deposit accounts.

22. See table 2.3 for method of calculation.

23. Simpanan Pedesaan means Rural Savings; Simpanan Kota means Urban Savings.

24. Actually the unit desas lend at rates that are substantially higher than standard bank rates because the operating costs of microfinance are much higher than those of conventional banking.

25. For further discussion, see World Bank (1996b).

26. The long-term loss ratio was 2.1 percent at the end of 1996, 2.2 percent at the end of 1997, 2.1 percent at the end of 1998, and 2.1 percent at the end of 1999. Portfolio status was 3.6 percent at the end of 1996, 4.7 percent at the end of 1997, 5.6 percent at the end of 1998, and 3.1 percent at the end of 1999. The 12-month loss ratio was 1.6 percent at the end of 1996, 2.2 percent at the end of 1997, 1.9 percent at the end of 1998, and 1.7 percent at the end of 1999. See table 2.2 and box 12.3 for definitions of the loss ratios used by BRI's unit desas.

27. BRI's unit desas have been visited by delegations from many countries. In Asia these include Bangladesh, Bhutan, Cambodia, China, India, Japan, Lao PDR, Malaysia, Nepal, Pakistan, the Philippines, Sri Lanka, Thailand, and Vietnam. In Latin America they include Bolivia, Brazil, Colombia, the Dominican Republic, Ecuador, Mexico, and Peru. In the Middle East and Africa they include Egypt, the Gambia, Israel, Kenya, Madagascar, Palestine, South Africa, Sudan, Tanzania, Uganda, and Zimbabwe, and in Europe and North America they include Canada, Kazakhstan, Poland, Switzerland, the United Kingdom, and the United States.

28. For information about BancoSol, see Drake and Otero (1992); Agafonoff and Wilkins (1994); Glosser (1994); Rhyne and Rotblatt (1994); Christen, Rhyne, and Vogel (1995); Mosley (1996); Gonzalez-Vega and others (1997); Berenbach and Churchill (1997); CGAP (1997c); Loubière (1997); Rock (1997); Krutzfeldt (1997, 1998); Churchill (1998); Otero (1998); Chu (1998a, 1998b, 1999); Campion and White (1999); and Rhyne (forthcoming).

29. Other early BancoSol investors included Bolivian institutions, private Bolivian investors, Calmeadow Foundation, and ACCIÓN International.

30. By October 1994 PRODEM had transferred to BancoSol a total of $8.8 million in exchange for shares in the bank.

31. PRODEM then created a new rural lending program and later created a regulated nonbank financial institution.

32. Portfolio at risk, a measurement of portfolio quality, is defined as the total outstanding balance of loans with late payments divided by the total outstanding loan portfolio.

33. The World Bank survey (Paxton 1996) included credit unions and banks as well as NGOs, but only the data for NGOs are used here. Only institutions that were founded in or before 1992 and had more than 1,000 active clients were included in the study. The survey covered 150 NGOs, but 10 were omitted in this comparison because of incomplete data.

34. See table 2.8 for the sources used for data on the Grameen Bank.

35. While many of the NGOs are not permitted to mobilize voluntary savings, the Grameen Bank has chosen not to emphasize the mobilization of voluntary savings.

36. The data from BRI's unit desa system, as well as being audited, have been subjected to international scrutiny (see Yaron 1992b, 1994; Christen, Rhyne, and Vogel 1995; and Yaron, Benjamin, and Piprek 1997; for later analyses see references in volume 2). The NGO data were self-reported.

37. The 18,822 credit unions in Africa, Latin America and the Caribbean, and developing Asia represent 55 percent of the 34,212 credit unions reporting data to WOCCU for 1996. However, these credit unions had only 4 percent of the total value of loans reported by WOCCU for 1996 and only 2 percent of the total value of savings.

38. All types of savings and deposit accounts are included.

39. This discussion excludes institutions that collect compulsory savings because they are not permitted to mobilize voluntary savings.

40. It should be noted that Grameen also provides housing loans, charging an 8 percent annual interest rate. Grameen's interest rates are stated as effective rates on the declining balance of the loan, unlike BRI's unit desas which charge 1.5 percent a month, or an 18 percent a year flat rate on the original loan balance. Grameen's annual effective interest rate on its general loans (not including its compulsory savings, which adds to the effective interest rate paid by the borrower) is 20 percent. BRI's unit desas' flat rate of 1.5 percent a month is equivalent to about a 32 percent annual effective rate for a one-year loan with monthly payments; the rate is 0.5 percent a month higher if payments are not made on time. BRI's units have no compulsory savings requirement.

41. "In the mid-1990s, Grameen got most of its funding from the Bangladesh Bank, the central bank, with some marginal funding coming from money markets. More recently, Grameen has been seeking funding through bond sales. Grameen takes the position that the Bangladesh Bank loans and the bond sales are unsubsidized. . . . [However,] the Bangladesh Bank had been offering Grameen about a 40 percent discount on interest. In recent years, Grameen has made a major shift to financing via bonds [guaranteed by the government]. These rates are, if anything, more favorable for Grameen than the Bangladesh Bank lending rate" (Morduch 1998b, p. 17).

3 | Voices of the Clients

In this chapter poor people from 16 developing countries tell about their experiences in using institutional microfinance services. The voices of these clients demonstrate unmistakably that poverty and lack of education do not preclude sound business knowledge, clear judgment of the comparative advantages of available options, or the ability to overcome obstacles. Their stories illustrate the many ways in which institutional credit and savings services have helped these people to expand and diversify their enterprises, to increase their incomes, to improve the quality of life for themselves and their dependents, and to create employment for others. The clients also speak of how access to microfinance can help in times of severe household difficulty, and of the role it can play in promoting their self-confidence. Each of the voices heard here belongs to a client of a microfinance institution; these clients are among the 10 percent or so who have access to such services in developing countries. Their accounts demonstrate eloquently the rationale for developing commercial finance in sustainable institutions: it is the only way that the other 90 percent of the population of the developing world can have similar access to microfinance products and services.

"I am a carpenter, so I save in wood." In the early 1980s, before the transformation of Bank Rakyat Indonesia's (BRI's) microbanking system, I was talking with a carpenter and his wife in their small home in rural Java. Because I was studying Indonesian rural demand for financial services, I asked the couple what they liked and did not like about saving in wood. The carpenter, SB, replied, "For me, it is good to save in wood because I can buy when the price is low. However, it is not good to save in too much wood because the wood gets warped and discolored. Then, when you sell whatever you have made, the price goes down. It would be better to buy some wood and to put the rest of the savings in the bank." His wife added, "Besides, when he buys too much wood it takes up half our house, and we are too crowded."

In many ways microfinance clients are similar the world over

Ten years later, while conducting research on savings demand for BancoSol, I was sitting with a carpenter and his wife in their home in Santa Cruz, Bolivia. I asked them what they liked and did not like about saving in wood. The carpenter, PN, said, "It is good to save in wood because you can buy when the price is low. But some wood deteriorates and the price of what you make goes down—so it is better not to buy too much at one time. I would prefer to buy less wood and save in a bank." His wife added, "The times when he has bought too much wood it took up a lot of room in our house and then it was very crowded for the family."

These are true stories. After years of field work in a variety of developing countries, I have found that in many ways microfinance clients are similar the world over. Coming from widely varying cultures, economies, and environments, there are, of course, differences among them. But in my experience, market women in Kenya talk essentially the same business language as market women in Bolivia. Farmers from India and Mexico share similar concerns about crop finance. And in Dhaka (Bangladesh) and Jakarta (Indonesia) slum dwellers who want to store their small savings safely seek a place with many of the same characteristics. When I interviewed them, neither SB in Indonesia nor PN in Bolivia had access to a bank with the types of savings accounts they wanted; they now save at BRI and BancoSol respectively.

This chapter tells of the experiences of people who are clients of microfinance institutions; where possible, the accounts are given in their own words. With the few exceptions noted, the voices heard here are from the 1990s. The statements were selected from oral and written histories of microfinance clients that I have compiled. Some were told to me by the people themselves, some are from published sources, and some were sent to me by microfinance practitioners and other colleagues working in dozens of countries.[1] The criteria used to select the statements included were: reliability of the sources of information, expressions that are broadly representative of views stated frequently by clients of microfinance institutions, and geographic, cultural, and gender diversity among a wide range of the economically active poor.

This is not a chapter for statisticians; nothing here is statistically significant. These microfinance clients cannot be considered representative of any larger group, and even their own experiences vary considerably. But the voices recorded below help to shape our understanding of the role of finance in the lives of the poor.

Five questions are addressed here:

- Do poor people understand microfinance products and services, and do they know how to use them?
- Can microfinance help the economically active poor expand and diversify their enterprises and increase their incomes?
- Can access to financial services enhance the quality of life of the clients of microfinance institutions?
- Can access to microfinance help the economically active poor in times of severe household difficulty?
- Can successful microfinance institutions promote the self-confidence of their clients?[2]

Although these issues are interlinked, they are discussed separately to highlight the clients' views on each topic. Other information emerges as well. We learn how these microfinance clients manage their resources; how they save "up," "down," and "through"; for what purposes their loans and savings are used; from what sources they repay their loans; how they earn sufficient returns to pay the interest on their loans; how they build income-earning opportunities with savings; and how they create employment for others. Those to whom we listen in this chapter demonstrate clearly that appropriate financial products and services help them to overcome obstacles, improve their enterprises, and increase their incomes and quality of life.

Because the focus is on clients, the microfinance institutions that serve them are not discussed here. But most of these institutions are examined elsewhere in the book—the Indonesian ones in volume 2, and many others in volume 3.

The people who speak here are, to varying degrees, poor. But they are among the small percentage of poor people in developing countries who are fortunate enough to have access to the services of financial institutions.

Do Poor People Understand Microfinance Products and Services, and Do They Know How to Use Them?

During the early 1980s, when the Indonesian government was beginning to consider changing BRI's unit *desas* to a commercial microbanking system, Indonesian officials expressed considerable concern that "our villagers are not 'bank-minded.'" As discussed in chapter 11, at that time there were widely prevailing views in the government and the financial sector that the country's rural population was poor and uneducated, did not understand formal sector credit terms and would not repay bank loans, did not trust banks, and either did not save at all (because they consumed all they earned) or preferred to save in animals or gold (because they were not "mature enough" to save in banks).

Those to whom we listen here demonstrate that institutional microfinance has helped them overcome obstacles, improve their enterprises, and increase their incomes and quality of life

I have since found similar attitudes to be common among government officials and bankers in many countries, although they have sometimes referred only to microcredit but not to microsavings—or the reverse. Such views typically are expressed about both the rural and urban poor. There seems to be considerable concern in the formal financial sector about whether low-income people are sufficiently educated, motivated, and financially knowledgeable to manage their resources rationally and to make effective use of financial services. Some examples of clients' perceptions are given below.

Indonesia: Understanding interest rates

In the early 1980s TS, an Indonesian farmer who owned a small plot of riceland, went to his local BRI unit to make a payment for his subsidized BIMAS loan. At that time BRI's unit desa system lent at a 12 percent nominal annual effective interest rate and paid 15 percent annual interest on small savings. I happened to be at the unit when TS came in, and we began to talk about his loan, and then about his savings.

> *"Do you think any sensible government would lend at 12 percent and pay 15 percent on savings? That could ruin the country"*
>
> —*An Indonesian farmer, in disbelief at the country's regulations in the early 1980s*

MSR: Do you also save here at the unit?

TS: No, but I have a savings account at the market bank [a nearby secondary bank].

MSR: How much interest does your bank pay you?

TS: 12 percent a year.

MSR: But BRI pays 15 percent a year interest on savings. Since you have to come here anyway to make your loan payment, why don't you save here and get the higher interest rate?

TS: I have seen the poster that says BRI pays 15 percent. But the printer made a mistake—the poster is wrong.

MSR: Why do you think the printer made a mistake?

TS: We have a good government with a lot of smart people. They know what they are doing. Do you think any sensible government would lend at 12 percent and pay 15 percent on savings? That could ruin the country. Our government would never do that!

Kenya: Demand for savings products

Working in 1994 for the Kenya Rural Enterprise Programme (K-REP) on potential savings demand, I met NR, a woman who owns and runs a small shop in Nairobi where she sells radios, radio parts, and occasionally a small television set; the shop also repairs radios. At the time NR was a K-REP borrower with a $125 outstanding loan. I explained three types of savings and deposit accounts to NR and asked her whether, if K-REP were to offer these instruments, any of them would be of interest to her. They were an interest-bearing savings account permitting an unlimited number of withdrawals, a savings account with a higher interest rate in which withdrawals were limited to 2 per month, and a fixed deposit account featuring the highest interest rate of the three products but including a penalty provision for withdrawal before maturity. She replied immediately to my question:

> I would want to have all three accounts because they are useful for different purposes. The account that allows withdrawals at any time would be good for me because I can afford to buy only one radio part at a time. As soon as I sell the part, I buy another—so this type of account would be good for buying parts. I would use the account that allows withdrawals twice a month for my repair service. I have an employee who repairs radios, and I pay him every two weeks. I could deposit his salary in that account as I would need to withdraw from it only twice in a month. Also, I have to save to buy radios, and even more to buy television sets. I use my loan for this purpose, but I also use my savings to buy radios and television sets. I would use the fixed deposit account to save for these; the higher interest rate would help me to acquire inventory faster.

Bangladesh: Managing scarce resources

TB is a client of the Association for Social Advancement (ASA), a microfinance institution in Bangladesh. Her story shows clearly the complex decisions that the poor make in managing their scarce resources.

> I have had three [ASA] loans [all of which were repaid on time]. As soon as I got the first one I bought a goat with some of the money and gave the rest to my brother to use in his firewood business, though I kept some back to make the repayments. Then after a few months I sold the goat, borrowed another 1,000 taka ($83) from my father and took a lease on a third of an acre of land. The second loan came a year later. At first I used the loan to buy paddy so I could husk and sell rice, and then our own paddy crop came in. We sold it for cash and repaid my father, and took another lease on a bigger piece of land. I let the rice husking business run down by using all the income to feed the family—we have two daughters. When the money ran out I asked my brother to give me the repayment money for a few weeks. When the third loan came in we kept it until we had sold our paddy crop and then we bought a rickshaw, so we are borrowing from my father to eat and repay the ASA loan. But when the next ASA loan comes in we'll have the rickshaw and we'll take another lease. If Allah is good to us we shall be in a better condition then.
>
> —Rutherford 1995, p. 120–21

TB's story illustrates the complex decisions that the poor make in managing their scarce resources

Peru: Credit as a launch pad

DM was born in a rural area in Peru and orphaned at an early age; after marriage, she migrated to Lima with her husband and two young children.[3] They became squatters on the urban periphery of Lima, living in a house made of hanging straw mats arranged around a dirt floor. DM was interviewed many years later in 1996; by that time she and her husband had six children and numerous grandchildren—and many things had changed.

One of the original borrowers of Acción Comunitaria del Perú (ACP, which later created a microfinance bank, Mibanco; see chapter 19), DM received her first loan in 1982. She used the money to stock her small market stall, a business that she still operated at the time of the 1996 interview. She sells staple food products, operating the business out of her stall in the morning and out of her home in the afternoon and evening. Her husband works as a casual laborer, and he and three of their children help in the food-selling enterprise.

DM has used the profits from her market stall as the "launch pad" for their six children. The oldest son is a lawyer, a middle son is an Air Force pilot, and their only daughter is a social worker; all of them have established separate households and manage their household economies. The remaining three sons continue to be members of the parental household. Two of them operate microenterprises. One runs a combined printing business and paper goods store located across the street from the family home; he has also established a beauty salon in the store that is contracted out to local beauticians. The other son has an electrical appliance repair shop located in an adjacent house.

In addition, the household owns a photocopy machine and provides copying services; one main client is the nearby police station. At the time of the interview DM was launching the couple's youngest son, who was 18 at the time, in his own computer graphics business.

DM qualifies for and receives loans from Acción Comunitaria on the basis of her market stall. At the time of the interview she had a six-week loan of $1,860, being repaid in six weekly installments of $334 (for a total repayment of $2,004). DM distributes the proceeds of each loan she receives among the various enterprises in the household's economic portfolio.

At the time of the interview DM had taken 91 successive loans from Acción Comunitaria.

At the time of the interview DM had taken 91 successive loans from Acción Comunitaria del Perú

Bangladesh: Saving for the future

SafeSave, a savings-based cooperative that provides financial services to people in slum areas of Dhaka, interviewed a number of its clients in 1997-98.[4] The following interview was conducted by S. K. Sinha of SafeSave. The respondent, AF, is an elderly widow.

> SKS: I see you save pretty regularly but you have never withdrawn or borrowed money. Can you tell me why you save?
>
> AF: For my future, like everyone else does.

SKS: What do you plan for the future? What do you do for a living?

AF: As you see, I am a widow. I have no son anymore. If I don't save, what will happen to me when I can't work anymore?

SKS: Would you mind telling me what is your work?

AF: You see, I am an old woman. I can't work. So I go from door to door.

SKS: Please don't mind, do you mean you are a beggar?

AF: What else can an old woman like me do?

SKS: Is it hard work?

AF: Not very. I go out only a few hours, and I don't go every day. It is enough. The people are good. I don't need anything but food.

SKS: Even so, you save more than some working people do!

AF: Of course. They have jobs and sons. They don't need to save like I do, do they?

Indonesia: Using credit and savings products together

RT and BT, husband and wife, are long-term clients of Indonesia's Bank Dagang Bali (BDB). Their use of bank services provides an example of how microcredit and savings products can be effectively used together. Residents of Bali, they first became clients of BDB in 1980. At that time BT was a waitress and RT was a driver. With small savings from their quite low salaries, they opened a BDB savings account ("saving up"). When enough savings had accumulated, they bought a motorcycle that they rented out. They used the motorcycle as collateral for a BDB loan, and they used the loan ("saving down") and the income from the motorcycle to start a small restaurant with four tables. The business was profitable, and they used the profits to buy land. They then used the land as collateral for a bigger loan and opened a larger restaurant.

This process of depositing profits and using the savings to purchase assets that also serve as collateral for loans for additional enterprises has continued ever since. When I talked with BT in 1994, the couple owned 10 different types of enterprises. BT said, "Everything we have was built with our work and bank help. BDB trusts us and we trust them."

———

These voices show unmistakably how clearly low-income people understand the uses of finance—from AF in Bangladesh (who saves part of her income from begging because she has no family to whom she can turn in an emergency) to DM in Peru (who has used her access to microcredit facilities to establish her children in multiple enterprises). When TS told me why he thought BRI's announced interest rates must be a printer's error, I mentioned his statement to a high-ranking government official in Jakarta—who commented that TS knew more about finance than many of his colleagues in some ministries.

Interviewer: "Can you tell me why you save?" Client (a beggar): "If I don't save, what will happen to me when I can't work anymore?"

Financial experts would be hard pressed to teach people like the Peruvian market woman, the wife in the rural Bangladeshi farm family, or the Indonesian waitress how to maximize their resources or how to use available financial services better than they already do. If financial services suitable for their needs are available, these people know well how to use them.

Can Microfinance Help the Economically Active Poor Expand and Diversify Their Enterprises and Increase Their Incomes?

By necessity the economically active poor tend to be resilient and hard working; their failures are often temporary

Many microenterprises are . . . hedges, not ways to build a sustainable growing business. Few are dynamic firms. In the majority of developing countries only a minority of informal firms with four workers or less experience growth of *any* sort. Indeed, informal sector growth comes not from firm growth but from net gains in firm "births."

—Dichter 1999, p. 16

The clients of microfinance institutions speak differently about the growth of their enterprises. Their firms frequently grow. Some clients allow their microenterprises to grow into small businesses. Many, however, diversify their activities and open additional firms—both to accommodate family members and to avoid attracting the attention of formal sector authorities who might demand licenses, fees, bribes, and taxes from larger, visibly successful businesses.

The examples below provide a sense of the range of enterprises and households served by microfinance institutions and show how access to financial services can help the economically active poor develop their enterprises and increase their incomes. These clients manage money, they expand and diversify their businesses, they invest and save for the future, and they make use of financial products that are suitable for their needs. Not all are successful, but by necessity the economically active poor tend to be resilient and hard working; their failures are often temporary. Access to microfinance services can make a critical difference for the economic activities and incomes of households like these.

The Philippines: Use of microloans at the lower levels of the economically active poor

AA lives in a squatters' village in Manila (the Philippines). She and her four adult children inhabit a shelter built from scrap materials. AA and the other family members go early each morning to a garbage dump where they obtain glass jars that they make into kerosene lamps to sell. AA received a loan of $133 from Opportunity International for this enterprise.

Before she received the loan, AA had to search through the garbage at the dump to find jars; the jars she found were dirt-encrusted, and she had to scrub them before the lids could be painted, the wicks added, and metal handles attached. With the loan, however, AA can afford to buy jars that have already been washed by other informal sector workers at the dump. When AA began the enterprise using dirty jars, her household could make only 150 lamps a day; starting with clean jars, they can produce more than 300 lamps a day. They earn an average daily profit of $30 from their lampmaking enterprise, substantially more than they earned before AA received her loan (*Countdown 2005, The Newsletter of the Microcredit Summit Campaign* 1(2): 12, 1997.)

Honduras: Developing and financing an enterprise

MG, who provides primary support for three of her children and four grandchildren, held a job distributing plantain chips.[5] But her employer decided to close the enterprise, and MG was suddenly out of work. Realizing that she knew the business and that there was an established client base, MG opened her own plantain chip business, working out of her kitchen where she shucked and sliced the plantains and fried the chips. As the only chipmaker in the area, her business prospered.

Two changes occurred in the business environment, however: her success engendered competition, and the price of raw materials rose substantially, with cooking oil tripling in price in two years. MG realized that conditions had changed and that she needed to rethink her business strategy. She visited a local branch of Fundación Nacional para el Desarrollo de Honduras (FUNADEH), a private nonprofit institution that provides microcredit. MG received a loan of $230 that she used for working capital. "I invested in [larger] quantities of everything; it really saves on my costs." Three subsequent loans (of $308, $385, and $500) enabled her to meet expenses even with the higher prices of raw materials, to hire employees, to expand her enterprise, and to succeed in what had become a competitive business.

Three years after taking her first loan, MG employed four workers as well as two family members; this more than doubled the number of people she had employed previously. Her enterprise produces about 60 bags of chips a day for bulk sale to school cafeterias and minimarkets. Clients come from up to 40 miles away to purchase her 10-gallon bags of chips at $3 apiece. MG plans to further expand her business.

Uganda: Building income opportunities with credit

BR is a client of the Foundation for International Community Assistance's (FINCA's) Uganda program.[6] The mother of seven children, she runs a brickmaking enterprise. Although the making of bricks is an occupation that is traditionally associated with men in Uganda, BR manages the business herself. She and her husband operate a second household enterprise jointly: brewing *waragi,* a type of local gin. Despite substantial competition in the brickmaking business, BR produces high-quality bricks and her enterprise does well. Unlike other local brickmakers, BR manufactures her bricks near the road, making it easy for her customers to collect their purchases.

Before she became a FINCA client, BR could produce only between 1,000 and 1,500 bricks at a time. However, she invested the proceeds of her

Before she became a FINCA client, BR could produce only 1,500 bricks at a time. After investing in her enterprise, BR's productivity rose from 1,500 bricks to 5,000

successive FINCA loans in materials and equipment. Her profits enabled her to employ two men to help in the business and to make 5,000 bricks at a time. The loans have been invested in both household enterprises. Previously the household could brew only a single jerrycan of wiragi at a time,[7] but the profits from the brickmaking have helped to build the wiragi business and now three jerrycans can be brewed at once. These are complementary enterprises. The income from the brickmaking, which is the more profitable business, can be invested in both enterprises, while wiragi (unlike the bricks, which can take three weeks to produce) provides a continual cash flow.

BR said that she has gained confidence in her roles as wife, mother, and businesswoman. "Earlier I could not even express myself or stand before people." Now she has set aside bricks to build a house, she pays the children's school fees from the brickmaking business, and she and her husband have plans to build a pub. "I have a happy marriage and my husband respects me. My children are also happy and respect me because I can provide for them and feed them."

"Earlier I could not even express myself or stand before people. Now I have a happy marriage and my children respect me because I can provide for them"

Indonesia: Building income opportunities with savings

I met HS in 1994 when I selected a number of BDB clients for interviews. He owns a stand, about 4 meters by 2 meters, from which he sells snacks, soft drinks, cigarettes, and rice wine. HS emphasizes service, typically keeping his stand open from 9 am until 12 midnight. BDB's mobile savings team collects savings from him every day, and he holds accounts in other banks as well. He said, "I like doing business with BDB because they also believe in service. I could not take the time away from my work to go to the bank every day. But they come to me, so I can easily build up my savings." HS has no loans; his business strategy is to build income opportunities with his savings.

During the five-year period before I met HS, he had used his savings to purchase land and build a house. When I asked whether his family lived in the house, he replied that perhaps later on they might live there but that the immediate purpose of building the house had been to earn income. He rents the house to the local BDB branch manager.

Senegal: Gaining business experience

BG lives in a small village with her six children and her husband's two other wives.[8] For many years she cultivated peanuts on half an acre of land, always turning the crop over to her husband. In the late 1980s, however, BG joined her local village banking program (which is assisted by Catholic Relief Services) and began to develop other productive activities. She decided to invest in activities with which she was familiar, and she used her first loan of $67 to purchase a sheep and to buy $15 worth of peanuts from which to make oil. BG began to produce about 14 liters of peanut oil and 5 liters of peanut residue (which she sells as livestock feed) a week. She travels to the nearest market town every Sunday to sell her produce and to replenish stock needed for her food processing activities.

At the time of her first loan BG earned about $5 a week on the processed peanut products; she sold the sheep she had raised for $97. This sale enabled her to repay her $67 loan plus $10 in interest. In the second loan cycle BG borrowed $94; she bought two sheep for $59 and sold them after six months for $106. She doubled her output of peanut products and began to sell these in new markets, and she also began a rice and soap business. In the third and fourth loan cycles BG bought and sold two sheep during each cycle. By the fifth loan cycle she received a loan of $478 and used part of it to buy two calves.

BG contributes $5 a week to her family. From her profits she bought a few animals that she cared for and eventually developed a small herd of livestock. BG owns the herd personally. "I live in the same household as before. But I am no longer dependent on my husband for my livelihood or that of my children."

Nicaragua: Leaving the moneylenders behind

AD sells takeaway meals and snacks from a vending cart in front of her house.[9] She purchases ingredients in the early morning and cooks during the day; in the evenings she sells enchiladas, carne asada, rice and beans. Her sidewalk stand is open every evening, seven days a week. When AD started the enterprise, she had only the vending cart. For initial working capital, she took a loan of $100 from an informal moneylender, for which she had to pay interest of $5 a day. This is equivalent to a nominal monthly effective interest rate of 332 percent; the average annual inflation rate was about 10 percent. (See chapter 6, and table 6.1 for method of interest rate conversion.) AD said, "I felt I had somebody's hands around my throat every day."

Then AD saw an advertisement for Fundación de Apoyo a la Microempresa (FAMA), a microfinance institution in Managua. She took a $200 loan for three months from FAMA, using it to buy bulk quantities of rice, oil, and wood. This enabled her to reduce the operating costs of the enterprise. AD also started a hot lunch service. After repaying the loan, she took another for $260 with which she purchased tables and chairs; having a place at which people could eat sitting down encouraged more business in the evening. She stopped borrowing from informal moneylenders. All five of her children help in the business; after three years the growing enterprise supports a family of 10, including AD's aging mother.

Kenya: Expanding income rapidly

DT is a client of the Kenya Rural Enterprise Programme (K-REP). He started as a small farmer but was unable to support his family of 11 (his wife, himself, and their 9 children) with the income he earned from farming. He then became a retail trader of potatoes and cabbage, but the income he received was still too low to support his family. When the K-REP program was introduced in his area in 1991, DT joined and received a loan.

DT used half of his first loan of $370 to increase his stock of cabbage and potatoes, and half to help construct a small house with rental units on land he owned. He wanted to own a house both to avoid paying rent and to have a more reliable income stream by building units he could rent out. His income increased from both sources, and after repaying his loan, he took a second loan

HS, a saver at Bank Dagang Bali (BDB), used his savings to purchase land and build a house—which he rents to the BDB branch manager

for $545. He was now able to hire a pickup truck and to travel further to purchase larger quantities of cabbage and potatoes. As DT expanded his scale of operations, he obtained contracts to supply vegetables to the army, a hospital, and a university. He was then earning $125 a week. By the time he received his third loan of $690 his activities had expanded further, and he was earning about $345 a week. By 1994 he said that he could provide for his family and that he had saved more than $800, most of which he had deposited in a commercial bank.

DT estimated that before his first K-REP loan, his farm generated a gross income of about $42 a month (56 percent of his household income at that time), while the vegetable retailing business provided $33 a month (44 percent). After 1991 DT's vegetable business prospered and he bought dairy cows; by 1994 the farm fed his family and produced a surplus of $36 a month. The rental income brought another $36 a month, and the vegetable business netted $1,071 a month after operating expenses. Thus in three years DT was able to expand and diversify his household economy from a poor farm to a prospering set of microenterprises (Davalos and others 1994, pp.37–38).[10]

———

These accounts provide evidence from many countries that access to microfinance can help the economically active poor expand and diversify their enterprises and increase their incomes. The voices above belong to people who juggle complex financial decisions of many types. They make investments from both savings and loans. They often use their loans for multiple purposes and repay them from multiple sources. They use their financial opportunities to break old barriers (as in the example of BR's brickmaking enterprise). And they overcome setbacks (as MG did when facing increasing prices for raw materials and growing competition in her plantain chip business). These microfinance clients learn from their investing experiences, they develop new business connections, and they gain confidence. They create employment for household members and for others.

Can Access to Financial Services Enhance the Quality of Life of the Clients of Microfinance Institutions?

When used by clients in ways that expand household economic activities and increase incomes, microfinance services can contribute in multiple and far-reaching ways to the quality of life of household members.

Bangladesh: "Tell your husband that Grameen does not allow borrowers who are beaten by their spouses to remain members and take loans"
AB and her husband lived as squatters and worked for low wages as day laborers; AB suffered continual beatings from her husband. In 1993 they moved to a vil-

AD took a loan from an informal moneylender at a nominal monthly effective interest rate of 332 percent. "I felt I had somebody's hands around my throat every day"

lage about 70 miles west of Dhaka. There AB met a woman who told her that the Grameen Bank was forming a new group; she encouraged AB to join. AB said she was doubtful that anyone would want her in the group. The woman persisted: "We're all poor—or at least we all were when we joined." AB joined the group and applied for a loan of $60, which she received. She gave half of it to her husband, who had begun a small trading business, and used the other half to start a chicken-and-duck raising business of her own. Her husband continued to beat her.

When AB repaid her loan and began preparing a proposal for a $110 loan, her friend gave her some advice: "Tell your husband that Grameen does not allow borrowers who are beaten by their spouses to remain members and take loans." AB took the advice and received her second loan. She said that from that time on her husband did not beat her. Her poultry business continued to grow, and she is now able to provide for the basic needs of the household (Grameen Connections, 1998, p. 12).

Uganda: Overcoming malnutrition

TA is the first of three wives of a man whose family compound contains 18 family members: TA's husband (who is employed as a janitor-watchman at a feed store), TA and her two co-wives, her mother-in-law, six children, three grandchildren, and four orphans whose households were devastated by acquired immune deficiency syndrome (AIDS).[11] TA herself lost two brothers and a son to what is called there the "slim sickness." TA's husband's small salary was insufficient to feed the family. None of the wives was literate or had a source of income. As TA said, "The children were always getting sick and there was no money for medicine. The whole family was becoming thin and wasted." To add to the family income, TA started a small grocery stand on the edge of a lane passing their compound. The enterprise was poorly stocked, however, and there were few clients and little profit.

TA decided to join the local village bank, part of FINCA's Uganda program. She received a first loan of $75, which she used to purchase 50 broiler chickens. She purchased feed on credit from the store where her husband worked, and she used the profits from her grocery stand to make her weekly payments to the village bank. After two months she sold the chickens and bought a slightly larger flock. She used subsequent loans to expand the inventory of her grocery store and to add laying hens to the poultry business. By her seventh four-month loan she had reached FINCA/Uganda's maximum loan size of $600 and was managing a flock of more than 500 birds.

With her earnings TA was eventually able to put all six of her school-age children in a boarding school, to finance the construction of a four-room brick house, and to purchase a cow that yields her family one to two liters of milk a day. She has also accumulated about $600 in savings. The milk, eggs, and poultry have ended the family's chronic malnutrition. In addition, TA routinely purchases tablets and vaccinations for her family at a local health clinic.

"Tell your husband that Grameen does not allow borrowers who are beaten by their spouses to remain members and take loans"

"Now I don't have to ask my husband for anything," TA said. "My family is prospering, my husband is happy, and my children are healthy and in school."

Indonesia: Saving for children's education

JB migrated to Bali from Java in 1973 and began working as an itinerant peddler selling ice cream. By 1975 he was able to obtain a fixed place in the market where he has worked ever since. In 1994, when I met him, JB's average net daily income was about $4. His wife sold local cosmetics and medicines as an itinerant peddler in the same market, and she earned about the same amount as JB. JB had been a regular saver at the BDB for five years, and he usually made deposits daily. He also had a savings account in a second bank. In addition to the savings account at BDB, he is responsible for the savings of an organization of 12 ice cream sellers who are members of his extended family (the others are itinerant peddlers). The savings of the organization are deposited monthly in another BBB account.

JB and his wife use their savings primarily for their children's education: in 1994 one child was in primary school, one was in junior high, and one was in high school. The only other purposes for which JB and his wife had withdrawn their savings were medical expenses and ceremonial occasions.

Bolivia: Providing university educations for sons and daughters

"I could not finish school because I had to work, but my children are in university"

AM started a tiny business selling sweets in the late 1980s.[12] Her enterprise generated a small income, but she knew that if she could find the money to add more products, she could do much better. With that in mind, AM went to Fundación para la Promoción y Desarollo de la Microempresa (PRODEM), the nongovernmental organization (NGO) that later gave birth to BancoSol; she took out a first loan of $60. She used the PRODEM loan for working capital to stock a wider variety of goods: fruits, soft drinks, dry foods, and soap. The merchandise sold well, so she borrowed again to stock more items. Gradually, with 10 loans over five years, she built her business into a general shop where customers can buy a variety of articles, including clothing and shoes. Twelve years after her first loan, AM now has employees to help run the shop—which frees up some of her time to go to La Paz, where she can buy wholesale merchandise at a better price.

Having seen the effects of capital investment, AM borrowed $5,000 to invest in a minibus for her husband, who works as a driver in La Paz. With his own vehicle he generates a substantially higher income than was possible before.

AM said she is particularly proud that her shop is helping to finance four of her six children to attend university in La Paz. "I could not finish school because I had to work, but my children are in university."

———

Microfinance services can contribute in many ways to the quality of life of clients and members of their households. The earliest change is often an improvement in nutrition. Others that follow typically include prevention of disease and provision of medical care, improvements in housing, and education of children. Economic independence and an associated increase in self-confidence help those who are abused find ways to stop the abuse (as in the example of AB in Bangladesh) or to end the relationship. Where institutional microfinance is available, it often plays a critical role in decreasing child labor.

One of the most common byproducts of microfinance is sending children to school. TA's six school-age children were in boarding school in Uganda. JB, the Indonesian ice cream seller, had one child each in elementary, junior high, and high school. In Peru DM's children include a lawyer, a pilot, a social worker, and a computer graphics specialist. AM, who started with a small sweets shop in Bolivia, had four children in university. Being able to provide for old age, both one's own (AF in Bangladesh) and that of one's elderly relatives (AD's mother in Nicaragua) is another way in which the quality of life improves with the income increases that can accompany the use of microfinance.

Among the economically active poor, the quality of life is typically improved in small increments, matching the small, gradual income increases that generally characterize the successful use of microfinance. The family begins to eat more and to have more nutritious food, a room is added to the house, a child is sent to school, medicine is provided for an elderly parent. Eventually the children are "launched," a new house is constructed, grandchildren are sent to school, and the quality of life has improved.

Can Access to Microfinance Help the Economically Active Poor in Times of Severe Household Difficulty?

Microfinance has multiple roles; one of them is as a social safety valve. When disasters hit and people unexpectedly lose their jobs, homes, incomes, and assets, many survive by turning to self-employment in the informal sector. At such times access to microfinance can make a critical difference in these people's ability to care for their families and to turn around the household economy. In such circumstances microfinance also serves as a safety valve for the wider society; people who are able to feed and clothe their families are less likely to cause social disruption than those who cannot.

Mexico: Supporting the family after her husband left them

AL helped her husband build a small ceramics business.[13] In addition, she managed the administrative side of the enterprise, obtaining a $200 loan from Asesoría Dinámica a Microempresas (ADMIC) to expand the business. Her husband, however, drank heavily and squandered their money; the business neared bankruptcy. AL's husband abused her and then left her and their three children. Soon after, he opened a competing ceramics shop down the street.

Demoralized and ashamed, AL decided to sell the business. However, her children objected. Her eldest son, who was 17, said, "Mom, you can't do that.

The family begins to eat more and to have more nutritious food, a room is added to the house, a child is sent to school, medicine is provided for an elderly parent

You've worked so hard, suffered so much to keep it going, you just can't sell it." AL said later, "I knew he was right so I decided to throw myself completely into it, get us out of debt, and make it the successful business I always knew it could be."

AL turned to ADMIC, which lent her $640 to start over. With the new loan and the help of her children, AL pulled the business out of debt. The next year she received a loan of $1,280 and the business grew large enough that AL qualified for a loan from a standard bank. Since then AL has been able to borrow from banks, and her years of hard work have resulted in a successful business that employs 15 people from the local community. She says that she has gained greatly in self-confidence and that she is especially proud that her children have been able to stay in school.

Ethiopia: Supporting a displaced family with her husband in jail

AG and her family were displaced from Eritrea and began a new life in Ethiopia, where AG had relatives. Shortly after their arrival in Ethiopia, however, AG's husband, a former soldier, was arrested—leaving her with their four young children. At that time AG was working as a day laborer making *injera,* a local bread. She heard about the Women's Savings and Credit Program sponsored by Catholic Relief Services and decided that she wanted to participate in the program.

AG formed a solidarity group with four friends, and in 1994 she received her first loan of $25. She started making and selling injera on her own. After repaying the loan, she took out a second loan of $40 and rented a quarter hectare of land on which she was able to cultivate vegetables four times a year. She gradually increased the amount of land she rented, creating employment for herself and for her husband after his return. After her fourth loan of $130, she rented three hectares of land and had an abundant crop of onions, tomatoes, green peppers, and cabbage. AG paid off the loan, and she purchased a water pump for $915 that she both uses and rents out. She continues to expand her cultivation, and she and her family have become respected members of their new community.[14]

Ecuador: Rebuilding a business

EC comes from a long line of herbal healers; she learned curing from her mother, who ran an herbal stand in the public market and was well known for her healing abilities.[15] However, the market was closed to build a parking lot and her mother fell ill. EC decided to open a new stand; to do so, she borrowed $880 from an informal moneylender. Interest was 10 percent a month on the original balance, and EC had to make daily payments of $17 for principal and interest. This is equivalent to a 19 percent nominal monthly effective interest rate (see table 6.1 for method of interest rate conversion); the average annual inflation rate was about 30 percent. With sales averaging $22 a day, EC found that little was left for feeding and clothing her four children.

One day EC heard a radio advertisement for Banco Solidario, an Ecuadorian bank for microenterprises. She went there to apply for a loan, which she

EC used her loan from Banco Solidario to pay off her loan from a moneylender

received eight days later. She used the loan to pay off the moneylender. EC took out two subsequent loans from the bank, and each time she increased the inventory of her business. Her sales grew substantially, and the business is now providing stable support for EC and her family. She was able to buy a typewriter for her son (who is in junior high school) and a television set.

Indonesia: Starting over using savings

A BRI saver for 17 years, KL said he never realized how valuable his savings would turn out to be. He had worked for many years as an employee of a state-owned factory that produced jute sacks. But the factory, which had run at a loss for some time, was closed. Some 1,500 workers, including KL, were laid off. KL used his savings to build a small chicken pen behind his house in Central Java and to purchase the chickens needed to begin a chicken farming enterprise. He built up a flock of about 50 chickens and after that he was able to increase its size gradually. KL supports his wife and two children with the income he earns from his chicken business (BRI 1997b, p.14).

Argentina: Starting over using credit

JC began learning the window glass business when he was 19. Six years later he opened his own shop making and selling windows, but Argentina's inflationary crisis in the late 1980s soon forced him to close the business. He then took a job in a large glass factory. "The salary was so small and the inflation was so great! When I got paid, I would have to run to the store to buy all the food I could because the prices were going up every hour." In 1992 JC once again opened his own business. Because he had no money to rent space, he started the business in his house, stacking the glass in the living room and cutting it on the kitchen table.

"He really had nothing," a loan officer from Fundación Emprender remembered. "In fact, it was doubtful he would qualify for a loan. But he did have his skill." JC joined a borrowing group and received a loan of $500. He used the money for a cutting table, materials, and rent for a workshop. By 1996 JC had taken out 16 loans, and both his business and his income had grown significantly. He had rented a larger workshop and enlarged his house, and his two children were both in secondary school (ACCIÓN International 1997, p. 8).

Colombia: Facing an economic downturn

AR and her husband lived in Caracas, Colombia, where she had a clothing shop, and where they were able to live quite well.[16] Then there was a downturn in the economy and both husband and wife lost everything they had. They went home to Cartagena. "When I came back to Cartagena, I had no work, friends, nothing—and neither did my husband." AR's mother-in-law lent her $250 with which she sublet a tiny kiosk in the market. She started selling chickens and eggs. She learned about Fundación Mario Santo Domingo in Cartagena and received a loan for $230. The purpose of the loan: "I just wanted to buy chickens at a better price."

"He really had nothing. It was doubtful he would qualify for a loan. But he did have his skill"

Over time AR was able to secure a loan of $4,500, and she bought the permanent rights to her stall in the market. Now she has a telephone and two other spaces in the market; her husband works stocking their warehouse and supplying their two stalls. They have four part-time employees, all local teenagers. "But rather than pay them directly," AR said, "my husband has worked out a plan with their parents and he pays for their schooling. That way the money they earn goes to something really useful for them."

Kyrgyz Republic: Living through the collapse of the Soviet economy

"Who could have imagined," asked RP, a 45-year-old mother of 13 children, "that one day I would be a grain seller in the Osh bazaar?"[17] Four years earlier, RP had led a comfortable life. Her husband earned a steady income as an engineer, her eldest son worked in a gasoline refinery, RP had seasonal work on their collective farm, and her school-age children were all in school. The family had plenty to eat. In addition to their steady income, they had their own plot of land where they grew tobacco, potatoes, apricots, and apples.

As the Soviet system collapsed, however, their comfortable life began to unravel. RP's husband lost his job, the collective farm could no longer meet payrolls, food became scarce and expensive, and school and medicine were no longer free. In 1994 RP's eldest son was killed in an accident at the refinery. The family had to sell clothing and other assets in order to survive.

In March 1996 RP decided that self-employment was the family's only hope. With her widowed daughter-in-law and her two youngest children, she moved to the regional market city of Osh, 22 miles from her home. With $21 in working capital borrowed from a neighbor, RP began selling rice in the Osh bazaar. But she could purchase only half a sack of rice and could earn only $2 a day in profit. Then in April she heard that FINCA was making small working capital loans—starting at $40—to female sellers in the Osh bazaar. She and 11 other women organized a village bank and RP received her first loan. She could now earn $3 to $4 a day. But the next month the Osh market police confiscated her inventory because she had failed to pay the market tax. She took the problem to the village bank, and six of the members agreed to accompany RP to the district governor's office where she pleaded her case. After promising to pay the tax, the rice was returned to her.

Six months after joining her bank, RP received a second FINCA loan of $57, as well as an additional $25 borrowed from bank members' collective savings. She increased her inventory and turned a profit of more than $6 a day, half of which she gave to her husband and the children living with him on the collective farm. The additional income allowed RP to purchase butter, sugar and meat—luxuries she could not afford a few months before. Moreover, she was able to accumulate nearly $33 in savings.

———

Whether it is the dissolution of a marriage, the displacement of a household, the loss of a business, the loss of a job, the effects of hyperinflation, or the

AR received a loan for $230. The purpose of the loan? "I just wanted to buy the chickens that I sell at a better price"

collapse of an economy, poor people in developing countries—and some of the better-off who become poor—are all too often unexpectedly thrown out of work and onto their own resources. Most of the people discussed here had skills that they could use in handling the crises in which they found themselves. But they also had access to convenient and appropriate financial services.

Can Successful Microfinance Institutions Promote the Self-confidence of Their Clients?

Clearly, successful microfinance institutions can boost the self-confidence of their clients. The process happens in many ways and at many levels. An elderly beggar in Bangladesh and a woman who makes kerosene lamps from jars recycled from a Manila garbage dump are provided financial services and treated with dignity by their microfinance institutions. AB in Bangladesh was able to stop her husband's beatings because of the power of her statement that her bank did not approve. AD in Nicaragua, who "felt [she] had somebody's hands around [her] throat every day," managed to move from a moneylender to a microfinance institution, as did EC in Ecuador.

Female clients of microfinance institutions can learn how to become economically independent. As BG in Senegal (who used her loans to develop a variety of microenterprises), said, "I live in the same household as before. But I am no longer dependent on my husband for my livelihood or that of my children." TA, in Uganda, with her grocery and poultry businesses, ended her family's malnutrition, put her children in school, and financed a new house. "Now I don't have to ask my husband for anything," she said.

Under such conditions women can move on to new horizons. DM in Peru, used her staple foods shop to launch her six children into successful careers. BR, who previously "could not even express myself or stand before people," developed a profitable brickmaking business in Uganda—where brickmaking is considered men's work. BT and RT, the Indonesian waitress and driver, built 10 enterprises out of tiny savings from their jobs—by using credit and savings products together.

Both men and women can gain the confidence to overcome severe setbacks. In Mexico AL was devastated when her husband left her—but she was able to take over their failing ceramics shop and turn it into a larger, profitable enterprise. KL started over when he lost his job in Indonesia, using his savings to start a poultry enterprise. JC had to close his windowmaking shop in Argentina because of the country's inflation; later he started over with a loan from a microfinance institution. With loans for working capital, MG in Honduras learned how to steer her chipmaking enterprise through rising prices and increasing competition.

AG survived being displaced from Eritrea to Ethiopia as well as her husband's jail term, supporting their four young children with vegetable cultivation made possible by working capital loans. And RP in the Kyrgyz Republic

Whether it is the dissolution of a marriage, the displacement of a household, the loss of employment, the effects of hyperinflation, or the collapse of an economy, access to microfinance helps the poor to move on

survived the collapse of the Soviet economy. When the household lost its sources of income, RP moved to a market center where she at first earned a tiny income selling rice. But with microloans she was able to support the family members who were with her and to send money to her husband and their other children.

Self-confidence increases when adversity is overcome, when abuse is stopped, when women become respected members of the household and the community, when the household can keep its children in school and launch them in careers, when the family is well nourished, when medicines can be bought, when the elderly can be cared for, and when savings can be accumulated. Where their services are available, microfinance institutions help their clients to achieve these goals and to increase their self-confidence.

Each of the voices above belongs to a survivor. They are also among the lucky. Most of the developing world does not yet have access to the microfinance services that helped these people to build their enterprises, control their lives, and care for their families. Yet these voices illustrate the potential scale for sustainable microfinance. Somewhere between AA with her loan for making kerosene lamps in the Philippines and the beggar AF with her savings account in Bangladesh on the one hand, and DM and her "launch pad" shop in Peru and DT with his multiple enterprises in Kenya on the other hand, lies most of the population of the developing world.

Each of the voices above belongs to a survivor. They illustrate well the potential for sustainable microfinance

Notes

1. I used Ohio State University's Development Finance Internet discussion list, discussed in chapter 20, to request material for this chapter. I specified that I was interested only in institutions that the respondents judged to be good ones. It is not difficult to find negative comments from clients in poorly run institutions; my interest was in hearing as wide a variety of views as possible from the clients of successful institutions. The response was excellent—I received well over a hundred statements about clients from network participants, some of which I have edited and used here. Of course, because the clients' views were originally collected for different purposes at different times and places, the content of the information provided by the speakers varies considerably. While some data that would have been useful in recounting the various experiences were unavailable, a sense of the role of microfinance in the lives of the clients comes through. None of the client statements or stories that I did not use contradicts the general points made in this chapter. In fact, I sent out a second letter to the network asking for negative client voices because the ones I received were so uniformly positive. While there was insufficient space for many of the replies, I am grateful to all who contributed.

2. As a social anthropologist, I am skeptical about the quality of most studies of the impact of microfinance on clients' incomes and enterprises. Such studies are far more difficult to carry out at a high level of quality than most people realize. I have been living in villages in different countries when survey teams have come through asking people about their incomes, assets, debts, participation in development programs, use of credit, and so on. I have also been there when the teams leave and the respondents laugh among themselves about what they told the "silly people with the pen-

cils" (as one Indian villager put it). It is possible to obtain accurate answers to such questions—but it takes a highly skilled and experienced person about half a day to acquire accurate information about the five points mentioned above for just one household. Most impact studies do not have such resources. Yet, many are designed as though it were possible to obtain accurate information on complex and often sensitive topics in a short time, using enumerators with relatively little training. Some carefully limited microfinance impact studies using relatively easily observable proxies for income and assets have been carried out well. Examples include some of the studies conducted under the U.S. Agency for International Development's (USAID's) Assessing the Impact of Microenterprise Services (AIMS) project and some of those carried out by microfinance programs such as BRI, the Association for Social Advancement (ASA), and the Kenya Rural Enterprise Programme (K-REP). Overall, however, the microfinance industry has little systematic, reliable information on the impact of its services on its clients and their households. As the microfinance industry comes of age, well-designed, carefully conducted, and statistically significant studies of the impact of its services should be carried out.

3. This account was adapted from Elizabeth Dunn (1997, pp. 7–10).

4. The interview was contributed by Stuart Rutherford, SafeSave, Bangladesh.

5. This example was contributed by Robin Ratcliffe, vice president for communications, ACCIÓN International.

6. This example was contributed by Carole Douglis, FINCA International, Inc. FINCA sponsors an international network of village banks; FINCA/Uganda was the network's first African program.

7. A jerrycan is a 5 gallon (19 liter) flat-sided can for storing or transporting liquid, commonly used for gasoline.

8. This example was contributed by Jennine Carmichael, editor, *Innovation and Transfer,* Catholic Relief Services.

9. This example was contributed by Robin Ratcliffe, vice president for communications, ACCIÓN International.

10. The Kenyan shilling declined against the U.S. dollar during 1991–94. One dollar was worth 27.5 Kenyan shillings in 1991 and 56 shillings in 1994 (annual average; *IMF Yearbook 1996*). Therefore DT, who operates in the local economy, would have prospered more than indicated here during this period.

11. This example was contributed by Carole Douglis, FINCA International, Inc.

12. This example was contributed by Robin Ratcliffe, vice president for communications, ACCIÓN International.

13. This example was contributed by Robin Ratcliffe, vice president for communications, ACCIÓN International.

14. This example, from Guellich (1997), was contributed by Jennine Carmichael, editor, *Innovation and Transfer,* Catholic Relief Services.

15. This example was contributed by Robin Ratcliffe, vice president for communications, ACCIÓN International.

16. This example was contributed by Robin Ratcliffe, vice president for communications, ACCIÓN International.

17. This example came from FINCA's microcredit program in the Kyrgyz Republic.

Part  2

Theories of Local Finance: A Critique

Four main streams of literature about local finance are reviewed: supply-leading finance theory, the imperfect information paradigm, informal credit markets, and the savings of the poor

Four main streams of literature about local finance are reviewed in part 2: supply-leading finance theory, the imperfect information paradigm, informal credit markets, and the savings of the poor. In each case certain theoretical views, or aspects of them, have impeded the development of sustainable, commercial microfinance. Here we consider why these ideas arose and how the obstacles they caused are being overcome as part of the microfinance revolution. The literature reviewed is drawn from a more than 50-year time horizon and a wide variety of topics. Where there have been extensive critiques of the original ideas—as, for example, with supply-leading finance and the savings of poor households—these criticisms are also reviewed. Many of them have helped lay the foundations for commercial microfinance.

As used in this book, microfinance refers widely to all types of financial services that are provided to low-income people, both rural and urban. But microfinance is a recent term, and much of the literature discussed here predates its use. Thus the title "Theories of Local Finance" refers simply to theories about rural finance and about household and microenterprise finance in low-income urban neighborhoods. Most of the views examined here were formulated to consider agricultural credit, rural credit, informal credit, local savings, and the like. The definition of microfinance used in this book includes, for example, most agricultural credit and informal credit. The congruence in client base is sufficiently large that the theories behind the different types of local finance have helped—for better or worse—to shape the history of microfinance.

Chapter 4 considers supply-leading finance theory. Supply-leading finance refers to the provision of loans in advance of the demand for credit, for the purpose of inducing economic growth. This theory emerged in the 1940s and 1950s in the context of the post–World War II development of newly emerging nations. Agricultural growth was given high priority, with an emphasis on the high-yielding agricultural technologies that were beginning to become available. It was believed, however, that most farmers would be unable to purchase the inputs they would need to use the new technologies. These ideas led to the views that farmers would need credit, that poor farmers could not pay the full cost of commercial credit, and that to achieve substantial agricultural growth, finance would have to be provided in advance of the demand for it.

The result was decades of massive subsidized rural credit programs in which the realities were far different from the expectations. By the late 1970s and the 1980s there was large and growing criticism of the rationale behind these programs. Such programs often do not reach the poor. The credit subsidies become transformed into political payoffs for rural

Subsidized rural credit programs often do not reach the poor. The credit subsidies become transformed into political payoffs for rural elites and the programs typically have high defaults and high losses

elites. The programs typically have high defaults and high losses. They have high transaction costs for the borrowers, including bribes to staff for the rationed below-market loans. And the programs provide loan products that are inappropriate for the needs of poor borrowers. Yet such programs continue in many countries today. Because their interest rates on loans are too low to permit full cost recovery and profitability, these programs have limited the volume of financial services available to the poor—helping for decades to suppress the development of large-scale microfinance.

The imperfect information paradigm, the subject of chapter 5, concerns the behavior of rational actors in an environment where information is imperfect and costly. Asymmetric information refers to transactions in which one party has more information than the other party about the transaction. Thus in a market where a given product is sold, items of different quality can be offered to buyers who cannot observe the quality of the individual units that are for sale. The quality of the items is known only to the seller. As the theory has been applied to rural credit markets, loan applicants and borrowers are the informed, banks the uninformed. The assumption is made that banks cannot differentiate cost-effectively between high-risk and low-risk applicants. Thus the quality (risk profile) of loan applicants—their investment choices, honesty, risk tolerance, capacity and willingness to

Subsized credit programs have limited the volume of financial services available to the poor—helping for decades to suppress the development of large-scale microfinance

repay loans—is unknown to banks. Credit models that use the assumption that banks cannot differentiate among loan applicants have often concluded that banks may charge higher interest rates to offset the risks caused by the lack of information they have about loan applicants. These models also often conclude that although the higher interest rates increase the returns to successful loans, the average riskiness of the loan applicants may increase because low-risk borrowers may choose not to borrow at the higher interest rates.

A moral hazard problem also exists in credit markets. The limited liability of borrowers (agents)—especially when found in conjunction with the higher interest rates charged by banks (principals)—may result in high-risk investments (moral hazard) by borrowers. Both adverse selection and moral hazard can increase the likelihood of default in a bank's loan portfolio. One conclusion is that if interest rates are raised to compensate for these risks and low-risk borrowers drop out, increasing the average riskiness of loan applicants and decreasing the expected returns to lenders, the result may be credit rationing.

Unlike supply-leading finance theory, the imperfect information paradigm helps explain a wide variety of economic behavior. But it has been applied to developing country credit markets, and in some cases specifically to rural credit markets, without adequate knowledge of these markets as they actually operate. The result is that the conclusions of the

The conclusions of the imperfect information models and the realities of the markets are often far apart

models and the realities of the markets are often far apart. Thus the results of imperfect information credit models typically imply that it would be difficult for banks to operate profitably in the credit markets of developing countries because of risk related to asymmetric information and the adverse selection effect of interest rates. The conclusions of the models also imply that banks would have difficulty operating with extensive outreach in rural credit markets because, for the reasons discussed above, they are likely to resort to credit rationing.

The results of the models have more adverse implications for microfinance than do the realities of the markets

In profitable microfinance institutions the realities are different. Asymmetric information, adverse selection, and moral hazard exist in all credit markets. But they can be overcome in microfinance markets, at least to the extent that commercial microfinance institutions can—and do—maintain high repayment rates and operate profitably.

With the exception of peer group lending, imperfect information rural credit models do not incorporate most of the methods used by profitable microfinance institutions to minimize the problems of imperfect information. The problems caused by imperfect information are, therefore, better understood by the analysts than are the solutions. Consequently the results of their models have more adverse implications for microfinance than do the realities of rural credit markets.

Chapter 6 analyzes the role of informal commercial moneylenders in local financial markets. Three main arguments in the literature are considered. The first two, which are the best known—moneylending as a malicious, monopolistic business and moneylending as providing good value for borrowers—are both valid in some respects but not others. The third, moneylending as a variant of monopolistic competition, best explains informal moneylending. This logic has crucial policy implications for the microfinance revolution.

The dynamics of local socioeconomic processes, political alliances, and associated information flows limit the number of borrowers to whom a particular lender can safely provide credit. Within a community some knowledge is widely shared. But other information flows may be limited by occupation, ethnic identity, political affiliation, gender, religion, age, and the like. Informal moneylenders, as part of their communities, are affiliated with factions, groups, alliances, and networks; they have cost-effective access to reliable information flows only for some types of information and only for some segments of the local population.

In informal commercial markets lenders typically lend only to a small number of borrowers from whom they can collect relatively easily. These are often people over whom the lender already has some control through long-term interlinked transactions in other markets (through the lender's relationship to the borrower as commodity buyer, employer, landlord, and so on). Such linkages, along with information

A variant of monopolistic competition best explains informal commercial moneylending

flows from local networks, political alliances, religious affiliations, and others, make it possible for informal lenders to obtain high repayment rates. But they also limit the number of borrowers per lender.

Lenders, who typically do not want to increase market share, tend to maintain high interest rates. As a result there are usually many lenders in the market, each with a relatively small number of borrowers. Much of informal commercial lending can be explained by monopolistic competition in which products are differentiated and lenders are imperfect substitutes.

In contrast, banks—which are less constrained by the local political economy than are local moneylenders—can cost-effectively gain reliable information about borrowers that is much broader in scope than the information to which informal lenders normally have access. Banks are then able to distinguish between high- and low-risk borrowers well enough to serve microfinance markets profitably on a large scale. As participants in the local political economy, moneylenders must ration credit; banks need not.

The analysis in chapter 6 shows that among the 41 monthly effective interest rates charged by the moneylenders examined (in 13 countries), 93 percent were higher than the rates charged by the two commercial microfinance institutions with which they are compared. Of the money-

In informal commercial markets lenders typically lend only to a small number of borrowers from whom they can collect relatively easily

lenders' rates, 44 percent were between 6 and 12 times the institutions' highest rate, while 27 percent were between 13 and more than 250 times the highest institutional rate. While real (inflation-adjusted) interest rates could not be obtained because of some uncertainty about when the moneylenders' loans were made, average annual inflation in the countries concerned during the years in which the loans could have been made were below 20 percent in most cases.

The chapter also considers borrowers' transaction costs for obtaining credit. These costs are generally lower for a loan from an informal moneylender than for a loan from a financial institution. But commercial microfinance institutions make special efforts to keep transaction costs for borrowers low. And the difference in transaction costs is likely to be small compared with the large difference in interest rates between the banks and the moneylenders.

The high interest rates charged by informal commercial lenders are of particular significance for social and economic development because these rates tend to impede or preclude the growth of borrowers' enterprises, because the volume of informal commercial credit is very large in developing countries, and because institutional commercial microfinance is still not widely available. When sustainable financial intermediaries serve the microfinance market, creditworthy

Of the moneylenders' interest rates, 71 percent were between 6 and more than 250 times the highest institutional rate

It is the formal sector, not the informal sector, that has the potential to make microfinance markets competitive

low-income borrowers can gain access to loans at interest rates and total costs that are much lower than those typically charged by moneylenders. Moreover, the demand for microsavings services can also be met. This chapter's conclusion is crucial for the microfinance revolution: it is the formal sector, not the informal sector, that has the potential to make microfinance markets competitive.

Chapter 7 discusses savings and its role in commercial microfinance institutions. Like the literature on informal credit markets, the literature on mobilizing microsavings is contradictory and often distorted by unproven assertions and assumptions. In writings on rural financial markets, for example, views run the gamut from informed, thoughtful analyses about the importance of savings mobilization for households and economies to ignorant speculation and—most commonly—total neglect.

After examining the broad patterns of savings mobilization in developing countries, the chapter assesses the advantages and disadvantages, for savers, of informal savings methods such as saving in gold, animals, raw materials, rotating savings and credit associations (ROSCAs), and other informal savings and credit associations. Also discussed are important purposes for saving by low-income households in developing countries (emergencies, income and consumption smoothing, enterprise expansion, land purchase, ceremonies).

Informal savings and financial savings are then compared for each purpose. Financial savings provide many advantages for the economically active poor, because only the formal sector can deliver a combination of security, convenience, liquidity, confidentiality, service, and returns. But in many institutions in the developing world, savings remains "the forgotten half of rural finance" (and microfinance generally). Because policymakers, bankers, and donors often believe that there is little demand for financial savings instruments, they see no reason to develop financial institutions with voluntary savings programs.

Other views are also examined. One, a subject of much debate, is that it is very costly for financial institutions to mobilize small savings. Yet extensive evidence shows that savings can be mobilized cost-effectively from many poor savers on a large scale. There are two main reasons. First, most poor savers care much more about security, convenience, and liquidity than about returns. Second, commercial microfinance institutions that provide small loans and collect deposits from local residents mobilize savings from both lower- and higher-income households, as well as from associations and institutions located near the institution. Thus these institutions serve low-income borrowers and all local savers, resulting in

Only the formal sector can deliver to savers a combination of security, convenience, liquidity, confidentiality, service, and returns

larger average account sizes (and therefore in lower costs for savings mobilization). In contrast to collecting savings from only the poor, this approach enables institutional profitability. It also enables substantial funds to be made available for loans to low-income borrowers. Bank Rakyat Indonesia's (BRI's) unit *desa* system has shown that these methods of mobilizing savings can work on a nationwide scale.

The chapter concludes by analyzing who benefits from microfinance intermediaries that collect voluntary savings from the public. All who are involved benefit: the savers, the borrowers, the institutions, the government, and the economy. Only institutional commercial microfinance combines the mobilization of voluntary savings, a moderate cost of credit for borrowers, and the widespread provision of financial services to low-income clients.

The theories discussed in part 2 were selected because of their intrinsic importance for microfinance and because they have had powerful influences on policymakers and bankers. Throughout part 2, the emphasis is on bringing closer together theoretical assumptions and models and microfinance realities. Many of the ideas discussed here have, unwittingly in most cases, impeded the development of sustainable microfinance. With the advent of the microfinance

With the advent of the microfinance revolution, policies are being changed. Teaching is also changing. Change is needed in social science theories as well

revolution, policies are being changed. The teaching of microfinance is also changing, as the teachers become more experienced with microfinance markets. Change is needed in social science theories as well.

4 | Supply-leading Finance Theory

Supply-leading finance theory—supplying finance in advance of the demand for it—arose in the post–World War II era of the late 1940s and the 1950s. The theory came from the combination of three ideas: that the governments of newly emerging nations were responsible for their economic development, that it was crucial for economic growth that high-yielding agricultural technologies be adopted rapidly and extensively, and that most farmers could not afford the full costs of the credit they would need to purchase the inputs for the new technologies. In this context massive subsidized rural credit programs were established throughout much of the developing world. Poor farmers would receive below-market credit and, it was believed, produce higher yields and increase their incomes.

But the realities were different. In fact, credit subsidies, which are capital constrained, provide a triple threat to the development of viable financial institutions with wide outreach. They often:

- Finance at high cost influential local elites who capture the subsidies.
- Severely limit the volume of institutional microcredit available to the poor.
- Depress both savings mobilization and institutional sustainability—because the interest rates on loans are too low to cover the operating costs required for the effective combined operation of savings and credit programs, and too low to permit institutional profitability. The low level of institutional microfinance available in developing countries today is in many cases attributable to supply-leading finance theory and the credit subsidies it has engendered.

> Farmers need much more capital than they can afford to save.
> —Lewis 1955, cited in Penny 1983

> Supply leading finance is the creation of financial institutions and instruments in advance of demand for them in an effort to stimulate economic growth. This strategy seeks to make the allocation of capital more efficient and to provide incentives for growth through the financial system.
> —Patrick 1983, extracted from Patrick 1966[1]

Supplying Finance in Advance of Demand

Governments considered intervention in rural credit markets easier to implement than land reform or off-farm employment creation

Extensive reevaluation of the role of the state in economic development accompanied the independence of many of today's developing countries. It was widely believed that the governments of newly created nations held important responsibilities for the economic development of their people. This approach, usually formulated and stated in explicit contrast to colonial policies, was a product both of Keynesian economic thinking and of the postwar view that developing countries must pass through a series of stages to achieve the status of developed nations. Emphasis was placed on the obligations of governments to play multiple roles, including accumulating capital, planning investment, promoting industrial development and agricultural growth, developing infrastructure, and—in varying degrees, depending on the country—improving income distribution and increasing equity. It was in this context that supply-leading finance theory emerged in the 1940s and 1950s.

Supply-leading finance refers to the provision of loans in advance of the demand for credit, for the purpose of inducing economic growth. Prevailing ideas of the time were that the rural areas of developing countries were critically important for national development, that it was essential for economic growth that high-yielding agricultural technologies be adopted rapidly and extensively, and that their adoption would often require substantial credit subsidies—because it was believed that most farmers would need more capital than they could save, and that they could not pay the full costs of the credit they would need.

By the 1960s the growing assumption of responsibility for economic development by the governments of emerging nations coincided with the rapid spread of the new varieties of rice and wheat that ushered in the green revolution, and with the related issue of financing the inputs for the new agricultural technologies. Traditionally, many rural households borrowed primarily for consumption—to subsist in preharvest seasons, for emergencies, and for social and religious obligations. In the 1970s, however, rural households increasingly began to borrow for the growing expenses of production: initially for agriculture, and later for off-farm productive activities as well.[2]

Intervention by governments and donors in rural financial markets was considered essential, especially since private lending institutions typically did not engage in most types of rural lending. The avoidance of rural credit on the part of private financial institutions was partly a result of the extensively held—but unexamined—beliefs that few rural households would be willing or able to pay commercial interest rates, and that institutional commercial loans in rural areas would be difficult to collect. Another reason for the reluctance of private institutions to provide rural credit, one less recognized by governments, was the proliferation of financial regulations that made it difficult or impossible for financial institutions to provide credit profitably at the local level.

Government intervention in rural credit markets was also advocated because policymakers considered it easier to implement than such development alternatives as land reform or off-farm employment creation. In addition, it was thought that subsidized credit to farmers would offset urban bias, improving income distribution and reducing regional disparities.

Supply-leading finance theorists assumed that economic growth in rural areas could be induced through the financial system. As a result financial incentives for the adoption of new agricultural technologies, often in the form of subsidized credit, were provided to farmers in advance of the demand for them. These theorists believed that most farmers could not save enough for the inputs they needed and could not pay the commercial cost of credit. Savings was the "forgotten half of rural finance" (Vogel 1984b)—because it was assumed that in rural areas of developing countries there were little or no savings to be mobilized. Thus, with the emergence of the green revolution in the late 1960s and 1970s, large-scale subsidized credit programs proliferated in developing countries around the world. The approach was later expanded to nonagricultural borrowers.

Because it was assumed that subsidized credit was required to stimulate agricultural growth, agricultural finance came to be treated essentially as a crop input: its subsidies were considered similar to those provided for fertilizers and pesticides. Government planning for intervention in rural credit markets, as formulated by many policymakers of that period, was thus quite simple: large numbers of low and middle-income farmers would receive low-cost credit. Using the new agricultural technologies, these farmers would produce more crops and increase their incomes. It was even believed that the targeted farmers would "graduate" from subsidized agricultural lending programs once their incomes had risen.

The facts, however, did not substantiate the theories. It is perhaps relevant to note in this context that most supply-leading finance theorists were not financial specialists, but economists concerned primarily with the development of the real sector. By the late 1960s and early 1970s serious difficulties with subsidized rural credit programs had begun to become apparent. A major turning point came in 1972–73 when the U.S. Agency for International Development (USAID) supported a wide survey of credit programs (the Spring Review of Small Farmer Credit) in developing countries. This review (USAID 1973) analyzed for the first time many of the failures of subsidized credit programs. By the late 1970s and the 1980s criticisms of the rationale behind these programs

Criticisms of subsidized credit programs have filled the development literature. But many of these programs continue today

filled the development literature. However, many governments and donors maintained large subsidized credit programs long after their intrinsic defects were well known, and many of these programs continue today.

How Credit Subsidies Prevent Sustainable Microfinance

Documentation of the problems of subsidized credit programs and analysis of the reasons for their widespread failures have grown steadily for more than 30 years. Starting in the 1960s, views about rural finance tended to reflect a more general shift in economic thinking away from planning models and toward microeconomics. Emphasis was placed on analyzing the political economies and institutions in which development processes are embedded and on which their results depend. Credit subsidies were now examined in this quite different context.

Rural credit subsidies are ineffective and inefficient, and they do not promote equity

In 1968 D. H. Penny (1983, p. 58 extracted from Penny 1968) used data from Indonesian villages to test his hypothesis that "cheap credit is unlikely to be a useful growth stimulus." He studied eight villages in North Sumatra at different stages of agricultural development and concluded that supply-leading subsidized credit programs are ineffective in stimulating agricultural growth and typically have poor returns. Penny (1983, pp. 65–66) argued that "most farmers do not have to be bribed with cheap credit to adopt profitable innovations if there is a satisfactory market for the additional output."[3]

During the late 1960s and the 1970s a new view of rural financial markets emerged based on the works of Dale W Adams, F. J. A. Bouman, Gordon Donald, Claudio Gonzalez-Vega, Douglas H. Graham, David H. Penny, Robert C. Vogel, J. D. Von Pischke, and others.[4] Drawing on the experiences of a number of developing countries, these authors demonstrated the distortions and failures that result from subsidized rural credit programs (box 4.1). As their views began to influence studies of rural credit programs in developing countries, evidence quickly mounted that rural credit subsidies are both ineffective and inefficient, and that they do not promote equity. Some of the reasons are discussed below.

Large-scale subsidized programs generally do not reach low-income households

Because of capital constraints, subsidized loans are effectively rationed. The "iron law of interest rate restriction," formulated by Gonzalez-Vega (1976), holds that when interest rates are subsidized, rent-seeking behavior by borrowers, combined with the relatively high costs to lenders of making small loans, ensures that institutional loans are routinely channeled to larger borrowers.[5]

Subsidized credit programs, especially in state-owned institutions, often have high default rates

Subsidized loan programs have been widely reported to experience high default rates (World Bank 1984a).[6] This shortcoming is especially pronounced in subsidized rural credit programs in state-owned financial institutions. Partly be-

Box **4.1**

Excerpts from *Undermining Rural Development with Cheap Credit*, edited by Dale W Adams, Douglas H. Graham, and J. D. Von Pischke

The book from which these excerpts are taken is more than 15 years old. Unfortunately, many countries and financial institutions have yet to learn its lessons.

Cheap and abundant credit is often regarded as essential for rural development. This assumption has led donor agencies and governments in developing countries to aggressively promote loans to farmers. Their efforts have resulted in large increases in the volume of loans made and the creation of new agricultural credit agencies and rural credit projects. The intent of these activities was to help the poor increase agricultural production by encouraging them to use new technologies and by compensating farmers for government price and investment policies that damaged their interests. Among others, Brazil, India, Jamaica, Mexico, the Philippines, and Thailand have used agricultural credit programs as a main component of their rural development strategies.

Despite the optimistic expectations of their sponsors, the results of these programs have been disappointing. Loan-default problems are often serious. Most poor farmers are still unable to obtain formal loans, and those who succeed in using such credit are often unnecessarily and inequitably subsidized. Many agricultural banks and other specialized formal lenders serving rural areas are floundering, and as a result they often severely limit the range of services they provide. Few aggressively offer savings-deposit facilities, for example. Their medium- and long-term loan portfolios are supported almost entirely by resources provided by government and development assistance agencies rather than by resources mobilized directly from savers and investors.

These problems persist after three decades of development assistance. They endure in spite of the fact that some governments have nationalized their banks in efforts to expand credit access, while others have piled regulation on regulation in an attempt to improve the performance of rural financial markets. Despite institutional and cultural diversity, similar problems fester in a large number of countries. Credit programs tend to self-destruct, and policymakers are largely resigned to recurring institutional problems and poor financial results from rural credit programs. A few of these problems can be attributed to unique factors, but the most common symptoms imply universal explanations and raise serious questions about the effectiveness of treatments traditionally prescribed to overcome the problems.

Viewing credit as an input, like fertilizer, causes people to conclude that farmers have specific credit needs that can be met by delivering predetermined amounts of loans to farmers. This approach leads policymakers and sponsors to measure the impact of additional loans in terms of how many hectares of rice were financed, how many tons of fertilizer were used, how many additional sacks of potatoes were produced, and how borrowers' incomes were affected by the loans. This has resulted in credit-impact studies that were fruitless, because the underlying assumption that credit is an input—rather than part of the financial intermediation process—ignored the essential property of financial instruments, their fungibility.

Farm inputs are specialized by function. Seeds produce plants, fertilizer stimulates plant growth, and diesel fuel powers engines. A loan is not an input, because its fungibility gives the borrower command over any good or service that can be purchased. A loan provides additional liquidity or purchasing power for use in any of the borrower's production, investment, or consumption activities. Most farmers in developing countries have several farm enterprises, engage in multiple occupations, and have a number of potential uses for additional liquidity. Measurement of the impact of a loan requires the collection of costly information on all changes in these sources and uses of liquidity that are contemporary with loan receipt and then a comparison of the "with" and "without" loan situations. Because the "without-loan" case can be specified only through assumption and conjecture, loan impact can never be determined with certainty.

Low-interest credit is used by local elites for business and household expenses—and for onlending at higher interest rates

"Seeds produce plants, fertilizer stimulates plant growth, and diesel fuel powers engines. A loan is not an input, because its fungibility gives the borrower command over any good or service that can be purchased"

cause borrowers tend to be locally influential individuals (rather than the poor) and because lending is often seen as a political entitlement rather than a business transaction, lending institutions typically put little effort into collection and usually do not foreclose on collateral in case of default.

As Yaron, Benjamin, and Piprek (1997, pp. 25–26) put it:

> The financial performance of virtually all government-owned RFIs [rural financial institutions] has usually been extremely poor. Most RFIs have remained highly subsidy-dependent. In India arrears as a proportion of amounts due and overdue hover at around 50 percent in most states. The recovery rate of Mexico's BANRURAL was around 25 percent in the late 1980s (ignoring recoveries from the loss-making national agricultural insurance company). Recoveries for the smallholder Agricultural Credit Agency in Malawi plummeted from almost 90 percent to less than 20 percent during the most recent elections; the agency was subsequently declared insolvent. Inflation eroded the real value of the equity of government-owned RFIs throughout Latin America during the 1980s because of poor loan collection and agricultural on-lending rates that failed to keep up with inflation. The economic cost of this dismal performance has been enormous and has often put macroeconomic stability at risk. For example, agricultural credit subsidies totaled 2.2 percent of Brazil's GDP in 1980 and 1.7 of Mexico's GDP in 1986.

Subsidized credit, channeled to local elites, buys political support for governments—and once offered, is difficult to dislodge

The difference between credit as agricultural input and credit as finance is well understood by borrowers around the world—if not always by their creditors. Influential borrowers, often local political leaders, quickly learn to take advantage of the below-market financing available to them (especially desirable because of the high probability of avoiding repayment altogether). In many countries such low-interest credit is used by local elites for a wide range of business and household expenses, as well as for onlending at higher interest rates.

The subsidies, which come to be expected by the recipients, tend to be difficult to dislodge once begun. "Subsidized credit programs ... maintain and even enhance the position of rural elites ... Low interest rates represent a subsidy that (whether originally intended to do so or not) buys the support of constituencies" (Blair 1984, p.187).

An example from Zimbabwe provides an illustration of how a politicized microcredit program, capitalized and administered directly by the government, can rapidly fail financially—although it may achieve its political objectives (Fidler 1996b). In 1992 the government of Zimbabwe established the Social Development Fund, a $14 million revolving loan fund for small enterprises and microenterprises. Loans were offered at a subsidized annual effective interest rate of 10 percent (at a time when inflation was more than twice that). The fund was intended to help mitigate the effects of structural adjustment on the lower half of Zimbabwe's economically active population.

In reality, however, these loans were closer to political payoffs than to financial instruments. While much attention and publicity was given to disbursing the loans, little effort went into collecting them. There was no mechanism to follow up on late payments, and a loan officer for the program was not hired until three years after the first disbursements were made. By the end of 1995, 1,500 loans had been disbursed, the repayment rate was about 3 percent, and most of the funds allocated for the program had been lost in the three years of operation.

While this is an extreme example, a similar pattern of low loan repayment as part of the political process is found in subsidized credit programs in many parts of the world. Argentine provincial banks routinely lost their capital due to loans provided to rural elites without expectation of repayment (most of the banks involved have now been privatized or liquidated). In India in fiscal 1996 loan recovery for more than 14,000 branches of the country's Regional Rural Banks (RRBs) was reported as 56 percent of the amounts due. These and other rural banks in India are required to provide subsidized loans to a quota of poor people. But the banks often have little role in selecting the borrowers. Rather, the lists of the "poor" who will be that season's borrowers are often drawn up by influential local political committees—who seem to find that many of the poor are located within their households and among their relatives and supporters.

Also in rural India, as in many countries, government officials and politicians routinely announce loan forgiveness programs for microcredit borrowers—ostensibly in honor of some political event or anniversary, but in fact to garner votes for themselves. Borrowers then delay their loan repayments, waiting for the next forgiveness day. In rural China about half of the $100 billion in outstanding subsidized credit at the Rural Credit Cooperatives in December 1997 was estimated to be in loans made to township and village enterprises. Much of the credit is politically induced, and much of it is uncollectible. These are classic examples

Lists of "poor" borrowers who will receive credit subsidies often include local political leaders and their relatives and supporters

of moral hazard (see chapter 5), in which many or all borrowers have limited liability because lenders, in varying degrees, do not expect repayment.

Borrowers bear high transaction costs

Lending institutions providing subsidized credit typically impose time-consuming and cumbersome procedures that can result in high transportation costs for borrowers as well as in significant opportunity costs of the borrowers' time spent waiting in line and in making return visits. In addition, staff members of institutions offering subsidized, below-market credit often require bribes from potential borrowers. This process both raises the transaction costs to borrowers and encourages a culture of corruption among the staff. "The accommodation of officials capturing the baksheesh . . . (or irregular payment to a bank official for authorizing a loan) . . . impoverishes the financial intermediary, adversely affects financial discipline, and undermines the repayment culture" (Yaron, Benjamin, and Piprek 1997, p. 101). A team in which I was a participant visited a rural bank in India whose internal auditor estimated that more than half the staff of the bank was taking bribes from borrowers.

The bank's internal auditor estimated that more than half the staff was taking bribes from borrowers

For borrowers, corruption is just another transaction cost, though often an expensive one because multiple payments to different people may be needed. This is especially the case when extensive documentation is required for a loan because each document may require a bribe—not only to the credit officer involved but also to his or her assistants, who act as gatekeepers to the officer.

In contrast, in commercial microfinance institutions where nonsubsidized credit is available to all creditworthy borrowers, the incidence of bribery decreases dramatically.

Loan products are inappropriate for borrowers' needs

Loan products in subsidized credit programs are usually rigidly determined; the purposes, amounts, and terms of loans are prescribed with little or no regard to borrowers' needs and income flows. Loans can be too small or too large. Inadequate loans may occur, for example, when a poor woman is lent $100 to purchase a buffalo and is told to repay the loan by selling the buffalo's milk. But, under local market conditions a buffalo that would produce enough milk to repay a $100 loan costs $175. If the woman buys a $100 buffalo, she cannot generate enough income to repay the loan.

On the other hand, a borrower who requests a loan of $150 for six months in order to expand his small shop is told that the only loan available to him is for $500 for five years toward the purchase of a well and pumpset. In both cases the products are unsuitable for the clients' needs, effective use of the loan is discouraged, and the chances of loan recovery are small.

Bank staff time is used unproductively

Bank staff in subsidized credit programs typically spend their time in unproductive ways. For example, they may engage in futile monitoring of the end use of loans—which cannot be effectively monitored because credit is fungible. They may train borrowers in their business activities (which the borrowers already know better than the bank staff) or in new projects that neither one knows. Staff may fill out multiple, long forms and reports that contain largely useless, and unused, information—instead of completing a few well-designed reports that provide information needed for good management of the institution. And bank staff may spend their time attending training sessions and meetings that reinforce assumptions that do not hold and promote methods that do not work.

Subsidized credit prevents the development of sustainable financial institutions

Large-scale subsidized credit programs depress, in one way or the other, the development of sustainable financial intermediation at the local level. The low interest rates of subsidized loan programs discourage deposit mobilization, microlending, or both. In contrast, sustainable microfinance institutions with wide outreach typically offer both services and act as financial intermediaries.

Credit subsidies often depress savings because revenues are too low to cover the operating costs of effective savings mobilization. Savings mobilization can be carried out successfully in conjunction with subsidized rural credit programs, as in China and India. But in these cases lending activities have typically incurred high arrears and losses. Implementing both savings and lending effectively requires relatively high operating costs to cover sufficient management, staff, personnel training, security, supervision, transportation, management information systems, and the like. The revenues needed to cover these costs are generally unavailable in programs that provide large-scale subsidized credit.

Far from being sustainable, many institutions providing subsidized credit programs—especially state-owned agricultural credit institutions—suffer from political interference, haphazard governance, poor and often corrupt management, untrained and unmotivated staff, unwanted products, low repayments, high costs, and high losses.

A borrower who requests a loan for six months to expand his small shop is given a five-year loan for a well and pumpset

Subsidized Credit Programs for Microenterprises

In the mid-1980s, driven by the mounting international economic crisis, increasing attention began to be paid not only to agricultural loans but also to the financing of small enterprises and microenterprises and of low-income people more generally. Thus "the original concern with 'small farmer credit problems' has become only a proxy (shorthand) for a preoccupation with difficulties of access to financial services by particular groups of society" (Gonzalez-Vega 1993, p. 5; see also Otero and Rhyne 1994). Some formal institutions began to onlend subsidized government or donor funds to small and microenterprises in urban areas at below-market interest rates.

But other microfinance institutions, while funded by low-cost credit from governments and donors, began to lend to borrowers at or near interest rates that would enable full cost recovery. While such institutions vary considerably, some have been highly successful both in reaching low-income borrowers and in recovering loans. However, financial institutions funded primarily by grants and low-interest loans usually cannot mobilize substantial voluntary savings, raise much equity, or leverage significant commercial investment.

The best of these institutions become operationally self-sufficient but they remain perpetually dependent on outside funding; hence they are inherently unstable. Even donor-funded institutions that lend at rates that cover their operating costs and that maintain high repayment rates usually cannot raise sufficient capital to meet local demand for microcredit. Some boards and managers of nongovernmental organizations (NGOs) have come to recognize that because of capital constraints, their institutions can meet only a tiny fraction of the demand for microfinance in their service areas. As a result they have begun to create banks, such as BancoSol in Bolivia, Mibanco in Peru, and the Kenya Rural Enterprise Programme (K-REP) in Kenya (see chapter 19).[7]

However many governments and some donors continue to spend large amounts on credit subsidies, with poor results. There are far better ways to spend less money for much better results in microfinance

Supply-leading finance theorists believed that subsidized credit programs were needed to stimulate economic growth and agricultural production. Their assumptions were largely uninformed about the ways that real rural credit markets work. As a result governments and donors have provided massive amounts of money for credit subsidies for decades—with generally very poor results.

Many institutions providing credit subsidies suffer from political interference, poor management, unwanted products, low repayments, high costs, and high losses

Many countries (such as China, India, and Vietnam) continue subsidized rural credit programs today—with continuing low repayment and high defaults. Aware of the problems with subsidized rural credit, most maintain their programs for reasons of ideology or political expediency. Some, however, are beginning to experiment simultaneously with commercial microcredit programs. It is much to be hoped that the governments of such countries will find ways to overcome the political obstacles that have prevented them from initiating on a large scale the basic credit reforms that underlie the microfinance revolution.

Notes

1. See Leibenstein (1957) and Higgins (1968 [1959]). For early dissenting opinions on supply-leading finance, see Galbraith (1952), Li (1952), Mellor (1966), and Penny (1983, extracted from Penny 1968).

2. See Mears (1981) for discussion of the shift in Indonesia from borrowing for consumption to borrowing for production.

3. Commenting on the prevailing views among economists at the time, Penny (p. 59) wrote: "The weight of both expert and political opinion is against Galbraith and the few who share his views. But Galbraith, Li, and Mellor are right, and government rural credit programs will remain ineffective until governments come to a better understanding of the role of credit in peasant economies, and the attitudes of peasant farmers toward savings, investment, and debt."

4. For overviews and bibliographies on the problems of subsidized rural credit programs, see: USAID (1973); Donald (1976); Von Pischke, Adams, and Donald (1983); Adams, Graham, and Von Pischke (1984); Meyer (1985); Von Pischke (1991); Gonzalez-Vega (1993); and Hollis and Sweetman (1998).

5. For example, a study of subsidized agricultural credit in Costa Rica showed that about 80 percent of loans went to large farmers (Vogel 1984a). In Indonesia the channeling of expensive BIMAS credit subsidies to better-off farmers became so apparent that in 1983 the government banned from the program farmers who cultivated more than 1 hectare of irrigated riceland; the program ended shortly thereafter (see chapter 11).

6. For discussion of high default rates in subsidized rural credit programs, see USAID (1973); Donald (1976); Vogel (1979, 1981); Bangladesh Bank (1979); Adams and Graham (1981); Eaton and Gersovitz (1981); Von Pischke, Adams, and Donald (1983); Adams, Graham, and Von Pischke (1984); Schaefer-Kehnert and Von Pischke (1984); Adams and Vogel (1986); Mosley and Dahal (1987); Adams (1988); Hossain (1988); Braverman and Guasch (1986, 1989, 1993); Von Pischke (1991); Floro and Yotopoulos (1991); and Yaron, Benjamin, and Piprek (1997).

7. See volume 3 for further discussion of NGOs that have created banks or other regulated financial institutions.

5 The Imperfect Information Paradigm

Self-sufficient microfinance institutions are rare—unnecessarily so. As noted in chapter 4, supply-leading finance theory and subsidized credit programs have been a major constraint to the development of such institutions. Yet another problem has arisen from the application of the imperfect information paradigm to developing country credit markets—and in some cases specifically to rural credit markets—without sufficient understanding of the social, political, and economic dynamics of these markets. Models of the imperfect information school of credit markets are not concerned specifically with microcredit, but their general nature and the concern of their authors with less developed countries and rural credit markets have accorded them an increasingly important role in microfinance. Although the models have wider scope, comment here is limited to their relevance to microcredit markets in developing countries.

The imperfect information paradigm helps explain a wide variety of economic behavior. Asymmetric information, adverse selection, and moral hazard exist in all credit markets. Yet with the notable exception of peer group lending, models of imperfect information have not incorporated many of the methods used by successful banks and other institutions providing commercial microfinance to overcome these problems. Conversely, some methods that are included in the models have not proven effective in commercial microfinance.

It may not always have been the theorists' intention to provide models that explain the workings of actual credit markets. But because analysts understand the problems caused by imperfect information better than the solutions, their conclusions suggest unnecessarily bleak prospects for financial institutions operating in rural areas, and for microfinance generally. The literature on imperfect information has made seminal contributions to our understanding of economic behavior in multiple contexts. But parts of this literature have also helped prevent the growth of sustainable financial institutions serving low-income people in developing countries.

A number of imperfect information credit models have been constructed based on the assumption that banks cannot differentiate cost-effectively between low-risk and high-risk loan applicants, or can differentiate among observationally distinguishable groups of potential borrowers, but not among members within groups. This assumption is at variance with a large body of empirical data, as are conclusions that have been drawn from it. No attempt is made here to review all of the relevant literature, but five of the most common conclusions from imperfect information credit models have been selected for discussion and for comparison with experiences of financial institutions in microcredit markets.[1] These conclusions are that:

- Banks may raise interest rates to compensate for risks related to their inability to distinguish between high-risk and low-risk loan applicants.
- The higher interest rates may drive low-risk borrowers out of the market, increasing the average riskiness of the loan applicant pool.

The models typically assume that banks cannot cost-effectively differentiate between low-risk and high-risk loan applicants. Substantial evidence shows they can

- Borrowers with limited liability who are charged higher interest rates as a result of a bank's assessment of its asymmetric information risk may be induced to choose risky projects that increase the likelihood of loan default.

- As a response to an expected decrease in returns resulting from the higher average riskiness of loan applicants, banks may choose to keep interest rates low enough to avoid a high-risk profile and may ration available loan funds.

- If credit is rationed, loans are denied to applicants who are observationally indistinguishable from those who receive credit.

- Collateral may signal borrower creditworthiness and help banks attract low-risk borrowers, and this may decrease credit rationing (Bester 1985). But other analyses conclude that collateral requirements may have adverse selection effects, increasing the riskiness of loans and decreasing the expected returns to lenders; the possibility of credit rationing remains (Stiglitz and Weiss 1981, 1986, 1987).

In addition, it is often thought that formal institutions are unlikely to be able to compete successfully with informal commercial moneylenders because such lenders have access to better information about credit applicants than formal institutions can obtain cost-effectively (Braverman and Guasch 1986; Herath 1996).

While imperfect information models of rural credit markets vary considerably, overall their conclusions suggest that it would be difficult for banks both to operate profitably in developing country credit markets and to attain extensive outreach.

Because in some cases imperfect information theory has been specifically applied to rural credit markets (see Braverman and Guasch 1986, 1993; and Hoff and Stiglitz 1993, 1998), this chapter begins by discussing information flows in such areas. Rural areas of developing countries tend to share some general features even though their social, political, and economic structures can vary greatly. One commonality is that many types of information do not flow freely. Much information is valuable, and it tends to be segmented and to circulate within different groups, factions, alliances, and networks. Informal moneylenders, like everyone else in the locality, have access to reliable information only about some people and some activities in their communities. This is a crucial reason that informal

The conclusions of numerous models imply that banks are unlikely to operate profitably in developing country credit markets or attain extensive outreach

commercial lending is best described by a model of monopolistic competition (see chapter 6).

Yet the often-segmented social structures of rural communities in developing countries frequently provide a significant opportunity for banks—which need not participate in the local political economy to the same degree as local residents—to meet the demand of community members for financial services. To understand this better, the standard assumption cited above—that banks cannot differentiate between high- and low-risk loan applicants—and the five conclusions drawn from it are compared with the experiences of two banks that serve the microfinance market profitably and on a large scale: Bank Rakyat Indonesia's (BRI's) microbanking (unit *desa*) system and Bolivia's BancoSol. Both rural and urban microcredit markets are included in the analysis.

Although this chapter is about theoretical models, it is of major policy relevance. Because the imperfect information paradigm represents an important advance in thinking about economic behavior, the work on credit markets that it has generated, and its extension to rural credit markets, is well known. Yet on the basis of these models—which do not incorporate most of the lenders' methods for decreasing information asymmetries—it would be difficult for economists, bankers, financial analysts, donors, government decisionmakers, or others to muster much enthusiasm for advocating the entrance of commercial banks into rural credit markets or into microcredit markets (rural or urban).

The models typically conclude that "as the interest rate increases, the mix of prospective projects tilts in favor of riskier projects" (Hoff and Stiglitz 1993, p. 39). At BRI's unit desa system and at BancoSol, however, the banks can differentiate among high-and low-risk applicants with a high degree of accuracy, and interest rates are maintained at a level that is attractive to low-risk borrowers. Incentives in the form of products, prices, services, and options to reborrow at larger loan sizes motivate low-risk borrowers to select these banks. New borrowers are given small loans; loan size increases as capacity and willingness to repay promptly are demonstrated. Credit rationing—either because of risk or because of lack of funds—is unnecessary. All loans are commercially financed, and both banks are profitable without subsidy. Although operating in microfinance markets in which informal moneylenders are ubiquitous, these banks have attained wider outreach to clients than any of the other banks in their respective countries.

On the basis of these models it would be difficult to muster much enthusiasm for advocating the entrance of commercial banks into microfinance markets

The theory of rural organization based on rational peasants in environments where information is imperfect and costly provides a simple explanation for a wide variety of phenomena in LDCs [less developed countries] . . . This theory can be viewed as an important application of a more general paradigm, the "Imperfect Information Paradigm," which has been useful in explaining economic phenomena under a wide variety of settings . . . in developed and less developed countries.

—Stiglitz 1986, p. 257

BRI's unit desa system and BancoSol can differentiate among high- and low-risk applicants with a high degree of accuracy

Imperfect Information in Credit Markets

Key concepts of the imperfect information paradigm as applied to credit markets include asymmetric information, adverse selection, moral hazard, and credit rationing.[2] Many authors have written many pages about these ideas and their applications to rural credit markets. The purpose here is not to provide a comprehensive review of this literature[3] but rather to examine some of the main ideas in imperfect information credit models in the context of commercial microfinance institutions and their experiences in developing countries (see box 5.1).

Asymmetric information refers to situations in which one party to a transaction has more information about the transaction than the other; such unequal information can lead to adverse selection. The idea was developed by George Akerlof (1970) in his well-known article, "The Market for Lemons," which analyzes a stylized market for used cars. Adverse selection occurs in markets where products of different quality are sold to buyers who, because of asymmetric information, cannot observe the quality of the articles they purchase. In the used car example, the sellers are knowledgeable about the quality of each car offered for sale; the buyers are not. When buyers cannot distinguish, within a given type of used car, between cars of high quality and those of low quality (the "lemons"), the sellers—who know the quality of each car—can offer the lemons at the same price as the high-quality cars.

Stiglitz and Weiss (1981) developed a model of a competitive banking system in which the banks are similar to Akerlof's uninformed used car buyers; the borrowers, like the car dealers, are the informed.[4] Just as the quality of the cars is unknown to the buyers, so too the quality (risk profile) of the borrowers—their investment choices, honesty, risk tolerance, capacity and willingness to repay loans, and so on—is unknown to the banks.

As a result banks may charge higher interest rates to offset the risks caused by asymmetric information (the borrower knows more about her use of the loan and her repayment intentions than the bank does). While the higher interest rates increase the returns to successful loans, the average riskiness of loan applicants may increase because low-risk borrowers may choose not to borrow at the higher interest rates (the adverse selection effect of interest rates).

A moral hazard problem also exists in credit markets.[5] The limited liability of borrowers (agents)—especially when found in conjunction with the higher interest rates charged by banks (principals)—may result in high-risk investments by borrowers whose liability is limited and who may expect to default on their loans if their investments fail (moral hazard).[6]

Both adverse selection and moral hazard increase the likelihood of default in a bank's loan portfolio. If interest rates are raised to compensate for these risks and low-risk borrowers drop out—increasing the average riskiness of loan applicants and decreasing the expected returns to the lender—the result may be credit rationing. Thus the bank chooses to keep the interest rate low enough to avoid a high-risk profile—and to ration its available loanable funds (see Jaffee and Russell 1976; Keeton 1979; Stiglitz and Weiss 1981, 1987; Bester 1985; Riley 1987; and Hoff and Stiglitz 1993). A bank in this situation may decide to provide credit to some but not to others among observationally identical loan applicants; those not accepted as borrowers cannot obtain credit from the bank at any interest rate (Stiglitz and Weiss 1981, 1987). In this form of credit rationing the bank denies credit to prospective borrowers not because of lack of funds but because of perceived risk related to asymmetric information and moral hazard.

Other models by these and other authors extend the analysis to situations in which there are observationally distinguishable groups in the credit market. Stiglitz and Weiss (1987, p. 229) comment, however, that "in actual markets, lenders never have perfect information about the characteristics of their borrowers and can never perfectly monitor their actions. Our papers have shown that under these circumstances, credit rationing is likely to persist regardless of the number of operationally distinct groups."

Stiglitz and Weiss's (1981) application of imperfect information theory to credit markets suggests that raising collateral can increase the riskiness of loans and have adverse selection effects. But using the idea of market signaling developed by Spence (1973, 1974), Bester (1985) developed a different view. Bester (1985) suggested that collateral can signal creditworthiness and that lenders could use higher collateral requirements in combination with lower interest rates to attract low-risk borrowers. Thus credit rationing might not be needed in banks that offer contracts with different collateral requirements and interest rates. Stiglitz and Weiss (1986) responded that the possibility of credit rationing remains under some conditions in real credit markets, including adverse selection and moral hazard. Braverman and Guasch (1986) argued specifically that credit rationing would remain in real rural credit markets.

Another issue is raised by the common belief that informal commercial lenders have much better access to information about potential borrowers than financial institutions can obtain cost-effectively. Braverman and Guasch (1986) comment:

> The adverse selection and moral hazard problems seem much less severe for the informal or village money lenders than for the organized commercial lending institutions, indicated by the fact that the default rate for the latter is much higher than for the former. *Information available to the local money lender is more extensive, more accurate, and easier to obtain than for the formal institution.* Indeed, as experience has demonstrated, this is a major problem for organized lending, especially for government-backed institutions.
>
> —p. 1260, emphasis added

Later in this chapter these statements are compared with the experiences of Bank Rakyat Indonesia (BRI) and BancoSol, banks that consistently operate profitably in microcredit markets. It is shown that banks can, in fact, obtain extensive information about loan applicants and repeat borrowers, that they can

A common—but generally incorrect— belief holds that financial institutions cannot compete successfully with informal commercial lenders

substantially overcome the problems of adverse selection and moral hazard, and that they do not need to ration credit to avoid high risk. But most banks do not serve these markets on a commercial basis, and in most developing countries very little of the demand for rural credit and microcredit is met commercially by the formal sector. This disjuncture—caused largely by the inadequate information about microfinance markets that reaches most developing country bankers and policymakers—is a crucial policy issue that is addressed throughout this book.

Information Flows in Rural Communities of Developing Countries

To understand the effects of imperfect information on rural credit markets in developing countries, it is helpful to understand how information is spread in such areas.[7] The discussion begins with information channeling in the context of the local political economy and then moves to the more specific kinds of information flows available to informal moneylenders as members of their local communities. This analysis provides necessary background for the conclusions that follow: banks can both substantially overcome asymmetric information flows in rural credit markets and compete successfully with informal commercial moneylenders.

Rural communities in developing countries vary considerably. Some are relatively homogeneous, while others are heterogeneous. Some of the heterogeneous communities are characterized by intracommunity rivalries based on ethnic identity, religion, kin groups, land or water disputes, and the like, while others contain discrete groups with symbiotic relationships. Some communities are egalitarian while others are hierarchical. Some are sparsely inhabited while others are densely populated. Some are relatively static while others are dynamic. Some are peaceful with no civil unrest while others are at war. Over time the characteristics of specific communities may change, but the general patterns tend to persist.

One common feature of many rural communities—contrary to conventional wisdom among some analysts who have not lived in such areas—is that much local information does not flow freely. Typically, of course, everyone living in some locally defined area (such as a village; a group of villages, settlements, or neighborhoods; or a valley, hilltop, or small catchment area) shares a body of general local knowledge and has continuing access to some information about all the other people who live in that area. Similarly, some new information (for example, on official appointments and local accidents and deaths) spreads rapidly and widely. But much information is valuable, and it tends to be segmented and to circulate within specific groups and networks. Information flows may be limited by gender, occupation, ethnic identity, political affiliation, religion, age, and the like. Some information may be scarce, valuable, and privately owned by individuals or groups in the community; it can be bought, sold, traded, and inherited.

One common feature of many rural communities is that much local information does not flow freely

Much information is valuable and tends to be segmented and to circulate within specific groups and networks

The channeling of information is especially relevant for microfinance for two reasons. First, informal moneylenders, as part of their communities, are affiliated with factions, groups, alliances, and networks; thus they have cost-effective access to reliable information flows—but only for some segments of the local population. Second, among low-income people who have little real property or financial holdings, the nontangible property that they possess, such as information and social debts,[8] can be especially valuable.

People living in a rural community do not necessarily share all or even most of the same interests; there may be opposing groups, shifting factions, different economic and political interests, and so on. Poor laborers, for example, may try to gain information about employment opportunities in order to increase their incomes. But wealthier members of the same community may try to keep the laborers uninformed and poor—in order to maintain a cheap, available, and tractable labor supply (Robinson 1988). In 1964 S. K. Dey, then India's minister for community development and cooperation, commented that, "the so-called harmony that we have in the villages of which we say we are very proud, is just a harmony enforced by a powerful few on a powerless many."

While this is true in some cases and not in others, there are many ways, at any point in time, in which the interests of some community members can diverge significantly from those of others (and information tends to flow with interests). Thus some people want to use scarce government or communal resources to build a road on the north side of the village; others hold out for constructing a dam on the south side. Some people are engaged in long-standing land or water disputes with their neighbors, or in inheritance fights with their siblings or cousins, or in conflicts with a group of a different religious affiliation. Some village members are allied with local leader X, while others are allied with his rival, local leader Y. In each case information about such issues tends to be channeled to allies and withheld from rivals. In the course of field work over more than 30 years, I have attended many gatherings in villages of developing countries that were held so that one local group or faction could secretly plan how to defeat another (Robinson 1988).[9]

Of course, alliances can break down. Rural communities have their own versions of espionage, and misinformation, rumors, and gossip add to the complexity of local information flows. Overall, however, much information does not flow freely in many rural areas of developing countries.[10] Some is both channeled and restricted by groups and factions, as discussed above. Other information flows exhibit different patterns; some examples will be useful.

People who control valuable information in the form of special knowledge or skills (such as ritual specialists, makers of local medicines, or masters at local crafts—or increasingly in some areas, people with locally scarce computer skills or knowledge of English) can teach their heirs or sell or trade the information to pupils, apprentices, initiates, or others. Information about corruption and misdeeds can sometimes be purchased or traded as well.

One aim can be to control information so that it is kept away from a particular person or group. In a village where I lived in south India in the early

1970s, the dominant family—consisting of four brothers—split into two factions. The three eldest brothers (one of them the village head and the largest moneylender in the village) then imposed on the youngest a full economic and social boycott that was enforced for five years. Because of the power of the elder brothers, no one could work on the youngest brother's fields; sell, trade, or give him goods; visit his house; lend him money; marry his daughter; or speak to any member of his household. Villagers were threatened with severe punishment for any of these infringements, and they were expressly forbidden from conveying any information to the boycotted brother or the members of his household (Robinson 1988). Only the widowed mother of the four brothers was exempt, de facto, from the information boycott. The aim in this case was to cause economic, financial, political, and social harm to the boycotted household and to exhibit the power that made this possible.

In other instances the aim may be rather to withhold circulation of a particular piece of information. Thus certain types of information—for example, about acts that are illegal or considered immoral, or about assets that are not easily observable—may be tightly controlled by an individual or household. Among the approximately 2 million Luo people of Kenya, largely rural farmers and herders, there are two kinds of money (see Shipton 1989, ch. 4). Some money is considered good, some evil; the distinction is based on how the money was obtained and affects how it can be used.[11]

Evil money, including that gained from sales of land, gold, marijuana, and tobacco, is called "bitter money"; it is dirty and dangerous. Bitter money must be kept strictly apart from all transactions involving permanent wealth, especially cattle. Cattle can be purchased, for example, with "good" money gained from the sale of maize, but not with bitter money obtained from the sale of tobacco. But bitter money is convertible to good money, "which will 'stick' to its owner's homestead by a purification ceremony led by a ritual specialist" (Shipton 1989, p. 40). Such ceremonies are expensive, however. Thus tobacco earnings are sometimes quietly laundered by buying cattle, then using these cattle to purchase other cattle that will then "stick" to the homestead. The launderer, however, strives to keep information about this action out of circulation.

In a number of developing countries, savings collectors hold the savings of poor people—often women—for a fee (see chapter 7). Typically this is so that others in the women's households and neighborhoods will not gain information that the women have savings. In extensive work on rural savings in developing countries, I found that one of the most important attractions of a voluntary savings account in a bank is the bank's promise of confidentiality. Poor savers—who need their savings for emergencies, consumption smoothing, children's school fees, and the like—often do not want their extended families, neighbors, and sometimes even other household members to have information about their financial assets.

With many people in a village spreading, containing, and secreting information at the same time, local information flows can become quite complex. But what

With many people in a village spreading, containing, and secreting information at the same time, local information flows can be quite complex

about modern communication facilities? The extent of such facilities available in rural communities of developing countries covers a wide range, from almost none to a wide array of communication options. But today many rural areas of developing countries have some communication facilities, such as post, telephone, and telegraph, and in some places even fax and email. And, with better rural infrastructure and networks of bus and rail services, rural inhabitants tend to travel more, increasing their knowledge and gaining new kinds of information.

In addition, the media—newspapers, radio, television—are reaching an increasing number of rural settlements. However, people of village S in developing country D are more likely to learn from the media about the death of Princess Diana, the results of the World Cup soccer finals, the U.S. presidential election, their agricultural minister's announcement of new rice prices, or the effects of the current drought in their district than they are to acquire information about village S. They are, for example, unlikely to learn from the media that yesterday merchant M from village S paid district leader Y $100, and that in return district leader Y agreed to speak to the judge in the court case merchant M has pending against his cousin V, also a resident of village S and a supporter of Y's rival, district leader X. Most people in village S will not learn this from local information flows either.

Within a period of several years, informal money-lenders usually do not compete for the same borrowers

Imperfect Information and Rural Credit Markets

Rural credit markets in developing countries tend not to be competitive, especially for low-income borrowers. People may borrow from relatives, neighbors, and friends for no or low interest, but reciprocation may be required in nonfinancial forms. Often this type of credit is available only for emergencies or specific purposes; it is usually not suitable for working capital loans for financing ongoing enterprises. Rotating savings and credit associations (ROSCAs) are widely available, but participation can be risky, loans may not be available when needed, and savings may not be liquid (see Mutesasira and others 1999, p. 17). Most institutional rural credit is subsidized and capital constrained; it normally reaches relatively few borrowers, who are often rural elites. Formal sector financial institutions have generally not been interested in competing for low-income rural clients on a commercial basis (although where the microfinance revolution is strongest, this is changing).

Also operating in many rural credit markets are pawnbrokers, savings and loan associations, cooperatives, credit unions, finance companies, and other financial bodies that range along the continuum from informal to formal—although their legal status differs in different countries. There are exceptions, but aside from pawnbrokers, some finance companies that charge very high interest rates, and some cooperatives, many of these are not particularly interested in low-income borrowers. Usually most credit to low-income rural borrowers is provided by the informal commercial credit market, operating as a form of monopolistic competition (see chapter 6 and Hoff and Stiglitz 1993, 1998).

Informal commercial lenders

Informal moneylenders wear multiple hats in their communities. They have family relationships, neighborhood associations, religious affiliations, business networks, political alliances, and so on—and they have access to the information flows associated with these. In their moneylending activities, these lenders understand well that lending beyond their sphere of influence and control of information can lead to high defaults, lowering the quality of their loan portfolios. Thus these lenders tend to provide credit primarily to those with whom they have interlinked transactions in other markets: to their commodity suppliers or buyers,[12] employees, sharecroppers, tenants, and the like. These lenders may also be linked to their borrowers by kin, neighborhood, or political relations. For these reasons such lenders typically have reliable information and some control over borrowers. As a result default rates are normally low (see chapter 6).[13]

Because of the structure of information flows, the tendency in rural areas in many parts of the world is toward numerous informal commercial lenders operating in a given area, with a relatively small number of borrowers per lender (often fewer than 20, typically fewer than 50, and rarely more than 100). Within a period of several years, lenders usually do not compete for the same borrowers.

Aleem (1993) points out from his study of the Chambar rural credit market in Pakistan:

> Each lender in this environment is perceived by borrowers to be offering a different product; thus each faces a downward-sloping demand curve, which gives him some flexibility to price according to his own circumstances. Equilibrium in this model involves a distortion in the market; there are too many lenders in relation to the size of the informal credit market . . . This observation of "too many lenders" is not unique to the Chambar market. Similar observations have been made in studies of credit markets in other countries.
>
> —pp. 148–49; see also Hoff and Stiglitz 1993, 1998

Local politics, market interlinkages, and the structure of information transfers often limit the number of borrowers per lender and help maintain the high interest rates common to informal commercial credit markets. Aleem (1993, p. 150) makes the important point that "because of these [information] imperfections [in the market,] the [informal] lender does not have an incentive to cut interest rates to increase his market share, even when rates are well above his marginal cost of lending."

For informal commercial lenders the constraint tends not to be the availability of funds but rather the number of borrowers about whom the lenders can acquire reliable information and over whom they can maintain sufficient control to minimize the default rate. Informal commercial lenders typically do not want to increase market share or lower interest rates. Informal lending as a form of monopolistic competition is documented and further analyzed in chapter 6.

Informal commercial lenders typically do not want to increase market share or lower interest rates

Formal sector financial institutions operating commercially in rural credit markets

Given the nature of information flows in rural credit markets, banks and other financial institutions can gain wider access to local information than can informal moneylenders who live and operate in the same localities. There are four main reasons.

Banks and other financial institutions can gain wider access to local information than can informal moneylenders who live and operate in the same localities

- Formal financial institutions are not constrained by the local political economy to the same degree as are individuals or local groups. As relative outsiders to their service areas, these institutions can obtain access to multiple sources of local information.
- Staff of rural bank branches are often local people who maintain their social and political relationships; each has access to a particular set of information flows. Among them they have access to a wide information base. With well-designed staff incentives, much of this aggregate information can become available to the bank.
- Most informal moneylenders have other businesses, and they are often clients of the banks that operate in the areas where they live and work. Some are bank borrowers, some are savers, and some are both. They often do not perceive banks as competitors in the lending business, but rather as sources of financial services. Moneylenders know that banks typically do not engage in interlinked transactions. Moneylender A may have objections if one of his borrowers obtains credit from moneylender B, primarily because the act implies that the borrower is likely to have become moneylender B's employee, supplier, tenant, or the like. Moneylender A knows that moneylender B will lend only if he thinks there is a high probability that he can collect the loan; the loan implies that the borrower is now linked to B in another market. In contrast, moneylenders A and B both know that banks will not lure away their suppliers or employees; they are less likely to object if their borrowers become bank clients than if they borrow from another informal lender.
- Where banking services are appropriate for rural credit markets, bank clients include savers and borrowers, as well as many people who use both services. The records of voluntary savings accounts can provide the bank with good time series data about the income flows, assets, and financial transactions of each saver. The pattern of the savers' deposits and withdrawals and the amounts involved can be analyzed, providing considerable information that helps to identify potential low-risk borrowers among savers.

Imperfect Information Credit Models and Profitable Microbanks

The assumption that banks cannot differentiate between high- and low-risk loan applicants, and the related conclusions commonly found in imperfect information credit models, are compared here with the practices of BRI's microbanking system and BancoSol, two profitable microbanking institutions. BRI's microbanking system serves primarily rural clients but also provides services to low-income neighborhoods in urban areas in Indonesia. BancoSol serves urban microentrepreneurs in Bolivia.

The substantial differences between the conclusions of imperfect information credit models and the performance records of these banks require better understanding. The models analyze economic behavior under a set of conditions arising from imperfect information in credit markets. But both banks have learned to decrease the asymmetries sufficiently to have continuing high repayment rates and to earn high profits.

Both banks distinguish cost-effectively between high- and low-risk borrowers. In both cases low-risk borrowers are attracted by incentives (the banks' products, prices, and services), while nearly all high-risk borrowers are screened out by the banks' methods of evaluating borrowers' creditworthiness. BRI's unit desas lend only to individuals and require collateral for most loans; BancoSol lends primarily to individuals who are formed into solidarity groups and whose guarantees of one another's loans substitute for collateral. In both cases new borrowers are provided small loans and allowed to increase loan sizes by demonstrating prompt repayment.

The limited liability of the borrowers appears to be less relevant to their repayment than the multiple incentives that motivate them to repay on time—especially the option for prompt payers to obtain increasingly larger loans. Thus the problems caused by adverse selection and moral hazard are largely overcome in these banks, as they are in other commercial microfinance institutions operating in many parts of the world.[14] Under these conditions the institutions normally have no need to ration credit, either because of risk related to asymmetric information or because of lack of loanable funds.

A major assumption of imperfect information rural credit models is examined below, as are five of the main conclusions drawn from those models; these are compared with the experiences of BRI's microbanking division and BancoSol. The findings do not reflect all rural credit models or all microfinance institutions. The purpose is to explore the difference between the experiences of two profitable banks serving microcredit markets and some of the more common conclusions of imperfect information credit models.

The limited liability of the borrowers appears to be less relevant to their repayment than the multiple incentives that motivate them to repay on time

- *Assumption: Banks cannot differentiate cost-effectively between low-risk and high-risk loan applicants, or can differentiate among observationally distinguishable groups of potential borrowers but not among members within groups.* BRI and BancoSol distinguish cost-effectively between low-risk and most high-risk borrowers, using many proven methods.[15] The low-risk applicants are selected, borrowers are given strong incentives for prompt repayment, and repayment rates are high.

- *Conclusion 1: Because they cannot differentiate between high- and low-risk loan applicants, banks may raise interest rates to compensate for risks related to asymmetric information.* This situation has not arisen in BRI and BancoSol because applicants are differentiated, low-risk borrowers are selected, the banks emphasize collection methods and delinquency measurement and management, and loan loss provisioning is adequate to cover default. Though there are operating costs related to obtaining good information about borrowers, the banks are able to cover all costs and risks and to generate a profit while offering interest rates that are attractive to low-risk (and low-income) borrowers.

- *Conclusion 2: The higher interest rates charged by banks (to compensate for the risks related to asymmetric information) may drive low-risk borrowers out of the market, increasing the average riskiness of loan applicants.* BRI and BancoSol have not needed to raise interest rates because of the risk of default because nearly all high-risk borrowers are screened out, and low-risk borrowers are not driven away. Borrowers are offered multiple incentives; especially attractive is the option provided to prompt payers to reborrow at gradually increasing loan sizes. The strength of this incentive is closely related to the financing of these banks. Their loan portfolios are commercially financed, and the banks are profitable and not capital constrained. This means that borrowers are assured that they can reborrow in the future if they repay on time and if their enterprise remains creditworthy.

- *Conclusion 3: Borrowers with limited liability—because of information asymmetries, uncertainties, or contracts that prevent assignment of full damages—may be induced to choose risky projects that increase the likelihood of loan default.* Multiple, cost-effective incentives provided to borrowers can deter moral hazard because borrowers want to be able to repay their loans in order to retain the option to reborrow on what they consider attractive terms. Interest rates at BRI and BancoSol are typically far lower than the rates charged to low-income borrowers by informal moneylenders operating in the same areas. The loans offered by these banks are much in demand because they are tested products with procedures, amounts, maturities, repayment plans, and permitted uses that have been designed for the needs of low-income borrowers. Thus incentives are used to offset limited liability, and moral hazard effects are small—as evidenced by the banks' high repayment rates.

- *Conclusion 4: Credit rationing may occur as a response to an expected decrease in returns resulting from the higher average riskiness of loan applicants. In this type of credit rationing, credit is denied not because the lender lacks funds but because of the perception of increasing risk. For this reason it may not be profitable to raise the interest rate or collateral requirements when a bank has an excess demand for credit; instead banks may deny loans to borrowers who are observationally indistinguishable from those who receive loans (Stiglitz and Weiss 1987, p. 394; see also box 5.1).* BRI and BancoSol need not anticipate a decrease in expected returns for these reasons—because their screening methods are effective and their lending products are designed to minimize risk, and because low-risk borrowers are attracted by the banks' incentives. As a result rationing credit in order to avoid risk either does not occur or occurs only marginally.[16] In addition, because these banks are commercially financed and are not capital constrained, there is no need to ration credit because of lack of funds. Thus large-scale profitable outreach has been attained by both banks.

Banks can cover all costs and risks and generate a profit while offering interest rates that are attractive to low-risk (and low-income) borrowers

- *Conclusion 5: Collateral requirements may signal creditworthiness and may help banks attract low-risk borrowers; this may decrease credit rationing (Bester 1985). According to another view, however, collateral requirements may have adverse selection effects, increasing the riskiness of loans and decreasing the expected returns to the lenders; the possibility of credit rationing remains (Stiglitz and Weiss 1981, 1986, 1987).* But neither of these two conclusions about the role of collateral explains the experiences of BRI and BancoSol. First, a bank can maintain a high-quality microcredit portfolio without requiring collateral.[17] BancoSol does not require collateral for its peer group loans and has consistently maintained high repayment rates. BRI's microbanking division, which until 1992 was legally required to take collateral worth at least the value of the loan, has subsequently experimented in some regions with noncollateralized small loans to individuals through the Kredit Umum Pedesaan (KUPEDES) program, also with excellent repayment rates.[18] Neither bank requires compulsory savings as a condition of borrowing.

Second, BRI's collateral requirements for KUPEDES loans appear neither to help attract low-risk borrowers nor to increase the riskiness of loans. Low-risk borrowers are attracted by the multiple incentives that the bank provides. (Collateral is not perceived by borrowers as an incentive.) High-risk loan applicants familiar with BRI's unit desa operations are not necessarily dissuaded by its collateral requirements. Because of cultural mores, implementation problems, and concerns about the working conditions of locally hired staff and the long-term performance of the unit desas, BRI does not foreclose on loan defaults in the unit desas except under extraordinary circumstances.[19] Most of Indonesia's rural population knows this. At BRI's unit desa system, default does not necessarily imply foreclosure on collateral, provision of collateral is not a reliable predictor of creditworthiness, and lack of collateral is not necessarily an indicator of risk. For these reasons BRI's unit desas are moving away from collateral requirements for small loans.

Third, neither of the two statements above concerning the possible effects of collateral on credit rationing appears relevant to these banks. One bank requires collateral; the other does not. Both serve all borrowers deemed creditworthy and both have profitably achieved wide outreach.

Finally, it is thought that formal institutions are unlikely to be able to compete successfully with informal moneylenders because informal moneylenders have access to better information about credit applicants than formal institutions can obtain cost-effectively (Braverman and Guasch 1986, Herath 1996; see also the references in chapter 6). BRI and BancoSol operate in markets where informal moneylenders charging high interest rates are very active. Both banks compete successfully with moneylenders primarily because they undersell them by a large margin. There are three main reasons for this. First, the banks have access to wider information flows. Second, unlike most moneylenders, the banks have an incentive to attain wide client outreach. Loans and deposits are their primary business (rather than a way of retaining commodity suppliers, employees, or political supporters), and they want

At BRI's unit desa system, default does not necessarily imply foreclosure on collateral, and lack of collateral is not necessarily an indicator of risk

to gain market share. Accordingly, the banks price their products on a competitive, commercial basis. Third, since both banks serve large numbers of clients in many different regions of their countries, they gain benefits from financial intermediation, from economies of scale, and from better protection against covariant shocks than moneylenders can normally obtain.

———

Banks can (and do) provide microcredit profitably on a large scale. More banks and policymakers need to know this

Large-scale outreach is fundamental to the microfinance revolution. Supply-leading finance theory led to subsidized credit programs that ration credit because of capital constraints (and to losses that result from poor loan repayments and spreads that are too low for institutional viability). Imperfect information theory, as it has been applied to rural credit markets, suggests that banks may ration credit because of the risks generated by asymmetric information.

As has been shown by profitable microfinance institutions operating in different parts of the world, neither of these outcomes need occur. Banks that use commercial funds to finance microloans normally do not need to ration credit because of lack of funds. Banks that can differentiate cost-effectively between most high-and low- risk loan applicants, that provide loans of incremental size based on past repayment records, and that provide incentives to their borrowers for prompt payment, normally do not need to ration credit because of risk.

These are not only theoretical issues—they have critical policy relevance. Despite the challenges of asymmetric information in rural credit markets, banks can (and do) provide microcredit profitably on a large scale. More banks and policymakers need to know this.

Notes

1. The assumption and the conclusions are drawn from Stiglitz and Weiss (1981, 1986, 1987) except where otherwise noted.

2. For the development of various aspects of the imperfect information paradigm and its application to credit markets, see Akerlof (1970); Jaffee and Russell (1976); Stiglitz and Weiss (1981, 1983, 1986, 1987); Stiglitz (1986); Braverman and Guasch (1986, 1989, 1993); Wilson (1980, 1987); Bester (1985); Riley (1987); Hiller and Ibrahimo (1993); Herath (1996); and Hoff and Stiglitz (1993, 1998).

3. See Braverman and Guasch (1986) for a review of credit market theory at that time. The authors comment that, "this brief review demonstrates the limitations of current theory as an adequate base for policy analysis and reform of rural credit in LDCs [less developed countries]" (p. 1258).

4. Stiglitz and Weiss constructed various kinds of credit models; see also Stiglitz and Weiss (1983, 1986, 1987).

5. As defined in *The New Palgrave: A Dictionary of Economics*, moral hazard refers to "actions of economic agents in maximizing their own utility to the detriment of others, in situations where they do not bear the full consequences or, equivalently, do not enjoy the full benefits of their actions due to uncertainty and incomplete or restricted contracts which prevent assignment of full damages (benefits) to the agent responsible" (Kotowitz 1987, p. 549).

6. The limited liability of borrowers can be especially limited when the borrowers obtain credit from subsidized formal sector financial institutions in rural areas of developing countries. Such borrowers may, for example, be politically well connected and decide that they are powerful enough that their nonrepayment will have limited or no negative results. Or borrowers may choose to delay repayment until the next election brings a loan forgiveness day. Some borrowers may believe (based on past experience) that if credit is provided for a project that fails, they will be exempt from repaying their loans.

7. The discussion of information flows and their relation to credit markets here is limited to rural areas. It is worth noting, however, that while there are some differences between rural and urban microcredit markets, evidence from some microfinance institutions (such as BRI's microbanking division and PRODEM/BancoSol) indicates that there are many similarities between these markets.

8. Social debt refers to reciprocal obligations, most of which have an economic component, usually in kind or in labor. For example, in rural areas of many societies it is common among families who are roughly social and economic equals that, if B has contributed a goat to a funeral in A's family, A owes B a goat (plus perhaps a chicken) at a similar occasion. If A worked for two days helping B to harvest his crop (with no recompense except food), B must provide two days to help A with his harvest. Social debt tends not to be fungible. Except under extenuating circumstances such as serious illness, labor cannot usually be repaid with a goat, nor can the debt of a goat for a ceremony be repaid with labor. Social debts owed to a person or household can be a form of savings for the creditor; see chapter 7 for further discussion.

9. I was permitted to attend meetings held in secret because I was an outsider to the communities, and in some cases also because of my gender. I could attend women's gatherings because I am a woman; ironically, I could also attend men's gatherings because I am a woman. As the leader of one village faction in India said, "We don't mind if you come to our meeting tonight because you are a woman and you will not understand what happens"!

10. Such restricted information is, of course, not confined to developing countries. As Frank McCourt put it in *Angela's Ashes,* a 1999 Pulitzer Prize–winning novel about growing up poor in Ireland, "In every lane there's always someone not talking to someone or everyone not talking to someone or someone not talking to everyone" (p. 133).

11. Readers who find the concept of two kinds of money with different uses to be strange may find it useful to think of the distinctions between appropriate uses of "soft" and "hard" money.

12. There are two basic kinds of commodity credit relationships: one in which the lender buys from the borrower, and one in which the lender sells to the borrower. For example, in the first type a rice merchant supplies credit to rice farmers for their cultivation expenses and/or to lower-level traders who procure rice. After the harvest the merchant typically expects to purchase the rice at a previously agreed price and to receive the principal and interest of the loan. Both the negotiated rice price as a percentage of the local market price and the interest on the loan can vary substantially by country and region. In the second type, the merchant who supplies a carpenter with wood and the wholesaler who supplies a woman operating a market stall with the items she sells provide these items on credit. Such relationships may also be combined: A supplies B with the materials and specifications for a given product (garments, crafts, furniture); B makes the product and is required to sell it to A at a preset purchase price that includes the cost of the credit for the materials.

13. The statements about informal moneylenders made in this chapter are documented in chapter 6, where informal credit markets are analyzed and references are provided.

14. Many examples are provided in volume 3. The financial institutions discussed there vary widely in structure. They include state and private banks; commercial, agricultural, and specialized banks; credit unions and cooperatives; various types of NGOs; and village banks. The institutions also vary considerably in geographic location, size, age, and purpose. Yet many of them have found ways to overcome asymmetric information and moral hazard in microfinance, as attested by their continuing high repayment rates.

15. See box 2.1 for the credit methods in general use among self-sufficient microfinance institutions; most apply to these banks.

16. BRI's microbanking system requires collateral for most loans, and borrowers who cannot provide acceptable forms of collateral are denied credit. But the extent of this form of credit exclusion is relatively small because BRI accepts many forms of collateral including movable assets such as furniture, vehicles, and machinery. BRI research indicates that about 90 percent of Indonesian households have some form of collateral acceptable to the unit desas (BRI 1997b, p. 7). In BancoSol all members of a solidarity group guarantee the loans of the other members; these guarantees substitute for collateral. But the dramatic microfinance competition in Bolivia in 1999 resulted in new forms of risk for BancoSol and other Bolivian microfinance institutions (chapter 19).

17. In addition to the two banks discussed here, the experiences of many of the microfinance institutions discussed in volume 3 support this point.

18. The system of village credit organizations (BKDs) supervised by BRI also provides loans to individuals without collateral. The system, which has been profitable for decades, has higher interest rates than BRI's units and higher loan defaults. But "the cost of [BKD] loan losses [are] easily covered by interest margins" (BRI 1998a, p. 7).

19. The problems of foreclosure in rural areas are perceived similarly by bankers in other developing countries as well. See Vogel (1981) for discussion of a somewhat similar situation in Costa Rica.

6 | Informal Commercial Moneylenders: Operating Under Conditions of Monopolistic Competition

The role of informal commercial moneylending in local financial markets has been debated for decades. This chapter examines three main strains of these debates: whether such moneylending is a "malicious" monopolistic business, whether it provides good value for borrowers, and whether it is a form of monopolistic competition. Evidence is presented to show that the first two views are correct on some points, but not on others, and that the third best explains informal commercial moneylending. This logic has crucial policy implications for the microfinance revolution.

If much of informal moneylending can be explained by a form of monopolistic competition, then it can be argued that banks can cost-effectively gain reliable information about borrowers that is far broader in scope than the information to which informal lenders have access (chapter 5). With this information, banks can distinguish between high-risk and low-risk borrowers sufficiently to be able to serve microfinance markets profitably on a large scale. Because of the constraints that informal moneylenders face as participants in the local political economy, they must ration credit; banks need not. Leading commercial microfinance institutions have demonstrated that they can gain sufficient information to serve millions of borrowers profitably, with extremely high repayment rates.

The chapter begins with a discussion of microfinance markets and of the large share of these markets held by the informal financial sector. The focus then turns to the debates on informal commercial moneylenders, and to the characteristics of transactions between lenders and borrowers. Documentation shows that moneylenders in many parts of the world typically charge much higher interest rates to poor borrowers than are required for microfinance institutions to operate profitably. Borrowers' transaction costs for obtaining credit are generally lower for a loan from an informal moneylender than for a loan from a standard financial institution. But if a borrower obtains credit from a sustainable microfinance institution, the difference in transaction costs will likely be small relative to the much larger difference in interest rates.

When banks serve the microfinance market commercially, creditworthy low-income borrowers can gain access to loans at interest rates, and total costs, that are much lower than those typically paid for loans from moneylenders. Moreover, the demand for microsavings services can be met.

Finally, the chapter shows why informal commercial credit markets are normally not competitive, and analyzes the effects this lack of competition has on low-income borrowers. The chapter concludes that it is the formal sector, not the informal sector, that has the potential to make microfinance markets competitive.

Banks can cost-effectively gain reliable information about borrowers that is far broader than the information to which informal lenders have access

In developing countries both rural and urban microfinance markets are typically composed of informal lenders and deposit takers, of semiformal bodies, and of formal financial institutions. But these categories are constructs; reality falls along a continuum. In addition, the same individual, household, or group may participate in more than one part of the system at any given time. Thus a formal sector borrower may use her bank loan to provide informal credit to her employees. An informal lender may save his profits in the local bank (which then lends his money to formal sector borrowers). Proceeds from both formal and informal loans may be placed in rotating savings and credit associations (ROSCAs) or credit unions. People may borrow from banks to repay moneylenders and, especially in difficult times, they may borrow from moneylenders to repay banks.

Fungibility and arbitrage are key factors. A Costa Rican moneylender, for example, sent people to the local cooperative bank to take subsidized loans; he then "rented" the proceeds to onlend at higher interest rates.[1] Bank loans can also be used, de facto if not de jure, to produce goods for sales in informal black markets. Thus where marijuana cultivation is illegal, a merchant may take a bank loan (ostensibly for trade in, say, potatoes or rice) and use it to provide informal credit to marijuana cultivators.

Informal credit can be commercial (loans from moneylenders, traders, employers, commodity wholesalers, landlords) or noncommercial (from family, friends, neighbors). In between are a variety of ROSCAs, mutual aid associations, and informal finance companies. Some of these are commercially oriented, others are more socially oriented. But the social-commercial distinction forms a continuum. For example, even ROSCAs vary from essentially social to highly commercial (Bouman 1989; Von Pischke 1991; Rutherford 2000).

Informal Commercial Lenders in Microfinance Markets

In examining informal financial markets, this book focuses on commercial moneylenders—because of their importance to the microfinance revolution. Such moneylenders know the microfinance market well, and commercial microfinance institutions have borrowed many of their methods. Yet there remain widespread misunderstandings—both in the formal financial sector and in the economic development literature—about how informal moneylenders operate. Banks are generally unwilling to compete with moneylenders in microfinance markets. This is partly because bankers assume that informal lenders have better information about borrowers than the bankers can obtain cost-effectively, and partly because bankers believe that microfinance, with its small transactions, would be unprofitable for their banks.

For our purposes informal commercial moneylenders (for which the term moneylender is used here) include people whose only or primary occupation is moneylending or informal pawnbroking, as well as lenders whose primary occupation is in trading, farming, fishing, industry, and the like—in short, in-

Moneylenders know the microfinance market well, and commercial microfinance institutions have borrowed many of their methods

formal lenders of all types who provide credit with the expectation of profiting financially from the loan. Included are lenders who lend at their own risk as well as brokers who intermediate between savers and borrowers, in which case the savers bear all or part of the risk.

Better knowledge of moneylenders can help commercial microfinance institutions develop in two ways. First, much can be learned from moneylenders and their methods—from, among other things, their:

- Knowledge of the microcredit market.
- Development of personal relationships with clients.
- Tested methods of evaluating the repayment capacity and character of prospective borrowers.
- Methods of containing costs.
- Products—in most cases short-term working capital loans.
- Quick, easy credit procedures carried out in locations convenient for borrowers.
- Practice of repeat lending to borrowers who repay promptly, with gradually increasing loan sizes.

Many of these practices have been adapted for use by institutions serving this market (Christen 1989).

Second, better knowledge of informal commercial moneylending can help in examining the limitations and restrictions that moneylenders have by virtue of being members of their local communities—and that the formal financial sector generally does not have to the same degree. This analysis can help banks understand how they can operate profitably in microfinance markets that are also served by moneylenders.

Other types of informal lenders, such as ROSCAs, savings and loan associations, and mutual aid groups, are beyond the scope of this book, as is credit from family and friends. While the emphasis here is on the commercial moneylenders in the informal sector, references are provided, both in this chapter and elsewhere in the book, for readers who want to learn about other aspects of microfinance markets (see, among others, Bouman 1989; Germidis, Kessler, and Meghir 1991; Von Pischke 1991; Floro and Yotopoulos 1991; Adams and Fitchett 1992; Hoff, Braverman, and Stiglitz 1993; Ghate and others 1993; and Carstens 1995 MicroSave-Africa 1999, 2000; Rutherford 2000).

However, a brief comment needs to be made about the many loans that are taken from family, friends, and neighbors. Such loans usually carry no financial interest, or sometimes low interest, but they may entail social, political, and economic obligations ranging from providing free labor to committing reciprocal future loans, from providing information to rendering political support (see Carstens 1995). Loans from family, friends, and neighbors are typically made available for small amounts and short terms for consumption or emergencies; or in larger amounts for special occasions such as weddings and funerals, or for specific purposes such as buying land or building a house (as with loans from

Informal financial services, while of value to clients, are not economically efficient

the parents of a young couple). A study of four regions in China makes the important point that credit from family and friends tends to be nonfungible.[2] Thus if an informal loan is provided by a relative for housing construction, the loan normally cannot be diverted to meet the household's cultivation expenses. Credit from family and friends is generally not a substitute for commercial credit, informal or formal.

Informal financial markets include both credit and savings. This chapter concerns moneylenders and their loans; the savings side of informal finance is discussed in chapter 7. It has been argued that informal financial services, while of value to clients, are not economically efficient (Gonzalez-Vega 1994, 1995):

In contrast to informal finance, formal sector microfinance institutions can be economically efficient

> *Question:* Are informal financial services *efficient* from an economic perspective?
> *Answer:* Emphatically, NO ... The information costs for screening and monitoring borrowers who are not in close proximity (same village, same occupation, same social group) are too high. In consequence, informal finance cannot contribute substantially to the reallocation of purchasing and investment ability in the economy, critical in order to increase the productivity of resources. This reallocation transfers command over resources from low to high-rate of return activities. Thus, informal finance is socially inefficient, and does not fully contribute significantly to economic growth.
>
> —Gonzalez-Vega 1995, pp. 1–2

The discussion in this chapter highlights the argument made throughout this book that, in contrast to informal finance, formal sector microfinance institutions can be economically efficient.

The Size of Informal Credit Markets

If informal credit markets were small, or if they were large and operated competitively, this chapter would not be necessary in a book on the microfinance revolution. But informal credit markets are large (in part because the formal sector is usually missing from these markets), and moneylenders are generally noncompetitive. We first review the size of informal credit markets, then analyze how moneylenders operate.

There is little accurate knowledge about the market shares of informal credit markets.[3] All we really know is that these markets are large and that they tend to shrink somewhat with economic development. But the bank finance that enters rural credit markets along with development, and that accounts for much of the formal financial sector's share of these markets, tends to be in the form of subsidized agricultural credit. Since these loans often go to better-off households, the poor still depend heavily on informal credit markets. In Thailand, for example, loans provided by informal lenders are reported to have been reduced from 90 percent of the rural credit market in 1975 to 50 percent in 1985 (Siamwalla and others 1993, p. 161). Yet in 1984–85 extensive field work on rural credit found that "the credit needs of poorer farmers are still served by the informal market or not at all" (Siamwalla and others 1993, p. 155).

In 1973 Marvin Miracle estimated that more than 90 percent of the credit provided to small farmers in most developing countries went through the informal credit market—though, as he noted, this share was declining (Miracle 1973b, excerpted in Von Pischke, Adams, and Donald 1983, p. 214). This was probably generally true of urban microcredit markets as well.

The size of informal credit markets in developing countries is documented in four quite different studies published in the 1990s (Germidis, Kessler, and Meghir 1991; Von Pischke 1991; Hoff, Braverman, and Stiglitz 1993; and Ghate and others 1993). Each study is based on comparative material drawn from a number of countries, most of it concerned with rural credit markets. There is general agreement in these writings, as well as in others, that informal credit markets remain large, and that most loans in developing countries are provided by the informal sector. What most of the studies actually show, however, is that the market share of formal sector lending in rural credit markets is relatively small; the sizes of informal credit markets are usually estimated from the remainder. In addition, within informal credit markets there is typically no way to know how much credit is provided by moneylenders, how much by ROSCAs and other mutual aid and self-help groups, and how much by family and friends of the borrowers.

Across the four studies, the estimates of formal sector penetration of rural credit markets are quite consistent. Von Pischke's estimate, made in his 1991 *Finance at the Frontier,* is that "formal agricultural credit . . . probably does not reach more than 20 percent of farm households . . . in the majority of developing countries" (p. 173).

The second study, *The Economics of Rural Organization,* edited by Hoff, Braverman, and Stiglitz (1993) and published by the World Bank, documents the importance of informal credit markets based on comparative evidence from different countries. Citing a number of sources, Braverman and Guasch (1993, p. 54) state in one of the chapters that "it has been estimated that only 5 percent of farmers in Africa and about 15 percent in Asia and Latin America have had access to formal credit; on average across developing countries 5 percent of the borrowers have received 80 percent of the [formal] credit."

Reporting in the same volume on their study of rural credit in Thailand, Siamwalla and others (1993, p. 155) found that "almost 75 percent of those active in the credit market still used the informal sector; in many cases, those households also used the formal sector." This study also reports that institutional credit goes primarily to farmers with above-average incomes. Other studies in the volume report that a 1988–89 survey of four villages in northern Nigeria found that "only 7.5 percent of all loans (by value) come from banks, companies or projects" (Udry 1993, p. 91); and that a 1987–88 survey of four counties in China

Most loans in developing countries are provided by the informal sector

showed that "total informal debts outstanding at the beginning of the season surveyed are at least as large [in amount] as total formal debts and often considerably higher" (Feder and others 1993, p. 114).

The third study, titled *Informal Finance* and based on research on South and Southeast Asian countries, concludes that "the share of rural informal credit [by value], although declining in most countries, still accounts for about two-fifths of total rural credit in India and Thailand, one-third to two-thirds in Bangladesh, and more than two-thirds in the Philippines . . . The proportion of the total number of informal loans, or households borrowing from the informal sector, is higher in most cases than these volume-based estimates would suggest" (Ghate and others 1993, pp. 10–11).

The fourth study, published in 1991 by the Development Centre of the Organisation for Economic Co-operation and Development (OECD), provides extensive documentation on the shares of formal and informal finance in developing countries (Germidis, Kessler, and Meghir 1991; see especially table 1.3 and pp. 39–49). The examples that follow are drawn from the OECD volume (Germidis, Kessler, and Meghir 1991, pp. 42–44). The data used in this study, which were collected at different times by different people for different purposes, vary considerably by country. Moreover, all types of informal loans are mixed together in the informal loan category. And some sources provide the number of loans, while others cite the value of loans. Thus no attempt is made here to use this material for direct intercountry comparisons. Still, the data—which are from the 1970s and 1980s—are useful as indications of the generally large informal credit markets in developing countries:

- Bangladesh—if "all major studies since 1974" are taken into account, the mean size of credit from informal sources was estimated in 1983 to be about 60 percent, with a range from 30–90 percent.[4] But informal moneylenders were estimated to cover 77 percent of farmers' credit needs.
- India—the percentage of rural household debt from informal sources was 83 percent in 1961, 71 percent in 1971, and 39 percent in 1981. The decline was largely due to the quadrupling in the number of commercial bank branches after 1969, when banks were nationalized and increased emphasis was placed on subsidized credit programs.
- Indonesia— "during the early 1980s, only 17 per cent of . . . agricultural households received credit from the government's special programmes, which means that 83 per cent of [these] households received no formal credit at all."
- Republic of Korea—it was estimated in 1985 that informal credit accounted for 50 percent of the average outstanding loans of agricultural households.
- Malaysia—a 1986 survey found that 62 percent of the loans made to farmers were informal.
- Mexico—a 1985 OECD review found that 50–55 percent of agricultural credit needs were met by informal loans.
- Nigeria—the 1985 OECD review reported that, based on a representative sample from two states, 95 percent of the loans to farmers were from informal sources.

"The proportion of the total number of informal loans is higher in most cases than estimates based on loan volume suggest"

- Philippines—the share of rural household debt from informal sources was 60 percent in the 1950s and 1960s, 33 percent in the early 1970s, and 78 percent in the late 1970s. Much of the explanation comes from the fact that in the 1970s the Philippines maintained massive subsidized rural credit programs, but many were dropped in the late 1970s because of poor performance.
- Thailand—it was estimated in 1988 that 52 percent of the loans made to the agricultural sector were from informal sources.
- Zambia—57 percent of farmers' loans were obtained from the formal sector.
- Zimbabwe—in 1986 only 13 percent of small farmers received credit from formal sources.

Although circumstances and trends vary, there is no doubt that informal credit markets are widely prevalent in many developing countries and that informal commercial moneylenders play an important role in many of these markets. Moreover, in some of the areas (such as parts of India and Latin America) where the volume of institutional credit is reported to have become higher than that of informal credit, most borrowers—especially poor borrowers—still continue to receive their credit from informal lenders.

Debates about Moneylenders and Their Interest Rates

The demand for credit among low-income borrowers is typically for short-term working capital loans made available at convenient locations with easy processes, appropriate payment schedules, and quick delivery, and with interest rates that the borrowers can repay from household income sources while also permitting their enterprises to grow. For all but the last feature, there is widespread agreement in the literature: moneylenders provide such loans. But there is considerable controversy about their interest rates. It has long been observed that moneylenders often charge high interest rates; for decades there has been extensive debate about the reasons (see Von Pischke 1991 and Germidis, Kessler, and Meghir 1991).

Among the many reasons that have been suggested are the opportunity cost of funds, administrative costs, risk premiums, high default rates, scarcity of capital, insufficient collateral, borrowing for consumption, seasonal character of demand, low geographic mobility, low income and education among borrowers, and monopoly (or oligopoly) profits. Each of these may be important under certain circumstances. But none really gets at the crux of the issue, which is a variant of monopolistic competition.

There have been three main arguments in the debates about moneylenders and their interest rates; these are considered below.[5] Although some of the studies cited here focus on or include urban moneylenders (see Germidis, Kessler and Meghir 1991; see also Timberg and Aiyar 1984 for India; Malhotra 1992a for Bolivia; and Carstens 1995 for Mexico), most of the literature concerns rural

It has long been observed that moneylenders often charge high interest rates; for decades there has been extensive debate about the reasons

lenders. Thus much of the discussion that follows is about rural lending. However, many of the arguments made here apply to microfinance markets, both rural and urban.

"Malicious," monopolistic moneylenders

The oldest view in the debates is that "malicious" monopolistic moneylenders charge high interest rates, extracting substantial profits.[6] A variant of the monopolistic moneylender is the lender whose primary aim is to make the borrower default in order to gain his land, to force him into bonded labor, or to get him to sell the lender his produce at below-market prices. There is considerable evidence, especially from South Asia (where it has been recorded since at least the 1920s), that some informal commercial lenders gain monopoly profits collected in financial form, land, or labor—and that some are indeed malicious.[7]

In India hundreds of small studies and central, state, and local government reports produced over decades have documented exploitive credit practices.[8] These reports cover cases of lenders who charge high interest rates that often lead to loan default—and then to bonded labor, land alienation, or monopsony prices for the borrower's produce (that is, the borrower must sell her produce to the lender at the lender's price even if other buyers are available and willing to pay higher prices). Roth (1983) discusses "debt farming" in India: managing credit so that the debtor defaults and the lender gains control over his labor. "Debt farming," Roth says, is "a means to the capture of a long-term source of labour that is cheaper than is available under the conditions of the open labour market" (p. 62).

Some examples of "malicious" moneylending may be useful.

Monopsony prices for commodities.

> In Ramnad [India], every one of the *panaiyeri* [palm tree tappers] Nadars I interview is heavily indebted. After awhile, it doesn't matter how much jaggery [a type of brown sugar made from date palm syrup] they produce. They are not only repaying loans but are also selling the [jaggery] at absurdly low prices to the middlemen. They have to ... the same man [the lender] is also their wholesaler. (Sainath 1996, pp. 139–140)

Bonded labor.

> Sarjunu Bumihar has been bonded to Lachaman Sahu of Marda village in the Bhardaria block of Palamau District (south Bihar [India]). Initially he borrowed 40 [kilograms] of paddy in 1972 from the Mahajan (moneylender) for consumption purposes. He agreed to work for the Mahajan ... until the time he repays the debt. But, poor Sarjunu did not know the economies of the Mahajan. The interest charged was 100 percent for the first year, i.e. 40 kg paddy borrowed in 1972 became 80 kg in 1973 and

Exploitive credit practices include lenders who charge high interest rates that lead to loan default—and then to bonded labor, land alienation, or monopsony prices

at compound interest rate it became 160 kg. Compelled by the circumstances he had to borrow 40 kg of paddy again in 1974 at the same compound interest rate ... For a poor landless person like Sarjunu, having no avenues of other income, it is just impossible to pay back, under these circumstances. He has to work throughout the year [for the moneylender]. In case of absence some amount is deducted from his pay [which was 8 rupees per month, or 89 cents, plus a small amount of grain]. (Indian School of Social Science 1976, pp. 117–18)[9]

Land alienation. A study of the effects of nontribal incursions into tribal areas of Central India notes the effects on the Raj Gond and Koya tribes of Adilibad [Andhra Pradesh] with regard to indebtedness at "exorbitant rates from money lenders." Thus:

> 80% of Raj Gond households [have been] forced into indebtedness to non-tribal money lenders who charge high interest rates ... The Koyas are the worst off, 50% of them being [landless] agricultural labourers. [Among] those Koyas who have retained their lands . . . loans are taken for the leasing of land and plough bullocks. Net income shows a deficit with 92 percent of Koyas households indebted to non-tribal money lenders. The likelihood of repaying the loans with such interest rates is low, thus resulting in large scale land alienation.
> —Pingle and von Furer-Haimendorf 1998, pp. 152–53

The general argument that high interest rates result at least partly from informal lending monopolies has been summarized as follows:

> Proponents of this view underline a number of particularities of informal sector lending to explain the emergence of such lending monopolies. First, moneylenders operate in areas where few individuals have a sufficient amount of loanable funds, while low geographical mobility restrains the entry of new lenders into the credit market, and makes it expensive for prospective borrowers to shop around for alternative credit sources. As a result, the number of potential lenders in a given area is limited, and the degree of market power thus conferred on them may range from pure monopoly (one lender to a village) to some point short of perfect competition.
> —Germidis, Kessler, and Meghir 1991, p. 180

Over the past 40 years the availability of institutional credit has increased widely in rural areas of developing countries—but at different rates in different areas. Multiple forms of informal credit can coexist within the same area. In un-

Multiple forms of informal credit can coexist within the same area. But in underdeveloped regions nonexploitive lenders may be rare

derdeveloped regions, however, nonexploitive lenders may be rare. In addition, the access of local borrowers to institutional lenders may be prevented by the borrowers' current exploitive lenders (Robinson 1988, pp. 131–33). The prevalence of lenders with a high degree of monopoly depends on a variety of factors, including the level of development, distribution of income, and availability of communication facilities in the area, as well as more general historical, geographical, and political considerations.

Informal moneylenders: "value for the people"[10]

A 1992 book on informal finance was dedicated to "the much maligned moneylender because of her ability to walk barefoot where bankers fear to tread"

A strongly held belief by traditionalists is that moneylenders are evil and charge exorbitant rates of interest. The emerging view is that moneylenders generally perform a legitimate economic function. Their operations are frequently more cost-effective and useful to the poor than those of the specialized farm-credit institutions, cooperatives and commercial banks that governments use to supplant moneylenders ... The emerging perspective is that informal financial arrangements, based on voluntary participation by rural people, are generally robust and socially useful. Widespread use of informal finance suggests that it is well suited to most rural conditions.

—Von Pischke, Adams, and Donald 1983, p. 8

This statement, made in the introduction to the classic 1983 volume, *Rural Financial Markets in Developing Countries,* signaled a new view of informal finance associated primarily with the Agricultural Economics Department of Ohio State University (United States). The views of rural financial markets developed there are responsible for many of the pathbreaking ideas of the past 25 years on the deficiencies of subsidized credit and the importance of the largely unrecognized but vast unmet demand in rural areas for deposit services.[11] The school of thought developed at Ohio State University also generated views about informal moneylenders that remain controversial (see Von Pischke 1991 and Germidis, Kessler, and Meghir 1991).

Dale W Adams, Anthony Bottomley, F.J.A. Bouman, J. D.Von Pischke, Martin W. Wilmington, and others have argued extensively against the idea that large numbers of private lenders exploit rural borrowers through excessively high interest rates made possible by credit monopolies. Their aim was to refute what came to be called the myth of the malicious moneylender (see above), to demonstrate that interest rates for informal commercial loans reflect primarily the lenders' transaction costs and risks,[12] and to argue, therefore, that most rural lenders are neither exploitive nor malicious. Their view is that most moneylenders provide small loans quickly and conveniently, with simple procedures and at generally reasonable interest rates, thus serving the interests of the poor.[13]

Thus:

Field studies do not support the myth [of the malicious moneylender]. Karam Singh ... [in a 1968 study of a village in northern India] estimated, using linear programming analysis, that monopoly profits approximated 9 percent of amounts loaned, while interest rates paid by borrowers exceeded 140 percent per annum . . . More than half the staggering rate to borrowers reflected the opportunity cost of capital in the village, and about one-quarter was contributed by the risk premium.

—Von Pischke 1991, p. 179

Adams and Delbert Fitchett dedicated a 1992 book they edited on informal finance to "the much maligned moneylender because of her ability to walk barefoot where bankers fear to tread." In their seminal statements opposing credit subsidies, Adams, Von Pischke, and others also tended to assume that removing formal sector interventions would leave behind local, informal, competitive credit markets. This, however, was generally not the case:

> This critical literature [in Von Pischke, Adams, and Donald 1983] stressed the distortions introduced by government policies [for credit subsidies] and, in doing so, tended to idealize the informal credit markets that did exist or that might have existed in absence of the massive government intervention in the credit market. There was a presumption that an intervention-free rural financial market would approximate the perfect competition model.
>
> —Siamwalla and others 1993, p. 170

Extensive evidence on noncompetitive rural credit markets that has been available since at least the 1920s seems to have been ignored in the enthusiasm of the 1970s and 1980s for eliminating intervention in rural credit markets—since the assumption of a competitive informal credit market was essential to that argument.

Two different arguments in these debates need to be disentangled: malicious moneylenders, and transaction costs and risks. Whether malicious moneylenders exist is not a question of myth or reality. They are real, as anyone who has lived in underdeveloped parts of rural India, for example, can testify. I once asked the headman of an Indian village (in the Telangana area of Andhra Pradesh) about loans he had made to people who had been unable to repay, and who had then become his bonded laborers. One question I asked was why the full-time work of a bonded laborer paid only the interest on the loan (there were no additional wages from which a borrower could repay the principal or subsist—thus leading to further borrowing). The headman replied, "If you put too much oil in your engine, it will not start. People are the same" (Robinson 1988, p. 9).[14]

Such lenders represent one end of the continuum of informal moneylenders. But while some informal moneylenders are malicious and exploitive, many are not.[15] The "value for the people" view argues that informal commercial lenders offer services that are cost-effective and useful to the poor, and that their interest rates reflect the real costs of loanable funds. As Bouman (1989, p. 9) put it, the informal sector "allows low income people access to services not available

"There was a presumption that an intervention-free rural financial market would approximate the perfect competition model." It did not

to them elsewhere and at a relatively low cost."[16] The Ohio State University school of thought and other theorists explain the high interest rates of many moneylenders by the lenders' transaction costs and risks. We will return to this aspect of the debates later in this chapter in a discussion of the operations of informal moneylenders and their risks and transaction costs. Meanwhile, the third argument in the debates is considered: that informal moneylenders are best explained by monopolistic competition.

Informal moneylending as monopolistic competition

The theory of monopolistic competition was developed by Chamberlin (1933) and Robinson (1933); see Negishi (1987) for definitions, history, and overview of the concept. But this theory has only recently been applied to rural credit markets (see Robinson 1992b, 1994a; Aleem 1993; and Hoff and Stiglitz 1993, 1998). Monopolistic competition has been defined as:

> the market situation in which there is a large number of firms whose outputs are close but not perfect substitutes, either because of product differentiation or geographical fragmentation of the market. The fact that products are not homogeneous means that any one firm may raise its price relative to the prices of its competitors without losing all its sales, so that its demand curve is downward-sloping rather than a horizontal line straight line (as in perfect competition). The combination of a large number of firms as if in perfect competition, with downward-sloping curves as in monopoly, is responsible for the term "monopolistic competition."
>
> —Penguin, *A Dictionary of Economics,* 1975, p. 289

An area served by informal moneylenders can be thought of as a Swiss cheese. There is free entry to the cheese, but not to the holes

While there have been a number of variations and interpretations of the theory, it is generally agreed that monopolistic competition is characterized by easy entry into the market, product specialization or geographic separation, and a downward sloping demand curve. In the classic monopolistic competition model, firms can earn economic profits in the short term. But because free entry into the market drives down the profits of individual firms, firms cannot make economic profits over the long term.[17]

An informal commercial moneylender can normally obtain good information only about a relatively small number of borrowers (see chapter 5). Thus in informal credit markets moneylenders, who frequently have interlinked transactions with their borrowers in other markets, are imperfect substitutes. These markets are characterized by product differentiation: moneylending services vary in terms of borrower access, types and amounts of loans, and other factors (Aleem 1993). In addition, Gonzalez-Vega (1995) emphasizes that informal markets are typically local and fragmented.

A variant of the monopolistic credit model is useful for explaining informal credit markets. The variant differs from the classic model in two closely related ways. First, entry is free only to a point. New lenders may enter the market freely—

so long as they lend to borrowers who are not served by (and often linked in other ways) to other moneylenders in the area. An area served by informal moneylenders can be thought of as a Swiss cheese (with many holes). The moneylenders with their borrowers are the holes, while the rest of the public, left unserved, is the cheese. There is free entry to the cheese, but not to the holes.

Second, and directly related, long-term economic profits are possible. The large number of lenders in these markets can give the illusion of competition. But new entrants into the market typically have (or establish) linkages in credit and other markets with people who are not currently linked with other moneylenders. Thus the new entrants normally do not compete for the borrowers of established lenders—whose borrowers are typically also their commodity suppliers, employees, tenants, and the like. Therefore, the new entrants tend not to drive down interest rates. Excess profits are not competed away, and it is possible for lenders to gain economic profits over the long term.

Thus lender B normally does not lend to the borrowers of lender A or lender C because lender B knows that it can be difficult to collect in an area or network controlled by A or C. For example, N is a long-term supplier of coffee beans to lender A, a coffee merchant who provides working capital credit to N. If N requests a loan from lender B, B is unlikely to lend to N so long as N remains linked with lender A. Lender B will usually decide that collecting loans on lender A's turf is too risky.[18]

The logic of the argument can be simply stated (box 6.1). Normally there are multiple lenders in the market, each with a relatively small number of borrowers. Lenders generally do not want to increase their market shares (because of the risks of lowering the quality of their portfolios if they lend outside the areas over which they exert influence), have access to good information, and maintain interlinked transactions with borrowers. Those who want to expand their lending typically do so through credit layering: providing credit to linked borrowers who then onlend to their own interlinked borrowers.

Lenders tend not to lower their interest rates because they know that the borrowers linked with them cannot easily find another informal lender, and because lenders typically do not want a significant increase in the number of their borrowers. Having no incentive to do otherwise, moneylenders maintain high interest rates and ration credit. Monopolistic competition also explains the frequent reports of a wide range of interest rates charged at the same time in the same area.

The crucial point for our purposes is that because informal moneylenders tend to operate under conditions of monopolistic competition, their low-income borrowers generally pay much higher interest rates for credit than would be necessary if commercial microfinance were widely available through financial institutions with broad outreach. As is discussed later, this generally holds true not only for interest rates, but for the total cost of borrowing.

Moneylenders range from helpful to malicious, although they generally lend at high interest rates throughout the range

The three views in a development perspective

The three views on moneylenders, discussed further below, do not represent discrete categories. There are degrees of monopoly power, and informal com-

- Informal commercial microcredit markets tend not to be competitive.
- Lenders typically make credit easily available to a relatively small number of selected borrowers with whom they often have other interlinked transactions (for example, as the borrower's commodity buyer, landlord, or employer).
- Lending to borrowers in another lender's network or territory is perceived as risky. Lenders do not want to lend beyond their sphere of influence and their control of information because of the risks inherent in collecting loans outside the relatively small area where the lender controls information flows, maintains interlinked transactions, and is politically connected. Larger lenders with influence over a more extensive area tend to operate through credit layering (lending to a few subordinates who onlend to others), with credit layering operating at each layer.
- For these reasons, established lenders typically ration credit. They generally do not want to increase their share of the market, they know that the borrowers linked with them cannot easily find another informal lender, and they have little or no incentive to lower interest rates.
- Not all creditworthy loan applicants borrow from informal lenders. Some are excluded because they are not part of a lender's network. And for some the cost of borrowing is too high.
- Interest rates on loans are typically high and cover a wide range. Poorer borrowers are often charged the higher interest rates within the moneylender's range because they have low bargaining power and because the lender's transaction costs are essentially the same for larger and smaller loans. If the same interest rate were charged, the smaller loans would be less profitable.
- Borrowers' transaction costs are generally low, and loans are delivered quickly and conveniently, with minimal procedures.
- Repayment rates tend to be high because lenders have good information about borrowers, because lenders usually have control over borrowers in other ways, and because borrowers want to preserve their option to borrow again.
- Borrowers tend to have long-term relationships with one lender. They may borrow also from family and friends and from the formal sector—but usually not simultaneously from another informal lender.
- Lenders are typically constrained in their moneylending activities not by the availability of funds but by the number of borrowers from whom they can collect with low risk.
- As a result of these characteristics, informal commercial credit markets are best explained by a variant of monopolistic competition in which economic profits can be maintained for the long term.

mercial moneylenders range from helpful to malicious, although they generally lend at high interest rates throughout the range. However, discussion of these views provides important background for understanding both how rural credit markets have been perceived and how they work.

Malicious, monopolistic moneylenders. Such moneylenders exist, but they do not represent the majority of informal moneylenders. They are mostly found in underdeveloped areas; thus in India they are much more common in less-developed Bihar and the Telangana region of Andhra Pradesh than in better-developed Punjab or Kerala. Government intervention can help in areas where such lenders operate to force borrower default and thus to gain access to land, cheap labor, or below-market commodity prices. But economic development generally, along with employment generation and broad-based education opportunities, are the most effective ways to combat this type of moneylender.

Value for the people. Informal commercial lenders provide small loans quickly and conveniently using simple procedures, and collectively they serve many of the creditworthy among the poor. To this extent they provide value for the people, especially since in most parts of the developing world the formal financial sector does not. The relevant question here is, do borrowers need to pay such high interest rates? In most cases the answer is no—if commercial microfinance institutions are present in the area. But in most cases the formal financial sector is still absent from these markets.

Because of the widespread authority of the Ohio State University school of thought on rural financial markets, it has come to be widely believed that informal commercial lenders provide credit to low-income rural borrowers at reasonable interest rates. If this were so, there would be less urgency to develop commercial institutional microfinance. From a development perspective, the result has been a view that there is no compelling reason to "fix what is not broken."

But evidence is provided later in this chapter to show that moneylenders in many parts of the world charge interest rates to poor borrowers that are often far above the rates charged by commercial institutions that provide microfinance profitably. As will be discussed, a loan from a moneylender generally has lower transaction costs than a loan from a financial institution. But commercial microfinance institutions try to minimize transaction costs to borrowers; as a result the total cost of borrowing from such institutions is typically much lower than the cost of borrowing from moneylenders. Given the large share of the microcredit market that moneylenders hold in many developing countries, the high costs their borrowers pay for loans can have a substantial negative effect on development.

However, banks can obtain information throughout their entire service area (if they have learned how), while informal moneylenders are restricted in their access to information. As noted, a moneylender typically has very good information about her borrowers and loan applicants—but for a relatively small number of people.

Monopolistic competition. The main reason that most moneylenders charge high interest rates is not because the lenders are malicious monopolists. And as will be discussed later, the main reason is not transaction costs and risks. It is that moneylenders operate under a variation of monopolistic competition. As will be shown, the political, economic, and social processes operating at the local levels of many developing countries tend to result in conditions that favor the operation of moneylenders under monopolistic competition. This situation is deeply imbedded in the social structure and is unlikely to change significantly in the short or medium term, except that lenders may drop out of the market under particular conditions.[19]

Most moneylenders operate under a variation of monopolistic competition that is usually deeply imbedded in the social structure

Moneylenders operating under monopolistic competition can earn varying degrees of monopoly profits. As show below, those with higher degrees of monopoly power may become malicious. But malicious moneylenders are a small subset of informal commercial lenders.

Policy implications

The interest rates charged by informal commercial moneylenders to poor borrowers are of particular significance for social and economic development because high rates tend to impede or prevent the growth of borrowers' enterprises, because in most developing countries both the volume of informal commercial credit and the number of borrowers are large, and because institutional commercial microfinance is still not widely available as an alternative.

The three views on moneylenders lead in very different policy directions. In underdeveloped areas that have malicious moneylenders turning loans into bonded labor and land alienation, the appropriate policy response requires high-level political will (to discredit and undermine local elites who want to keep the poor poor); direct government intervention in making, and especially in implementing, appropriate laws and regulations; and general economic development, with an emphasis on employment creation, infrastructure development, communications, and education.

The value for the people view of moneylending leads to a kind of benign neglect. If informal credit markets are believed to work well, then developing profitable financial institutions providing microcredit will be a low priority on policy agendas. Proponents of the value for the people argument are correct in stating that moneylenders provide valuable services for their clients; many (though not all) do so. But because informal credit markets typically are not competitive, low-income borrowers pay an unnecessarily high price for credit. As will be shown, the view that informal commercial lenders provide credit to low-income borrowers at moderate (or "affordable" cost) is generally incorrect.

The monopolistic competition model of informal commercial lending discussed here is directly related to the microfinance revolution. Informal commercial lenders are unlikely to reduce their interest rates significantly, though they may decrease the number of their borrowers or drop out of the market. But banks can gain much wider information cost-effectively and can profitably lend at much lower interest rates (and total costs to borrowers) than can informal moneylenders. The appropriate policy response is to encourage formal sector financial institutions to serve the microfinance market.

In this context it is important to make clear that the products of microbanks and moneylenders are different, although they overlap. A moneylender—with his high-quality information, effective methods of processing loans, quick customized service, and low borrower transaction costs—is efficient at the low end of the market and on a small scale. Banks do not provide $5 loans at 11 o'clock at night, as many moneylenders do. But the comparative advantages of banks include their cost-effective access to widespread information, their economies of scale, and their opportunities for diversifying risk. Three points of critical importance for the microfinance revolution stand out in the comparison between microbanks

There are three views on moneylenders, and they lead in very different policy directions

and informal commercial lenders. Efficient microbanks provide loans at a much lower cost to their borrowers, they serve large numbers of the economically active poor, and they provide not only credit but also voluntary savings services.

Characteristics of Informal Commercial Loans from Moneylenders

The literature on moneylenders is difficult to compare and to analyze because the data, like those on the extent of informal credit, have been collected under different conditions, for different purposes, at different periods, and in many parts of the world. In aggregate, studies of informal commercial credit markets cover multiple loan types. The results are often reported with only partial information about the loan terms; interest rates and repayment rates are frequently provided without indication of how these were calculated. Reports differ substantially concerning lenders' transaction costs, risks, and profits. Yet in many ways the practices of informal moneylenders seem quite consistent throughout much of the developing world.

Flow credit and stock credit

People at all socioeconomic levels participate in informal commercial credit markets, and many are both lenders and borrowers. The poor typically borrow for consumption, working capital, medical expenses, ceremonies, emergencies, and the like. The better-off tend to borrow for investment (for example, in land, housing, business expansion or diversification, children's education), for consumer durables (vehicles, furniture, electronic appliances), for elaborate ceremonies, for working capital, and in some cases for political reasons (to campaign for local office, to support a candidate for district or provincial office who, if elected, can be expected to provide favors and opportunities).

Loans with repayment periods of less than one year (usually for consumption or working capital) are termed *flow credit* because the information most relevant to the creditor concerns the borrower's income flows. In contrast, *stock credit* (usually for long-term investment) refers to loans with terms of a year or more; the lender is primarily interested in the borrower's assets, liabilities, and collateral. Flow credit tends to dominate informal credit markets, but stock credit is also provided (Siamwalla and others 1993, p. 177).

Flow credit is provided for relatively small amounts and short terms. These loans are normally made available quickly, with little or no paperwork for the borrower and without regard to the intended use of the funds. Collateral is often not required.

The conditions of borrowing for stock credit are similar, with two exceptions (which may also apply when large amounts of flow credit are at stake). First, borrowers are typically limited to a few people the lender knows well and with whom he maintains extensive interlinked transactions in other markets. Second, collateral—generally worth more than the value of the loan—is required.

Whether or not lenders and borrowers are linked in other markets, lenders develop personal relationships with their borrowers, and they know their

Efficient microbanks provide loans at a much lower cost to their borrowers than do moneylenders. They also provide voluntary savings services

clients' businesses. They assess not only borrowers' repayment capacities but also their characters—whether they pay their suppliers on time, whether they are responsible in their dealings with buyers, whether they have a good reputation in the community. Informal commercial lenders are not especially interested in the purpose of the loan. "They [informal lenders] want to know if the borrower is generally financially solid. If the investment plan were to fail, the lender wants to be sure that the borrower can repay from income sources other than those committed to the investment plan" (Christen 1989, p. 23).

Lenders provide borrowers with incentives for timely repayment: the option to borrow again, as well as appropriate loan products with simple procedures, rapid delivery, and flexible repayment schedules. Transaction costs for borrowers, which include transportation and opportunity costs, tend to be low. For all these reasons, as well as their interlinked transactions in other markets, repayment rates are normally high.

A lender will normally not permit a defaulting borrower to borrow again (except in an instance of observable *force majeure*), and an interlinked borrower who defaults on his loan jeopardizes his job or business at the other end of the linkage as well. Depending on their relative positions in the community, the lender may be able to collect the loan by mobilizing community pressure on the borrower. If all else fails, the lender may bring to bear other sanctions on the defaulting borrower, including ostracism, informal economic sanctions, damage to the borrower's enterprise and reputation, and physical harm to the borrower or a family member.

Informal lenders typically do not use legal prosecution to collect loans from borrowers who have defaulted. Informal moneylending is illegal in some countries, and such recourse may not be possible. And even if a legal process is available, it is likely to be expensive and risky.

Interlinked transactions

As noted, lenders often have interlinked transactions with their borrowers in other markets. At the credit end of the linkage, lenders provide credit to their produce suppliers, agents, employees, sharecroppers, tenants, and the like.[20] The borrower has a job, a buyer for her produce, access to raw materials or to land for cultivation, and so on. The borrower has a strong incentive to repay the loan; lenders generally face low risk in providing credit to such borrowers (Bell 1993, p. 197).

Interlinked transactions can work to the benefit of both participants, or they can be exploitive. In addition to the generally high interest rates charged by the lender at the credit end, at the other end he may pay below-market prices to his grain supplier (borrower) or provide below-market wages to his employee (borrower). Like the presence of malicious moneylenders, however, the degree of exploitation possible in interlinked transactions seems to decline with economic development in the area. As Hellman (1994, p. 129) comments about Mexico, "the more distant the peasant from market, the more isolated the village, the more complete is the control of the moneylender who is the only one equipped to move the crop of a poor peasant from the field to the marketplace."

Lenders often have interlinked transactions with their borrowers in other markets

Informal moneylenders lend to linked borrowers in developed, as well as undeveloped areas. For example, a 1984 survey of 111 borrowers and 16 lenders in 14 villages in three rural provinces in the Philippines found that linked loans accounted for 79 percent of the volume of credit in the marginal regions of the study area and 82 percent in the developed regions (Floro and Yotopoulos 1991, p. 75). I observed in Indonesia that by the late 1970s, in contrast to earlier periods when economic growth and development were lower, many employees who had interlinked credit transactions with their employers were paid market wages, while linked producers were paid market prices. However, interest rates on the credit side of the linkage were still very high.

Although borrowers participating in interlinked transactions normally use only one informal commercial lending source for relatively long periods, they may also borrow simultaneously from family and friends and from the formal sector.

Availability of loanable funds

In general, loanable funds do not appear to be scarce in informal credit markets. Siamwalla and others (1993, p. 172) comment on the availability of funds in Thailand's informal rural credit markets: "In our extensive interviews with informal lenders in Thailand, there is very little evidence that the volume of their business is constrained by the availability of funds" (see also Aleem 1993). I found the same to be true when conducting field work in south India in the 1970s and 1980s and in much of Indonesia in the 1980s and 1990s. Aleem (1993, p. 138) reports that for the Chambar market in Pakistan, "rejection of applicants was not significantly linked to the non–availability of funds." This is primarily a result of the common pattern of multiple lenders: each has relatively few borrowers, and many lenders have multiple income sources. In addition, lenders may gain access to funds by obtaining subsidized loans from formal sector institutions. In his study of 14 noninstitutional lenders in the Chambar market, Aleem (1993, p. 149) found that: "On average, about 30 percent of the informal lender's funds come directly or indirectly from low-cost institutional sources. Indeed, a major benefit to the lender from nonspecialization [as a moneylender] was the access trading activities gave him to low-cost and subsidized institutional credit."

Extensive arbitrage is also reported from some areas of India. Moneylenders obtain substantial funds from subsidized loans that they onlend at high rates to small farmers (Bell 1993).[21] But this does not mean that the lenders necessarily increase the number of their borrowers, although they may engage in credit layering (as discussed below).[22] For the reasons already given, each lender tends to ration credit to a relatively small number of borrowers from whom she has a high probability of collection.

It has been argued that insufficient funds, information problems about borrowers, and opportunity costs limit arbitrage in rural India (Bell 1993). But except to some extent for insufficient funds, the limits on arbitrage apply to the credit disbursed by individual lenders, not to the number of such lenders in the system—and thus not necessarily to the aggregate amount under arbitrage.

Moneylenders are typically not capital-constrained. Generally the main constraint is the number of low-risk borrowers available to each lender

Overall, moneylenders are typically not constrained in their lending by capital. Generally the main constraint is the number of low-risk borrowers available to each lender.

The "Too Many Lenders" Problem

In his study of moneylenders in Pakistan, Aleem (1993) says that each lender is perceived by borrowers to offer a different product; each faces a downward-sloping demand curve. He then comments that:

> Equilibrium in this model involves a distortion in the market; there are too many lenders in relation to the size of the informal credit market . . . This observation of "too many lenders" is not unique to the Chambar market. Similar observations have been made in studies of credit markets in other countries . . . In the study, the author was surprised at the large number of lenders operating in the small market area.
>
> —pp. 148–49

Nearly two-thirds of the farmers interviewed said they would have problems obtaining credit if their current lender refused to give them a loan

The "too many lenders" problem should come as no surprise. Having multiple lenders in the market is a characteristic of the segmented nature of informal credit markets in many developing countries, and a hallmark of monopolistic competition. There are not "too many" lenders; there are many lenders because that is how the market operates. In informal commercial credit markets there is high demand for loans, but in general each lender wants to lend to relatively few borrowers. Each lender prices her own interest rates based on the conditions of her business and her ability to collect loans. Thus borrowers may pay different rates to the same lender, and lenders in the same area may offer different ranges of interest rates.

Given the generally high quality of lenders' information about their borrowers, a borrower can face considerable risk in seeking a loan from another informal commercial lender (see Roth 1983, ch. 1; Robinson 1988, ch. 4; Siamwalla and others 1993, p. 162). On the one hand, the new lender may refuse to lend to the borrower because of the risk of collecting loans in another lender's territory. On the other hand, the current lender may learn about the attempt, require immediate repayment of the loan, and terminate the business or employment linkage with the borrower.

Interlinked transactions and access to good information about their borrowers are crucial factors in enabling informal lenders to obtain high repayment rates. But these factors also constrain the number of borrowers per lender. As a result each lender typically provides credit to a relatively small numbers of borrowers (often fewer than 20 and usually fewer than 50). Moreover, within a given period—generally at least several years—each borrower is normally a client of only one informal commercial moneylender.[23]

Each lender serves a small number of borrowers

Siamwalla and others (1993, pp. 161–62) report from three surveys on rural credit carried out in Thailand between 1984 and 1987, one a national survey in six regions of the country:

> Informal lenders are very thick on the ground ... [each lender has] from one to forty-five borrowers, with the average loan portfolio being 36,000 baht (or $1,440) per lender.

A similar pattern in rural Chile was reported by Nisbet (1967, p. 81):

> In all cases [moneylenders] lived and operated within their respective *communas* [minor civil divisions], and their operations usually were found no more than 1 to 2 miles from a rural village or were confined to the rural neighborhood. Their effective geographic zone of operation, or their "rural credit market area", then, is much smaller than the communa unit. The number of moneylenders ranged from none to three, with a mean of one operating within a rural credit market area. In no case did a moneylender operate in an adjoining rural credit market area.[24]

In a paper on rural finance in Sri Lanka, Bouman (1984, p. 245) reported that "A money lender typically serves only 20 to 50 borrowers."

A borrower typically receives credit from one informal commercial lender

In a given period (usually several years) borrowers take loans from only one informal moneylender (see Gamba 1958; Nisbet 1967; Robinson 1988; and Siamwalla and others 1993).

> Nearly two-thirds of the farmers interviewed in 1980–1981 [in villages served by the market town of Chambar in Sind, Pakistan] said they would have problems in obtaining credit if their current lender were to refuse to give them a loan.
> —Aleem 1993, p. 151

> Of the 14 Chambar market lenders studied, 10 said they were not prepared to give loans to farmers borrowing from other lenders as well.
> —Aleem 1993, p. 137[25]

> In our 52-village survey [in the Nakhon Ratchasima Province of Thailand in 1985] ... the modal number of lenders resident in the village is three, and the modal number of outside lenders is two ... Of the households surveyed in NR Province who reported some borrowing from the informal sector, about five-sixths reported

Of the 14 market lenders studied, 10 said they were not prepared to give loans to farmers borrowing from other lenders

that they borrowed from only one informal source. Many of these also borrowed from formal sources, but . . . formal and informal lenders are non-competing. A more telling set of figures comes from our national survey [conducted in 14 villages in 6 regions of Thailand in 1987]. Seventy-two percent of the informal sector borrowers in that survey reported that they had not attempted to borrow from other informal lenders during the past three years.

—Siamwalla and others 1993, p. 162

Large lenders use credit layering

The constraints that prevent moneylenders from increasing their market shares affect even influential lenders whose economic and political activities extend broadly. High status at the village and district levels in developing countries is usually associated with extensive obligations, such as fulfilling broad-based responsibilities to one's dependents and constituents, and contributing or lending to district-level political leaders, factions, alliances, kin groups, or political parties.

This type of creditor is unlikely to expand his direct lending significantly, partly because there are other demands on his capital and partly because of reluctance to lend in areas where political opponents may be active. Larger lenders who have influence over wider areas tend to operate instead through various methods of credit layering. In one common version a large informal lender, instead of lending directly to end borrowers (except those with whom he has long-standing personal relationships), provides loans to smaller lenders with whom he has close connections. The smaller lenders, in turn, onlend to other lenders or to end borrowers with whom they have close ties.

Floro and Yotopoulos (1991) studied credit layering as part of their extensive 1984 survey of informal lenders and borrowers in rural areas of the Philippines. They found that:

> The large trader-cum-wholesalers in our sample rarely deal directly with small borrowers and tend to channel their credit through a group of credit agents who are usually rich farmer-clients . . . The rich farmers who act as credit-agents have extensive knowledge about local conditions, such as the time of harvest, and have personal information about the farmer-borrowers in their locality, such as their efficiency, level of yields, and other sources of income.
>
> —pp. 46–47

In a study of vegetable trading in an upland area of the Philippines, Russell (1985) found that in the area surveyed (a village of 472 households) there were 19 middle-level vegetable traders who provided credit to the vegetable growers of the village. The ratio was about four growers to one lender. Floro and Yotopoulos (1991, p. 46) comment on this study:

Production loans for 83 percent of the borrowers were extended by two wholesale agents through a vertical chain of traders, middlemen, and other intermediaries

What seemed to be a fairly competitive, small scale informal credit market, under further analysis turned out to be a multi-layered hierarchical relationship based on personalized trade networks. All middlemen were financed by the five vegetable traders who were the buyers for the majority of the vegetable growers. Furthermore, all five of these traders obtained their credit capital from two large Chinese vegetable wholesalers. Ultimately, production loans for 83 percent of the borrowers were extended by the two wholesale agents, by means of a vertical chain of traders, middlemen, and other local intermediaries.

I have observed similar credit layering systems in Indonesia for many kinds of products (grain, vegetables, fruit, cattle, coffee). The system works the same way throughout: at each level informal lenders lend directly to borrowers with whom they have personal relationships, interlinked transactions, or both, and about whom they have good information. The political, business, social, and kin relationships operating horizontally at each level, and vertically across levels, provide the information flows and controls that enable lenders in credit layering systems to recover their loans—from a limited number of borrowers—with relatively low risk. In the many parts of the world where informal lenders operate under a system of monopolistic competition, that system is deeply imbedded in all layers of the region's social structure.

One view is that high interest rates of informal commercial lenders are accounted for primarily by transaction costs and risk

Transaction Costs and Risks for Informal Commercial Moneylenders

Lenders' transaction costs and risk premiums have been debated at length. At Ohio State University's Department of Agricultural Economics, the view has been, rightly, that most moneylenders are not malicious monopolists. But according to this school of thought the observed interest rates of informal commercial lenders are accounted for primarily by transaction costs and risk. This view cannot be accepted as a general explanation. In some cases it is true; in others it is not.

The transaction costs of lending
Transaction costs for lenders include the costs of collecting information about potential borrowers and updating information about repeat borrowers; assessing collateral when relevant; and extending, recording, and collecting loans. Overall transaction costs are generally higher for initial borrowers and lower for repeat borrowers.

It has been argued for decades that high interest rates are a result of high transaction costs as well as risks. Three examples:

- Wilmington (1983 [1955], p. 255)—"Village merchants, landowners, and persons with no other occupation commonly lend money to small farmers in the developing world. Their interest rates tend to be very high, and they are often denounced by intellectuals and city dwellers. But their costs and risks are also high, and their services are adapted to their clients."

- Bottomley (1975, p. 243)—"The high cost of administering small loans and persistent repayment problems lead to high interest rates in informal rural money markets in the developing world."
- Von Pischke (1991, p. 175)—"The basic flaw in the malicious moneylender myth is that it interprets quoted lending rates of interest, often of stratospheric heights, as evidence of monopolistic practices. High prices do not prove monopoly, however. How many observers would conclude, for example, that because a car costs more than a box of matches that the manufacturer or retailer of the car gouges consumers?"

Another view is that transaction costs (along with risk premiums) do not explain the high interest rates charged—because these costs are low

Another view, also widespread, is that transaction costs (along with risk premiums) do not explain the high interest rates charged—because, in fact, these costs are low!

- Bouman (1989, p. 9)—"Informal intermediaries . . . survive on the basis of competitiveness, financial viability and low cost operations."
- Germidis, Kessler, and Meghir (1991) find explicitly that lender transaction costs in the informal sector are low because of low overhead; low default risk; good, cheap information on the creditworthiness of potential borrowers; and interlinked credit contracts. Thus:

> Transaction costs in the informal sector are low (administrative expenses such as premises and overhead costs are low or non-existent) . . . Default risk is minimized by informal lenders in a number of ways. Information on the credit worthiness of potential borrowers can be obtained easily and relatively cheaply, since lenders usually live and work in the circumscribed area of their financial operations, which also allows for effective follow-up on outstanding loans. Lenders employ an additional means of minimizing default risk: through interlinked credit contracts, i.e. with *ex ante* or *ex post* tie-in arrangements established between the credit market on the one hand and the land, labor, or product markets on the other, through the overlapping personae of moneylenders, landlords, employers, or produce dealers."
>
> —p. 18

A study by Aryeetey and others (1996) found that in Ghana, Malawi, Nigeria, and Tanzania transaction costs in banks for standard loans ranged between 12 and 19 percent of the amounts lent. In contrast, the transaction costs for informal lenders providing microloans were generally less than 3 percent—primarily because these loans carried low overhead costs. Thus the transaction costs of the informal lenders were lower than those of the banks despite the fact that the average bank loan was substantially larger than the average loan provided by the informal lenders.

Risks

Moneylenders manage risk in a number of ways. A distinction must be made, however, between lenders who lend their own or borrowed funds and bear the risk of default, and those who act as brokers, matching savers with borrowers and charging the borrowers a commission. In the latter case, all or part of the risk may be borne by the savers. Thus in a study of moneylenders in Bolivia, "Seventy-five percent of informal financiers surveyed were 'brokers.' The majority did not bear the risk of default" (Malhotra 1992a, p. 6). Another example of lenders who match savers and borrowers comes from the owners of Bank Dagang Bali (BDB) in Indonesia (see chapter 10); before opening the bank in 1970, its owners operated as informal brokers of this type.

Managing risk through interlinked transactions is especially common. In their study of informal credit markets in the Philippines, Floro and Yotopoulos (1991, p. 87) found that:

> Examining the impact of market interlinkage on the interest rate, it can be noted that unlinked loans have in general significantly higher interest rates, whether contractual or effective, than linked loans. Moreover, for both linked and unlinked loans, the nominal interest rate is lower in developed areas and higher in the marginal areas. These trends indicate, in part, the importance of the risk premium; the risk of default is greater in unlinked loans and, other things equal, it is greater in the poorer agricultural areas.

Moneylenders accept forms of collateral ranging from land to watches, from telephone lines to antique shawls

Other methods of risk management include screening techniques that enable careful selection of borrowers; interest rates that incorporate a range of risk premiums, enabling the lender to match the premium with the borrower's risk profile; and, particularly for large loans, collateral requirements.

Moneylenders often use collateral to manage the risk of large loans. But they generally accept a much wider range of loan guarantees than do banks. Informal moneylenders accept forms of collateral ranging from land to watches, from telephone lines[26] to antique shawls—although the type of security is matched with the size of the loan. Thus for large loans, collateral in the form of land, buildings, or vehicles is often required.

Because they typically live and work near their borrowers, informal moneylenders face risks from covariant shocks. Unlike many banks, the business activities and risks of informal lenders are usually not regionally diversified, and lenders and borrowers are often subject to the same external shocks. The effect on lenders is heightened by market interlinkages with borrowers. Thus lenders may be unable to collect loan payments when the region is faced with drought, flood, pest attack, epidemics, macroeconomic shock, warfare, or other collective shock. Under these circumstances lenders may face substantial losses. However, lenders and borrowers who live in the same area and who participate in the same local political economy often search for ways to maintain ongoing economic relationships during such crises. Thus some lenders may forgive interest payments, while others may collect only interest and reschedule loan payments. In some areas lenders and borrowers expect to share risks in cases of observable external shocks (Udry 1993).

Are the transaction costs and risks of informal commercial lenders high or low?

Are the transaction costs and risks of informal commercial lenders high or low? The answer is "both"—depending on the circumstances

The answer to this question is "both"—depending on the circumstances. Lenders' transaction costs and risks can be high. But they can also be low, especially for repeat borrowers. As Long (1968, p. 276) pointed out more than 30 years ago, there is considerable variation in informal financial markets:

> In most Asian countries, the agricultural credit markets . . . are not classifiable either as fully competitive or fully monopolized. Competition may prevail in one village market while the next is under the control of a single lender. Even within a village one borrower may have several sources of loans, while another lacking alternatives may be forced to pay monopolized rates.

Consistent with Long's argument, Floro and Yotopoulos (1991) demonstrate not only that lenders price their loans with different risk premiums, but that lender transaction costs vary depending on a number of interlinked variables. These include the type of contract, the type of lender (farmer-lenders are distinguished from trader-lenders in their aims and their preferred clients), whether the loans are linked to other transactions, and the extent of layering in the informal credit market.

Overall, lenders' transaction costs and risks can be high, but—especially when there are interlinked transactions with borrowers in other markets—they are often low. Thus, by themselves, transaction costs and risk premiums cannot account for the high interest rates typically charged in informal commercial credit markets.

What Interest Rates Do Moneylenders Charge?

Extensive data on moneylenders' interest rates in many countries date back to at least the 19th century, and in some cases longer. Moneylenders' terms and interest rates are described in detail in Henry Mayhew's classic study of poverty in 19th century London, *London Labour and the London Poor*. For example, Mayhew (1968 [1861–62], vol. 1, p. 30) describes the costermongers (peddlers selling fruit, vegetables, fish, and other food in the streets using carts, barrows, or baskets) among whom:

it is estimated that not more than one-fourth of the entire body trade upon their own property. Some borrow their stock money, others borrow the stock itself, others again borrow the donkey-carts, barrows, or baskets, in which their stock is carried around, whilst others borrow even the weights and measures by which it is meted out.

Mayhew continues:

> The reader, however uninformed as to the price the poor usually have to pay for any loans they may require, doubtlessly need not be told that the remuneration exacted for the use of the above-named commodities is not merely confined to the legal 5£ per centum per annum; still many of even the most "knowing" will hardly be able to credit the fact that the ordinary rate of interest in the costermongers' money-market amounts to 20 percent per week,[27] or no less than 1040£ a year, for every 100£ advanced.
>
> But the iniquity of this usury in the present instance is felt, not so much by the costermongers themselves, as by the poor people whom they serve; for of course the enormous rate of interest must be paid out of the profits on the goods they sell, and consequently added to the price, so that coupling this overcharge with the customary short allowance—in either weight or measure, as the case may be—we can readily perceive how cruelly the poor are defrauded, and how they not only get often too little for what they do, but have to pay too much for what they buy.

By themselves, transaction costs and risk premiums cannot account for the high interest rates typically charged in informal commercial credit markets

Mayhew provides many details of costermongers' borrowing for their stock, barrows, and baskets, and examines closely borrowing by poor people in other occupations as well. Among the costermongers, "it is seldom that a lower sum than 10s is borrowed and never a higher sum than 2£ . . . Sometimes a loan is effected only for a day, generally a Saturday, as much as 2s, 6d being sometimes given for the use of 5s; the 5s being of course repaid in the evening" (vol. 1, p. 30). If calculated as an effective monthly interest rate, this is a rate of 19,175,000 percent (see table 6.1 for method of calculation).

The nature of the data

While data about moneylenders' interest rates are extensive, they are difficult to compare and analyze. The problems mentioned earlier about data on informal commercial credit markets hold most strongly for information on interest rates—which are often considered sensitive, even secret, matters. This is especially the case in countries that have usury laws. Overall, accurate interest rate information is often difficult to obtain, especially from lenders.

Shipton (1991, p. 23) comments on the wide range of interest rates found in the Gambia: "The wide variation may result in part from the secrecy surrounding interest charges. Not only is it common for researchers to receive inaccurate reports, but there are also uncertainties and disagreements in the rural population itself as to what rates are conventional." In his study of moneylenders in Pakistan, Aleem (1993, p. 134) says that "interviews [with lenders] were carried out with the understanding that the interviewees would not have to provide information on interest rates charged; information on the costs of borrowing was obtained from the demand side."

On several occasions I have been living in Indian and Indonesian villages when survey teams came through asking questions about credit. Moneylenders were very active in these villages, charging poor borrowers nominal monthly effective interest rates from about 10 to more than 100 percent and, in India, also managing credit in order to drive borrowers to default to gain their labor or land. Yet the survey teams were invariably informed that there had been moneylenders in the village in the past ("in our fathers' time," "in our grandfathers' time," "many years ago"), but certainly not any more!

Not surprisingly, authors writing about moneylenders are often ambiguous about such matters as linked and unlinked loans, whether the interest rates cited are charged on the original loan balance or on the declining balance, whether interest is collected up front, whether commissions are charged, whether interest is compounded, and about the definitions of terms used and whether (and how) calculations were made.

Although some studies on moneylenders and their interest rates are excellent,[28] data for the developing world generally cannot be accurately compared across countries (or in many cases even across regions) or well analyzed. Nevertheless, abundant evidence demonstrates two points.

First, there is a wide range of interest rates in informal moneylending, the result of multiple types of credit arrangements (see Germidis, Kessler, and Meghir 1991). This is clearly demonstrable. A corollary, which cannot be proven but which I believe to be widely applicable, is that poor people generally pay the higher interest rates in their lender's range. Without exception, all the informal moneylenders and borrowers with whom I have talked about credit and interest rates—over more than 30 years and in many developing countries—have told me that the high end of their interest rate ranges is primarily for poor borrowers and for high-risk borrowers. The moneylenders whom I know place the poor and the risky in two separate categories, although these can overlap.

Moneylenders generally do not lend to risky borrowers. But they typically add an extra risk premium to the interest rates of borrowers considered even slightly above the lenders' normal risk level. However, the poor are charged higher interest rates because they have low bargaining power, and because the transaction costs to lenders in making small loans are essentially the same as those in making larger loans. If interest rates were the same, smaller loans would be less profitable.

Second, in many parts of the world moneylenders' interest rates are much higher than the interest rates required to maintain profitable, self-sufficient mi-

The poor are charged higher interest rates because they have low bargaining power, and because the lenders' transaction costs are essentially the same for large and small loans

Source	Country, year(s)	Reported interest rate	Other available information	Monthly effective interest rate	Annual inflation rate [a]
1. Von Pischke 1991	Philippines, late 1980s	20%/day	Maturity: 1 day	23,638%	Range during 1987–90: 3.8–14.1%
2. Von Pischke 1991	Philippines, late 1980s	20%/6 days	Maturity: 6 days Number of payments: 1	149%	Range during 1987–90: 3.8–14.1%
3. BRI 1996a	Indonesia, early 1990s	5–10%/day	Maturity: 1 day	332–1,645%	Range during 1990–95: 7.5–12.5%
4. BRI 1996a	Indonesia, early 1990s	100%/week	Maturity: 1 week Number of payments: 1	1,939%	Range during 1990–95: 7.5–12.5%
5. Floro and Yotopoulos 1991	Philippines, 1984	6.2–32.0%/month on declining loan balance	Rates are lower in developed regions	6.2–32.0%	50.3% (1984)
6. Germidis, Kessler, and Meghir 1991	Philippines, 1980s	100% markup on purchase price of consumer items	Payments: daily installments	30%[b]	Range during 1980–82: 10.2–18.2%
7. Siamwalla and others 1993	Thailand, 1984–87	2–10%/month	Typical maturity: 6 months. Rates are lower in developed regions	2–10%	Range during 1984–87: 0.9–2.5%
8. Sutoro and Haryanto 1990	Indonesia, 1988	13.4–14.8%/month (on average) on declining balance		13.4–14.8% (on average)	8% (1988)
9. BRI-CPIS unpublished	Indonesia, 1980s	5–40%+/month flat rate	Rates of 5–10% were not found among poor borrowers	5–67%+[c]	Range during 1980–90: 4.7–18.0% and above
10. BRI 1997b	Indonesia, early 1990s	20%/2 months	Maturity: 2 months Number of payments: 1	10%	Range during 1990–95: 7.5–12.5%
11. BRI 1996a	Indonesia, early 1990s	50%/month flat rate	Payments: daily installments	132%	Range during 1990–95: 7.5–12.5%
12. Mosley 1996	Indonesia, 1993	5–60%/month on declining loan balance		5–60%	12.5% (1993)
13. Hossain 1988	Bangladesh, 1982	125% average annual rate		10.4% (on average)	12.5% (1982)
14. Montgomery, Bhattacharya, and Hulme 1996	Bangladesh, 1992	10%/month		10%[d]	4.3% (1992)

Table continues on next page

Table **6.1**

(continued)

Source	Country, year(s)	Reported interest rate	Other available information	Monthly effective interest rate	Annual inflation rate [a]
15. Aleem 1993	Pakistan, 1980–81	18–200% annual rates on declining loan balance; 78.7% average annual rate		1.5–16.7%	11.9% (1980 and 1981)
16. Rutherford 2000	India, 1995–97	For a 1,000 rupee loan, 150 rupees deducted upfront as fee; borrower then makes 10 weekly payments of 100 rupees each		14%	Range during 1995–97: 7.2–10.2%
17. Robinson unpublished	Bolivia, 1992–94	8–20%/month flat rate		8–44%[e]	Range during 1992–94: 7.9–12.1%
18. Robinson unpublished (1994)	Bolivia, 1994	10%/day	Maturity: 1 day. Found in some rural areas	1,645%	7.9% (1994)
19. Malhotra 1992a	Bolivia, 1989	6–10%/month	In urban areas	6–15%[f]	15.2% (1989)
20. Mosley 1996	Bolivia, 1993	3–5%/month	In urban areas	3–5%	8.5% (1993)
21. IAIC cited in Mosley 1996	Bolivia, 1991	12%/month		12%	21.4% (1991)
22. Carstens 1995	Mexico, early 1990s	10–30%+/month		10–30%+	Range during 1990–94: 7.0–26.7%
23. ACCIÓN unpublished	Nicaragua, 1997	5%/day	Payments: daily installments	332%	1996: 11.6% 1997: 9.2%
24. ACCIÓN unpublished	Ecuador, 1997	10%/month flat rate	Maturity: 2 months Payments: daily installments	20%	1996: 24.4% 1997: 30.6%
25. Buckley 1996a	Kenya, 1992	25%/month	Typical maturity: 1 month	25%	29.5% (1992)
26. Robinson unpublished	Kenya, 1994	10–25%/month flat rate		10–25%[g] 15–35%[h]	29% (1994)
27. Shipton 1991	The Gambia, 1985–90	50–150%/ 6–8 months; 100%/6–8 months most common; annual rate can range to 1,000%	Typical maturity: 6–8 months Number of payments: 1. Interest rate may or may not be time dependent	6.2–25.0%[i]	Range during 1985–90, excluding 1986: 8.3–23.5% 1986: 56.6%
28. Buckley 1996b	Malawi 1993	100%	Interest rate not time dependent[j]	17–100%[k]	19.7% (1993)

Table **6.1**

(continued)

Note: The table does not include reports published after 1980 if the data about the loans were collected before then. Calculations of effective monthly interest rates are made using the formula $R = (1 + I)^n - 1$, where R is the nominal effective monthly interest rate, I is the nominal interest rate for the period reported, and n is the number of such periods in a month (see Rosenberg 1996). Because of the ambiguity of many of the dates, the interest rates are not adjusted for inflation. However, annual inflation rates for the approximate years cited are provided. In the absence of information about whether rates are calculated on the original balance (flat rate) or on the declining balance, and whether there are commissions or upfront interest payments, the more conservative assumption is made. It should be noted, however, that these common practices can increase effective rates substantially. For example, use of a flat interest rate calculation may raise the effective interest rate by 50–100% or more. Conversions from daily or weekly rates to monthly rates have assumed 30 days a month and 4.35 weeks a month. These calculations were made with the help of Richard Rosenberg, whose advice is gratefully acknowledged.

a. Annual inflation rates as measured by the consumer price index, reflecting the annual percentage change in the cost to the average consumer of acquiring a fixed basket of goods and services. Taken from International Monetary Fund, *International Financial Statistics Yearbook 1998*.

b. Assumes a six-month loan.

c. The low end (5%) assumes a one-month, one-payment loan. The high end (67%) assumes a six-month, weekly payment loan.

d. Assumes a one-month, one-payment loan. Although the authors do not specify, experience in Bangladesh leads me to believe that for loans with multiple installment payments, the interest would generally be charged on the original loan balance; the effective interest rate would then be higher.

e. The low end (8%) assumes a one-month, one-payment loan. The high end (44%) assumes a loan at the 20% rate with daily payments.

f. The low end (6%) assumes a one-month, one-payment loan. The high end (15%) assumes a six-month term with monthly payments of principal and interest.

g. Assumes a six-month, one-payment loan.

h. Assumes a six-month, monthly payment loan.

i. The normal range is from 6.2% for a one-payment, eight-month loan at 50% to 25.0% for a one-payment, eight-month loan at 150%. However, Shipton also reports loans up to an annual interest rate of 1,000%.

j. The author does not specify, but it appears that the expectation would be for the loan to be repaid within an agricultural season. The same interest would be charged if the loan were used by the borrower for a week, for a month, or for a whole season.

k. The low end (17%) assumes a six-month, one-payment loan. The high end (100%) assumes a six-month, monthly payment loan.

crofinance institutions. Even when borrowers' transaction costs are included, as demonstrated below, the total cost of borrowing from a moneylender is typically much higher than that of borrowing from a Bank Rakyat Indonesia (BRI) or a BancoSol (Bolivia).

Examples of nominal interest rates of moneylenders in developing Asia

Examples of nominal interest rates in informal credit markets in Asia are provided below; the data used are drawn from a wide variety of sources and from six countries.[29] The selections are from developing Asia simply because I am most familiar with this region; some examples from other parts of the developing world are provided in the next section. Table 6.1 and figure 6.1 summarize the data on the loans that were made during 1980–97, both in Asia and elswhere, and convert the lenders' stated interest rates into monthly effective rates for purposes of comparison. Figure 6.1 provides examples of interest rates in 13 countries from the 28 sources shown in table 6.1. Wherever ranges of interest rates are given in table 6.1, both the high and the low ends of the range are included in figure 6.1, which covers a total of 41 interest rates.

The definitions of the terms used, the types of interest rates cited, and the level of information about loan terms vary considerably among the different sources. Thus the interest rates are cited below as reported in each source. Where

Figure **6.1**

Monthly effective interest rates: informal commercial moneylenders compared with BRI's unit desas and BancoSol

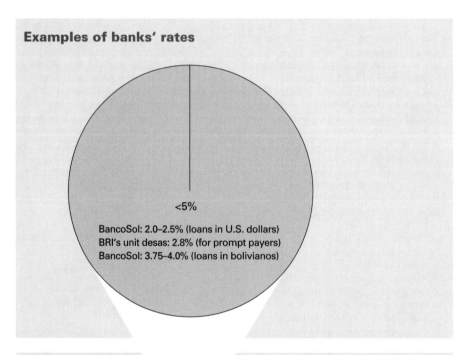

Examples of banks' rates

<5%

BancoSol: 2.0–2.5% (loans in U.S. dollars)
BRI's unit desas: 2.8% (for prompt payers)
BancoSol: 3.75–4.0% (loans in bolivianos)

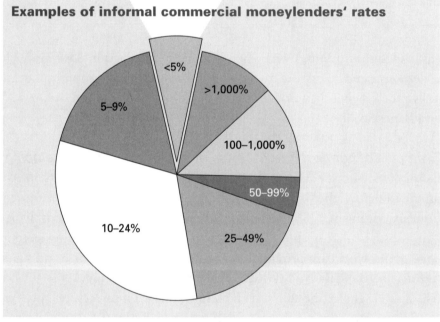

Examples of informal commercial moneylenders' rates

<5%
>1,000%
100–1,000%
50–99%
25–49%
10–24%
5–9%

Note: Examples of informal commercial moneylenders' rates are drawn from table 6.1. See the note to table 6.1 for methods of calculation. Because of ambiguities about dates in many sources, the interest rates are not adjusted for inflation. See table 6.1 for annual inflation rates. Whenever a range of interest rates is given in table 6.1, the high (H) and low (L) ends of the range are both reported here. Reference numbers for the 28 examples in table 6.1 are as follows: >1,000%: 1, 3H, 4, 18; 100–1,000%: 2, 3L, 11, 23, 28H; 50–99%: 9H, 12H; 25–49%: 5H, 6, 17H, 22H, 25, 26H, 27H; 10–24%: 7H, 8, 10, 13, 14, 15H, 16, 19H, 21, 22L, 24, 26L, 28L; 5–9%: 5L, 9L, 12L, 17L, 19L, 20H, 27L; <5%: 7L, 15L, 20L. With the exception of 1998 and 1999 in Indonesia (when none of the Indonesian loans cited here was taken), annual inflation rates (measured by the consumer price index) in Bolivia and Indonesia have been below 15 percent since BancoSol opened in 1992 and since BRI's unit desas began to operate commercially in 1984.

information is available on whether interest is charged on the original or declining loan balance, whether commissions are charged, and the like, these data are included. Often, however, this kind of information has not been provided. Because the dates to which the data refer are often unclear, it has also not been possible to use real, inflation-adjusted interest rates; all interest rates cited are nominal. Still, with three exceptions the annual inflation rates in all the Asian countries cited were less than 15 percent during all the years in which the reported loans could have been made. In other countries annual inflation ranged from 7 percent to 57 percent (see table 6.1 and figure 6.1).[30] The overall picture on interest rates is remarkably consistent: credit from moneylenders is generally expensive for developing country borrowers, especially poor ones.

The examples from Asia are grouped into four broad categories of informal commercial moneylending. The first three are classified by length of loan maturity; the fourth is a general category for all loans in which the lender's expectation is not repayment but borrower default. After the anticipated default the lender gains possession of the borrower's land or labor, or is able to buy from the borrower at monopsony prices.

As in other aspects of moneylending, these categories do not represent discrete types. Rather, they are found along a continuum. Thus the boundaries of the first three categories— very short-term loans, short- and medium-term loans (less than one year), and long-term loans (more than one year)—are flexible and can vary considerably in different areas and for different types of loans. Loans that aim at borrower default are a special case. In some areas all four loan categories can be found together (parts of India; see Robinson 1988 and Bell 1993), while in other areas none is common (parts of China; see Feder and others 1993).

This discussion of interest rates refers only to those of informal commercial moneylenders. It does not include informal loans from family, friends, or neighbors, or credit from ROSCAs or other informal organizations.

Very short-term credit. Loans with maturities of a day, a week, or a few weeks are especially common among the poorest borrowers in both rural and urban areas, and these loans often carry very high interest rates. Such credit is typically used for working capital, consumption, or both. There are many variations. Table 6.1 provides conversions to monthly effective interest rates for some of the examples provided. The differences between the stated interest rate and the effective interest rate, which can be very large, are due to practices common among moneylenders such as charging "flat" rates on the original (rather than the declining) balance, requiring upfront interest payment, charging a commission, and requiring daily repayment (see table 6.1 for the method of calculation of the effective interest rates). In many cases, however, information was unavailable on whether the stated interest rates were on the original or declining balance, compounded or not compounded, and so on. In every case the most conservative assumption was made. The actual rates are probably considerably higher in most cases.

An example from the Philippines demonstrates informal urban supplier credit. A street vendor obtains fresh produce each morning for 50 pesos and repays

A street vendor obtains fresh produce each morning for 50 pesos and repays 60 pesos each afternoon. This borrower is paying an effective monthly interest rate of 23,638 percent

60 pesos each afternoon (Von Pischke 1991, pp. 184–85; see also Germidis, Kessler, and Meghir 1991, pp. 89–90). The street vendor is paying an effective monthly interest rate of 23,638 percent (see table 6.1, no. 1). This rate, 20 percent a day, is common in parts of Asia and Latin America, where it is widely known as "five-six" terms (six units are returned for five units borrowed).[31] In another example from the Philippines (see table 6.1, no. 2), vendors obtain 1,000 pesos of dried fish from a wholesaler each Monday morning and repay 200 pesos each day for six days (Monday through Saturday) (Von Pischke 1991, p. 184). This represents an effective monthly rate of 149 percent. Also found in Indonesia, five-six terms are known there as *sepuluh kembali duabelas*—literally, "10 comes back 12."

Two examples of short-term rural credit in Indonesia (see table 6.1, nos. 3 and 4) were discussed in box 1.1. AC, a market woman who sells bean sprouts daily in the local market, paid a 5–10 percent daily "commission" to her supplier (equivalent to a nominal monthly interest rate of 332–1,645 percent). RM, who makes stoves from scrap metal, paid 100 percent interest to a local moneylender for a one-week loan repaid at the end of the week (equivalent to an effective monthly rate of 1,939 percent) (BRI 1996a, pp. 6–8).

Short- and medium-term credit. Loans with maturities ranging from a few weeks to one year are common in informal commercial credit markets. Such loans are typically used for working capital, consumption, investment, or combinations of these. A borrower who repays promptly may take multiple loans sequentially within a single year. Loan security may or may not be required; loan terms depend primarily on the amount of the loan and the relationship between lender and borrower (smaller loans may have higher rates). Some examples of interest rates charged are provided below.

In their 1984 survey of three provinces in the Philippines, Floro and Yotopoulos (1991, pp. 86–87) found that monthly effective interest rates for informal lending in the study area ranged from 6.2–32.0 percent. In addition, unlinked loans carried higher rates than linked loans, and both types of loans had lower rates in developed than in marginal areas. Germidis, Kessler, and Meghir (1991, pp. 89–90) report on the "Bombay merchants" in the Philippines, trader-lenders who take orders for consumer goods, usually appliances, and sell these to clients on installment—typically with a 100 percent markup on the price (a 30 percent effective monthly interest rate, assuming a six-month loan).

Based on three major surveys (1984–87), Siamwalla and others (1993, p 168) found that "in much of Thailand except the commercialized Central Plains, the informal [effective] interest rate usually hovers around 5 to 7 percent per month for a loan of 8,000 baht (US $320) for a period of six months . . . Some of the more remote provinces report a rate of 10 percent per month, while the rate in the Central Provinces is only 2 or 3 percent per month" (see table 6.1, no. 7).

In Indonesia, BRI's KUPEDES Development Impact Survey (Sutoro and Haryanto 1990) found that in 1988 the average effective monthly interest rate charged by informal moneylenders was 13.4 percent. For loans from commodity

There is wide variation in loan terms, which depend primarily on the amount of the loan and the relationship between lender and borrower

wholesalers, which were usually working capital advances, the monthly effective rates averaged 14.8 percent. But there have been wide variations in interest rates. Research conducted in Indonesia throughout the 1980s found that moneylenders' monthly effective interest rates to low-income borrowers ranged from about 5 percent to more than 1,900 percent.[32] Mosley (1996, p. 38) found effective monthly rates from 5–60 percent (see table 6.1, no. 12).

At the lower end of this range, as shown in box 1.1, is NP, a woman who produces bean curd (see table 6.1, no. 10). In the early 1990s she paid 20 percent interest for a one-payment, two-month loan (equivalent to an effective monthly rate of 10 percent). She borrowed 100,000 rupiah ($46), the maximum allowed, and returned 120,000 rupiah two months later (BRI 1997b, p. 7). A commonly found interest rate, also shown in box 1.1, is that paid by JR and TR, husband and wife shopkeepers in Yogyakarta (see table 6.1, no. 11). In the early 1990s they paid interest of 50 percent for a one-month loan; payments were made daily (BRI 1996a, p. 5). This rate is equivalent to an effective monthly rate of 132 percent.

In Bangladesh, Hossain (1988, p. 22) estimated the average annual rate of informal commercial interest in 1982 to be 125 percent (an average monthly effective rate of 10.4 percent). A 1992 study reported that moneylenders' interest rates in Bangladesh were "commonly around 10 percent a month or tied to unpalatable conditions" (Montgomery, Bhattacharya, and Hulme 1996, p. 127; see table 6.1, nos. 13 and 14).

Aleem's (1993, p. 147) detailed study of effective interest rates paid to moneylenders by farmers in Sind, Pakistan, in 1980-81 reports that "on an annual basis, the average cost of borrowing from informal sources was 78.7 percent. . . . the standard deviation [was] 38.1 percent, with rates ranging from a low of approximately 18 percent (still well above the 12 percent rate charged by banks) to a maximum of 200 percent" (see table 6.1, no. 15).

There is wide variation in the informal interest rates reported for India, generally depending on the degree of economic development in the particular region. Thus reported interest rates charged by informal commercial lenders in India in the 1970s and 1980s range from 2–8 percentage points a year above bank rates (of 13–16 percent) in urban areas,[33] through rates up to 300 percent a year in rural areas,[34] and finally to bonded labor in which the interest on the loan is repaid by the borrower's full-time work and which may, therefore, continue for many years.[35]

Rutherford (2000, p. 18) reports on a system in Vijayawada (Andhra Pradesh, India) in the 1990s, exemplified by a borrower who borrowed 1,000 rupees (see table 6.1, no. 16). The borrower agreed to repay 1,000 rupees of principal and 150 rupees of interest. But the borrower received only 850 rupees because the 150 rupees in interest was collected at the beginning of the loan. The borrower then paid 10 weekly installments of 100 rupees each. The effective monthly interest rate was 14 percent because the interest was paid up front and the borrower did not have the use of the entire 1,000 rupees—even though he paid interest on the full amount.

The loan was for 1,000 rupees but the borrower received 850 rupees because interest was collected up front. The effective monthly interest rate was 14 percent

Long-term loans. Much less common than the first two categories, long-term loans—those for more than one year—are normally provided in larger amounts than shorter-term loans and are typically used for investment capital. These are stock credit loans, according to the terms of Siamwalla and others (1993, p. 177), because the lender is interested less in the borrower's income flows than in her assets and liabilities. The loans can vary from several hundred to many thousands of dollars. An informal moneylender tends to make only a few large loans at any given time, and only to very well-known customers who are usually linked with the lender in other ways.

Interest rates for such loans appear to be similar to those charged for working capital loans, but collateral in the form of land, business assets, or vehicles is typically required. There is, of course, substantial variation among countries and regions in terms of the loan value that is perceived as representing a large loan. Thus in the early 1990s the point at which a loan from a moneylender was considered large enough to require collateral in the form of land or business assets was reported to be about $400 in rural Thailand (Siamwalla and others 1993, p 163) and $5,000 or more in urban Bolivia (Malhotra 1992a, p. 7).

There are many variations in the arrangements for collateral. Even within one type—land, for example—there are major differences in how the collateral requirements can affect both borrower and lender. These requirements depend on a number of factors, including the size of the loan, the quality of the land and the owner's water rights, the financial position of the borrower, and the relative power of the lender and borrower. In one arrangement a land title is simply deposited with the lender for security, while the borrower continues to use the land.

In usufruct loans, however, the lender uses the borrower's land until the loan principal is repaid, the use of the land being considered the interest on the loan. This type of loan is discussed by Siamwalla and others (1993, p. 166) for Thailand and by Floro and Yotopoulos (1991, pp. 78–79) for the Philippines (where it is called *sanglang-buhay,* or "live mortgage"). In contrast, *sanglang-patay* ("dead mortgage") refers to usufruct loans where the collateral is highly productive land; in this case use by the lender of the borrower's land, usually for three to five years, repays both principal and interest. Finally, in some undeveloped areas in rural India, locally powerful lenders may forcibly take possession of the borrower's land and hold it until the borrower returns both the loan's principal and interest (Robinson 1998).

Long-term loans may be related to local politics. When the lender is powerful, political support may be required from the borrower as part of the loan repayment. In some cases such support can substitute for repayment of part of the loan capital. In other cases it may substitute for collateral or for interest.

On the other hand, the locally powerful leader may be the borrower. When loans are made by political supporters to candidates for office, or to government officials, the loans may be repaid by the latter, in full or in part, through political favors. For example, in a village in Andhra Pradesh, India, the

When the lender is powerful, political support may be required from the borrower as part of the loan repayment

village headman and his elder brother made a loan to the member of the (state) legislative assembly (MLA) for their district. The loan was repaid partly in cash, partly in the MLA's support for the village head's reelection, and partly in helping the lenders to obtain contracts for a road and for a toddy shop.

In such instances, however, if adequate political support is not forthcoming from the lender, the borrower may refuse to repay the loan. On a different occasion the same village headman and his brother made a loan to another candidate for MLA who subsequently lost the election. The losing candidate judged the headman's support for him to be have been insufficient (and the headman's power to be relatively low since he had not supported the winning MLA candidate) and so refused to repay the loan (see Robinson 1988).

Loans can remain unpaid for a long time when they are linked with shifting political alliances and rivalries, especially if the creditor is less powerful than the debtor. Sometimes the borrower repays years later, when he again wants support from the lender. Sometimes the loan capital ends up with neither the borrower nor the lender. In one such case in Andhra Pradesh a lender had been unable for years to collect a loan from a borrower who was wealthier and more powerful than he. The borrower would not repay the loan, and the lender knew that he could neither force the borrower to repay nor collect through the courts. Finally, the lender sent the borrower's signed promissory note as the lender's contribution to a powerful Hindu temple in south India. The temple collected from the borrower immediately.

Loans to force borrower default. In some loans the lender's primary aim is not to collect interest payments but eventually to force the borrower to default. This aim may be accomplished by charging high and often compound interest on a relatively small loan. It may also be accomplished by providing a loan (or series of loans) larger than the borrower can afford. Either approach will likely drive the borrower to default. Through such default, the lender acquires the borrower's mortgaged land, a cheap long-term supply of attached or bonded labor, or monopsony power in setting commodity prices.

These loans, found for example in parts of South Asia and Latin America, are usually illegal. Nevertheless, they remain fairly common in some rural areas. A 1981 survey of bonded labor in India concludes that "the moneylender does not demand any security; money can be given at any hour of the day or night; in most cases no formalities are observed.... The main interest of the moneylender is to secure a source of cheap labour for himself, if possible, on a long-term basis" (Marla 1981, p. 4). In his discussion of "debt farming" in Bihar, Roth (1983, p. 62) elaborated the many ways in which credit is used to capture cheap labor for the long term (see also Sharma 1978 and Robinson 1988).

Bonded labor is a subset of what is known as "attached labor": a system whereby a laborer takes a loan, after which his labor (or that of a household member) belongs to the creditor until the loan is repaid (under a variety of payment systems). If the laborer is paid a sufficient wage, he can work off the loan within an agreed period But in bonded labor, one type of attached labor, the

In bonded labor the presumption is that the laborer's work cannot provide both subsistence and loan repayment within the stated period

presumption is that the laborer's work cannot provide both subsistence and loan repayment within the fixed period. For example, the laborer's full-time work may pay only the interest on the loan.

A report on debt bondage, especially in Latin America and South Asia, comments:

> Technically bonded laborers can end their state of servitude once the debt is repaid. But the fact of the matter is that this rarely occurs. Since debtors are often illiterate and lack basic math skills, they are easy prey for deception by moneylenders. A combination of low wages and usurious interest rates make it impossible to repay the initial debt. In many cases the debt increases because the employer deducts payment for equipment and tools or charges fines for faulty work. Sometimes the labor pledged is used to repay the interest on the loan but not the principal.
> —U.S. Department of Labor 1995, p. 2

Some female bonded laborers are required to provide sexual services to the lender, in addition to their agricultural or domestic labor

In 1972–73 I lived in a village of 732 people (139 households) in the Telangana region of Andhra Pradesh; I also visited there frequently during the late 1970s and early 1980s (Robinson 1988). The village, just 35 miles from the city of Hyderabad, the state capital, was still undeveloped. In 1973 I documented 55 cases of attached labor there; 20 were children under 12 or laborers who had been attached while under 12. Of the 55 attached laborers, 21 were clear examples of long-term bonded labor, which was, and is, illegal.

In this area, as in some other underdeveloped parts of India, a bonded laborer's full-time work pays only the interest on the loan; it neither repays the loan principal nor provides subsistence. Other members of the laborers' households provide their food. In most cases the laborer ends up having to reborrow from his lender or employer, perpetuating the bondage. The lender's only concern in such cases is to ensure that the laborer has enough food to be able to work. Some female bonded laborers are required to provide sexual services to the lender, in addition to their agricultural or domestic labor.

At the time I lived in the village, borrowers who had defaulted on loans and become bonded laborers as a result had been bonded for periods ranging from one month to more than 30 years. A few had inherited the bondage from a parent after the parent's death.

In the late 1970s, however, the central and state governments made strong attempts to implement the laws against bonded labor that were on the books. By 1980 attached labor in the village had decreased from 55 to 30 cases; only one was a child. Among the 30 attached laborers were 5 instances of long-term bonded labor (see Robinson 1998). While I do not have subsequent data from the village, bonded labor in the area appears to have decreased during the 1980s and 1990s as the area became more developed.

Without question, malicious moneylenders exist in backward areas of developing countries. However, loans intended to force borrower default can be decreased and even eliminated with economic development and government efforts. It is worth noting, though, that loans whose purpose is to force borrowers to default are found not only in backward regions of developing countries, but in developed countries as well.[36]

Examples of nominal interest rates of moneylenders in other parts of the developing world

Informal commercial moneylending is less common in some parts of the world (China, parts of Africa) than in others (South Asia, parts of Latin America). Yet it seems remarkably similar wherever it is found. Examples of interest rates charged by moneylenders in Latin America and Africa are given below. Again, the data are scattered and incomplete, and real interest rates cannot be provided. Four of the seven countries considered here had annual inflation rates that were above 20 percent for some of the years in which the loans discussed were provided. In all but one instance, however, annual inflation rates were below 31 percent.[37]

Working in Bolivia with urban and rural microentrepreneurs during 1992–94, I found that people I knew were paying informal moneylenders monthly interest rates that ranged from 8–20 percent, equivalent to effective monthly rates of 8–44 percent (see table 6.1, no. 17).[38] When they paid in multiple installments, the rate was always calculated on the original loan balance. In some rural areas I found loans of 10 percent a day (see table 6.1, no. 18): the borrower received a loan of 100 bolivianos one day and repaid 110 bolivianos the next day (equivalent to a monthly effective rate of 1,645 percent).

Malhotra (1992a, p. 6) cites commissions of 6–8 percent a month for urban Bolivian moneylenders, most of whom are brokers (*tramitadores*) who match savers with borrowers; the brokers do not bear the risk of these loans. She also makes reference to an urban moneylender whose rate was 10 percent a month (p. 4; see table 6.1, no. 19). Mosley (1996, p. 21) quotes informal moneylender interest rates of 3–5 percent a month in urban areas in 1993 (see table 6.1, no. 20). The Inter-American Investment Corporation (1991, cited by Mosley 1996, p. 30) quotes 12 percent a month for moneylenders in Bolivia in 1991 (see table 6.1, no. 21), but annual inflation was higher in 1991 (21.4 percent) than in the later years cited above. Using the most conservative assumptions about interest rates unless specific information is available to show otherwise, these rates are treated here as effective interest rates. In practice they are likely to be flat interest rates on the original loan balances, so the effective rates could be higher.

Carstens (1995, ch. 3) analyzes the many types of informal commercial lenders in Mexico; effective interest rates there range from about 10 percent to more than 30 percent a month (see table 6.1, no. 22).[39] In chapter 3 we heard from AD in Nicaragua, who paid $5 a day interest for a $100 loan from her local moneylender for working capital for her foodstand. As she put it, "I felt I had somebody's hands around my throat every day." She did—her effective monthly interest rate was 332 percent (see table 6.1, no. 23). EC, the herb dealer from Ecuador, paid 10 percent a month interest on the original balance of a two-month loan of $880, making daily payments (equivalent to an effective monthly rate of 20 percent; see table 6.1, no. 24)).

Effective interest rates in Mexico range from about 10 percent to more than 30 percent a month

In Malawi "most respondents reported that moneylenders generally got a 100 percent return on their loans whether the loan was to be repaid in a week, a month, or a season"

Buckley (1996a, p. 285) reports that short-term loans in Kenya, usually for one month, normally carry a monthly interest rate of 25 percent (see table 6.1, no. 25). In 1994 I found moneylender interest rates in Kenya ranging from 10–25 percent a month on the original loan balance (see table 6.1, no. 26). Shipton (1991, p. 123) reports that in the Gambia, "merchants and other rural lenders commonly charge interest of 50 to 150 percent over six to eight months [equivalent to a 6–25 percent effective monthly rate], but rates vary enormously outside this range" (see table 6.1, no. 27). "The figure of 100 percent [is] the most commonly recorded—but the rates may vary between 0 and over 1,000 percent if calculated in monetary values and on an annual basis" (p. 238). These are typically loans that are repaid in one payment at harvest time.

In some areas the amount of interest on loans is fixed but the maturity of the loan may vary. For these loans, interest rates do not necessarily accrue at a constant rate over time. Thus in rural Gambia a three-month loan often carries the same stated interest (100 percent) as a six-month loan (Shipton 1991, p. 127). Buckley (1996b, p. 361) reports a similar arrangement for Malawi: "most [respondents] reported that moneylenders generally got a 100 percent return on their loans irrespective of the time-frame [see table 6.1, no. 28]. Whether the loan was to be repaid in a week, a month, or a season, the standard cost was a doubling of the original amount lent."

Shipton (1991, p. 128) comments that loans in rural Gambia that are not paid when due at harvest time do not necessarily keep accruing interest charges. If payment is not made until the following year's harvest, interest may be charged for the use of the loan over the second year—or it may not; this is negotiable. "Linear time is not taken for granted in loan arrangements. Rather there are at least several modes or idioms, temporal or a temporal, linear or nonlinear, for constructing agreements. Which will be chosen is negotiable, if not at the time of the deal, then in renegotiation later. In rural Gambia, time is an optative element."

What Are the Transaction Costs and Other Noninterest Costs for Borrowers?

Among all the debates about moneylenders, there seems to be little or no dispute about borrowers' transaction costs: typically they are low. Moneylenders are conveniently located for people who need microcredit; they live in the same or a nearby village, or in the nearest market town. Loan procedures are minimal, and cash is available quickly. Loan amounts, maturities, and payment schedules are flexible. There is little transportation cost or opportunity cost of time spent traveling or waiting. For small loans, collateral is often not required. However, not all demand is met. Potential borrowers with no links to a lender may be unable to obtain a loan at all, or may receive credit only at a very high interest rate.

Borrowers' transaction costs in obtaining credit from financial institutions are nearly always higher than those incurred in borrowing from moneylenders.

But there is a wide range of transaction costs for obtaining microloans in financial institutions. In Jaipur (India) LS, a small farmer, described to me his transaction costs in applying for a 5,000 rupee loan (about $150) at the local Regional Rural Bank (RRB) in 1995. The RRBs, local banks established and maintained with very large, continuing government investment, were begun in 1975 to provide subsidized loans to small and marginal farmers and to landless laborers. Each RRB is owned by a sponsoring commercial bank. As is discussed in chapter 7, the RRBs have generally been successful in mobilizing savings, but most have a dismal lending record. LS described his experience as an RRB loan applicant:

> In order to get the signatures I needed for the loan application, I made four trips to see to the *patwari* [village officer in charge of land records], and four trips to the *tehsildar* [revenue officer]. On the fourth trip to the patwari I could finally meet him. But I still could not get in to see the tehsildar. Then I asked a friend who is a relative of the tehsildar's servant to accompany me to the tehsildar's office. My friend came with me on my fifth trip. I paid the tehsildar's servant 25 rupees and got the signature. Then I had to make trips to two local banks and a cooperative in order to obtain "no dues" certificates [attesting that the applicant did not have outstanding or previously defaulted loans from these institutions]. Everywhere I went I had to pay. I had to find a loan guarantor and pay him 100 rupees. Next I went to the notary to obtain a "no encumbrance" certificate, for which the fee was 250 rupees. Including the transportation costs, I paid 900 rupees in all. In order to pay these expenses, I borrowed 1,000 rupees from a moneylender in my village for six weeks at 3 percent a month. However, my loan application was denied by the bank because the branch manager of the RRB did not have authority to give loans outside the credit target of the government's IRDP[40] loans.

At banks fixed loan categories often do not match the borrowers' cash flows and enterprise needs

Like most RRBs, this one limited its loans because its interest rates were subsidized, it was capital constrained, and its default rate was high.[41] There was considerable political interference in borrower selection and repayment. Losses were high, and each new subsidized loan meant a further loss to the bank.

In the end LS was out 900 rupees, plus the interest paid to the moneylender, plus the extensive opportunity cost of his time. Of course, not all microloan applicants bear such heavy transaction costs from banks (and some get the loans). But in my experience the high end of the transaction cost continuum is heavily populated by microloans from formal lenders—except in commercial microfinance institutions, which typically make a strong effort to keep these costs low.

Borrowers can also face other costs arising from a mismatch between the loan product and the enterprise. Loans are given for specific projects and amounts, and for set maturities. At banks fixed loan categories often do not match the borrowers' cash flows and enterprise needs. In 1996 a farmer in Rajasthan (India) wanted a small six-month loan for working capital for a tea stall he operated; instead he was given a larger three-year loan to develop his land. In eastern Uttar Pradesh (India) crop loans for paddy and sugarcane were too small to permit purchase of the required inputs. The same was true of loans for buffalo.

There may also be substantial opportunity costs of the borrower's time. Finally there may be psychological costs. Low-income borrowers from many countries have told me that when they enter a (conventional) bank branch, they are usually treated rudely. They must wait for long periods while better-dressed people are served. Staff speak to them abruptly and harshly, sometimes making jokes about them and refusing to answer their questions. Under such circumstances many rational borrowers will prefer an informal moneylender with high interest rates to a formal institution with other kinds of high costs. But is this the only choice?

The answer is no. Profitable, commercial microfinance institutions make a major effort to reduce borrowers' transaction and opportunity costs. Staff, who are well trained and motivated by incentives, are generally friendly and helpful to poor clients. Procedures, while not as simple as at the moneylender's, are nevertheless easy and quick. The institution's outlets are placed at locations that are convenient for clients. Waiting time is minimized. Loan products are flexible, and within limits can be tailored to customer's needs.

For example, BRI's unit *desas,* which provide loans to individual borrowers, have a standard package of loan terms. Within this package, however, borrowers are offered considerable flexibility in meeting their credit needs. Loans are available for a variety of maturities, from 3 months to 24 months for working capital loans and 36 months for investment loans. Repayment terms include monthly payments, seasonal payments, single payments (for loans with maturities of one year or less), and loans with grace periods up to 9 months. Prepayment of loans, with a rebate of the unearned interest, is permitted for most loans.

The possible combinations of maturities and payment terms offer 36 possible variations. Each of these is printed in loan tables that are used to determine which of the terms most closely meet the borrower's needs. Using the loan tables and reviewing the payment schedule with the borrower helps make loan arrangements transparent, helping the borrower customize her loan and reducing the chance that the staff member will try to collect extra fees or provide special terms to favored customers.

Loan application and approval are simple. Potential borrowers discuss their needs with the unit desa's credit officer, manager, or both. Applicants fill out a short loan application. If necessary, unit staff help applicants fill out the form. After the application has been filed, the credit officer visits the potential borrower at his workplace or home, appraises the activity for which the loan has been requested, and collects information on household economic activities and income flows. If an applicant is new, the credit officer will also ask neighbors, village officers, and the applicant's suppliers and buyers about his character. For

Borrowers'

transaction costs at

BRI's unit desas

are higher than

most borrowers

incur when

obtaining credit from

moneylenders. But

the total cost is

typically much lower

a repeat borrower, the application process is similar but shorter, and the field visit is less detailed. Collateral is normally required, but for smaller loans many different forms are acceptable, including motorcycles, bicycles, furniture, televisions and, tools. Some small loans are provided without collateral. "No encumbrance" certificates from notaries and "no dues" certificates from financial institutions are not required, nor are there other formalities except demonstration of ownership of the collateral. If land is used as collateral and if full title is not available, tax bills and tax receipts are acceptable.

Most loan decisions are made by the unit desa manager, although larger loans must be approved at the supervising branch. A loan decision for a new borrower typically takes four or five business days; loans that must be approved at the branch take slightly longer. A repeat borrower can usually obtain a decision within two or three days. Loans are normally disbursed immediately after approval is granted. A 1996 BRI survey of 1,341 borrowers found that 76 percent said they had received their loans within a week of applying for them; only 2 percent said it took more than two weeks (BRI 1996b). Borrowers reported unit staff to be friendly and helpful (98 percent) and to provide quick service (95 percent).

Borrowers' transaction costs at the unit desas are undoubtedly higher than most borrowers incur when obtaining credit from moneylenders. But when the difference in interest rates is considered, the total cost is typically much lower at the unit desas.

The Costs of Borrowing: Comparing Moneylenders with Bank Rakyat Indonesia's Unit Desas and BancoSol

The examples of interest rates discussed in this chapter are shown in table 6.1, excluding loans taken before 1980. Like the voices of the clients in chapter 3, the examples in table 6.1 do not represent a scientific sample. The table does, however, demonstrate the wide range of moneylenders' interest rates and types of loan arrangements reported from developing countries.

The table omits all loans made to force default, because there is no reasonable way to calculate the interest rate or cost to the borrower of a $25 loan that results in years of bonded labor or of acceptance of monopsony prices. Without such loans, the stated interest rates in table 6.1 range from about 2 percent a month (equivalent to an effective monthly rate of 2 percent, in the commercialized Central Plains of Thailand) to 20 percent a day (equivalent to an effective monthly rate of 23,638 percent, in Manila, the Philippines).

The stated interest rates in table 6.1 have been converted, as accurately as possible given the data, to monthly effective interest rates. But as noted, conservative assumptions have been used in the conversions to effective interest rates. Thus unless interest rates were specified as having been charged on the original balance (flat rates), they were assumed to be charged on the declining balance. Similarly, unless up-front interest payments, commissions, and the like were specified, it was

Up-front interest payments, commissions, and the like are common practices that substantially increase moneylenders' effective rates

assumed that they were not part of the loan. These are, however, common practices that substantially increase effective rates. Thus in many cases the actual effective monthly interest rates are likely to have been higher than shown in table 6.1.

Comparison is made in figure 6.1 between the monthly effective interest rates of the moneylenders shown in table 6.1 and those of BRI's unit desas and BancoSol. Because of the ambiguity in the dates of many of the entries, the rates in table 6.1 and figure 6.1 are not adjusted for inflation. However, table 6.1 shows annual inflation rates for the year (or range of years) when the loans from moneylenders were made.[42] Most of the annual inflation rates were less than 20 percent, and only two—the Philippines in 1984 (50.3 percent) and the Gambia in 1985 (56.6 percent)—were above 50 percent. With the exception of Indonesia in 1998 and 1999, annual inflation in Bolivia and Indonesia have been below 15 percent since BancoSol opened in 1992 and since BRI's unit desas became commercial microbanks in 1984. (The Indonesian loans in table 6.1 and figure 6.1 were made before 1998.)

It should be emphasized that figure 6.1 compares moneylenders' interest rates with two of the most efficient banks providing services to microfinance clients. The purpose is to show that as the microfinance revolution engenders more banks like these, many borrowers will have a lower-cost credit option than most now have. They will also gain access to regulated and supervised savings facilities appropriate for their needs.

Table 6.1 and figure 6.1 both contain some entries that represent single loans, while some represent averages, and others ranges of different-sized samples. Some entries are based on large and careful studies, others on only a few incidents. In addition to this statistical nightmare, many of the relevant data are missing: If there are multiple installment payments, is the interest calculated on the original or the declining loan balance? Is a commission paid? Is the interest paid at the beginning of the loan? Is the lender using the borrower's collateral? Is the interest rate compounded? Often we do not know, and the most conservative assumption is used.

The conversions were made to monthly rather than to annual rates because most loans from moneylenders are short term (although the borrower may reborrow frequently). Representing a mid-range between daily and annual rates, monthly rates are suitable for microfinance analysis.

The informal commercial moneylenders represented in figure 6.1 often charge far higher effective monthly interest rates than do BRI's unit desas (2.8 percent for most loans) and BancoSol (3.75 percent for loans in bolivianos and 2.0–2.5 percent for loans in U.S. dollars). Of the 41 monthly effective rates charged by moneylenders that are shown in this table, only 2 are below 5 percent—and neither is likely to be available to poor borrowers. One is from the Central Plains of Thailand, a well-developed, commercialized area; monthly effective rates elsewhere in rural Thailand range from 5–10 percent (Siamwalla and others 1993, p. 168). The other is the lowest in a range of the several reports from Bolivia shown in table 6.1; its data are drawn entirely from La Paz and the adjoining municipality, El Alto (Mosley 1996, p. 21).

Of the moneylenders' monthly effective interest rates, 27 percent are 50 percent or higher, and 22 percent are 100 percent or higher. Some are in thousands of percent

Thus, of the moneylenders' monthly effective interest rates shown in figure 6.1, 93 percent are above the rates of BRI's unit desas and BancoSol. Moreover, it is unlikely that many low-income borrowers have access to the loans within the other 7 percent.

As shown in figure 6.1, 76 percent of the moneylenders' monthly effective interest rates are 10 percent or higher, 44 percent of the rates are 25 percent or higher, 27 percent are 50 percent or higher, and 22 percent are 100 percent or higher. Some of the monthly effective rates charged by the moneylenders are in thousands of percent.

Given that with two exceptions, annual inflation in these countries and years was less than 31 percent, and that in many cases it was less than 15 percent, these are very high interest rates. More than three-quarters (76 percent) of the moneylenders' monthly effective interest rates are more than three times BRI's rates and BancoSol's rates for loans in dollars, and they are more than twice BancoSol's rates for loans in bolivianos. Figure 6.1 shows that 44 percent of the moneylenders' rates are at least nine times BRI's rate and BancoSol's dollar rate, and more than six times BancoSol's boliviano rate. More than a quarter of the moneylenders' rates (27 percent) are at least 18 times BRI's rate and BancoSol's dollar rate, and 12 times BancoSol's boliviano rate. As noted, when calculating the moneylenders' rates, all ambiguities were resolved by using the most conservative assumption; thus the actual difference between the moneylenders and the banks is likely to be considerably larger.

Given the lack of available data on borrowers' transaction costs, it is not possible to examine or to compare these, as has been done for interest rates. Yet it seems likely that many poor borrowers would probably prefer to bear the transaction costs of a loan from a BRI or a BancoSol if they could obtain credit at an interest rate that is one-third, one-tenth, or even one-twentieth the rate charged by their local moneylender.

Assuming five people to a household among the 4.5 billion people living in low- and lower-middle-income economies in 1999 (World Bank, *World Development Report 2000/2001*), there are 900 million households in those economies. If, estimating conservatively, we assume that informal commercial moneylenders supply credit to 30 percent of these households at least once a year,[43] this would mean that there are 270 million households borrowing from informal moneylenders in a year. Undoubtedly, however, many of these households borrow multiple times within a year.

Some of these households would not be acceptable borrowers to BRI, BancoSol, or other commercial microfinance institutions. Some households may have requirements (such as loans provided the day the application is made, or loans with one or two day maturities) that do not fit the constraints of most microfinance institutions. Still other households might consider the transaction costs too high—for example, travel expenses and time spent traveling from distant villages, provision of collateral at BRI, or the opportunity cost of time spent making weekly payments at BancoSol. There can be a mismatch in even the

44 percent of the moneylenders' rates are at least nine times BRI's rate; 27 percent are at least 18 times BRI's rate

best microfinance institutions between the terms of the loan and the business opportunities of the borrower.

Nevertheless, faced with paying 3 times the bank rates—or 9 times, 18 times, or more—many of the 270 million households would surely opt for a sustainable commercial microfinance institution if one were available to them. Moreover, many additional potential clients might want to save in these institutions. And the development effects on such clients and their households—higher incomes, better nutrition and health, improved housing, more children in school, decreased child labor—could reach more than 1 billion people.

Making Microfinance Competitive

Where informal commercial lenders and commercial microfinance institutions coexist in the same area, they are generally not close substitutes

Von Pischke (1991, p. 185) comments on the five-six terms found in the Philippines and elsewhere: "Monopoly profits of the sort implied by these examples would surely attract vigorous competition that would severely erode returns." Bouman (1984, p. 283) comments that "one should not expect monopoly profits to be terribly important since . . . competitive forces generally prevail." But as noted, this is not what typically happens in informal credit markets.

Rural credit markets have generally not been competitive—and especially not with regard to low-income clients. Most institutional rural credit is subsidized and capital constrained; it normally reaches relatively few borrowers, often rural elites. Most formal sector financial institutions have not been interested in competing for low-income rural clients on a commercial basis. Cooperatives, savings and loan associations, and credit unions also operate in rural credit markets, but many of these institutions are not particularly interested in serving the poor. Nongovernmental organizations (NGOs), which often do serve the poor, typically operate on a very small scale. While noncommercial loans from family, friends, and neighbors may be arranged, these are usually provided only for emergencies, for small amounts, and for special occasions—and they are normally unsuited as working capital finance.

Much of the volume of rural credit is usually provided by the informal credit market, operating in a form of monopolistic competition. Each lender provides loans to a relatively small number of borrowers with whom he is typically connected through linkages in other markets or political, kinship, or other ties, and from whom he has a high probability of collecting the loan. Lenders normally do not want to increase market share and have little incentive to lower interest rates. As noted in chapter 5, however, such lenders are often bank clients themselves and frequently have no objection if their borrowers receive bank credit (figure 6.2).

In the absence of an institutional alternative that provides access to commercial microcredit, borrowers tend to stay with informal commercial lenders despite the high costs of credit. Under these circumstances the prices for credit stay high. Much of the argument appears to hold for urban informal microcredit markets as well, although the evidence is much stronger for rural credit markets.

Figure **6.2**

**Meeting the demand from low-income
clients: informal commercial
moneylenders and commercial**

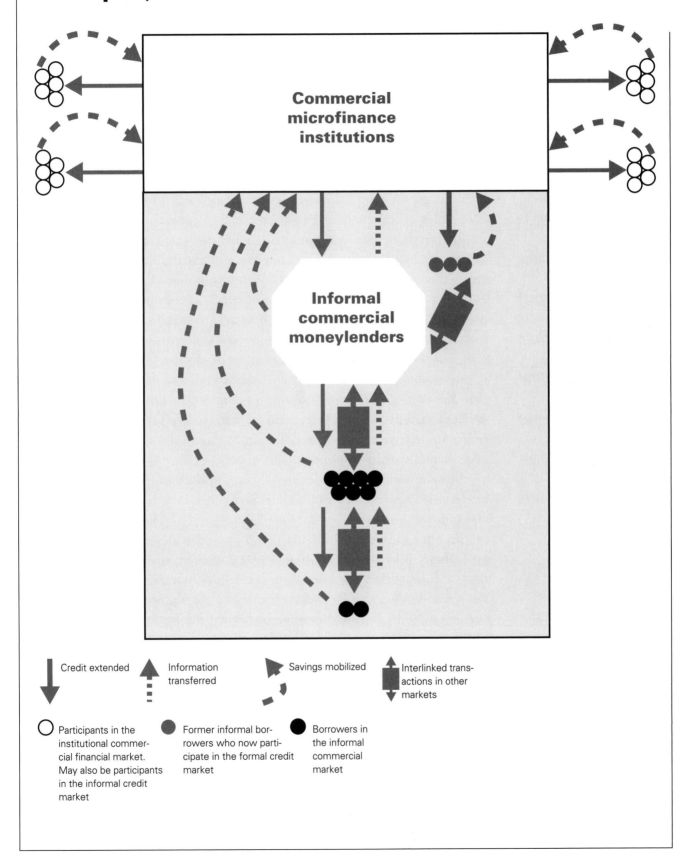

**Commercial
microfinance
institutions**

**Informal
commercial
moneylenders**

Credit extended

Information
transferred

Savings mobilized

Interlinked trans-
actions in other
markets

Participants in the
institutional commer-
cial financial market.
May also be participants
in the informal credit
market

Former informal bor-
rowers who now parti-
cipate in the formal credit
market

Borrowers in
the informal
commercial
market

As shown in figure 6.1, BRI's unit desas, BancoSol, and other commercial microfinance institutions can provide microcredit profitably at much lower interest rates than most moneylenders charge. These banks are sustainable for the long term. Why have they not been derailed by adverse selection and competition from the informal financial market? The reason is that they sorted out which information about informal lenders was correct (and learned from it), which was false (and discarded it), and which problems were true but not immutable (and overcame them)—and discovered where their comparative advantages lay.

Where informal commercial lenders and commercial microfinance institutions coexist in the same area, they are generally not close substitutes. Both can operate profitably. Unlike informal commercial lenders, however, formal institutions providing commercial microfinance aim for volume, try to achieve economies of scale, and have better protection against covariant shocks. Such institutions price their loan products competitively, and they provide incentives and training to managers and staff in order to expand their businesses and increase their profitability. Because the institutions maintain many small branches in areas convenient for customers, and because they offer loans with simple procedures, borrowers' transaction costs tend to be relatively low. These costs may still be higher than the transaction costs of borrowing from moneylenders. But the difference in interest rates tends to be so great that the total cost of borrowing from banks, especially for poor borrowers, is generally far lower than the cost of borrowing from moneylenders. In addition, banks can offer savings instruments and services that are attractive to low-income clients. And unlike moneylenders, commercial microbanking serves the public—all savers and all creditworthy low-income borrowers.

Most important, profitable microfinance institutions—again unlike moneylenders—engender competition. This has been clearly demonstrated in Bolivia and Indonesia, where other commercial microfinance institutions entered the market after the first microbanks demonstrated wide outreach and sustained profitability. Rhyne and Christen (1999) document the emergence of microfinance competition in a number of other developing countries as well. It has long been known that large-scale financial intermediation is crucial for economic growth.[44] For the first time in history, the intermediation process has begun on a large scale for low-income clients.

The formal sector, not the informal sector, has the potential to make microfinance competitive, and thus to contribute to economic growth and to development. This is one of the main forces driving the microfinance revolution.

Notes

1. As recounted by the late W.M. Gudger.
2. Feder and others (1993). "The data indicate that the institutional and non-institutional credit markets are segmented, and that non-institutional credit is generally non-fungible, and that consequently the bulk of the fungible credit is provided

Financial intermediation is crucial for economic growth. For the first time in history, the intermediation process has begun on a large scale for low-income clients

by institutional sources" (p.109). "The informal loans are often tied to large, exogenous, lumpy and highly visible special consumption purposes such as funerals and weddings, or to non-productive investment purposes such as the construction of residential housing . . . No interest is usually charged on informal loans" (p. 126).

3. See Germidis, Kessler, and Meghir (1991) for a recent review of studies on the share of formal and informal credit in rural areas of developing countries. The predominance of informal over formal credit sources is carefully documented there; see particularly table 1.3 and pp. 39–49. See also Von Pischke (1991); Hoff, Braverman, and Stiglitz (1993); and Ghate and others (1993).

4. Atiq Rahman (1992) reviewed data on informal moneylenders in Bangladesh in the 1980s and concluded that the informal credit market accounted for about two-thirds of the volume of rural credit in the country.

5. A fourth view, associated with George Stigler of the Chicago school, is that imperfections in credit markets are unimportant, and that high interest rates would reflect high default rates and high information costs. See Hoff and Stiglitz (1993, p. 36) for discussion of Stigler's view, which is not considered here.

6. See Von Pischke, Adams, and Donald (1983, part I) for discussion of "evil" moneylenders (a categorization that they refute); see Von Pischke (1991, ch. 8) for discussion of the history of what he calls the "malicious moneylender myth."

7. For discussion of monopolistic and exploitive moneylending in developing countries, see, among others, Darling (1978 [1925]); Thorner (1953); Gamba (1958); Government of India (1960); Chaudhuri (1976); Mundle (1976); Indian School of Social Sciences (1976); Rao (1977); Sharma (1978); de Silva and others (1979); Government of the Philippines (1980); Vyas (1980); Marla (1981); Kamble (1982); Roth (1983); Basant (1984); Dhanagare (1985); Robinson (1988); Bell (1988, 1989); Sainath (1996); and Pingle and von Furer-Haimendorf (1998).

8. For a classic account of the use of the debt mechanism to acquire land in India, see Darling (1978 [1925]); see also Reserve Bank of India (1954a, b); Bhaduri (1977); Roth (1983); Robinson (1988); and Pingle and von Furer-Haimendorf (1998). For the acquisition of attached labor through debt, see Government of India (1960); Kumar (1965); Harper (1968); Breman (1974); Indian School of Social Science (1976); Chaudhuri (1976); Mundle (1976); Rao (1977); Sharma (1978); de Silva and others. (1979); Bardhan and Rudra (1980); Vyas (1980); Marla (1981); Kamble (1982); Roth (1983); Basant (1984); Binswanger and Rosenzweig (1984); and Robinson (1988). For review of the relation of debt to price stipulation in the case of trader-lenders and producer-borrowers, see Bell and Srinivasan (1985). See Floro and Yotopoulos (1991) and Carstens (1995) for comparable material from the Philippines and Mexico, respectively.

9. Although this example is from the 1970s (it was chosen because it explains the process so well), bonded labor continues in underdeveloped parts of South Asia and elsewhere—but it tends to decline with social and economic development (see Robinson 1988 for an example from India).

10. The title of this section is drawn from the title of chapter 8 of Von Pischke (1991). More than half the chapter, entitled "Value for the People: Informal Finance," concerns informal commercial moneylenders.

11. See Von Pischke (1998) for an account of the history of the Ohio State school and its role in the financial systems approach to development finance.

12. For discussion of transaction costs and risk, and arguments explaining the interest rates of rural lenders as a reflection of these, see Bottomley (1975); Singh (1983); U Tun Wai (1980); Adams and Graham (1981); Wilmington (1983) Von Pischke, Adams, and Donald, eds. (1983); Adams and Vogel (1986); Bouman (1989); Ahmed (1989); and Von Pischke (1991). See Siamwalla and others (1993) for a critique of the "idealization" of the informal credit market as represented in the literature defending the

high interest rates of rural moneylenders on the basis of high transaction costs and risk. For discussion of interlinked transactions and of lender transaction costs and risk in linked and unlinked loans in informal rural credit markets in the Philippines, see Floro and Yotopoulos (1991).

13. See Von Pischke (1991, ch. 8) for a summary and overview of these arguments.

14. Moneylending in India has some special characteristics related to the Hindu caste system. Thus the village headman cited above used an untouchable (harijan) villager as his loan collector. Because of the collector's extremely low ritual status in the community, if he beat, or even touched, a defaulting borrower from a higher caste (both of which he did on occasion), the latter automatically became "polluted" and disgraced. The borrower's low ritual state, thusly incurred, can be overcome. But by the collector's action the borrower is put into a situation of extreme shame and of ritual impurity that can be expensive to counteract.

15. This point was argued by U Tun Wai of the International Monetary Fund in the 1950s (U Tun Wai 1957). See also U Tun Wai (1992).

16. See also Gonzalez-Vega (1993, p. 23).

17. However, several authors have adapted the monopolistic competition model to show that free entry cannot be relied on as a sufficient condition to eliminate long-term economic profits (Eaton 1976; Eaton and Lipsey 1978).

18. Under some circumstances lender B might decide to lend in lender A's territory. This could occur if lender B considers lender A weak and decides to attack or undermine him for political or financial reasons. But lender B will probably not attempt to gain many of lender A's borrowers, as lender B would then have to expand lending beyond his ability to enforce collection. In this situation, lender B might use credit layering in A's territory, as discussed later in this chapter. See Robinson (1988) for documentation and analysis of such cases in India.

19. Such conditions could include circumstances in which lenders could not enforce their interlinked contracts (farmers find a way to sell their rice more profitably and do not supply rice to their merchant or creditor), in which usury laws were strongly enforced and harshly punished, in which a series of co-variant shocks caused continuing losses for lenders, or in times of hyperinflation.

20. Interlinked transactions can be defined as those "in which all parties trade in at least two markets on the condition that the terms of all trades between them are jointly determined" (Bell and Srinivasan 1985, p. 73). "Such interlinkages assume economic significance when the prices of commodities transacted through interlinked markets differ from what their prices would have been if they were not interlinked" (Gangopadhyay and Sengupta 1986, p. 112). For discussion of interlinkages among rural markets, see Neale (1969); Bhaduri (1973); Bardhan and Rudra (1978); Bardhan (1980; 1984; 1989); Braverman and Srinivasan (1981); Braverman and Stiglitz (1982); Binswanger and Rosenzweig (1984); Braverman and Guasch (1984); Hart (1986b); Robinson (1988); Ray and Sengupta (1989); Floro and Yotopoulos (1991); Yotopoulos and Floro (1991); Hoff, Braverman, and Stiglitz (1993); Carstens (1995).

21. However, some informal commercial lenders in India lend wholly or predominantly from their own equity.

22. In a recent paper that discusses monopolistic competition among moneylenders in rural credit markets in developing countries, Hoff and Stiglitz (1998, p. 512) find that "an increase in subsidized institutional credit to large landowners need not increase their on-lending to small landowners."

23. For early reports of the many lenders operating in rural credit markets, each lending to relatively small numbers of borrowers, see Moore (1953); Government of Ceylon (1954); Gamba (1958); Bottomley (1964); Nisbet (1967) and Wilmington (1983). For more recent examples, see Siamwalla and others (1993) for Thailand; Aleem

(1993) for Pakistan; Philippine Presidential Committee on Agricultural Credit (1980); Ladman and Torico (1981) for Bolivia; Harriss (1983) for India; Bouman (1984) for Sri Lanka; Varian (1989) for Bangladesh; and Carstens (1995) for Mexico. See also Bell and Srinivasan (1985); Floro and Yotopoulos (1991); and Von Pischke (1991).

24. Nisbet (1967) points out that similar findings on informal commercial loans were reported from Ceylon in 1950–51 (Government of Ceylon 1954), India in 1954 (Reserve Bank of India 1954a, b), and Malaya in 1958 (Gamba 1958).

25. Aleem does not state whether the statement refers only to borrowing from informal lenders or from lending institutions as well. However, Siamwalla and others (1993, p. 162) report that in Thailand "formal and informal lenders are non-competing." I have found this to be generally true for Indonesia as well.

26. In 1992 in Bolivia, telephone lines, which cost $1,500, were an acceptable guarantee for loans of $750–$1,000 (Malhotra 1992a; see also for discussion of the wide range of security accepted by Bolivian moneylenders).

27. If calculated as an effective monthly interest rate, this would be 121 percent (see table 6.1 for method of calculation).

28. See, for example, Roth (1983) for rural India, Timberg and Aiyar (1984) for urban India, Floro and Yotopoulos (1991) for the Philippines, Shipton (1991) for the Gambia, Siamwalla and others for Thailand (1993), Aleem (1993) for Pakistan, Carstens (1995) for Mexico, and Rutherford (2000) for Bangladesh.

29. For discussion of country financial policies and informal lending, see Germidis, Kessler, and Meghir (1991); see Floro and Yotopoulos (1991) for the Philippines and Siamwalla and others (1993) for Thailand.

30. The exceptions were the Philippines, which had an annual inflation rate of 18.2 percent in 1980 and 50.3 percent in 1984; and Indonesia, which had an inflation rate of 18.0 percent in 1980.

31. Loans on five-six terms may be provided with other maturities (for example, weekly or monthly) as well, in which case their monthly effective rates are lower (see table 6.1, no. 10).

32. This unpublished research was conducted by BRI, CPIS, and HIID as part of demand research for appropriate unit desa products; see volume 2 for discussion.

33. Timberg and Aiyar (1984, p. 57); the study was of informal lenders in urban credit markets in the 1970s. See also Bouman (1989).

34. Roth (1983), p. 46. The data are for the 1970s.

35. Robinson (1988). The references are from the 1970s and early 1980s. References on bonded labor are provided in notes 7 and 8.

36. The automobile title pawn business as practiced in some parts of the United States is an example. A title lender makes a loan to a person with a clear title to an automobile, based on the value of the car. The borrower gives the lender the right to transfer, in the name of the borrower, title to the car should the borrower default on the loan. Caskey (1996, p. 42) reports on the statement of a title lender whom he interviewed: "Some [title pawn lenders], including himself [the lender interviewed], are in the business primarily to make profits from the finance charges. These lenders notify borrowers as soon as they become delinquent and urge them to repay their loans. They attempt to keep borrowers' payment obligations to a level that the borrowers can handle because these lenders do not want to repossess cars. They believe that they will maximize their long-run profits by lending multiple times to borrowers who consistently redeem the titles. Other lenders view the title loan business as a way to acquire used cars at bargain prices. These lenders will not notify a borrower who becomes delinquent. Rather, they wait quietly for the grace period to expire and then repossess the car. Such lenders also encourage debtors to refinance their loans, adding the interest payment to the loan principal. With the principal balance potentially growing at 25 percent a month, their hope

is that the borrower will quickly accumulate a larger debt than he can handle, and the borrower will be forced to default." In the United States "predatory" lending is recognized as a problem, and in 1999 the Federal Reserve convened a nine-agency working group to attack predatory practices (Gramlich 2000). Annual interest rates up to 2,000 percent have been cited in the United States (*Business Week*, 24 April 2000, pp. 107–16). The same article comments: "High-interest loans to the poor and hard-pressed are hardly novel. But what is new is the invasion of mainstream financiers into what was once the sole province of check cashers, pawn shops, and the like" (p. 107).

37. The exception was the Gambia, which in 1986 had an annual inflation rate of 56.6 percent.

38. I was working in Bolivia to advise financial institutions, especially BancoSol, on demand research for savings products. While I did not conduct research on moneylenders, I learned about the economic activities of more than 100 microentrepreneurs and their households (in different parts of the country) through extended discussions with members of these households. As we discussed the households' savings and loans, information about informal loans—their own and others—was sometimes provided.

39. Carstens also reports that credit from urban stores selling furniture, appliances, and other consumer goods is provided at an annual effective rate of about 166 percent, while at semiurban stores the rate is marginally higher (p. 159).

40. Integrated Rural Development Programme; this program gives small subsidized loans with a grant component to the "poorest" potential borrowers in the area. Because the recipients are often politically determined, the loans typically do not reach many of the poor. The IRDP credit target for a branch is typically quite small.

41. This incident occurred in 1995. Since then most interest rates have been deregulated, and a process of RRB reform has begun. But much remains to be done.

42. Where there was no information about the dates of the loans discussed in the sources, a range of several years before the publication date was used.

43. These very rough estimates assume that China, which does not appear to have extensive informal commercial moneylending, is offset by South Asia, which appears to be well above average.

44. Pioneers in the 1960s and 1970s in analysis of the interaction of the financial sector with other sectors of the economy include Raymond Goldsmith, John Gurley, Edward Shaw, and Ronald McKinnon.

7 | Savings and the New Microfinance

In 1984 Robert Vogel (1984b) called savings "the forgotten half of rural finance."[1] For more than 20 years Dale W. Adams, his colleagues at Ohio State University, and others have argued that there is large demand for financial savings in rural areas of developing countries,[2] and that savings is more crucial for microfinance clients than credit. Yet savings remains forgotten in much of institutional microfinance, rural and urban.

All over the world, however, the economically active poor save in a variety of forms, financial and nonfinancial. They save at home, in rotating savings and credit associations (ROSCAs), and in other savings and loan associations. Some even pay collectors to hold their savings safely.

Opinions on the role of savings in institutional commercial microfinance, as expressed in the literature on rural development and local financial markets, vary greatly—from utter neglect[3] to aggressive skepticism (Schmidt and Zeitinger 1994) to advocacy of specialized deposit institutions for microsavings (Gadway and O'Donnell 1996) to the strong advocacy of savings mobilization of the Ohio State school and others.

This chapter examines the role of public savings in institutional commercial microfinance. It begins with an overview of five broad patterns of savings mobilization in developing countries. Then it analyzes the demand side of microsavings: in what forms do people save, and for what purposes? Next it considers the reasons that efforts to collect the savings of low-income people have been neglected for so long in so many countries. The focus then shifts to the experiences of savings mobilization in commercial microfinance institutions and to the conditions required for formal sector institutions to mobilize the savings of the poor. The chapter ends with a discussion of who benefits from savings services in commercial microfinance institutions.

Throughout, the focus is on voluntary savings mobilized from the public (as opposed to compulsory savings required from an institution's members as a condition of obtaining a loan). Voluntary savings are discretional. People choose to save excess liquidity for future use; our interest here is in how this excess liquidity can be mobilized by financial institutions serving low-income people.

Some people save to smooth income and consumption flows: farmers save at harvest time to get through the pre-harvest "hungry" season, while entrepreneurs with businesses that have high and low seasons save for the low seasons during the high seasons. Many low-income people count as excess liquidity all but basic necessities in order to save for emergencies, investment opportunities, social and religious obligations, children's education, and other purposes. The better-off among the poor may spend more on consumption, but they typically save as well. As one Indonesian villager commented, "My investment opportunities are not the same throughout the year. I save while I look for the right openings."

In developing countries most poor people (except some of the destitute) save—and often save regularly. They know that they must save for emergencies because their other options are limited; they also save for the future of their families and their businesses.[4] But do they

Mobilizing voluntary savings— both as a service and as a source of finance for loans— is a basic tenet of the microfinance revolution

save in financial form? In some countries, yes. In many others, very little. But the latter is changing, as will be seen in volumes 2 and 3 of this book. In contrast to the microcredit focus of the poverty lending approach, the importance of voluntary savings—both as a service and as a source of finance for loans—is a basic tenet of the microfinance revolution.

Mobilizing Microsavings: Five Broad Patterns

As noted in chapter 2, the collection of voluntary savings by microfinance institutions falls into five major patterns.[5] The first consists of institutions that have successful microcredit programs but that are not permitted to mobilize savings from the public; many of the better donor-subsidized nongovernmental organizations (NGOs) fall into this category. Second are institutions that are successful in lending but that, although permitted to mobilize savings from the public, choose not to collect voluntary deposits or are unsuccessful in doing so. These are usually institutions that have little incentive to mobilize savings because they are well supplied with cheap donor or government funds—funds that are either provided directly or channeled through apex organizations. Bangladesh's Grameen Bank is a good example of this pattern.

The third pattern is the reverse of the second: institutions providing subsidized credit that are successful in savings but weak in lending. China's Rural Credit Cooperatives, India's Regional Rural Banks, and Niger's Caisses Populaires d'Épargne et de Crédit are examples—the first two on a vast scale and the third on a small scale. The fourth pattern comprises institutions that fail in both lending and savings; many subsidized microfinance institutions fall into this category.

These four patterns are typically associated with credit subsidies. Under both kinds of subsidized models (credit driven and savings driven), financial institutions have not, and cannot, meet the demand for microfinance—for credit and savings services. Even the best of the institutions that operate with subsidized loan portfolios are effective either in capturing savings or in providing microloans. They cannot afford to be effective in both because they do not have a large enough interest rate spread to cover the operating and financial costs required for the profitable implementation of both services simultaneously. Of course, it is also possible for nonsubsidized institutions (such as savings banks that are not allowed to lend) to provide only one kind of financial service.

The fifth pattern, however, consists of microfinance institutions that are successful in both credit and savings. These are, of necessity, commercial financial institutions with a large enough interest rate spread to cover all the costs and risks, including financial costs, associated with the sustainable provision of microfinance services. Institutions that provide commercial microfinance have strong incentives both to provide deposit instruments that are appropriate for small saver demand and to lend out the deposits locally in small loans. Such institutions can meet the high demand for credit and savings services and can provide other financial services as well, such as money transfers and salary and pension payments.

There are two subsets in this model. In one, as in Bank Rakyat Indonesia's (BRI) unit *desa* system and Bank Dagang Bali (BDB), all loans are financed by savings. In the other, exemplified by BancoSol, loans are funded in part by savings and in part by other commercial sources of finance. The first of the subsets tends to be associated with mature microfinance institutions—since in the

Institutions that operate with subsidized loan portfolios cannot afford to be effective in both savings and lending

long run the demand for public savings tends to be higher than the demand for microcredit. The second subset is especially useful for successful microcredit institutions that want to add savings to their lending activities, as it allows them to do so gradually. Both enable large-scale financial intermediation for low-income clients.

Pattern 1: Microfinance institutions that are not permitted to mobilize voluntary savings

Most NGOs and some other nonbank financial institutions (depending on the country) are not permitted to collect voluntary savings from the public. They are restricted to mobilizing compulsory savings that are required of borrowers to obtain loans; in some cases these institutions may mobilize voluntary savings from member-borrowers. Although there are occasional exceptions in countries with very weak banking systems, the reasoning behind this general prohibition is sound. Such institutions are not publicly regulated and supervised, and if they mobilized voluntary deposits, the savings of the poor would be placed at risk. Recently in some countries, especially in Latin America, new types of regulated nonbank financial institutions have been developed. These organizations are permitted to collect some types of savings from the public and are able to meet some forms of savings demand and to attain wider outreach in the provision of microcredit.

Pattern 2: Savings as the forgotten half of microfinance

Policymakers and bankers in many parts of the developing world have been taught to believe that the poor do not save, cannot save, do not trust financial institutions, and prefer nonfinancial forms of savings (Robinson 1994b). These were also the reasons given in Indonesia in 1983 to explain why BRI's 3,600 unit desas had mobilized only about $18 million in the previous ten years. Most government and bank officials faulted the rural population, saying that they were poor and uneducated, and needed to be taught financial discipline. It was easier to blame the poor, especially since no one understood that the problem of low financial savings in rural areas was on the supply side.

Yet with mandatory interest rates of 12 percent for loans and 15 percent for savings, every rupiah mobilized was a loss for BRI—as TS, the poor Indonesian rice farmer, pointed out (chapter 3). Only one savings instrument was available to would-be savers, and it limited withdrawals to two a month. Because most people wanted to be able to withdraw their money whenever they needed it, especially in case of emergency, this instrument was in little demand. The poor savings record of BRI's unit desas at that time was not a result of low demand; it was a direct result of bad policy by the government and the bank. Indonesia's economically active poor were saving all along, but in nonfinancial forms, in cash held at home, and in informal savings and credit associations.

After the government deregulated interest rates in 1983 and BRI developed savings instruments and services that were appropriate for local demand, the bank mobilized massive—and stable—local savings (chapter 13). By the end

The poor savings record of BRI's unit desas in the 1970s was a direct result of bad policy by the government and the bank

of 1996 unit desas had mobilized 7.1 trillion rupiah ($3 billion) in 16.1 million accounts. Despite the economic and political crisis that began in Indonesia in mid-1997, clients have continued to save in the unit desas. In rupiah terms savings more than doubled during the crisis (though the real value of the unit desas' savings substantially decreased because of the steep decline in the value of the rupiah).

In many developing countries, however, banks tend not to mobilize microsavings because they assume a lack of demand, because they think that collecting savings in small accounts would be unprofitable, and because many state-owned banks are given continuous access to subsidized government funds. A review of rural credit in developing countries reports: "Commercial banks and state-funded institutions have not mobilized much rural savings. The estimate of the percentage of loanable funds from rural sources has ranged from 5 percent to 40 percent, with the median much closer to the former than the latter figure" (Braverman and Guasch 1986, p. 1256).[6]

The Grameen Bank is the best-known example of the pattern of successful lending and low emphasis on voluntary savings. As shown in table 2.8, both Grameen and BRI's commercial unit banking system began their current approaches to microfinance at about the same time in the mid-1980s. By the end of 1995 they had a similar number of loans outstanding (2.1 million at Grameen and 2.3 million at BRI's unit desas). But Grameen, which collects compulsory savings from its members, had about 2.1 million accounts,[7] while BRI's microbanking division had 14.5 million accounts. Bangladesh, which had only 63 percent of Indonesia's population in 1995, is a poorer country. Still, the value of Grameen's savings in 1995 ($133.3 million) was just 5 percent of the BRI units' ($2.6 billion).

Much of that difference can be attributed to the two institutions' different approaches to mobilizing savings. Grameen's savings were nearly all in compulsory savings from poor members. In contrast the BRI units, which have no compulsory savings requirement, actively mobilize savings from the public. BRI can afford to do so because the unit desas are a commercial system with a spread between loan and deposit interest rates that provides the operating costs needed to maintain both effective large-scale lending and savings activities. Grameen recently indicated that it is placing more emphasis on savings. But as long as it continues to receive heavily subsidized funds from the Bangladesh Bank and from donors, Grameen will not have an incentive to mobilize substantial savings. In 1985–96 the average nominal interest rate of Grameen's borrowed funds was 3.7 percent; the average real rate was 1.6 percent (Morduch 1998b, p. 35).

Pattern 3: High savings, with lending as the forgotten half of microfinance

Pattern 3 is the reverse of pattern 2: pattern 3 institutions capture savings from rural households, sometimes in massive amounts. But they do not lend effectively. Pattern 3, common in Asia and parts of Africa, is often found in state-owned financial institutions that channel government-subsidized credit to rural

Under its new commercial approach that began in 1984, BRI's unit desas had mobilized $3 billion in 16 million accounts by 1996

borrowers. With billions of dollars in locally mobilized deposits, these institutions show that banks can mobilize large amounts of rural savings, much of it in small accounts.

However, the spread between interest rates on subsidized loans and rates on deposits is too small to cover the costs required for an institution to deliver both credit and savings services effectively. These banks tend to invest the savings they collect in securities or to deposit them in the interbank market. The savings are not lent to many rural borrowers—and especially not low-income ones.

In India, for example, the widespread network of Regional Rural Banks (RRBs) was established to provide loans to small and marginal farmers and to landless laborers. The RRBs, which are owned by sponsoring commercial banks, have been quite successful in mobilizing deposits. By 31 March 1996 they had more than 37 million active deposit accounts, averaging about $200 per account, for a total of more than $7.4 billion.

Until 1996 the RRBs provided only subsidized loans, and many have been unable to lend funds to rural borrowers without incurring extensive losses. In March 1996 the outstanding loan portfolio was about $2.1 billion. Cumulative losses were reported to be $615 million, though real losses were much higher because adequate provisioning had not been made for large, uncollectible portions of the portfolio, and interest payments had been accrued that are unlikely to be collected. The losses were almost entirely attributable to poor loan repayment; in March 1996 loan recovery was reported at 56 percent of amounts due. As a manager of one of the commercial banks that own the RRBs said in 1996, "We instruct our RRBs not to lend outside of IRDP,[8] but only to collect savings. We need the savings, not the losses that come from the loans."

By the early 1990s the Indian government had concluded that it could no longer sustain the continuing burden of RRB losses. A reform program for the RRBs, begun in 1993, has helped somewhat. Interest rates for most loans have been deregulated. Collection rates gradually improved, and losses have slowly decreased. But these results were achieved by shifting away from the RRBs' original mission. Thus RRB loans are now often made to higher-income, larger borrowers, rather than to the poor borrowers for whom the credit is intended. Meanwhile, large amounts of excess liquidity are deposited in the banks that own the RRBs, where they are deposited in the interbank market or lent to larger borrowers in urban areas.

A second example of this pattern is found in China. There the nationwide network of more than 50,000 Rural Credit Cooperatives (RCCs), under the control of the People's Bank of China (the central bank),[9] provides financial services to rural areas (see Park 1998). As in the Indian RRBs, loans are subsidized and losses are high. In December 1997 the RCC system had $141 billion in savings, more than 85 percent of it from rural households. The outstanding loan portfolio at that time was $100 billion. In 1997–98 Chinese officials estimated that at least a third of the RCCs operate at a loss—and in poor areas, more than half.

Banks that are successful in savings but weak in lending tend not to lend the savings to many rural borrowers— and especially not low-income ones

There appear to be three main reasons for the RCC losses: a cap on loan interest rates that remains too low for institutional sustainability (although improvements in the regulations have been made in recent years); a high loan delinquency rate, especially for loans to township and village enterprises; and a combination of high costs for mobilizing savings and low rates received on RCC bank deposits and government bonds. The substantial and continuing RCC losses put at risk a large portion of the savings of the country's rural households. The government could face serious difficulty if it were to have to bail out these savers.

In 1996 the government substantially increased pressure on the formal financial sector to reduce losses and bad loans. In a response similar to that found in India, this resulted in major cutbacks in lending in many RCCs. Instead, more rural savings were deposited in the central bank. By 2000 the RCC system had a negative net worth, raising serious concerns about the risk to depositors and about potential social and economic unrest in rural areas (see chapter 17).

Overall, pattern 3 institutions mobilize large amounts of savings from rural households, many of them low-income households. But there are severe problems with the pattern 3 approach. Most low-income households and enterprises do not have access to institutional credit, the mobilizing institutions are not financially viable, rural investment remains low, and losses on the lending side put at risk the savings mobilized.

Pattern 4: Failing at both savings and lending

With subsidized microcredit it is possible to have good lending and poor savings, poor lending and good savings, or institutions that fail at both—of which there are many. The literature is rife with accounts of such failures, especially in state-owned agricultural banks and development banks more generally. *Undermining Rural Development with Cheap Credit* (Adams, Graham, and Von Pischke 1984) and other writings from Ohio State University document and analyze many subsidized credit failures. Most of the failed institutions have been unsuccessful not only in their microcredit efforts, but in savings mobilization as well. The Vietnam Bank for the Poor (chapter 19) is, unfortunately, an excellent example.

Pattern 5: Profitable financial intermediation

In microfinance institutions, sustainable, large-scale financial intermediation between borrowers and savers is incompatible with subsidized credit. Successful lending and savings programs for low-income clients are found together only in commercial institutions. If the financial intermediary is to be profitable, the spread between interest rates on lending and savings must cover all the costs of both services—and operating costs are relatively high in microfinance. As noted, institutions with substantial subsidized lending do not have a large enough spread to carry out both services effectively. In contrast, profitable microfinance institutions design credit and deposit instruments together to meet microfinance demand and price them to enable institutional profitability.

Before BRI began its unit desa savings program, the bank carried out extensive studies of savings habits among rural Indonesians in order to design ap-

Successful lending and savings programs for low-income clients are found together only in commercial institutions

propriate savings instruments; this research was later extended to low-income people in urban areas. Liquidity was found to be in high demand. Yet BRI found that liquid instruments are labor-intensive and so can be costly for the institution. BRI also found, however, that most liquid account holders at the unit desas did not consider the rate of return they obtained on their savings to be important. Thus it was possible for BRI to set interest rates that permitted unit desa savings products to meet demand while also enabling institutional profitability. Since 1989 all unit desa loans have been funded by locally mobilized savings.

Policy implications

Savings mobilization is both a service in high demand and a source of finance for microloans. Yet not all microcredit institutions should capture voluntary savings (Robinson 1997a)—and not all microloans need be financed by savings (Otero 1994; Chu 1997, 1998b, 1999).

First, microfinance institutions that are permitted to mobilize public savings should be regulated and publicly supervised by competent, well-informed supervisory agencies (although in practice there are occasional exceptions because of extraordinary circumstances; see chapter 18). They should also have accountable owners and managers and a record of high loan repayment and good financial management. Microfinance institutions that do not meet these basic criteria should not collect savings from the public.

Second, other commercial sources of funds—such as debt and investment—are also appropriate for financing microfinance loan portfolios. Although not discussed in this chapter, these can be important funding sources for self-sufficient microfinance institutions, normally in combination with savings mobilization.

As commercial microfinance intermediaries, BDB and BRI's microbanking system pioneered savings mobilization from low-income people, in the case of BRI on a large scale. BancoSol initiated the other approach, gaining access to domestic and international commercial investment to finance its loan portfolio. This strategy allowed BancoSol to introduce savings mobilization services gradually, with the necessary demand research and pilot projects undertaken—but without constraining the growth of the bank's loan portfolio.

While other commercial sources of funds are important for the development of microfinance, voluntary savings from the public are potentially the largest and most immediately available source of finance for microcredit programs. Of course, well-designed savings instruments and services are in great demand on their own.

A growing number of institutions are seeking to meet the criteria that would permit them to mobilize public savings. This is, in three ways, a direct result of the microfinance revolution. First, there is increasing recognition of the evidence for the huge demand for institutional microsavings programs—evidence long ignored in many countries. The demand is specifically for programs that provide low-income clients with security, convenience, confidentiality, prod-

Not all microcredit institutions should capture voluntary savings—and not all microloans need be financed by savings

ucts providing different ratios of liquidity and returns, access to loans, and prompt, friendly service. Second, it is now known that formal sector financial inter-mediaries can meet this demand profitably. Third, in the second half of the 1990s interest in the accurate documentation of the performance and costs of mo-bilizing savings in microbanking institutions, and in the careful study of demand for microsavings, grew dramatically. (See Hannig and Wisniwski 1999—an ex-cellent study by the German Agency for Technical Cooperation for CGAP's Working Group on Savings; and the UNDP-DFID–sponsored series of sem-inal papers on the savings of the poor in Africa—which include Mutesasira and others 1999; Mutesasira 1999; Mugwanga 1999; Rutherford and others 1999; Wright 1999a, b; Wright and others 1999; and MicroSave-Africa 1999.)

Profitable financial intermediation on a large scale also has another kind of policy implication, one of critical importance for the poor. Most poor people have assets (houses, farms, businesses) for which they lack legal title. As de Soto has shown (1989, 2000), these assets are "dead capital"—capital that cannot be used to cre-ate capital. This is because such assets are properties without legally enforceable transactions. People with such assets usually cannot use them as collateral for loans or mortgages, cannot sell shares in their businesses, cannot collect debts through the legal system, and so on. The poor own vast amounts of dead capital:

> Even in the poorest countries, the poor save. The value of savings among the poor is, in fact, immense—forty times all the foreign aid received throughout the world since 1945. In Egypt, for instance, the wealth that the poor have accumulated is worth fifty-five times as much as the sum of all direct foreign investment ever recorded there, including the Suez Canal and the Aswan Dam. In Haiti, the poorest nation in Latin America, the total assets of the poor are more than one hundred fifty times greater than all the foreign investment received since Haiti's independence from France in 1804. If the United States were to hike its foreign-aid budget to the level recommended by the United Nations—0.7 percent of national income—it would take the richest country on earth more than 150 years to transfer to the world's poor resources equal to those they already possess.

> But they hold these resources in defective forms: houses built on land whose ownership rights are not adequately recorded, unincorporated businesses with undefined liability, industries located where financiers and investors cannot see them. Because the rights to these possessions are not adequately documented, these assets cannot readily be turned into capital, cannot be traded outside of narrow local circles where people know and trust each other, cannot be used as collateral for a loan, and cannot be used as a share against an investment.

> —de Soto 2000, pp.5–6

A growing number of institutions are seeking to meet the criteria that would permit them to mobilize public savings

Microfinance is an important part of the solution to poor people's problems with dead capital. Savings accounts in regulated financial institutions are legally recognized assets, often the first that poor families acquire. Their bank accounts are fungible assets—live capital. Banks are legally accountable for their savers' deposits, and deposits can be used as collateral for loans and mortgages—which open up possibilities for acquiring real property with legal title. A microentrepreneur with title to her business site and a farmer with title to his land are able to invest in these enterprises with reasonable assurance that their investments will not suddenly disappear. Regulated microfinance institutions provide voluntary savings accounts that are appropriate for low-income savers and legally recognized, they accept some dead capital as loan collateral (or do not require collateral), and they provide a mix of financial products and services. Microfinance is often the first step in the process by which the poor acquire live capital.

Savings accounts in regulated financial institutions are legally recognized assets, often the first that poor families acquire

Forms of Informal Savings

Developing countries show considerable similarity in the informal methods used by the poor for saving, in the reasons they save, and in the ways they match the type of savings with the saving purpose. The discussion below is drawn primarily from extensive work in Indonesia, but it is also informed by field work that I have conducted in India, Sri Lanka, China, Kenya, Bolivia, and Mexico, and by conversations about local savings held with people in many developing countries in Asia, Africa, and Latin America. All the forms of local savings considered here are found in some version in all countries; there appear to be no major differences among the savers interviewed in the various countries except that some forms of savings are more available or more valued in some places than in others. This discussion is not intended as a complete account of the forms in which poor people save; it simply covers some of the most common of these.

The people whose savings habits are explored here are drawn from urban and rural areas. They operate microenterprises (as traders, producers, and service providers), they are farmers and fishers, they are government and private sector employees. In many cases the savers' households have multiple sources of income.

However, pastoralists are not covered in this discussion, for two reasons. First, I have little experience with herding societies. Second, my limited observations indicate that the views about savings held by pastoralists, and their opportunities for savings, may differ in important ways from those of farmers, microentrepreneurs, employees, and others. Given adequate grazing land and water, reliable labor, and a suitable market for their animals, pastoralists may prefer to increase herd size rather than deposit their savings in banks. This strategy may provide them with both adequate liquidity and higher returns than would be obtained from banks and other financial institutions.

In general, however, low-income households in developing countries save informally in a variety of forms. It is difficult to distinguish between savings and investment in this context, at least as perceived by the people themselves. In some cases savings and investment can be clearly differentiated—for example, people save in cash, grain, and small animals in order to manage irregular income streams. But poor savers also say that they save in cash or grain to buy gold, that they save in gold to buy land, and that they save in land to buy better land. There are complexities in distinguishing among perceptions of saving and investment that I have not tried to unravel here, and they are a good topic for further investigation. For simplicity, the term savings is used throughout this book to refer to both savings and investment unless otherwise specified.

Forms in which people save commonly include cash; grain and cash crops; animals; gold, silver, jewelry, and other valuables; land; rotating savings and credit associations (ROSCAs) and regular savings and credit associations (RESCAs; also known as accumulating savings and credit associations, or ASCAs); raw materials and finished goods; construction materials; cash or grain lent out for profit; deposits with informal savings collectors; and labor obligations.

The saver must match the form of savings with the purpose. As discussed in chapter 2 (see also chapter 17), the primary need of poor savers is to swap small savings flows for lump sums needed for a variety of purposes (Rutherford 2000). Cash and gold can generally be used as savings for all purposes. Emergencies are typically met with cash (assuming inflation is under control), gold, grain, small animals, and other liquid assets. Medium-term savings or investment goals (paying for religious ceremonies, purchasing tools or machinery, managing irregular income streams) can be met, in addition to cash and gold savings, by saving in such forms as grain, cash crops, animals, and ROSCAs. Other forms of saving are the raw materials needed for an enterprise (cloth, wool, leather, wood) or the finished goods themselves—as, for example, when a weaver stocks finished pieces until she needs to buy more raw materials or pay her children's school fees. People may save for housing construction by stockpiling construction materials. Long-term goals (children's education, pilgrimages, preparing for old age) may be met by saving in a variety of forms, including cash, gold, jewelry, animals, and land. Each of these forms of informal savings has advantages and disadvantages (table 7.1).

Cash

Cash is liquid and convenient. In monetized areas it is generally thought important to hold some cash in the house, primarily for emergencies. In addition, cash is considered useful because business opportunities sometimes arise unexpectedly—for example, the opportunity to purchase raw materials for household enterprises at a low price. However, many households keep more cash at home than they consider desirable because they do not know what else to do with it.

Security is a major reason for not wanting too much cash in the house. Equally important, however, is the view that if one has cash on hand, it is difficult to avoid lending to family, friends, and neighbors. A possible decline in the value of currency because of high inflation or devaluation is of concern to some, but the extent of the concern varies greatly according to the saver's experience with

Many households keep more cash at home than they consider desirable because they do not know what else to do with it

Form	Advantages	Disadvantages
Cash	• Convenience • Liquidity	• Security problems • Social expectations for use of cash on hand • Potential decrease in real value due to inflation or currency devaluation • Lack of returns
Grain and (not easily perishable) cash crops	• Hedge against poor crops • Some liquidity • Can be stored at harvest and held until prices rise • Can be sold in increments to smooth consumption	• Storage problems • Quality deterioration in some cases • Community expectation that grain will be lent or given if needed in pre-harvest season or other times of shortage • Lack of returns if sold when prices are low • Some cash crops are subject to sharp international market fluctuations
Animals	• Generally high returns from propagation [a] • Relatively high liquidity • Animal by-products (milk, eggs, wool) • Animal labor	• Opportunity cost of household labor used to care for animals • Liquidity problems caused by indivisibility of animal • Scarcity of grazing land or water in some areas • Risk of illness or death of animal • Risks of shareherding • Markets may be seasonal; price variability may be high
Gold and other valuables	• Liquidity • Hedge against inflation and currency devaluation • Possible capital gains • Can serve as status symbol	• Security problems • Uncertain price fluctuations and possible capital loss • Lack of returns
Land[b]	• Rural: Source of livelihood; base for enterprise, residence, or both • Urban: Base for enterprise, residence, or both • Serves as status symbol • Investment value	• Titling difficulties • Rural: Cultivation of small plots can be risky for low-income households (in some areas higher incomes can be earned from nonfarm activities) • Urban: Possible loss in case of urban development • In countries with land ceilings, purchase of land beyond the legal limit can be risky • Variable liquidity • Land taxes
ROSCAs and RESCAs/ASCAs	• Generally secure • Savings available in a lump sum • Social benefits from membership • Mechanism for encouraging regular savings	• Can be risky (especially RESCAs/ASCAs) • Not as useful for members who receive funds late in a ROSCA cycle • Generally lack liquidity (though practices vary) • Vulnerable to collapse if managers are corrupt, members are undisciplined, or collective shock occurs
Raw materials and finished goods	• Raw materials can be purchased in bulk when prices are low • Finished goods can be stored and used as needed, or sold when prices are high	• Deterioration of stored materials • Need for secure storage space • Risk that materials become outdated • Lack of returns
Construction materials	• Materials may be purchased when prices are low and sold when prices rise • Often the only available option for housing construction or renovation	• Security problems • Deterioration of materials • Risk of damage to partially constructed buildings • Lack of returns (unless sold at a profit)

Table **7.1**

Form	Advantages	Disadvantages
Lending to others in cash or in kind	• Generally high returns	• Limit on the number of borrowers from whom the lender can collect with low risk • Transaction costs of making and collecting loans • Generally undiversified portfolio • High risk at times of regional shock or political upheaval
Deposits with savings collectors	• Security • Convenience	• Negative returns • Risk of losing all or part of the savings stored with an unregulated and unsupervised informal collector • Lack of liquidity in some cases
Labor obligations and expected reciprocation for past contributions	• Provides access to a supply of labor as needed for specific purposes • Enables fulfillment of some social and religious obligations without drawing from more liquid savings sources • Possible returns	• Lack of fungibility • Uncertain returns

Note: The table excludes savings in pastoral societies.

a. It is widely reported that this is especially true for pigs.

b In dry areas land may be widely available and water rights more highly valued. In addition, in some land tenure systems (as in some tribal areas of central India) trees may be owned separately from the land on which they grow. Thus people may save in rights to water and in trees, as well as in land.

such events. Another disadvantage of saving in cash is the lack of returns. In my experience, however, microsavers rarely mentioned this shortcoming.

Young people sometimes store cash with trusted elders, but when those elders die, the savers often have difficulties storing their savings safely.

> When my mother was still alive I used to give her a few shillings every day . . . She looked after it for me really well, and every January there was always enough for the school fees. Now that she's dead I just haven't got anyone I can trust like that. It's much harder to make sure I've enough for the fees. We may not be able to send our youngest to school this year.
>
> —An East African woman, quoted in Rutherford and others 1999, p. 42

> Old people are very trustworthy. A lot of young people used to keep their money with their grandparents. The sad thing is, most grandparents and grownups have died. So it is a problem. Now most people have to buy chickens, transform them into goats and then later to cows which they afterwards have to sell to have a lump sum of money.
>
> —A Ugandan vegetable farmer, quoted in Mutesasira and others 1999, p. 9

Grain and cash crops

Attitudes toward saving in grain tend to be similar to those expressed about cash. Stored grain is relatively liquid and serves as a hedge against poor crops. Almost everyone wants to have enough grain or other staple food on hand to meet a reasonable level of unexpected need above anticipated requirements, but farmers often do not want to store grain beyond a particular time or above a certain amount.[10] Farmers with other forms of savings or sources of income try to save their grain until the low prices typically found at harvest time have increased. But stored grain requires space, it must be protected against vermin and theft, and it can deteriorate if stored too long. In addition, there is often a strong ethic that a household that has stored grain (which is usually easily visible) must give or lend it as requested by family, friends, and neighbors in the pre-harvest, "hungry" season. Farmers say that it can be difficult to keep stored grain while also maintaining good relations.

Farmers also try to save cash crops that are not easily perishable, such as cloves, nutmeg, rubber, cotton, and coffee, until prices rise.[11] Depending on the price, farmers then sell all or part of the crop. At that time they may switch to another form of savings, such as cash, gold, or animals. Households that do not have sufficient income from other sources and that cultivate crops with long growing seasons must save in some form to manage their irregular income streams.

Some cash crops, such as those mentioned above, are subject to international market price fluctuations, making it difficult for farmers to estimate the value of their savings in this form. In general, farming households wait, if possible, until the price for their crops is high, then sell them and save in another form. If they cannot afford to wait until prices rise, they typically sell gradually, as the household needs the income for consumption.

Animals

In developing countries, rural households that can afford to do so typically keep a few large animals. These vary according to the environment, but cows, goats, sheep, horses, donkeys, and pigs (except in Muslim areas) are common. Poultry and other smaller animals are also kept. Animals can provide good returns given normal propagation, and in most circumstances they can be sold fairly rapidly. In addition, some animals provide by-products (milk, eggs, wool), and some are sources of labor that can be both used by the owner and rented out.

However, in areas where employment is available and where children are in school, many households—except those whose members breed or trade animals as a primary source of livelihood—do not want to care for more than a few large animals. They perceive the opportunity costs of household members' time and the liquidity problems caused by the indivisibility of animals. There is also the risk of an animal's illness or death, and in some cases there may be uncertain markets for animals or their by-products.

Households with working adults and children in school often say that caring for more than a few animals is too much work. Particularly in regions where

"Young people used to keep their money with their grandparents. The sad thing is, most grandparents and grownups have died"

—*A Ugandan vegetable farmer*

grazing areas or water are scarce, or where space is limited, caring for animals is considered onerous and time-consuming. In some cases animals are given out on a shareherding basis, to be cared for by people who live near better grazing lands. Shareherding is analogous to sharecropping: the owner of an animal gives it to be cared for by a shareherder, and the animal's progeny are divided between the owner and the shareherder. However, it is difficult for owners to monitor from afar the care and propagation of their animals under a shareherding arrangement.

Gold, silver, jewelry, and other valuables

Gold, silver, jewelry, and similar valuables are fairly liquid, can easily be pawned, can serve as a hedge against inflation or currency devaluation, and may provide capital gains. If made visible to the community, gold and other valuables can also serve as status symbols and can sometimes be used as collateral for loans.

Still, savers often say that while gold and other valuables may be good long-term investments, they are not suitable for the ordinary savings needs of most households. Jewelry, other small valuables, and ceremonial objects are prized household possessions. Beyond these, however, many people say they do not want to save in gold, silver, and jewelry because of the security problem. Such valuables must be hidden from outsiders who might steal them and from insiders who might appropriate them, claiming shared rights. As an Indonesian villager said, "If we have gold in the house, we cannot sleep peacefully." Another commented, "In the old days there was always somebody at home. Now we are sometimes all away from the house at the same time. How can we leave the gold behind?"

Land

In rural areas land serves as a source of livelihood, residence, and status. In urban areas land serves as a permanent base for a microenterprise, household residence, or both, and as a status symbol. In all areas where land is valuable and privately owned, its ownership is a long-term investment that can increase in value over time. Land ownership, as well as land control obtained through rentals, mortgage foreclosures, and other mechanisms, is a high priority for many rural households. Ownership of housing sites is also a priority for urban dwellers.

It usually takes a long time to purchase land. The potential buyer must consider size, location, price, soil type, water availability, and other variables when locating a suitable piece of land. Obtaining clear land title is not always possible—and even when it is, procuring land title can be expensive and time-consuming. Without clear title, the use of rural land may be subject to dispute and litigation; in urban areas such land may be lost to urban development. The often lengthy process involved in purchasing land is perceived by prospective buyers as a reason for holding savings, especially in liquid forms. Households waiting for suitable land to become available save, for example, in cash or gold so that their funds will be available when an appropriate piece of land is found. In addition, I have known farmers who sold land in order to obtain the funds needed to clear the title on a better piece of land that they owned.

Gold, silver, and jewelry must be hidden from outsiders who might steal them and from insiders who might appropriate them, claiming shared rights

Not everyone wants land, however. Land ownership by low-income households can be risky; it is not always possible for small landholders to provide the labor resources, capital for inputs, and water required for cultivation. Low-income rural households sometimes turn down opportunities to invest in land because they calculate nonfarm economic activities to be more profitable. Sometimes they sell their land at a loss. As family planning and education become more widespread, older people may sell land because they do not have children who can manage and work it. Other disadvantages of land as savings include land taxes and the fact that land is often illiquid.

In countries with land ceilings, such as India, buying land beyond the legal limit may be risky. While these ceilings are usually not implemented effectively, landowners can become politically vulnerable if they own large amounts of land above the ceiling. Thus in some areas, there is a growing emphasis on controlling the use of land that one does not own, rather than on purchasing land.

It should also be noted that in some dry regions where land is plentiful and water is scarce, water rights are more valuable than land rights.

ROSCAs and RESCAs

ROSCAs and RESCAs/ASCAs are found in many variations and at many financial levels throughout developing countries (see Rutherford 2000). In ROSCAs all members are both savers and borrowers; in RESCAs/ASCAs all members are savers but not all are necessarily borrowers.

> A favorite ROSCA pattern is the one of twelve participants making monthly contributions, which will take exactly one year for completion. It the individual contributions amount to $10, one of the participants will pocket a fund of $120 each month. ROSCA with weekly or even daily contributions—and therefore weekly or daily drawings—usually have more members, but the cycle seldom exceeds one year. The capital of the ROSCA-fund does not grow during its lifecycle.★ Each time the members convene and submit their contributions, a new fund is formed but is depleted immediately again. The RESCA-fund, on the other hand, grows over time, while loans are taken and repaid at regular intervals.
>
> ★ In some countries, however, members may agree to increase contributions—and hence the fund—to match inflation.
>
> —Bouman 1989, pp. 52–53

ROSCAs, RESCAs/ASCAs, and other informal savings and loan associations are extremely popular in most developing countries, and many people are members of more than one such group. For low-income people these groups can permit reasonably secure savings and facilitate regular savings habits. They enable members to accumulate savings from income flows and to receive them in a lump sum that can be used for a specific purpose. The social benefits that

Low-income rural households sometimes turn down opportunities to invest in land because for them nonfarm economic activities are more profitable

arise from membership in ROSCAs and RESCAs/ASCAs are sometimes more important than the financial benefits.

Many such groups are consumer-oriented, with members saving primarily for household goods ranging from cooking pots to refrigerators and televisions. Others are related to a wide range of activities: religious, ceremonial, travel, work-related, educational, sports, and others. However, participation in ROSCAs or RESCAs/ASCAs is typically not the household's primary mode of savings.

Although practices vary, ROSCAs and RESCAs/ASCAs may not be particularly liquid from the viewpoint of the borrower. A member who needs money early in the cycle may not be able to receive it until late in the cycle. Since those who receive funds early benefit more than those who receive funds late, some ROSCAs auction the dates of receiving funds. Some ROSCA managers receive benefits (such as receiving the funds at the beginning of the cycle) in return for their management duties. While ROSCAs work well generally, they are vulnerable to collapse if managers are corrupt, members are undisciplined, or a collective shock occurs. Rutherford and others (1999) and Mutesasira and others (1999) provide examples of the risks to the poor from membership in ROSCAs and RESCAs/ASCAs.

Raw materials and finished goods

Saving in raw materials is common among goods producers. People like to save—up to a point, in raw materials. Shoemakers save in leather, garmentmakers save in cloth, metalworkers save in metal stocks, carpenters save in wood, knitters save in wool, crafts producers save in the materials of their crafts, and so on. The advantages are that the materials can be purchased when prices are low and saved for later use. The disadvantages are that stored materials may deteriorate, secure space is required for storage, and materials sometimes go out of fashion.

Thus a dressmaker operating a microenterprise in Kenya commented that when she had made a big sale the previous year, she had not known what to do with the money. Eventually she decided to use the cash to purchase a large bolt of cloth. But she later had to sell more than half the cloth below cost because the design had gone out of fashion and there were no orders for clothes made from this material at a price that would cover costs.

Microentrepreneurs who produce or trade goods also frequently save in finished goods that are ready for sale. If they have excess cash, they produce or purchase more goods than they expect to sell in the near future, holding the extras as savings. The advantages and disadvantages of this form of savings are similar to those of saving in raw materials.

Construction materials

For microenterprises that are engaged in construction as a business, saving in construction materials falls into the category of saving in raw materials. But many other people also save in construction materials. Houses are often built or ren-

While ROSCAs work well generally, they are vulnerable to collapse if managers are corrupt, members are undisciplined, or a collective shock occurs

ovated bit by bit. As excess cash becomes available, small quantities of bricks, lumber, or cement are purchased, especially when prices are low. These materials may be used for construction or sold when prices rise.

> When I got some money I made bricks, when I got some more money I built up to the window level. I have now roofed the house and God willing I will get more money and finish the house.
>
> —A low-income Ugandan, quoted in
> Wright and others 1999, p. 26

The poor often entrust their savings to collectors who charge a fee for the service

The advantages of this form of saving are that the house is being constructed or renovated in the only way possible for most low-income households (gradually) and that the household can be seen as being upwardly mobile—although this is not always considered desirable. Another advantage is that unused materials can be sold if prices rise, or in emergencies. The disadvantages to saving in construction materials are that security can be a problem because bricks and bags of cement can easily disappear, and materials may deteriorate if left for long periods. In addition, incomplete construction is vulnerable to damage by natural causes.

Saving by lending

Many people, not just professional moneylenders, lend cash and grain. The advantages of this form of saving are the possible high returns to the lender. The disadvantages are a de facto limitation on the number of borrowers per lender, the transaction costs of making and collecting the loans, a general inability to diversify the portfolio, and risk, especially at times of regional shock or political upheaval.

Deposits with savings collectors

Savings services are in such great demand in developing countries that the poor are often willing to pay for the opportunity to save outside the house, entrusting their savings to paid collectors. Some collectors are informal, some are registered (see box 7.1 for reasons that poor people want to get their savings out of the house). For example, in Ghana—at a time when annual inflation was more than 30 percent—many people operating in the informal labor sector were paying savings collectors a 3.3 percent monthly fee to keep their money for them (Aryeetey and Steel 1994). The Ghana Cooperative Susu Collectors Association (GCSCA), a registered self-help cooperative organization with regional and district offices in 7 of Ghana's 10 regions, mobilizes savings from the poor through savings collectors. The clients (mostly women) save a fixed amount each day; at the end of each month the collector receives one day's savings as a commission (GCSCA 1999, 2000). Rutherford (2000) discusses savings collectors in India, and Mutesasira and others (1999) provide examples from Uganda (see also Rutherford and others 1999).

If you live in an urban slum or in a straw hut in a village, finding a safe place to store savings is not easy. Bank notes tucked into rafters, buried in the earth, rolled inside hollowed-out bamboo, or thrust into clay piggy banks, can be lost or stolen or blown away or may just rot…But the physical risks may be the least of the problem. Much tougher is keeping the cash safe from the many claims on it—claims by relatives who have fallen on hard times, by importunate neighbors, by hungry or sick children or alcoholic husbands, by your mother-in-law (who knows you have that secret hoard somewhere), and by landlords, creditors and beggars. Finally, even when you do have a little cash left over at the day's end, if you do not have somewhere safe to put it you will most probably spend it in some trivial way or other. I have lost count of the number of women who have told me how hard it is to save at home, and how much they would value a simple, safe way to save.

Source: Rutherford 2000, p. 2.

"The client is 'earning' interest at minus 30 percent APR"

In India informal savings collectors charge for holding the savings of poor clients. In one example from eastern India, women are furnished with cards containing 220 cells; the women save small prearranged amounts, marking off a box for each deposit.

> For example, one client may agree to save Rs 5 per cell, at the rate of one cell a day. This means that at the end of 220 days . . . she will have deposited 220 times Rs 5, or 1,100 rupees (. . . about $25 US). . . . When the contract is fulfilled—when the client has saved Rs 5,220 times . . . the client takes her savings back. However, she does not get it all back, since Jyothi [the collector] has to be paid for the service she provides. These fees vary, but in Jyothi's case it is 20 out of the 220 cells—or Rs 100 out of the Rs 1,100 saved. . . . We can calculate Jyothi's fee as a percentage of the cash she handles. Her fee, at Rs 100 in Rs 1,100, can be said to be 9 per cent. Or, we can look at it another way and work out the interest that her savers are earning on their savings. Obviously since they get back *less* than they put in, they are earning a negative interest rate, but what is that rate? . . . *On an average,* over the 220-day period [the saver] had half that amount, or Rs 550, deposited with Jyothi. On that Rs 550 she has paid an interest of Rs 100, or 18 percent over a 220-day period . . . the same as 30 percent over 365 days. So the *annual percentage rate* (APR) is about 30 percent. In other words, the client is 'earning' interest at *minus* 30 percent APR.[12]
> —Rutherford 2000, p. 14–15

In many such arrangements the savers' funds are not liquid, which is often perceived as a disadvantage. But there is evidence that in some cases these savings methods satisfy an "illiquidity preference" (see Aryeetey and Steel 1994). Thus a poor woman who wants to save to pay school fees and buy uniforms for her children can accomplish this with illiquid savings, which ensure that neither she nor anyone else can get to the savings until she is ready to use them for the designated purpose.

The advantages of this system include its convenience and the fact that the savings are out of the house, protecting them from other demands and to some extent from theft. The disadvantages are the negative returns and the risk that the savings collector, who often is not formally registered or supervised, may abscond with the funds.

Saving in labor obligations and expected reciprocation for past contributions

At the funeral of A's father, B provides two days' labor. B now has savings with A that will be withdrawn when a member of B's family dies

Low-income people also save in long-term obligations owed to them. Thus A helps B with his harvest; A can now save B's labor debt until it is needed (see Robinson 1975). Or, at the funeral of A's father, B provides two days' labor, while C provides a goat for the funeral meal. B and C both have savings with A that will be withdrawn when a member of each of their families dies. In planning a ceremony, the household or households responsible usually count their savings in labor and reciprocal obligations first, then deduct these from anticipated expenses in order to know the amount they must raise from their other forms of savings or from other sources of income and assets.

This system is common in many developing countries. In my experience in Sri Lanka and Indonesia, households kept careful, if informal, track of who owed whom what. In some cases the debt increases over time: A provides a goat to B for a wedding ceremony, then B provides a goat and some chickens for a similar ceremony in A's household. At the next round A provides two goats for B's ceremony, and so on. I have never found this to be perceived as an interest payment. But it may be an informal method for taking some account of inflation.

The advantages of saving in labor obligations owed to you are that this provides access to a supply of labor as needed and enables the fulfillment of social and religious obligations without exhausting more liquid forms of household savings. As a form of savings, the main disadvantage is the lack of fungibility: a goat owed by household D for a future funeral in household E is not the same as a goat that household E can use now to increase its herd.

Advantages and Disadvantages of Informal Savings and Financial Savings

Why do low-income people in developing countries save? Some of the most important reasons are reviewed below. Drawing on the experiences of BRI, BDB, BancoSol, and other institutions that mobilize microsavings, and on work by MicroSave-Africa (see, among others, Rutherford and others 1999; Wright 1999a; Mutesasira and others 1999; Mutesasira 1999; Mugwanga 1999; and MicroSave-Africa 1999), this section examines both the informal savings methods and the financial instruments used for each savings purpose. The advantages and disadvantages—as perceived by savers—of financial deposits and informal savings methods are shown in table 7.2. Many, probably most, savers who open bank accounts also maintain some informal savings.

The main advantage of financial savings instruments is the combination of security, convenience, liquidity, confidentiality, access to loans, and returns. And the savings are legally recognized. No informal savings mechanism offers this combination. The primary disadvantages are that

- The real value of the deposits may decline because of inflation or currency devaluation.
- There are transaction costs to the saver.
- A saver may need her funds when the bank is not open.
- Interest on the savings may be taxed (though the incomes of poor savers are often below the taxable minimum).
- There is a risk that the bank may fail or go bankrupt.
- For savers with very small accounts, no interest may be paid if the account is below a minimum monthly balance (though the minimum is usually quite low).

Because these disadvantages affect the various types of savings accounts discussed below, they are not discussed under each example. But other disadvantages are mentioned, as relevant. The advantages of financial savings may differ by instrument and by savings purpose and so are detailed below.

Only deposit accounts with no restrictions on withdrawals will draw savings that are being kept for emergencies

Emergencies and unexpected investment opportunities

Saving for emergencies is probably the most common reason for saving among low-income households in developing countries. The poor know that if a family emergency arises they will have few options, and the economically active poor tend to save in a variety of ways to deal with such situations. Low-income households also save to purchase materials needed for their enterprises, so that they can buy when prices are low. Informal savings used for these purposes are primarily cash, gold, and grain.

Interest-bearing, fully liquid accounts in secure and convenient financial institutions are much in demand for this purpose. In general, only deposit accounts with no restrictions on withdrawals will draw savings that are being kept for emergencies. The advantages of financial deposits are that the funds are secure, liquid, and in most cases earn returns.

Managing irregular income streams

Households and enterprises with uneven income streams (for example, from agriculture, fishing, and enterprises with seasonal variations) save when income is high for consumption in periods when income is low. Many informal savings methods are used for this purpose (see table 7.2). Depending on the nature of the income stream, liquid, semiliquid, and fixed deposit accounts can

Table **7.2**

Advantages and disadvantages for savers of informal savings and financial savings

Reason for saving	Primary forms of informal savings	Appropriate financial instruments	Primary advantages of financial products relative to informal savings	Primary disadvantages of financial products relative to informal savings
Emergencies and unexpected investment opportunities	Cash Gold and other valuables Grain and cash crops	Liquid accounts	Security and legal status Returns	
Managing irregular income streams	Cash Gold and other valuables Animals Grain and cash crops	Liquid, semiliquid, and fixed deposit accounts	Security and legal status Useful for consumption smoothing Returns provide income flows for low-income periods	Real value of savings may decline due to inflation or currency devaluation
Long-term investments (land purchase, children's education, housing construction, purchase of machinery)	Cash Gold and other valuables Animals Construction materials Land Savings collectors	Fixed deposit accounts; liquid and semiliquid accounts may also be used depending on the nature of the investment desired	Security and legal status Possibility of substantial returns over long periods	Transaction costs to the saver Interest may be taxed Savers with very small accounts may earn no returns
Social and religious obligations (life crisis ceremonies, religious holidays and pilgrimages, contributions to local funds and functions)	Cash Gold and other valuables Grain and cash crops Animals ROSCAs Reciprocal obligations Savings collectors	Fixed deposit accounts; semiliquid and liquid accounts may also be used	Security and legal status Through selection from a set of available instruments, financial savings can be customized to meet the needs of a wide variety of social and religious obligations	Risk of the institution's failure or bankruptcy
Old age and disability	Land Gold and other valuables Cash Animals	Fixed deposit accounts	Security and legal status Possibility of substantial returns over long periods	

Note: The table excludes savings in pastoral societies.

all be appropriate for this purpose. Multiple accounts—such as a combination of liquid and fixed deposit instruments—are often selected by savers to smooth consumption. The advantages of financial deposits in this case are that the funds are generally secure, the returns provide a flow of income in low-income periods, and, unlike most ROSCAs, for example, the savings are available when they are needed.

Long-term investments

Households often save to finance long-term investments such as land purchase, children's education, and house construction. Microentrepreneurs save for purchases such as machinery, vehicles, and land, and for construction. Saving for these types of investments can be done in a variety of forms (see table 7.2). Financial savings are often preferred, when these are available.

> "Like most parents, we have faced a lot of trouble with school fees, and only that [Uganda Women's Finance Trust] savings account could come to my rescue." Alice's husband's business had once again hit a snag, and so the children returned to school while the fees remained unpaid. It did not take long before her son was sent back home from school. This was a severe crisis since he was about to sit for his final exams. The school informed the family that it was not in the habit of offering exams on credit. "The only place I could find money was in my UWFT savings account." She paid the fees and her son was able to sit for the exams.
> —A Ugandan woman, quoted in Mutesasira and others 1999, p. 23

When financial instruments are available, fixed deposit accounts are commonly selected for saving for long-term goals. But semiliquid and liquid instruments are also used. The selection of instruments depends on the nature and timing of the planned investment, and use of more than one type of account is common. BDB offers special fixed deposit accounts for education and housing. For long-term investments, the advantages of financial deposits are the security of the funds and the possibility of substantial returns over long periods. The main disadvantages are the potential for the decline in the real value of the deposits because of inflation or currency devaluation and the risk that the institution may fail.

Social and religious obligations

While the forms vary, people everywhere commonly save for life crisis ceremonies, especially birth, puberty, marriage, and death; for religious holidays and pilgrimages; and for social obligations such as contributions to family, neighborhood, or village functions and collections. Nearly every form of informal savings is used for these purposes.

Where institutional microfinance services are available, fixed deposit accounts are often used. Other types of accounts are also used for this purpose, depending on the nature of the anticipated needs. BRI offers a special fixed deposit account for pilgrimages to Mecca, and BDB offers one for ceremonies. In Bolivia BancoSol clients use their regular fixed deposit accounts to save for festivities connected with saints' days.

The primary advantage of financial savings for this purpose is the use of a set of deposit instruments offering different ratios of liquidity and returns. By

BRI offers a special account for pilgrimages to Mecca, and BDB offers one for ceremonies. BancoSol clients use accounts to save for saints' days

using these instruments in different proportions, financial savings can be customized by the saver to meet a wide variety of social and religious obligations.

Old age and disability

Saving for old age and disability takes both direct and indirect forms. Indirect forms may include saving for investment in children's education and marriages, with the expectation that the parents will be cared for in old age by the children thus supported.[13] Direct forms involve saving in such forms as land, gold, cash, and animals.

Microsavings generally cannot be mobilized cost-effectively in areas that are very sparsely settled or where basic infrastructure is lacking

When financial instruments are available, fixed deposit accounts are often used for both direct and indirect savings of this type. Other instruments are also used, however. BDB offers a special long-term fixed deposit account designed for retirement savings. Advantages of financial deposits include the security of the savings and the possibility of substantial returns earned over long periods. The main disadvantages are the possible loss of the value of the savings due to inflation or currency devaluation and the possible failure of the institution.

The recent experience of BRI's unit desas is instructive in this regard. As a result of the Indonesian economic crisis that began in mid-1997, the value of the rupiah against the dollar fell sharply—from 2,383 rupiah at the end of 1996 to 4,650 rupiah at the end of 1997, to 8,025 rupiah at the end of 1998; by the end of 1999 the rupiah was valued at 7,430 to the dollar. Nevertheless, unit savings in rupiah terms more than doubled, from 7.1 trillion rupiah ($3 billion) at the end of 1996 to 17.1 trillion rupiah ($2.3 billion) at the end of 1999. During this period the number of deposit accounts increased by 8.0 million, from 16.1 million to 24.1 million. BDB also saw an increase in its savings and in the number of accounts during the same period.

The real value of the savings in these and other Indonesian banks declined as a result of the crisis. However, most unit desa clients are low-income people operating in the local economy. Their response seems to indicate that, even in a crisis, such savers still find a well-managed, secure, convenient bank with appropriate products and services to be among their best savings options (chapter 15).

Why Does the Formal Sector in So Many Countries Fail to Mobilize Microsavings?

In some countries government regulations—such as mandated interest rate spreads that are too low for institutional profitability—impede the mobilization of microsavings. Other obstacles may result from authorities' inability to supervise institutions that capture voluntary microsavings. Where they exist, these issues are crucial (see chapter 20). Other obstacles are found under particular circumstances. Thus savings generally cannot be mobilized cost-effectively in areas that are very sparsely settled, where basic infrastructure is lacking, or where monetization is low. To resolve these kinds of problems, there is no alternative but to change the regulation or improve the infrastructure.

However, three major obstacles to mobilizing microsavings remain in the minds of beholders in the formal financial sector. Despite substantial evidence to the contrary, it is still widely believed that the poor do not save, or will not save in banks; that the aggregate value of savings of the poor is too small to be worth capturing in the formal sector; and that banks could not collect small savings profitably.[14] These mistaken perceptions can largely be overcome with information, incentives, and political will.

Different views on mobilizing small savings

In the late 1960s and the 1970s many articles demonstrated the distortions that had resulted from subsidized rural credit programs. Some of these writings also highlighted the potentially vital but seriously neglected role of rural savings in developing healthy financial institutions and in improving rural financial markets.[15]

A number of economists argued, as Adams (1978, p. 548) put it, that "financial markets influence the forms in which savings are expressed, as well as the total amount of potential consumption which is diverted to savings." Adams, Bouman, Vogel, and others suggested that appropriate savings instruments providing positive real rates of return to the household can induce rural people to put more of their savings into financial form. This, in turn, "may increase the average rate of return realized by the household on its savings portfolio and induce the household to divert more of its income to S (savings-investment activities)" (Adams 1978, p. 550).

In addition, evidence collected over more than 30 years has shown that household savings are extensive in developing countries, even in low-income economies.[16] In fact, households are especially induced to save in countries where complementary markets (such as credit and insurance) are still at a low level of development. A 1962 United Nations study showed that household savings made up one-half to two-thirds of total savings in seven Asian countries (UN 1962; see Adams 1978 for discussion). Since then substantial savings by both households and enterprises have been reported from developing countries worldwide. Informal savings, as well as savings in formal financial institutions, have been widely documented in Asia, Africa, and Latin America.[17] A journal, *Savings and Development* (published by the Centre for Financial Assistance to African Countries, Milan) has been providing extensive documentation of savings in developing countries since 1977.

Yet financial institutions, governments, and donors often ignore or discount the worldwide evidence that low-income people save. Even massive household financial savings in developing countries like China and India are disregarded by much of the rest of the world.

A 1996 survey of donors is instructive. The survey, carried out by Women's World Banking and the United Nations Development Programme, asked the heads of donor agencies that fund microfinance programs to rank 12 issues of institutional development, such as credit management capacity and business planning (Women's World Banking 1996). Savings ranked 10th! While some donors

A 1996 survey asked the heads of donor agencies that fund microfinance programs to rank 12 issues of institutional development. Savings ranked 10th!

have begun to recognize the importance of savings mobilization in recent years, others may be concerned that sustainable microfinance programs could render their roles superfluous.

Because many policymakers and bankers assume that there is not much demand among poor people for financial savings instruments, they see no reason to give high priority to the development of financial institutions with voluntary savings programs. Underlying this view is an even more basic assumption—that most rural economies in developing countries do not generate enough business to be attractive to formal sector financial institutions (Bouman 1989).

Summarizing the conventional wisdom on this issue, Bouman (1989, pp. 122–24) states:

> Most rural economies of Asia can be characterized as penny economies in which money transactions between participants in the economy are very frequent, small-sized and measured, as it were, in dimes and quarters rather than dollars .... Like many other businesses, banks survive on volume and penny economies do not generate sufficient business volume.[18]

Yet in 1997 China's Rural Credit Cooperatives held $141 billion in savings; more than 85 percent was from rural household deposits. Similarly, in March 1996 India's more than 60,000 rural bank branches (of commercial banks, Regional Rural Banks, and cooperatives) held more than $26 billion in savings (Gupta 1997).[19]

Despite these sizable savings, the "penny economy" view of the developing world persists—unverified and too often unquestioned. An important result of the neglect of savings and of the view that local economies do not generate sufficient business is that most people do not have the opportunity to save in financial products appropriate for their needs, to earn returns on their deposits, and to leverage credit with savings. In addition, with their low savings, financial institutions serving the local levels of developing countries generally cannot meet the demand for microcredit. While other sources of commercial funds could be accessed to fund microloan portfolios, it is unlikely that anyone with a "penny economy" view of microfinance would attempt to do so.

Germidis, Kessler, and Meghir (1991, p. 23) comment about the neglect of savings:

> The excessive reliance on external sources of finance and the resulting atrophy of domestic financial circuits and markets also meant that the public authorities were foregoing the possibility of tapping the potential sources of savings which are present in the developing countries. These are often underestimated because the postulate that developing countries have a low or nonexistent savings capacity is, unfortunately, accepted without

Some donors may be concerned that sustainable microfinance programs could render their roles superfluous

question. . . . Yet even in the least developed countries, there is a savings capacity that is often undetected and frequently neglected.

In most developing countries domestic savings are accumulated mainly by households. Thus mobilizing domestic savings should be an important concern for institutions collecting savings, but this has been true in only a few developing countries (such as China, India, and Indonesia). Elsewhere, limited progress had been made on this front even by the end of the 1990s. Policymakers and bankers considering microfinance receive a lot of bad advice on formal sector mobilization of voluntary microsavings: there is no significant demand for institutional savings services because the poor cannot save, or will not save in banks; and "penny economies" do not generate enough business volume to be attractive to banks. In addition, there are two other kinds of common but generally wrong advice: if microsavings are collected, this effort should be carried out by specialized savings institutions, not by financial intermediaries; and banks are unlikely to be able to mobilize microsavings profitably.

The argument for specialized savings institutions that do not provide credit (see Gadway and O'Donnell 1996) is compelling only in regulatory environments where no other choice is possible. Under other circumstances government-supervised, sustainable microfinance intermediaries can be encouraged to mobilize savings from the public (see Jackelen and Rhyne 1991; Rhyne and Otero 1991; Christen, Rhyne, and Vogel 1995; Schmidt and Zeitinger 1996; and Robinson 1997a). Institutions that begin with savings and move to credit in a second stage represent a possible approach, but one that is usually not necessary. Because there is typically high demand for both services, financial intermediation is normally the better approach for a microfinance institution that is qualified and licensed to mobilize public savings. In addition, microfinance has relatively high operating costs, and in most cases the most profitable way to use locally mobilized deposits is to lend them out to creditworthy small borrowers.

In most cases the most profitable way to use locally mobilized deposits is to lend them out to creditworthy small borrowers

Can mobilizing the savings of the poor be financially viable?

One of the most hotly debated issues in microfinance is whether banks can collect small savings profitably. Schmidt and Zeitinger (1994, p. 18) have taken the lead in promulgating the argument that it is very expensive to mobilize savings in accounts with balances below $500:

> [An] institution . . . should think twice before it starts taking up an activity [savings mobilization] which may be as difficult as lending to the target group [poor people, especially small and microentrepreneurs] and which inevitably proves to be a very expensive source of funds. . . . The mobilization of small-scale savings is so expensive that one must ask why an intermediary which, in its lending operations, is already attempting to develop

a market that is difficult and expensive to serve, should be expected to deliver this additional range of services, which are costly and extremely difficult to provide.

While it is essential that microfinance institutions monitor carefully the costs of mobilizing savings, as well as the costs of delivering credit, it is incorrect to claim that capturing small savings is prohibitively expensive for financial institutions. This view is yet another red herring that draws policymakers and bankers away from developing profitable, large-scale microfinance institutions that provide financial intermediation among borrowers and savers. It is, of course, possible to mobilize small savings unprofitably. But this is certainly not the only option. There are five main problems with the Schmidt and Zeitinger (1994, 1996) argument on the high cost of mobilizing small savings.

Inadequate evidence. As the Consultative Group to Assist the Poorest's Working Group on Savings has put it:

> Schmidt/Zeitinger (1994) argued that mobilizing microsavings is costly ... [Their] skeptical conclusions question the possibility of significant mobilization of microsavings ... The validity of these conclusions remains open, however, due to the scarce underlying empirical evidence. In addition, the authors did not consider economies of scope and synergies between savings mobilization and credit operations.
> —Hannig and Wisniwski 1999, pp. 10–11

The general argument made by Schmidt and Zeitinger—that mobilizing microsavings is a high-cost activity—is based primarily on one 1993 study that examined the cost of mobilizing savings for accounts smaller than $500 in Peruvian municipal savings banks (*cajas municipales de ahorro y credito Peru*). Schmidt and Zeitinger (1994, p.15) cite the finding of that study, by Rochus Mommartz, that it cost the banks 40 percent a year to administer these accounts.[20] However, these banks faced exceptionally difficult circumstances at that time. In the 1980s Peru suffered hyperinflation, negative real income growth, and massive bank failures. These conditions diminished the capacity of many households to save and undermined public confidence in formal financial institutions.

A large share of the savings accounts of the municipal savings banks was held in very small accounts; in 1994 more than half the savings accounts in a study of two such banks were smaller than $10 (Bredenbeck 1997). Thus the banks had a large number of tiny interest-bearing accounts that would necessarily be costly to mobilize and to administer. In contrast, sustainable microfinance institutions that collect savings cost-effectively target a broader client base—everyone, including the very poor, located near the local branch—and typically use tiered interest rates paid on the minimum monthly account balance; they normally pay no interest on very small accounts.

It is, of course, possible to mobilize small savings unprofitably. But this is certainly not the only option

The economic situation in Peru began to turn around in the 1990s, and the municipal banks were able to mobilize more savings. While recent figures for the cost of savings at the banks are not available, their overall savings position has improved considerably. By 30 September 1998 the municipal savings banks held about $71 million in more than 118,000 accounts (Burnett, Cuevas, and Paxton 1999, p. 24). The average account size was $600. These figures suggest that the cost of mobilizing savings has fallen substantially, as this typically occurs when the average account size increases.

Overlooked evidence. The institutions that have the longest history of mobilizing savings in the microfinance context—and that document the opposite view in the argument—have been ignored or misrepresented in the presentation of the issues. BDB and BRI are widely recognized for their profitable savings mobilization among low-income borrowers and savers. Yet Schmidt and Zeitinger ignore BDB and seriously misrepresent BRI (1994, pp. 14–15).

> *[BRI's unit desa system] offers considerably higher interest rates on savings than, say, BRI itself, thus raising the suspicion that many deposit customers of BRI may simply have shifted their deposits to another part of the same conglomerate,* and that the Unit Desa's success has come at the expense of BRI and other big banks. In macroeconomic terms as well as in terms of improving the supply of deposit facilities, the value of these savings services is therefore quite limited. (emphasis added)

Schmidt and Zeitinger are wrong about BRI's unit desas. Interest rates on savings instruments at BRI's branches, which serve larger clients and do not provide microfinance services, are generally higher, not lower, than interest rates at the unit desas. This pricing policy reflects the higher costs at the units relative to the branches.

Thus in 1996 BRI branches offered two savings instruments: TABANAS, the national savings instrument, and an instrument known as Smart BRI. In December 1996 the interest rates on these accounts ranged from 13 to 15 percent. At the unit desas interest on savings accounts ranged from 10 to 13 percent.[21] Fixed deposit accounts were 14 to 15 percent at both the branches and the units. Thus Schmidt and Zeitinger are mistaken in claiming that the unit desas offer considerably higher interest rates than BRI. This claim was also incorrect in 1993-94, when their paper was written.

It is also worth noting that in 1996 the average size of the 16.1 million unit desa savings and deposit accounts (of all types) was $185, which strongly suggests that the system mobilizes its savings from its own smaller clients rather than from the larger savers in BRI branches. In contrast, the average account size in the branches was $1,015. In addition, small savers in Indonesia interviewed over a 10 year period consistently rated convenience to be far more important than returns. Schmidt and Zeitinger's view that "many deposit cus-

The institutions with the longest history of mobilizing micro-savings profitably collect savings from the public

tomers of BRI may simply have shifted their deposits to another part of the same conglomerate" does not reflect reality.

Schmidt and Zeitinger (1994, pp. 14–15) continue:

> The Asian experience seems to indicate that, although a relevant demand exists, it is difficult for target group-oriented institutions to mobilize a significant volume of "micro-deposits". Although we do not have data on the administrative costs of mobilizing savings, the high interest costs of mobilized funds alone would support the hypothesis that mobilizing small savings deposits is an expensive proposition in Asia.

Thailand's Bank of Agriculture and Agricultural Cooperatives increased its savings from $281 million in 1986 to $5 billion in 1996

But the Asian evidence does *not* support this proposition. A study by CGAP's Working Group on Savings analyzed the cost of savings in BRI's unit desa system in 1996 and estimated that the total cost of mobilizing savings and deposits, including the liquidity cost and reserve requirement, was 15.4 percent of the deposit balance (Maurer 1999, p. 134).[22] BRI's annual effective interest rates for the units' KUPEDES loans were between 26 and 32 percent, and the spread was quite adequate for the profitability of the unit desa system; the system has been profitable since 1986.

Schmidt and Zeitinger ignore BDB, which has profitably engaged in small-scale savings mobilization in Indonesia since 1970, and they do not offer evidence from any other Asian country to support their position on the high cost of mobilizing small savings in Asia.

It is strange for Schmidt and Zeitinger to claim that it is difficult for target group–oriented institutions to mobilize a significant volume of microdeposits in Asia. During the 1990s Thailand's Bank of Agriculture and Agricultural Cooperatives (BAAC) made a major effort to raise voluntary savings. BAAC increased its (heavily rural) savings from $281 million in 1986 to $5.4 billion in 1996 (both figures in 1996 dollars; BAAC 1997). Moreover, in 1997 GNP per capita in China was $860 and in India it was $310; in rural areas of both countries per capita income was generally lower than the national average. Given that China and India together account for more than two-thirds of Asia's population and that both have mobilized massive rural household savings, the evidence indicates that mobilizing small savings in Asia is, in fact, not "difficult."

Overemphasis on returns. Schmidt and Zeitinger's argument assumes that interest rates for savers with accounts smaller than $500 need to be high to counterbalance a lack of confidence in the institution. While this can happen under certain circumstances, two crucial points have been missed. First, institutions worthy of trust have numerous ways of building confidence among their clients. Second, most small savers are not sensitive to interest rates; they are far more concerned about security, convenience, liquidity, and confidentiality.

Do clients require a high return on microsavings? Burkina Faso's Réseau des Caisses Populaires (RCP), a savings and credit cooperative, provides a useful perspective. At the end of 1994 it had $4.8 million in savings from 64,000 member-savers, with an average account size of $75. The RCP had more than 17 times as many savers as borrowers—even though it paid no interest on savings. At the same time, the RCP had a ratio of one staff member to 582 savers, with $44,545 in savings for each staff member (Webster and Fidler 1996).

As noted, informal savings collectors and local cooperatives in some developing countries charge poor savers for collecting and holding their money; for the savers the returns are negative. The collectors know the extent of the demand, and they know that many of the poor are desperate for secure, convenient places to store their savings safely—and are willing to pay for this service.

In institutional commercial microfinance, banks design and price their loan and savings products together. What matters is the spread between lending and savings interest rates and the efficiency of the bank. An efficient bank that provides financial intermediation to microfinance clients—and that understands the extent of the demand for both savings and credit—has two basic options in setting and in adjusting its spread as necessary. First, given that moneylenders typically charge much higher interest rates for small loans and have high repayment rates, the nominal interest rates on an efficient bank's small loans can be set at the level required for institutional profitability. Second, at least some of the poor are so much in need of a secure place to store their savings that they pay savings collectors for such a service. Thus banks can set tiered interest rates, paying lower rates on smaller accounts than on larger ones, reflecting the higher cost of mobilizing and administering the smaller accounts. This is common practice at BRI's unit desas, BDB, and other microbanks that serve large numbers of small savers.

I have yet to meet a borrower who has left an efficient microcredit program with appropriate products, simple procedures, and good, prompt service, simply because the interest rate on loans was too high (see also Rosenberg 1996, p. 10). Nor have I met a microsaver provided with security, convenience, a choice of instruments providing different ratios of liquidity and returns, and good, prompt service, who closed her savings account of $500 or less because the interest rate was too low.

Overestimated frequency of transactions. Schmidt and Zeitinger assume that administrative costs are high in mobilizing small savings because the poor have a preference for liquidity; the implication is that on average there is high turnover in these accounts. Yet the study by CGAP's Working Group on Savings (Maurer 1999, p. 134) estimates the administrative costs of mobilizing savings in BRI's unit desas in 1996 to be just 2.2 percent of the deposit balance.

Poor savers do value liquidity highly—but in most cases because they want to have the option of withdrawing whenever they want, not because they want to use their accounts frequently. A 1987 study of BRI savers showed that in the fully liquid SIMPEDES account, the average number of transactions per month was slightly less than two. In general, small savers tend not to have high turnover in their accounts. Thus a preference for liquidity need not result in frequent

I have yet to meet a microsaver provided with security, convenience, and good products and services who closed her savings account because the interest rate was too low

transactions and high administrative costs. A second important reason that administrative costs need not be prohibitively high is given below.

Unrecognized importance of serving the public in containing administrative costs. Schmidt and Zeitinger's argument does not take into account the implications for savings mobilization that arise from the experiences of self-sufficient commercial microfinance institutions that serve the public (as opposed to serving only the poor). In such institutions loans are limited by a cap on the maximum loan size. But savings of any amount above a very small minimum are mobilized from low-, middle-, and high-income households, as well as from associations and institutions located near the institution's local outlet. Thus the institution serves small borrowers and all savers. Schmidt and Zeitinger (1994) argue that mobilizing funds from higher-income clients is difficult and expensive for microfinance institutions, but they do not provide evidence. BRI's unit desa system and BDB provide unmistakable evidence that this need not be the case. (See also Hannig and Wisniwski 1999 for a comparison of costs of savings mobilization in six microfinance institutions.)

Compared with microfinance institutions that collect savings only or mainly from members, the strategy of mobilizing savings from the public—individuals, organizations, institutions—results in larger average savings account sizes and, in most cases, in lower administrative costs for savings mobilization. Thus collecting savings from the public enables widespread service to poor savers, results in a higher volume of funds for small loans, and helps attain institutional profitability.

Collecting public savings enables widespread service to poor savers, makes more funds available for small loans, and helps attain institutional profitability

The Mobilization of Public Savings by Sustainable Microfinance Institutions

New microfinance institutions or those that fall into pattern 2 (good lenders but weak savings mobilizers) must consider three issues if they want to mobilize public savings. Are the necessary preconditions in place for collecting savings from the public? What products and services are suitable for the potential savers in their areas? And what is the appropriate sequencing in building the savings program? The answers to these questions will vary somewhat depending on the country and region. But sound savings programs in microfinance institutions are generally based on a number of common underlying principles.

Preconditions

There are five main preconditions for a microcredit institution to begin mobilizing public savings. The first three, however, are beyond the control of the institution. First, the mobilization of voluntary microsavings by an institution engaged in profitable financial intermediation requires an enabling macroeconomy and some political stability. Microfinance institutions cannot be expected to operate sustainably in countries suffering from hyperinflation or in regions experiencing continuing warfare or endemic and severe civil strife.

Second, an appropriate regulatory environment is required—or at least non-enforcement of inappropriate regulations. As discussed in chapter 20, commercial institutions that provide microfinance need appropriate regulations on such matters as interest rates, capital requirements for opening an institution, capital adequacy ratios, liquidity ratios, accounting and audit standards, requirements for opening branches, and reporting requirements (for discussion, see Berenbach and Churchill 1997; Christen 1997c; Churchill 1997b; Rock and Otero 1997; Ledgerwood 1999; and Christen and Rosenberg 1999).

Third, for the protection of their customers, especially savers, microfinance institutions that mobilize voluntary savings need to be publicly supervised. In most cases this means that the government must be willing to modify its banking supervision practices (so that the rules for microfinance institutions are suitable for their activities) and ensure that the supervisory body is able to monitor these institutions effectively. Thus the supervisory authorities must not permit unqualified institutions to mobilize public savings nor allow more institutions than can be effectively supervised to collect savings. It is important, however, that the country develop a capacity to supervise enough institutions to enable microfinance demand to be met.

These three preconditions are essential for the safe collection of public savings. If a country is experiencing hyperinflation or if its regulations stipulate interest rates on loans that are too low for institutional sustainability, these conditions must be changed before its financial institutions can mobilize voluntary microsavings profitably.

The fourth condition concerns the history, capability, and performance of the financial institution. Before mobilizing voluntary public savings, a microcredit institution should have demonstrated accountable ownership, effective governance, and consistently good management of its funds. It should be financially solvent, with a high rate of loan recovery, regularly earning good returns. In several developing countries I have met low-income people who entrusted their savings to small, unsupervised institutions and lost their life savings. Their anger was outweighed only by their despair. Only institutions with good records should be permitted to mobilize public savings—especially when the savings of the poor are concerned.

This condition—a good track record—refers to pattern 2 institutions that want to start capturing public savings. It is also possible, however, for banks to establish microfinance divisions or subsidiaries that begin their credit and savings programs simultaneously. In this case those entrusted with the institution's governance and management must ensure that appropriate products, services, pricing, and staffing are instituted, that everyone in the institution is held accountable for his or her performance, and that the emerging track record consistently demonstrates a high rate of timely loan repayment, prudent asset-liability management, and good financial management generally.

I have met low-income people who lost their life savings in small, unsupervised institutions. Their anger was outweighed only by their despair

The fifth condition is the allocation of high-level management resources to the institution's microfinance effort. As will be discussed in part 3, banks may be reluctant to appoint their best managers to microfinance divisions or subsidiaries. If that is the case, the institution should halt its microfinance efforts. The provision of simple, appropriate products to a large number of microfinance clients spread over a large area, with profitable intermediation between savers and borrowers, may look simple to an observer of a low-level outlet with a staff of, say, four people. But large-scale microfinance is a complex effort at the head office, and it requires high-level, experienced, open-minded, and dedicated managers. Efforts to mobilize public savings should begin only when all five preconditions have been met, although some leeway is possible for some issues of regulation and supervision. In many countries microfinance regulation and supervision and microfinance institutions are evolving simultaneously.

Designing and pricing savings instruments

The first step in designing and pricing savings instruments for the microfinance market should be careful market research and the design of savings and deposit instruments and services appropriate for demand in this market. Offering savers a selection of instruments that provide different ratios of liquidity and returns has proven popular with clients—and important for institutional profitability. Except for fixed deposit accounts, the minimum amount required to open an account and minimum monthly balances should be kept low.

Three basic deposit instruments are useful when an institution starts mobilizing voluntary savings; other products can be added as needed. (See Christen 1997a; Calvin 1995; Ledgerwood 1999; Bass and Henderson 2000 and Wright 2000 for discussion of microsavings products and their pricing) A basic combination is an interest-bearing liquid savings account, a higher-interest semiliquid savings account, and a fixed deposit account. The characteristics and uses of such instruments by specific banks are considered in volumes 2 and 3. A brief overview of the philosophy behind this combination of accounts is provided here.

Because most households and enterprises consider rapid access to at least some of their financial savings to be essential, interest-bearing liquid savings accounts are in great demand. Liquid accounts are also important for mobilizing deposits from people who have not previously had voluntary savings accounts. Even depositors who do not require high liquidity for the management of their finances often feel safer, especially in the beginning, if they know that they can obtain their funds at any time during the hours the institution is open. In addition to depositing savings from income flows, small savers often deposit cash previously held in their houses, as well as the proceeds from stocks held in other forms and converted to cash. But such deposits tend to be forthcoming only when savers are sure that they will have easy access to their savings. Many savers test the institution by depositing a small amount of savings in the beginning and then withdrawing in order to see how long the process takes and whether the funds are available as advertised.

Because unlimited numbers of withdrawals and deposits are permitted in the liquid instruments, interest rates must be kept relatively low. Such accounts

Banks are often reluctant to appoint their best managers to microfinance divisions. In that case the institution should halt its microfinance efforts

can be labor intensive and incur relatively high administrative costs. The absolute cost of administering a savings account is essentially constant regardless of the size of the account, but a small account is expensive to administer relative to the size of the deposit that the bank receives from the account. As noted, microbanking makes use of liquid accounts with tiered interest rates based on minimum monthly balances. Very small accounts receive no interest; interest rates are gradually increased on accounts with higher monthly balances. Only the highest tier need be at, or near, market rates. Typically only the largest of the account holders are interest sensitive; the rest tend to be content with appropriate products, security, liquidity, confidentiality, and good service. But market or near-market rates are important for the larger account holders, who tend to be interest sensitive. It is important to meet these savers' requirements because their deposits raise the average account size, making it possible for the institution to serve the public, including small savers, profitably.

Microfinance institutions that mobilize funds from the public collect deposits from better-off clients who live or work near the local branch. In addition to the liquid account, instruments appropriate for these clients that can be easily administered (such as fixed deposit accounts) should be made available. In addition, some microenterprise clients experience considerable enterprise growth and expand into substantial businesses with more extensive banking needs. These clients also require a choice of savings instruments, including fixed deposit accounts. Farmers and others with seasonal incomes may also use fixed deposit accounts for some of their savings, as is also common with people saving for long-term goals.

To be competitive, fixed deposit accounts must offer market rates, or near-market rates, to all account holders.[23] BDB, BRI's unit desas, BancoSol, China's Rural Credit Cooperatives, and India's Regional Rural Banks all offer fixed deposit accounts. Choices of maturities vary in different countries from 1 month to more than 10 years; those most in demand tend to be from about 6 months to 2 years. Many fixed deposit account holders also hold liquid accounts.

A third type of savings account—semiliquid accounts of varying kinds—falls between liquid and fixed deposit accounts in liquidity, returns, and often in institutional labor requirements. Semiliquid accounts may pay interest on all deposits while restricting withdrawals. One purpose of this type of product is to provide opportunities for holders of very small accounts to obtain returns on their deposits. In BRI's experience, however, many low-income savers opt for fully liquid accounts instead, forgoing interest in favor of liquidity.

Semiliquid accounts are generally not as important for microfinance as the other two account types. But in addition to being useful for the clients who choose them, the availability of a product that pays interest on all (or nearly all) accounts can be politically important. People with very small financial savings are generally ineligible for fixed deposit accounts because these normally have relatively high opening balances. Such savers would also typically not receive interest on liquid accounts because their monthly balances would be

In many countries microfinance regulation and supervision and microfinance institutions are evolving simultaneously

below the minimum for interest payments. This leaves an opening for political criticism of the bank for paying interest to rich savers but not to poor ones. Such criticism can be deterred by offering a semiliquid account with the characteristics described above. A client with very small savings can then choose freely between the liquid account that provides no interest for such small accounts and the interest-bearing semiliquid account.

Semiliquid accounts are appropriate for people who want to maximize returns rather than liquidity, but who do not want to tie up their savings for the time required for a fixed deposit account, or who do not have enough savings to meet the fixed deposit minimum. Semiliquid accounts are also used by clients to save for regular expenses that come due once or twice a month, such as rent or wage payments to employees.

In most cases the three account types should be offered together; many microsavers select two and in some cases all three instruments. Once the savings program is well established, other products can be added: special accounts to save for pilgrimages, education, housing, retirement, marriages, and other important events are popular. But in keeping with the general idea (discussed in volume 2) that microfinance must be kept simple so that it can be managed at the lowest level by locally hired managers, microbanks should not offer a wide range of instruments—either for savings or for credit. It is preferable to concentrate on a few products appropriate for the needs of microfinance clients. If a financial institution is initially able to offer only one product to microsavers, it should be a fully liquid, interest-bearing account with tiered interest rates. It is better, however, to offer a package of two or three products as discussed above, so that savers can customize their use of the products according to their needs.

Pricing of savings products must be carried out in conjunction with pricing of loan products, and with an intimate knowledge of the microfinance market. Within reasonable limits, a financial institution providing microfinance has considerable flexibility in pricing loan and savings products (except savings products for large account holders). Microfinance institutions need to set (and to adjust as necessary) the spread between interest rates on loans and on savings so that the spread is sufficient for the institution to be able to provide profitably both the products and services that are in demand.

Appropriate products will be effective in mobilizing savings from low-income clients only if accompanied by friendly, helpful service. Banks that give the impression that they serve only "serious people who have bundles of money" (a Ugandan bicycle delivery boy quoted in Rutherford and others 1999) will not succeed in mobilizing microsavings. The clients must be made to feel that the institution is there to serve them.

Sequencing a savings program

Some institutions serving microsavers begin with savings services, some start with savings and loans together, and some add voluntary savings mobilization to ongoing microcredit institutions. In all cases careful attention must

Microfinance must be kept simple so that it can be managed at the lowest level by locally hired managers

be paid to sequencing in developing the capacity to mobilize public savings. (See chapter 13 for a detailed analysis of the sequencing for savings mobilization undertaken by BRI's unit desas in the 1980s) The discussion below assumes that the preconditions discussed above have been met and that the institution is a bank or other licensed financial institution that is regulated and publicly supervised.

The institution's owners and managers should start by learning about international best practices in microfinance—and specifically about microfinance institutions that have mobilized voluntary savings. (Lessons can be learned from both the successes and the mistakes of other institutions.) Second, careful market research should be carried out in the prospective service area, and staff selected and trained for a pilot phase. Good examples of demand research are those carried out by BRI's unit desas (chapter 13) and by MicroSave-Africa for East Africa (Mutesasira and others 1999; Mugwanga 1999; Rutherford and others 1999; Wright and others 1999).

Third, a pilot project should be conducted and evaluated. This step is essential because, until the extent of the demand and the costs of different products (including labor) are known, only temporary interest rates can be set. If necessary (which is likely), a second-stage pilot project with revised products and prices should be carried out in a number of areas and evaluated carefully. Pilots are required to ensure that instruments are priced correctly, that operating costs are understood, that spreads enable profitability, that staff members are trained, and that information and communication systems work—before the institution attracts large amounts of savings.

While the number of borrowers can be controlled by the number of loans approved, savers cannot be turned away. Once an institution has opened its doors to public savings, it must have the capacity to provide the services the clients have been promised. Poor service or faulty cash management can easily drive away savers. During the pilot phase attention should also be given to the planning, logistics, management information systems, asset-liability management, and wider staff training that will be needed to expand the savings program.

Fourth, after the pilots have been evaluated and their results determined to be satisfactory, the institution can expand its savings services gradually throughout its branches, conducting staff training as the expansion moves from region to region. The key word here is gradually. Institutions should restrain themselves from expanding too quickly after pilots have been deemed successful. As the rollout takes place, staff, systems, buildings, equipment, methods of cash management, and the like must be in place before the collection of public savings begins in that region.

One bank manager who sought to expand directly from the pilot phase to immediate savings mobilization in all the bank's branches learned the hard way. Systems were not ready, staff members were insufficiently trained, and logistical problems were still severe when the bank's promotion campaign went into effect, advertising the availability of voluntary savings products at all branches. When the savings program opened, savers found long lines, har-

While the number of borrowers can be controlled by the number of loans approved, savers cannot be turned away

ried staff, and disgruntled customers. I talked with a saver who had opened a liquid account at her local branch as soon as these were available. I met her again two weeks later when she was standing in a long line, waiting to make a withdrawal from her account. While waiting, she told me that this was the third time she had tried to withdraw funds from her account, but on the other two occasions she had not been successful because the computer had been down. As she got to the window this time, she again asked to withdraw funds. The cashier was unable to access her computer file. Finally the exasperated customer said, "I would like to close my account." The cashier went away, came back a few minutes later, and said, "I am sorry, but you cannot close your account now because the computer is not working." The bank lost about a year in its savings efforts because it moved too quickly at the rollout stage; it then had to go back and put in place what should have been taken care of first.

Fifth, after successful introduction of savings services throughout the institution, the emphasis should switch from the logistics of expansion to the techniques of market penetration. Expansion is a necessary but insufficient condition for massive deposit mobilization. Well-run institutions that offer appropriate deposit facilities and services can quickly mobilize savings from people who live or work near the institutions' outlets. Market penetration of an outlet's wider service area, however, requires additional methods. These include developing a systematic approach to identifying potential depositors, implementing staff incentives based on performance, developing effective methods of communicating within the institution lessons learned from clients, undertaking additional market research, overhauling public relations, and engaging in massive staff training.

The length of time for each stage in the sequence will vary according to local conditions and the size of the institution. Still, a reasonable timeframe would be to complete the first four steps in about two years (three if necessary) and then be ready for rollout. Depending on the number of branches, the rollout should take from six months to a year. Market penetration is an ongoing process. But unless there are special problems in the institution or in the economy, a savings program in a large, well-managed bank should be well into the market penetration phase five years after taking the first step—by that time the bank should be financing a rapidly increasing share of its microloan portfolio from savings. And it should be studying investment strategies. In 10 years there may excess liquidity in the microfinance system because many microfinance clients want to save all the time in an institution that meets their needs, but to borrow only some of the time.

This sequencing may appear lengthy and cumbersome, but a voluntary savings program should be introduced gradually and carefully. Otherwise the institution stands to lose the trust of its clients—and eventually its own viability. An institution that introduces voluntary savings in an appropriate sequence should be able to meet local demand for savings services and to finance from its savings a growing volume of microcredit, enabling it to increase both outreach and profitability.

An institution that introduces voluntary savings in an appropriate sequence should be able to meet local demand and to finance a growing volume of microcredit

Who Benefits?

Who benefits from profitable microfinance institutions providing extensive voluntary savings services? The answer is almost everyone involved: individuals, women, households, and enterprises; groups, organizations, and institutions; the implementing financial institutions, governments, and donors; and the economy. Self-financing of investment is especially important for low-income households and microenterprises. The dearth of institutional deposit facilities at the local levels of most developing countries has an adverse effect on savers in general, and on low-income people in particular.

The many benefits of effective institutional savings mobilization are summarized below. These benefits assume careful government supervision of the financial institutions involved. If such supervision is not available, the deposits of poor savers may be at risk. As noted, supervision quality and capacity must be addressed by governments before microfinance programs are permitted to mobilize voluntary local savings. With good supervision, however, voluntary savings mobilization can help social and economic development in a number of ways.

Benefits to individuals and enterprises

When voluntary savings are locally mobilized by microfinance institutions, households and enterprises can benefit (see table 7.2). Microenterprises can self-finance in full or in part their working capital needs, as well as save toward investment needs. Savings accounts not only provide security, legal recognition of the asset, and returns, they also improve household financial management.[24] In addition, women have—in many cases for the first time—the opportunity to hold their savings in their own names.

Substantial growth in an institution's deposits can significantly increase the amount of credit available to small entrepreneurs, enabling them to obtain loans at a much lower cost than is otherwise available to them in the informal commercial market.

In addition, saving to build credit ratings and to leverage loans with deposits is of particular importance for low-income households and microenterprises because many of them lack the types of collateral acceptable for formal sector loans. Their deposits can be used as collateral for loans, which can then contribute to enterprise growth and rise in income. Savings accounts help low-income households smooth income flows and consumption patterns.

Many households and enterprises hold savings accounts and loans simultaneously. This strategy permits financial stocks to be held for emergencies, while loans, which are used for working and investment capital and in some cases for consumption, are repaid from income flows. A common misconception in microfinance is that an individual, household, enterprise, or association is either a borrower or a saver. In fact, many are both.

Benefits to groups, organizations, and institutions

Deposit instruments that permit savings to be held in the name of organizations can provide significant benefits to the depositing institution. BRI's pro-

Who benefits from profitable microfinance institutions providing extensive voluntary savings services? The answer is: almost everyone

vision that the unit desas' SIMPEDES (fully liquid) savings accounts may be held in the name of a group, organization, or institution opened a substantial new market for deposits (chapter 13). New savers included schools, village treasuries, government offices, religious institutions, development programs disbursing funds for rural projects, and a plethora of local organizations including voluntary agencies, informal savings and loan associations, and employee, women's, youth, religious, and sports associations. Previously, the group's president or treasurer had usually held the organization's funds at home in cash, providing easy opportunities for corruption and mismanagement. The members of many such groups prefer the new arrangement, though some group leaders think otherwise.

Thus on the day that SIMPEDES accounts were introduced in one region a street fight broke out in front of a unit desa between members of the local horse cart association and its treasurer. The members had heard that the new account allowed funds to be deposited in the name of organizations, and they wanted their group funds deposited in the name of the horse cart association. However, the treasurer objected. Only when the members threatened to elect a new treasurer were the funds deposited in the bank.

Such savings accounts refer only to the group savings of ongoing organizations that exist for other purposes, not to individual savings deposited in a group account—which is generally not a good idea. Group savings of the first type have been reported to improve the financial security of the group, to decrease opportunities for corruption, and to improve the accountability and financial management of group funds. The group, of course, also earns returns on the deposits.

Benefits to the implementing financial institutions

Deposits mobilized in conjunction with commercial credit programs enable the growth of sustainable microfinance institutions. Dependence on governments and donors for financing loan portfolios can be eliminated because the portfolios can be fully financed commercially. BRI and BDB finance all their loans from locally mobilized deposits, and both have been consistently profitable. Microfinance programs that are able to generate equity from profits can leverage commercial investment as well, as in the case of BancoSol. Finally, properly supervised financial intermediation imposes stringent financial discipline on a microfinance institution, benefiting both the institution and its clients.

Benefits to governments and donors

Governments and donors benefit because the funds they previously provided to finance microcredit portfolios can be used for other development purposes. Governments also gain because of the benefits to their economies and to the society more broadly.

Benefits to the economy, development, and equity

Institutional savings mobilization at the local level deepens financial markets. Higher domestic savings then enable higher gross domestic investment, con-

Institutional savings mobilization at the local level deepens financial markets, contributing to economic growth and equity

tributing to higher economic growth. And as microfinance helps the poor move out of poverty, equity improves.

———

Institutional commercial loans and informal commercial credit both have the capacity (present or potential) to meet much of the demand for microcredit. But borrowers usually must pay far more for informal commercial credit than for institutional loans. Microfinance institutions that mobilize public savings can make lower-cost institutional microcredit more widely available.

Whether microfinance intermediaries increase domestic savings or simply transfer these from the informal to the formal sector is not known (and should be investigated). But savings mobilization enables poor people to self-finance investment and to acquire and use "live capital," and it provides microbanking institutions with capital to lend out in small loans. Thus it seems reasonable to suppose that savings collection by microbanking institutions eventually helps increase domestic savings. In addition, many savers say that access to voluntary savings accounts imposes better discipline on them, and they save more.

Overall, microfinance fosters growth in low-income segments of the economy and improves the distribution of income. Charity is not required for microfinance and so can be directed toward other poverty alleviation tools for the very poor. Only institutional commercial microfinance combines the mobilization of voluntary savings, a moderate cost of credit for borrowers, and the widespread provision of financial services to low-income clients.

Notes

1. Deposit and savings accounts have been defined in a variety of ways. In the banking industry deposit generally refers to "an amount of funds consisting of cash and/or checks, draft, coupons, and other cash items that may be converted into cash upon collection," while a savings account refers to "money that is deposited in a bank, usually in small amounts periodically over a long period, and not subject to withdrawal by check" (J. Rosenberg 1993, pp. 107, 308). Because these distinctions are not always relevant in the microfinance market and because others are more important, the terms deposit and savings (when used to describe accounts and services) are used synonymously in this book.

2. See, among others, Adams (1973, 1978, 1984b, 1988); Bouman (1977, 1984, 1989); Lee, Kim, and Adams (1977); Mauri (1977); Von Pischke (1978, 1983b, 1991); Bourne and Graham (1980); Miracle, Miracle, and Cohen (1980); Howse (1983 [1974]); Von Pischke, Adams, and Donald (1983); Adams, Graham, and Von Pischke (1984).; Sideri (1984); Vogel (1984b); Agabin (1985); Adams and Vogel (1986), *Savings and Development* (various issues, 1977–99).

3. For example, a 1993 World Bank volume, *The Economics of Rural Organization* (Hoff, Braverman, and Stiglitz 1993), mentions savings on just 6 of its 568 pages. Although savings is a fundamental component of rural economics, it was forgotten in this book, as in many others.

4. This has been true of poor people I have met in every developing country I have visited. I do not know whether it holds for poor people in centrally planned

economies or in countries with extensive welfare programs. In developing countries the poor save in part because their only safety nets (family, friends, neighbors) are typically also poor, and options can be limited for emergencies, illness, and old age.

5. Other patterns such as savings banks that are not allowed to provide microcredit, or choose not to do so, are outside the scope of this discussion. But some examples are discussed in chapter 19.

6. For discussion of the problem of neglect of savings in local financial markets, see Adams (1978); Adams and Graham (1981); Vogel (1984b); Adams and Vogel (1986); Germidis, Kessler, and Meghir (1991); and Von Pischke (1991).

7. Yaron, Benjamin, and Piprek (1997, annex, p. 137) comment about the 2.1 million savings accounts, "Although no data on number of savers are available, this should be the minimum number since saving is obligatory."

8. The Integrated Rural Development Programme, a government-subsidized rural credit program, is highly politicized, has a very poor repayment record, and often does not reach the poor. The Indian government requires the RRBs to provide IRDP loans

9. In 1996 the RCCs were separated from the state-owned Agricultural Bank of China, where they had been located since the early 1960s. The RCCs became a separate institution managed by the Leading Group on Rural Financial Reforms, which was later absorbed by the People's Bank of China.

10. In addition to price, the decision on how much grain to store rests on the availability of grain in the local market, and on storage capacity and cost.

11. In some forest areas, a similar pattern is found among people who save in honey they collect. They store the honey (for as long as they can afford to) until the price is high.

12. As the author points out (p. 24), he used a simplified formula here in contrast to that required by law in the United Kingdom, which is the formula used in chapter 6 of this book: (1 plus the interest rate for the period quoted) to the power of the number of such periods in a year, minus 1. Had Rutherford used this formula, the saver's negative annual interest rate would have been higher.

13. Expectations for support of aging parents vary by culture. For example, in patrilineal (descent through the male line) societies a married woman may not be permitted to support her parents, as her responsibility is to her husband's family. In matrilineal societies (descent through the female line) a man will normally be expected to support his mother's brothers in old age, rather than his father.

14. For an example of the assumption that propensity to save is low in most rural areas and that rural savings mobilization is difficult, see Braverman and Guasch (1986).

15. See Adams (1973, 1978, 1984b, 1988); Bouman (1977, 1984, 1989); Von Pischke (1978, 1983b, 1991); Von Pischke, Adams, and Donald (1983); Adams, Graham, and Von Pischke (1984); Vogel (1984b); and Adams and Vogel (1986).

16. See Howse (1983 [1974]); Mauri (1977); Lee, Kim, and Adams (1977); *Savings and Development* (various issues 1977 to the present); Bourne and Graham (1980); Miracle, Miracle, and Cohen (1980); Sideri (1984); Agabin (1985). See Kelley and Williamson (1968) for a study of household savings in Indonesia.

17. See Mauri (1977); Von Pischke (1978, 1983b, 1991); Bouman (1979); Vogel (1984a); Adams (1984a, 1984b); Germidis, Kessler, and Meghir (1991); and Hulme and Mosley (1996).

18. Many Asian rural areas are among the most densely populated in the world. Given this view, one would have to consider the rural economies of Africa and Latin America as farthing economies!

19. Gupta, who was deputy governor of the Reserve Bank of India, the central bank when he wrote this paper, noted that: "the Indian financial system has an impressive record of mobilisation of savings from households. Savings in the form of financial assets account for 50 percent of such savings with bank deposits constituting

28.2 percent of financial assets. Deposits mobilised by rural financial institutions (commercial banks, RRBs, and cooperatives) have increased from US $217 million in 1969 to over US $26 billion at present. The success of savings mobilized by rural financial institutions is largely attributable to the public confidence in the financial system arising out of the ownership pattern of such institutions, deposit insurance, and the remarkable absence of bank failures over the last four decades." (p. 7).

20. Schmidt and Zeitinger cite two other institutions in their argument that mobilizing savings in accounts smaller than $500 is very expensive. One is the Badan Kredit Kecamatan (BKK) of Indonesia, credit organizations supervised by the provincial government of Central Java that mobilize voluntary savings. But the BKKs are primarily concerned with credit delivery. The other institution is BancoSol of Bolivia—which had just begun mobilizing voluntary savings at the time of the Schmidt and Zeitinger paper. Neither example provides evidence for Schmidt and Zeitinger's conclusion that mobilizing small voluntary savings is necessarily a high-cost activity.

21. At the rural unit desas, no interest was paid on accounts with balances under $4; in urban units no interest was paid on accounts with balances under $10. At the branches no interest was paid on savings accounts under $20. However, it is most unlikely that, given the distances and transaction costs involved, urban branch clients would seek out units in which to deposit their savings in order to receive interest on the $10 to $16 in their balances on which interest was not paid in the branches.

22. The study found that the interest cost was 12.4 percent and the administrative cost 2.2 percent. See chapter 13 for discussion.

23. An exception might be made in remote areas where there is little competition and where the bank may have higher transaction costs. This would hold both for fixed deposit accounts and for the highest tier in liquid savings accounts.

24. Microfinance clients often say that holding loans and deposit accounts has helped them improve household and enterprise management.

Glossary and Acronyms

ACCIÓN International	a nonprofit microfinance organization based in Somerville, Massachusetts (United States) that works with an extensive network of microfinance institutions in Latin America, the United States, and Africa
ACEP	Agence de Crédit pour l'Entreprise Privée (Senegal)
ACP	Acción Comunitaria del Péru (Peru)
ADMIC	Asociación Dinámica a Microempresas (Mexico)
ADOPEM	Asociación Dominicana para el Desarrollo de la Mujer (Dominican Republic)
AIMS	Assessing the Impact of Microenterprise Services, a project funded by USAID's Office of Microenterprise Development
arbitrage	the purchase of goods or securities in one market for immediate resale in another market to profit from a price discrepancy. Some informal commercial money-lenders take subsidized loans from banks and use some or all of the loan funds to lend to borrowers (often poor ones) in the informal credit market at higher interest rates.
ASA	Association for Social Advancement (Bangladesh)
ASCA	accumulating savings and credit association (also known as RESCA)
asymmetric information	a situation in which one party to a transaction has more (or different) information about the transaction than

	does the other party. In credit markets, the borrower has more information about his or her creditworthiness than does the lending institution.
attached labor	a system in which a borrower takes a loan from an informal lender and becomes "attached" to the lender: the borrower's labor (or that of a member of his or her household) belongs to the creditor until the loan is repaid (under a variety of payment systems)
BAAC	Bank for Agriculture and Agricultural Cooperatives (Thailand)
BancoSol	Banco Solidario (Bolivia)
BDB	Bank Dagang Bali (Indonesia)
BIMAS	*bimbingan massal* (mass guidance), the Indonesian government's subsidized agricultural credit program operated through BRI, 1970–85
BKD	Badan Kredit Desa (Indonesia)
BKK	Badan Kredit Kecamatan (Indonesia)
bonded labor	a subset of *attached labor* found especially in underdeveloped areas. The terms of the loan do not permit the borrower's work to provide both subsistence and loan repayment within the period specified. This practice typically aims to establish a long-term supply of cheap labor for the lender.
BRAC	Bangladesh Rural Advancement Committee (Bangladesh)
BRI	Bank Rakyat Indonesia (Indonesia)
BRK	Bankin Raya Karara (Niger)
CDF	Credit and Development Forum (Bangladesh)
CGAP	Consultative Group to Assist the Poorest, a multidonor international consortium formed in 1995 to assist the development of microfinance internationally. The CGAP Secretariat is at the World Bank in Washington, D.C.
compulsory savings	savings required as a condition of obtaining a loan. Also called forced or mandatory savings, such savings usually cannot be withdrawn until the loan is repaid or longer, and sometimes not until the borrower leaves the institution. Compulsory savings raise a loan's effective interest rate.
CPI	consumer price index
CPIS	Center for Policy and Implementation Studies (Indonesia)
desa	village (Indonesian)
DFID	Department for International Development (United Kingdom)

DPIS	Development Program Implementation Studies. A HIID project, 1979–83, funded by Indonesia's Ministry of Finance.
effective interest rate	interest rate calculated on a declining balance basis— that is, the real cost of the money actually in the client's hand from time to time, in contrast to a flat interest rate calculated on the original loan balance. The computation of effective interest rates should incorporate all fees, commissions, compulsory savings, and other costs paid by the borrower to the lender for the use of the borrowed money during each period of the life of the loan. But in practice these costs to the borrower are often omitted in stated effective interest rates.
FAMA	Fundación de Apoyo a la Microempresa (Nicaragua)
Finamérica	Financiera América (Colombia)
financial intermediaries	organizations that provide financial products and services (credit, savings, payment services, transfer facilities), intermediating between borrowers and lenders/savers
FINCA	Foundation for International Community Assistance. A nonprofit antipoverty organization based in Washington, D.C. that promotes the village banking method of microcredit delivery internationally.
flat interest rate	interest rate calculated on the original face amount of the loan (rather than, as in *effective interest rate,* on the declining balances owed after successive installment payments)
FUNADEH	Fundación Nacional para el Desarrollo de Honduras (Honduras)
FUNDES	Fundación para el Desarrollo Sostenible (Switzerland)
GCSCA	Ghana Cooperative Susu Collectors Association (Ghana)
GDP	gross domestic product
GEMINI	Growth and Equity through Microenterprise Investments and Institutions, a project funded by USAID in the 1990s
GNP	gross national product
HIID	Harvard Institute for International Development
IDB	Inter-American Development Bank
IMF	International Monetary Fund
informal commercial moneylenders	unregulated lenders whose subsidiary, primary, or sole occupation is the provision of credit with the expectation of profiting from the loan. Some lend at their

own risk, others intermediate between savers and borrowers—in which case the savers bear all or part of the risk.

interlinked transactions	transactions in which the parties trade in two or more markets and the terms of the trades are jointly determined. For example, a rice merchant provides loans to farmers who are also the merchant's rice suppliers; the terms for the loan and the purchase of the rice are set jointly.
IRDP	Integrated Rural Development Programme (India)
KIK	Kredit Investasi Kecil—Small Investment Loan Program (Indonesia)
KMKP	Kredit Modal Kerja Permanen—Small Permanent Working Capital Loan Program (Indonesia)
K-REP	Kenya Rural Enterprise Programme (Kenya)
KUPEDES	Kredit Umum Pedesaan, the loan product of BRI's unit desas. KUPEDES is an acronym for general rural credit, but after 1989—when these loans were offered in urban units as well as rural ones—KUPEDES became widely known as general purpose credit.
leverage	use of equity as a lever to obtain additional funds by borrowing or taking deposits
LPD	Lembaga Perkreditan Desa (Bali, Indonesia)
MBB	*The Microbanking Bulletin*
MFI	microfinance institution
microfinance	small-scale financial services provided to low-income clients
MicroRate	Private Sector Initiatives Corporation, known as MicroRate. A private microfinance rating company based in Washington, D.C.
MicroSave-Africa	a multidonor project in Africa that provides training and assists in the capacity-building efforts of microfinance institutions working to provide secure, appropriate savings services for poor people
monopolistic competition	a market in which a large number of firms provide outputs that are closely similar but are not perfect substitutes, due to product differentiation or geographic segmentation. Informal commercial moneylenders often operate under conditions of monopolistic competition.
monopoly	a market with only one seller
monopsony	a market with only one buyer
moral hazard	occurs when an individual acts to maximize his or her own welfare to the detriment of others in a situation

where the individual does not bear the full consequences of his or her actions because of information asymmetries, uncertainties, or contracts that prevent assignment of full damages. In the credit market context, the lender cannot fully monitor or enforce contracts because the lender cannot observe the borrowers' use of the loan funds. Yet the borrowers' limited liability provides an incentive to use loan proceeds for risky investments.

NGO	nongovernmental organization
OECD	Organisation for Economic Co-operation and Development
portfolio at risk	a measurement of portfolio quality, defined as the total outstanding balance of loans with late payments divided by the total outstanding balance of the loan portfolio
PRODEM	Fundación para la Promoción y Desarrollo de la Microempresa (Bolivia)
RCC	Rural Credit Cooperative (China)
RCP	Réseau des Caisses Populaires (Burkina Faso)
RESCA	regular (nonrotating) savings and credit association, also known as ASCA
RFI	rural financial institution
ROSCA	rotating savings and credit association
RRB	Regional Rural Bank (India)
savings collector	an individual or association that holds the savings of clients (usually poor savers) and charges a fee for the service. Savings collectors typically operate in the informal, unregulated economy, but some are registered entities.
SBP	Sustainable Banking with the Poor, an international collaborative project sponsored by the World Bank and other donor agencies to promote microfinance
SEWA	Self-Employed Women's Association (India)
SIMASKOT	*simpanan kota* (urban savings), a savings product offered in BRI's urban unit desas
SIMPEDES	*simpanan pedesaan* (rural savings), a savings product offered in BRI's rural unit desas
subsidized credit	Credit in which interest rates and other fees do not cover the full cost of making and collecting the loans. The full cost of providing microloans, as a percentage of the loans, is higher than the market rate for standard bank loans (so the market rates of conventional loans are usually subsidized rates if used for microloans).
subsidy dependence index (SDI)	percentage increase in the average yield obtained on a loan portfolio needed to compensate for the elimination of all subsidies in a financial institution

supply-leading finance	provision of loans (usually subsidized) in advance of demand for credit in order to induce economic growth
TABANAS	*tabungan nasional,* a national savings product (Indonesia)
transaction costs	When a lender (formal or informal) provides a loan to a borrower, both parties bear transaction costs. For the lender such costs include obtaining information about the creditworthiness of the borrower, administering the loan, and collecting it. Transaction costs that borrowers may incur include the opportunity cost of time spent traveling, preparing a loan application, and (in group lending programs) attending meetings; transportation costs; and bribes to officials.
UNDP	United Nations Development Programme
unit *desa*	The lowest level permanent outlet of BRI's microbanking system. Unit desas are located at the subdistrict level and provide financial services to the villages (desas) of that subdistrict.
USAID	U.S. Agency for International Development
UWFT	Uganda Women's Finance Trust
voluntary savings	savings deposited voluntarily in a financial institution.
WOCCU	World Council of Credit Unions
WWB	Women's World Banking

Bibliography

ACCIÓN International. 1991. "Exposing Interest Rates: Their True Significance for Microentrepreneurs and Credit Programs." Somerville, Mass.

———. 1997. *1996 Annual Report*. Somerville, Mass.

Adams, Dale W. 1973. "The Case for Voluntary Savings Mobilization: Why Rural Capital Markets Flounder." In U.S. Agency for International Development, *Spring Review of Small Farmer Credit*. Washington, D.C.

———. 1978. "Mobilizing Household Savings through Rural Financial Markets." *Economic Development and Cultural Change* 26 (3): 547–60.

———. 1984a. "Are the Arguments for Cheap Agricultural Credit Sound?" In D. W. Adams, D. H. Graham, and J. D. Von Pischke, eds., *Undermining Rural Development with Cheap Credit*. Boulder, Colo.: Westview Press.

———. 1984b. *Do Rural Savings Matter?* Studies in Rural Finance, Economics and Sociology Occasional Paper 1083. Ohio State University, Columbus, Ohio.

———. 1984c. "Effects of Finance on Rural Development." In D. W. Adams, D. H. Graham, and J. D. Von Pischke, eds., *Undermining Rural Development with Cheap Credit*. Boulder, Colo.: Westview Press.

———. 1988. "The Conundrum of Successful Credit Projects in Floundering Rural Financial Markets." *Economic Development and Cultural Change* 36 (2): 355–67.

Adams, Dale W., and Delbert A. Fitchett. 1992. *Informal Finance in Low-Income Countries*. Boulder, Colo.: Westview Press.

Adams, Dale W., and Douglas H. Graham. 1981. "A Critique of Traditional Agricultural Credit Projects and Policies." *Journal of Development Economics* 8 (3): 347–66.

Adams, Dale W., and Robert C. Vogel. 1986. "Rural Financial Markets in Low-Income Countries: Recent Controversies and Lessons." *World Development* 14 (4): 477–87.

Adams, Dale W., and J. D. Von Pischke. 1992. "Microenterprise Credit Programs: Déjà Vu." *World Development* 20 (10): 1463–70.

Adams, Dale W., Douglas H. Graham, and J. D. Von Pischke, eds. 1984. *Undermining Rural Development with Cheap Credit.* Boulder, Colo.: Westview Press.

Agabin, Meliza H. 1985. "Rural Savings Mobilization: Asian Perspective and Prospect." *CB Review* 37 (1): 7–15.

Agafonoff, Alex, and D. Wilkins. 1994. "Developing Financial Instruments to Support Poverty-Oriented Financial Institutions—Banco Solidario S.A." Opportunity International, Chicago, Ill.

Ahmed, Zia U. 1989. "Effective Cost of Rural Loans in Bangladesh." *World Development* 17 (3): 357–63.

Akerlof, George A. 1970. "The Market for 'Lemons': Quality Uncertainty and the Market Mechanism." *Quarterly Journal of Economics* 84 (3): 488–500.

Aleem, Irfan. 1993. "Imperfect Information, Screening, and the Costs of Informal Lending: A Study of a Rural Credit Market in Pakistan." In K. Hoff, A. Braverman, and J. E. Stiglitz, eds., *The Economics of Rural Organization: Theory, Practice, and Policy.* New York: Oxford University Press.

Aryeetey, Ernest, and William Steel. 1994. "Savings Collectors and Financial Intermediation in Ghana." Paper presented at the 37th annual meeting of the African Studies Association, 3–6 November, Toronto.

Aryeetey, Ernest, Hettige Hemamala, Machiko Nissanke, and William Steel. 1996. *Financial Market Fragmentation and Reforms in Sub-Saharan Africa.* World Bank Technical Paper 356. Washington, D.C.

BAAC (Bank for Agriculture and Agricultural Cooperatives). 1997. "The Bank for Agriculture and Agricultural Cooperatives: Savings Mobilization Case Study." Paper presented at a workshop on institutional commercial microfinance for the working poor, sponsored by Bank Rakyat Indonesia and the U.S. Agency for International Development, 12–13 June, Jakarta.

Bangladesh Bank. 1979. *Problems and Issues of Agricultural Credit and Rural Finance.* Dhaka.

Bardhan, Pranab K. 1980. "Interlocking Factor Markets and Agrarian Development: A Review of Issues." *Oxford Economic Papers* 32: 82–97.

———. 1984. *Land, Labor and Rural Poverty: Essays in Development Economics.* Delhi: Oxford University Press.

———, ed. 1989. *The Economic Theory of Agrarian Institutions.* Oxford: Clarendon Press.

Bardhan, Pranab K., and Ashok Rudra. 1978. "Interlinkage of Land, Labor, and Credit Relations: An Analysis of Village Survey Data in East India." *Economic and Political Weekly* 13 (6/7): 367–84.

———. 1980. "Types of Labor Attachment in Agriculture: Results of a Survey in West Bengal, 1979." *Economic and Political Weekly* 15 (35): 1477–84.

Basant, Rakesh. 1984. "Attached and Casual Labor Wage Rates." *Economic and Political Weekly* 19 (9): 390–95.

Bass, Jacqueline, and Katrena Henderson. 2000. "The Microfinance Experience with Savings Mobilization." USAID Microenterprises Best Practices Project. Weidemann Associates and Development Alternatives, Washington, D.C.

Bell, Clive. 1988. "Credit Markets, Contracts, and Interlinked Transactions." In H. Chenery and T. N. Srinivasan, eds., *Handbook of Development Economics.* Amsterdam: North-Holland.

———. 1993. "Interactions between Institutional and Informal Credit Agencies in Rural India." In K. Hoff, A. Braverman, and J. E. Stiglitz, eds., *The Economics of Rural Organization: Theory, Practice, and Policy.* New York: Oxford University Press.

Bell, Clive, and T. N. Srinivasan. 1985. "An Anatomy of Transactions in Rural Credit Markets in Andhra Pradesh, Bihar, and Punjab." World Bank, Washington, D.C.

———. 1989a. "Interlinked Transactions in Rural Markets: An Empirical Study of Andhra Pradesh, Bihar and Punjab." *Oxford Bulletin of Economics and Statistics* 51 (1): 73–83.

———. 1989b. "Some Aspects of Linked Product and Credit Market Contracts among Risk-Neutral Agents." In P. K. Bardhan, ed., *The Economic Theory of Agrarian Institutions.* Oxford: Clarendon Press.

Berenbach, Shari, and Craig Churchill. 1997. "The Regulation and Supervision of Microfinance Institutions: Experience from Latin America, Asia, and Africa." Occasional Paper 1. Microfinance Network, Washington, D.C.

Bester, H. 1985. "Screening versus Rationing in Credit Markets with Imperfect Information." *American Economic Review* 75 (4): 850–55.

Bhaduri, Amit. 1973. "Agricultural Backwardness under Semi-Feudalism." *Economic Journal* 83: 120–37.

———. 1977. "On the Formation of Usurious Interest Rates in Backward Agriculture." *Cambridge Journal of Economics* 1 (4): 341–52.

Binswanger, Hans P., and Mark R. Rosenzweig, eds. 1984. *Contractual Arrangements, Employment, and Wages in Rural Labor Markets in Asia.* New Haven, Conn.: Yale University Press.

Blair, Harry W. 1984. "Agricultural Credit, Political Economy, and Patronage." In D. W. Adams, D. H. Graham, and J. D. Von Pischke, eds., *Undermining Rural Development with Cheap Credit.* Boulder, Colo.: Westview Press.

Boomgard, James, and Kenneth J. Angell. 1990. "Developing Financial Services for Microenterprises: An Evaluation of USAID Assistance to the BRI Unit Desa System in Indonesia." GEMINI Technical Report 6. Development Alternatives, Bethesda, Md.

———. 1994. "Bank Rakyat Indonesia's Unit Desa System: Achievements and Replicability." In M. Otero and E. Rhyne, eds., *The New Role of Microenterprise Finance: Building Healthy Financial Institutions for the Poor.* West Hartford, Conn.: Kumarian Press.

Bottomley, Anthony. 1964. "Monopoly Profit as a Determinant of Interest Rates in Underdeveloped Rural Areas." *Oxford Economic Papers* 16 (1): 31–37.

———. 1975. "Interest Rate Determination in Undeveloped Rural Areas." *American Journal of Agricultural Economics.* 57 (2): 7–16.

———. 1983. "Interest Rate Determination in Underdeveloped Rural Areas." In J. D. Von Pischke, D. W. Adams, and G. Donald, eds., *Rural Financial Markets in Developing Countries: Their Use and Abuse.* Baltimore, Md.: The Johns Hopkins University Press. Extracted from *American Journal of Agricultural Economics* 57 (2): 279–91 (1975).

Bouman, F. J. A. 1977. "Indigenous Savings and Credit Societies in the Third World." *Savings and Development* 1 (4): 181–214.

———. 1979. "The ROSCA: Financial Technology of an Informal Savings and Credit Institution in Developing Countries." *Savings and Development* 3 (4): 253–76.

———. 1984. "Informal Saving and Credit Arrangements in Developing Countries: Observations from Sri Lanka." In D. W. Adams, D. H. Graham, and J. D. Von Pischke, eds., *Undermining Rural Development with Cheap Credit.* Boulder, Colo.: Westview Press.

———. 1989. *Small, Short and Unsecured: Informal Finance in Rural India.* Delhi: Oxford University Press.

Bourne, Compton, and Douglas H. Graham. 1980. "Funding and Viability of Rural Development Banks." *Savings and Development* 4 (4): 303–19.

Braverman, Avishay, and J. Luis Guasch. 1984. "Capital Requirements, Screening and Interlinked Sharecropping and Credit Contracts." *Journal of Development Economics* 14 (3): 359–74.

————. 1986. "Rural Credit Markets and Institutions in Developing Countries: Lessons for Policy Analysis from Practice and Modern Theory." *World Development* 14 (10/11): 1253–67.

————. 1989. "Rural Credit Reforms in LDCs: Issues and Evidence." *Journal of Economic Development* 14 (1): 7–34.

————. 1993. "Administrative Failures in Rural Credit Programs." In K. Hoff, A. Braverman, and J. E. Stiglitz, eds., *The Economics of Rural Organization: Theory, Practice, and Policy.* New York: Oxford University Press.

Braverman, Avishay, and T. N. Srinivasan. 1981. "Credit and Sharecropping in Agrarian Societies." *Journal of Development Economics* 9 (3): 289–312.

Braverman, Avishay, and Joseph E. Stiglitz. 1982. "Sharecropping and the Interlinking of Agrarian Markets." *American Economic Review* 77 (4): 695–715.

Bredenbeck, Kirsten. 1997. "Savings Mobilization: Lessons from the Peruvian Municipal Savings Banks in Trujillo and Sullana." *Savings and Development* 31 (1): 87-107.

Breman, Jan. 1974. *Patronage and Exploitation: Changing Agrarian Relations in South Gujarat, India.* Berkeley: University of California Press.

BRI (Bank Rakyat Indonesia). 1994. *BRI Village Units.* Jakarta.

————. 1996a. *BRI Unit Products.* Jakarta: International Visitors Program.

————. 1996b. *Keberadaan dan Prospek KUPEDES Sebagal Sumber Pembiayaan Usaha Kecil.* Jakarta: BRI Urusan Perencanaan dan Litbang.

————. 1997a. *BRI Unit Organization and Management.* Jakarta: International Visitors Program.

————. 1997b. *Introduction to BRI's Unit Banking System.* Jakarta: International Visitors Program.

————. 1998a. *Badan Kredit Desa.* Jakarta: International Visitors Program.

————. 1998b. *Developing the BRI Unit System: Policy Issues.* Jakarta: International Visitors Program.

Buckley, Graeme. 1996a. "Financing the Jua Kali Sector in Kenya." In D. Hulme and P. Mosley, eds., *Finance Against Poverty.* vol. 2. London: Routledge.

————. 1996b. "Rural Agricultural Credit in Malawi." In D. Hulme and P. Mosley, eds., *Finance Against Poverty.* vol. 2. London: Routledge.

Burnett, Jill, Carlos Cuevas, and Julia Paxton. 1999. "Peru: The Cajas Municipales de Ahorro y Credito." Case Studies in Microfinance. World Bank, Sustainable Banking with the Poor project, Washington, D.C.

Calvin, Barbara. 1995. "Operational Implications of Introducing Savings Services." Paper Delivered at the MicroFinance Network Conference, 8 November, Cavite, Philippines.

Campion, Anita, and Victoria White. 1999. "Institutional Metamorphosis: Transformation of Microfinance NGOs into Regulated Financial Institutions." Occasional Paper 4. MicroFinance Network, Washington, D.C.

Carstens, Catherine Mansell. 1995. "Las Finanzas Populares en Mexico: El Redescubrimiento de un Sistema Financiero Olvidado (English draft)." Institute Technologico Autonome de Mexico, Mexico City.

Caskey, John P. 1996. "Consumer Financial Services and the Poor." Swarthmore College, Swarthmore, Penn.

Castello, Carlos, Katherine Stearns, and Robert P. Christen. 1991. "Exposing Interest Rates: Their True Significance for Microentrepreneurs and Credit Programs." Discussion Paper 6. ACCIÓN International, Somerville, Mass.

CGAP (Consultative Group to Assist the Poorest). 1997a. "Anatomy of a Microfinance Deal: A New Approach to Investing in Micro-finance Institutions." Focus Note 9. World Bank, Washington D.C.

———. 1997b. "CGAP Year Two—A Synopsis: June 1995–June 1997." World Bank, Washington, D.C.

———. 1997c. "The Challenge of Growth for Microfinance Institutions: The BancoSol Experience." Focus Note 6. World Bank, Washington, D.C.

———. 1997d. "Effective Governance for Micro-finance Institutions." Focus Note 7. World Bank, Washington D.C.

———. 1997e. "How CGAP Member Donors Fund Micro-finance Institutions." Focus Note 11. World Bank, Washington D.C.

———. 1997f. "State Owned Development Banks in Micro-finance." Focus Note 10. World Bank, Washington D.C.

———. 1998a. *Business Planning and Financial Modeling for Microfinance Institutions: A Handbook.* Technical Tool Series 2. New York: Pact Publications.

———. 1998b. "Commercial Banks in Microfinance: New Actors in the Microfinance World." Focus Note 12. World Bank, Washington, D.C.

———. 1998c. "The Consultative Group to Assist the Poorest: A Microfinance Program." Focus Note 1, revised edition. World Bank, Washington, D.C.

———. 1998d. "Cost Allocation for Multi-Service Microfinance Institutions." Occasional Paper 2. World Bank, Washington, D.C.

———. 1998e. "Savings Mobilization Strategies: Lessons From Four Experiences." Focus Note 13. World Bank, Washington, D.C.

———. 1998f. *Status Report to the Executive Directors of the World Bank July 1995–March 1998.* World Bank, Washington D.C.

Chamberlin, E. H. 1933. *The Theory of Monopolistic Competition.* Cambridge, Mass.: Harvard University Press.

Chandavarkar, Anand G. 1987. *The Informal Financial Sector in Developing Countries.* Occasional Paper 2. South East Asian Central Banks Research and Training Center, Kuala Lumpur.

Charitonenko, Stephanie, Richard H. Patten, and Jacob Yaron. 1998. "Indonesia: Bank Rakyat Indonesia, Unit Desa 1970–1996." Case Studies in Microfinance. World Bank, Sustainable Banking with the Poor project, Washington, D.C.

Chaudhuri, Kalyan. 1976. "Bonded Labor." *Economic and Political Weekly* 11 (11): 415–16.

Chaves, Rodrigo A., and Claudio Gonzalez-Vega. 1996. "The Design of Successful Rural Financial Intermediaries: Evidence from Indonesia." *World Development* 24 (1): 65–78.

Chen, Martha Alter. 1991. *Coping with Seasonality and Drought.* New Delhi: Sage Publications.

Christen, Robert Peck. 1989. "What Microenterprise Credit Programs Can Learn from the Moneylenders." Discussion Paper 4. ACCIÓN International, Somerville, Mass.

———. 1997a. *Banking Services for the Poor: Managing for Financial Success.* Somerville, Mass.: ACCIÓN International.

———. 1997b. "Highlights." *MicroBanking Bulletin* 1 (November).

———. 1997c. "Issues in the Regulation and Supervision of Microfinance." In R. Rock and M. Otero, eds., *From Margin to Mainstream: The Regulation and Supervision of Microfinance.* Monograph 11. Somerville, Mass.: ACCIÓN International.

Christen, Robert Peck, Elisabeth Rhyne, and Robert Vogel. 1995. *Maximizing the Outreach of Microenterprise Finance: The Emerging Lessons of Successful Programs.* USAID Program and Operations Assessment Report 10. Washington, D.C.: U.S. Agency for International Development.

Christen, Robert Peck, and Richard Rosenberg. 1999. "The Rush to Regulate: Legal Frameworks for Microfinance." CGAP Occasional Paper 4. World Bank, Consultative Group to Assist the Poorest, Washington, D.C.

Chu, Michael. 1997. "Reflections on Accessing Capital Markets." In C. Churchill, ed., *Establishing a Microfinance Industry: Governance, Best Practices, Access to Capital Markets.* Washington, D.C.: MicroFinance Network.

————. 1998a. "Key Issues of Development Finance." ACCIÓN International, Somerville, Mass.

————. 1998b. "Microfinance: Funding Opportunities in Emerging Markets." Paper presented at Goethe University's second annual seminar on new development finance, September, Frankfurt.

————. 1999. "Tapping Capital Markets: Microfinance as an Emerging Industry." ACCIÓN International, Somerville, Mass.

Churchill, Craig, ed. 1997a. *Establishing a Microfinance Industry: Governance, Best Practices, Access to Capital Markets.* Washington, D.C.: MicroFinance Network.

————. 1997b. "Regulation and Supervision of Microfinance Institutions." Occasional Paper 2. Microfinance Network., Washington, D.C.

————. 1998. *Moving Microfinance Forward: Ownership, Competition, and Control of Microfinance Institutions.* Washington, D.C.: MicroFinance Network.

CPIS (Center for Policy and Implementation Studies). 1988a. *Report on Informal Sector Labor.* Jakarta.

————. 1988b. *Savings Report No. 9.* Jakarta.

Credit and Development Forum. Various issues. *CDF Statistics* (published semiannually). Dhaka.

Darling, Malcolm L. 1978 [1925]. *The Punjab Peasant in Prosperity and Debt.* 4th ed. Columbia, Mo.: South Asia Books.

Davalos, Maria, J. Sebsted, M. Manundo, W. Kiiru, and C. Neill. 1994. *Evaluation Report of the USAID Kenya Rural Enterprise Program Cooperative Agreement.* Washington, D.C.: U.S. Agency for International Development.

de Silva, G. V. S., and others. 1979. "Bhoomi Sena: A Struggle for People's Power." *Development Dialogue* 2: 3–70.

de Soto, Hernando. 1989. *The Other Path: The Invisible Revolution in the Third World.* New York: Harper & Row.

————. 2000. *The Mystery of Capital: Why Capitalism Triumphs in the West and Fails Everywhere Else.* London: Bantam Press.

Dhanagare, D. N. 1985. "Rural Development, Poverty, and Protest." *Contributions to Indian Sociology* 19 (2): 349–58.

Dichter, Thomas. 1999. "NGOs in Microfinance: Past, Present and Future—An Essay." World Bank, Sustainable Banking with the Poor project, Washington, D.C.

Donald, Gordon. 1976. *Credit for Small Farmers in Developing Countries.* Boulder, Colo.: Westview Press.

DPIS (Development Program Implementation Studies). 1983–84. "DPIS Reports." Nos. 1–5. Jakarta.

Drake, Deborah, and María Otero. 1992. *Alchemists for the Poor: NGOs as Financial Institutions.* Monograph 6. Somerville, Mass.: ACCIÓN International.

Dunn, Elizabeth. 1997. "Diversification in the Household Economic Portfolio." Assessing the Impact of Microenterprise Services (AIMS), Washington, D.C.

Eaton, B. C. 1976. "Free Entry in One-Dimensional Models." *Journal of Regional Science* 16: 21–33.

Eaton, B. C., and R. G. Lipsey. 1978. "Freedom of Entry and the Existence of Pure Profit." *Economic Journal* 88: 455–69.

Eaton, Jonathan, and Mark Gersovitz. 1981. "Debt with Potential Repudiation: Theoretical and Empirical Analysis." *Review of Economic Studies* 48 (2): 289–309.

Feder, Gershon, Lawrence J. Lau, Justin Y. Lin, and Xiaopeng Luo. 1993. "The Nascent Credit Market in Rural China." In K. Hoff, A. Braverman, and J. E.

Stiglitz, eds., *The Economics of Rural Organization: Theory, Practice, and Policy*. New York: Oxford University Press.

Feith, Herbert. 1988. "The Interest Rate Structure and Factors Affecting Interest Rate Determination in the Informal Rural Credit Market in Sri Lanka." *Savings and Development* 12 (3): 249–67.

Floro, Segrario L., and Pan A. Yotopoulos. 1991. *Informal Credit Markets and the New Institutional Economics: The Case of Philippine Agriculture*. Boulder, Colo.: Westview Press.

Gadway, John F., and M. G. O'Donell. 1996. "Financing Micro-Enterprises and Rural Smallholders."

Galbraith, John Kenneth. 1952. "The Role of Credit in Agricultural Development." In E. K. Bauer, ed., *Proceedings of the International Conference on Agricultural and Co-operative Credit*. vol. 1. Berkeley: University of California Press.

Gamba, Charles. 1958. "Poverty and Some Socio-Economic Aspects of Hoarding, Saving and Borrowing in Malaya." *Malayan Economic Review* 3 (2): 33–62.

Gangopadhyay, Shubhashis, and Kunal Sengupta. 1986. "Interlinkages in Rural Markets." *Oxford Economic Papers* 38 (1): 112–21.

Germidis, Dimitri, Dennis Kessler, and Rachel Meghir. 1991. *Financial Systems and Development: What Role for the Formal and Informal Financial Sectors?* Paris: Development Center, Organisation for Economic Co-operation and Development.

Ghana Cooperative Susu Collectors Association. 1999. "Ghana Cooperative Susu Collectors Association." Accra.

———. 2000. "Performance Indicators, June 2000." Paper presented at the Small Enterprise Education and Promotion (SEEP) Network's "New Directions in Village Banking: A Consultative Forum," 11–15 December, Leesburg, Va.

Ghate, Prabhu, Arindam Das-Gupta, Mario Lamberte, Nipon Poapongaskorn, Dibyo Prabowo, and Atiq Rahman. 1993. *Informal Finance: Some Findings from Asia*. New York: Oxford University Press.

Glosser, Amy. 1994. "The Creation of BancoSol in Bolivia." In M. Otero and E. Rhyne, eds., *The New World of Microenterprise Finance: Building Healthy Financial Institutions for the Poor*. West Hartford, Conn.: Kumarian Press.

Gonzalez-Vega, Claudio. 1976. "On the Iron Law of Interest Rate Restrictions: Agricultural Credit Policies in Costa Rica and Other Less Developed Countries." Ph.D. diss. Stanford University, Department of Economics, Stanford, Calif.

———. 1992. "Do Financial Institutions Have a Role in Assisting the Poor?" Economics and Sociology Occasional Paper 2169. Ohio State University, Rural Finance Program, Columbus.

———. 1993. *From Policies to Technologies, to Organizations: The Evolution of the Ohio State University Vision of Rural Financial Markets*. Economics and Sociology Occasional Paper 2062. Ohio State University, Rural Finance Program, Columbus.

———. 1994. "Stages in the Evolution of Thought on Rural Finance: A Vision from the Ohio State University." Economics and Sociology Occasional Paper 2134. Ohio State University, Department of Agricultural Economics and Rural Sociology, Columbus.

———. 1995. "Is Informal Finance Desirable?" Microenterprise Development Brief 2. U.S. Agency for International Development, Washington, D.C.

Gonzalez-Vega, Claudio, Mark Schreiner, Richard Meyer, Jorge Rodriguez, and Sergio Navaja. 1997. "BancoSol: The Challenge of Growth for Microfinance Organizations." In H. Schneider, ed., *Microfinance for the Poor?* Paris: Development Center, Organisation for Economic Co-operation and Development.

Government of Ceylon [Sri Lanka], Department of Census and Statistics. 1954. *Final Report of Economic Survey of Rural Ceylon, 1950–51*. Colombo.

Government of India. 1960. *Agricultural Labor in India: Report on the Second Inquiry, 1956–57. Volume 1: All India.* New Delhi.

Government of the Philippines. 1980. *Presidential Committee on Agricultural Credit.* Manila.

Grameen Foundation. 1998. *Grameen Connections: The Newsletter of Grameen Foundation USA* 1 (1): 12.

Gramlich, Edward M. 2000. Speech presented at the Fair Housing Council of New York, 14 April, Syracuse, N.Y.

Guellich, Margaret, ed. "Aster's Story." *The Wooden Bell* 8 (5). Catholic Relief Services, Baltimore, Md.

Gulli, Hege. 1998. *Microfinance and Poverty: Questioning the Conventional Wisdom.* Washington D.C.: Inter-American Development Bank.

Gupta, R. V. 1997. "Policy and Environment in Establishing Sustainable Microfinance Institutions in India." Paper presented at a workshop on institutional commercial microfinance for the working poor, sponsored by Bank Rakyat Indonesia and the U.S. Agency for International Development, 12–13 June, Jakarta.

Hannig, Alfred, and Sylvia Wisniwski, eds. 1999. *Challenges of Microsavings Mobilization: Concepts and Views from the Field.* Consultative Group to Assist the Poorest Working Group on Savings Mobilization. Eschborn, Germany: Deutsche Gesellschaft für Technische Zusammenarbeit (GTZ).

Harper, Edward B. 1968. "Social Consequences of an 'Unsuccessful' Low-Caste Movement." In James Silberg, ed., *Social Mobility in the Caste System in India.* The Hague: Mouton.

Harriss, Barbara. 1983. "Money and Commodities: Their Interaction in a Rural Indian Setting." In J. D. Von Pischke, D. W. Adams, and G. Donald, eds., *Rural Financial Markets in Developing Countries: Their Use and Abuse.* Baltimore, Md.: The Johns Hopkins University Press.

Hart, Gillian. 1986a. "Exclusionary Labor Arrangements: Interpreting Evidence on Employment Trends in Rural Java." *Journal of Development Studies* 22 (4): 681–96.

———. 1986b. "Interlocking Transactions: Obstacles, Precursors, or Instruments of Agrarian Capitalism?" *Journal of Development Economics* 23 (1): 177–203.

———. 1986c. *Power, Labor and Livelihood: Processes of Change in Rural Java.* Berkeley: University of California Press.

Hart, Keith. 1986. "The Informal Economy." *Cambridge Anthropology* 6 (1–2): 845–56.

Hellman, Judith Adler. 1994. *Mexican Lives.* New York: The New Press.

Herath, G. 1996. "Rural Credit Markets and Imperfect Information: A New Perspective." *Savings and Development* 20: 241–53.

Higgins, Benjamin H. 1968 [1959]. *Economic Development.* 2d ed. London: Constable.

Hillier, Brian, and M. V. Ibrahimo. 1993. "Asymmetric Information and Models of Credit Rationing." *Bulletin of Economic Research* 45: 271–304.

Hoff, Karla, Avishay Braverman, and J. E. Stiglitz, eds. 1993. *The Economics of Rural Organization: Theory, Practice, and Policy.* New York: Oxford University Press.

Hoff, Karla and Joseph E. Stiglitz. 1993. "Imperfect Information and Rural Credit Markets: Puzzles and Policy Perspectives." In K. Hoff, A. Braverman and J. E. Stiglitz, eds., *The Economics of Rural Organization: Theory, Practice, and Policy.* New York: Oxford University Press.

———. 1998. "Moneylenders and Bankers: Price-Increasing Subsidies in a Monopolistically Competitive Market." *Journal of Development Economics* 55: 485–518.

Hollis, Aidan, and Arthur Sweetman. 1998. "Microcredit: What Can we Learn from the Past?" *World Development* 26 (10): 1875–91.

Hook, Richard. 1995. "The Experience of Bank Rakyat Indonesia." In E. Brugger and S. Rajapatirana, eds., *New Perspectives on Financing Small Businesses in Developing Countries.* San Francisco, Calif.: International Center for Economic Growth and Fundación para el Desarrollo Sostenible (FUNDES).

Hossain, Mahabub. 1988. *Credit for Alleviation of Rural Poverty: The Grameen Bank in Bangladesh.* IFPRI Research Report 65. Washington, D.C.: International Food Policy Research Institute.

Howse, C. J. 1983. "Agricultural Development without Credit." In J. D. Von Pischke, D. W. Adams, and G. Donald, eds., *Rural Financial Markets in Developing Countries: Their Use and Abuse.* Baltimore, Md.: The Johns Hopkins University Press. Extracted from *Agricultural Administration* 1 (4): 259–62 (1974).

Hulme, David, and Paul Mosley. 1996. *Finance against Poverty.* London: Routledge.

IDB (Inter-American Development Bank). 1995. *The IDB and Microenterprise: Promoting Growth with Equity.* Washington, D.C.

IMF (International Monetary Fund). 1997. *International Financial Statistics Yearbook 1997.* Washington, D.C.

———. 1998. *International Financial Statistics Yearbook 1998.* Washington, D.C.

———. 1999a. *International Financial Statistics 1999.* Washington, D.C.

———. 1999b. *International Financial Statistics Yearbook 1999.* Washington, D.C.

Indian School of Social Sciences. 1976. *Bonded Labor in India.* Calcutta: India Book Exchange.

Institute for Development of Economics and Finance. 1998. *Dimensi Teoritis dan Praktis: Kupedes Dan Simpedes BRI.* Jakarta: Divisi Bisnin Mikro BRI.

Jackelen, Henry R., and Elisabeth Rhyne. 1991. "Towards a More Market-Oriented Approach to Credit and Savings for the Poor." *Small Enterprise Development* 2 (4): 4–20.

Jaffee, Dwight M., and Thomas Russell. 1976. "Imperfect Information, Uncertainty and Credit Rationing." *Quarterly Journal of Economics* 90 (4): 651–66.

Kamble, N. D. 1979. *Poverty within Poverty: A Study of the Weaker Sections in a Deccan Village.* Bangalore: Institute for Social and Economic Change.

———. 1982. *Bonded Labor in India.* New Delhi: Uppal Publishing House.

Keeton, William. 1979. *Equilibrium and Credit Rationing.* New York: Garland Publishing.

Kelley, Allen C., and Jeffrey G. Williamson. 1968. "Household Savings Behavior in the Developing Economies: The Indonesian Case." *Economic Development and Cultural Change* 16 (3): 385–403.

Khandker, Shahidur R., Baqui Khalily, and Zahed Khan. 1995. *Grameen Bank: Performance and Sustainability.* World Bank Discussion Paper 206. Washington, D.C.

Kindleberger, Charles P. 1996 [1978]. *Manias, Panics, and Crashes: A History of Financial Crises.* 3rd ed. New York: John Wiley & Sons.

Kotowitz, Y. 1987. "Moral Hazard." In J. Eatwell, M. Milgate, and P. Newman, eds., *The New Palgrave: A Dictionary of Economics.* New York: Stockton Press.

Krutzfeldt, Hermann. 1997. "BancoSol: Group Lending in a Competitive Market." In C. Churchill, ed., *Establishing a Micro-finance Industry: Governance, Best Practices, Access to Capital Markets.* Washington, D.C.: Microfinance Network.

———. 1998. "Markets: Marketing Strategies in a Competitive Microfinance Environment." In C. Churchill, ed., *Moving Microfinance Forward: Ownership, Competition, and Control of Microfinance Institutions.* Washington, D.C.: MicroFinance Network.

Kumar, Dharma. 1965. *Land and Caste in South India: Agricultural Labor in the Madras Presidency during the Nineteenth Century.* Cambridge: Cambridge University Press.

Ladman, Jerry R. 1971. "Some Empirical Evidence on Unorganized Rural Credit Markets." *Canadian Journal of Agricultural Economics* 19 (3): 61–66.

Ladman, Jerry R., and Jose I. Torrico. 1981. "Informal Credit Markets in the Valle Alto of Cochabamba, Bolivia." In J. J. Brasch and S. R. Rouch, eds., *1981 Proceedings of the Rocky Mountain Council on Latin American Studies Conference*. Lincoln: University of Nebraska.

Ledgerwood, Joanna. 1999. *Microfinance Handbook, An Institutional and Financial Perspective*. Washington, D.C.: World Bank, Sustainable Banking with the Poor project.

Lee, Tae Young, Dong Hi Kim, and Dale W. Adams. 1977. "Savings Deposits and Credit Activities in South Korean Agricultural Cooperatives, 1961–75." *Asian Survey* 17 (12): 1182–94.

Leibenstein, Harvey. 1957. *Economic Backwardness and Economic Growth*. New York: Wiley.

Lewis, W. A. 1955. *The Theory of Economic Growth*. Homewood, Ill.: Irwin.

Li, C. M. 1952. "The Subsistence Farmer in the Process of Economic Development." In E. K. Bauer, ed., *Proceedings of the International Conference on Agricultural and Cooperative Credit*. vol. 1. Berkeley: University of California Press.

Long, Millard. 1968. "Interest Rates and the Structure of Agricultural Credit Markets." *Oxford Economic Papers* 20 (1): 276–87.

Loubière, Jacques Trigo. 1997. "Supervision and Regulation of Microfinance Institutions: The Bolivian Experience." In R. Rock and M. Otero, eds., *From Margin to Mainstream: The Regulation and Supervision of Microfinance*. Monograph 11. Somerville, Mass.: ACCIÓN International.

Malhotra, Mohini. 1992a. "Informal Financial Intermediaries in Bolivia." Development Alternatives, Bethesda, Md.

———— 1992b. "Poverty Lending and Microenterprise Development: A Clarification of the Issues." GEMINI Working Paper 30. Development Alternatives, Bethesda, Md.

Marla, Sarma. 1981. *Bonded Labor in India: National Survey on the Incidence of Bonded Labor*. New Delhi: Biblia Impex Private Ltd.

Martokoesmono, Soeksmono Besar. 1993. *Beyond the Frontiers of Indonesian Banking and Finance*. Rotterdam: Labyrint Publication.

Maurer, Klaus. 1999. "Bank Rakyat Indonesia (BRI), Indonesia." In A. Hannig and S. Wisniwski, eds., *Challenges of Microsavings Mobilization: Concepts and Views from the Field*. Eschborn, Germany: Deutsche Gesellschaft für Technische Zusammenarbeit (GTZ).

Mauri, Arnaldo. 1977. "A Policy to Mobilize Rural Savings in Developing Countries." *Savings and Development* 1 (1): 14–25.

Mayhew, Henry. 1968 [1861–62]. *London Labor and the London Poor: A Encyclopedia of the Condition and Earnings of Those Who Do Not Work, Those That Cannot Work, and Those That Will Not Work*. 4 vols. New York: Dover Publications.

McCourt, Frank. 1996. *Angela's Ashes*. New York: Simon and Schuster.

Mears, Leon. 1981. *The New Rice Economy of Indonesia*. Yogyakarta: Gadjah Mada University Press.

Mellor, John. 1966. *The Economics of Agricultural Development*. Ithaca, N.Y.: Cornell University Press.

Meyer, Richard L. 1985. "Deposit Mobilization for Rural Lending." United Nations Food and Agriculture Organization, Rome.

MicroBanking Bulletin. 1997. Issue 1 (November). Economics Institute, Boulder, Colo.

————. 1998. Issue 2 (July). Economics Institute, Boulder, Colo.

————. 1999. Issue 3 (July). Calmeadow, Toronto and Washington, D.C.

————. 2000a. Issue 4 (February). Calmeadow, Toronto and Washington, D.C.

————. 2000b. Issue 5 (September). Calmeadow, Toronto and Washington, D.C.

MicroSave-Africa. 1999. "Savings in Africa: A Collection of Savings from MicroSave-Africa." United Nations Development Programme and U.K. Department for International Development, Kampala, Uganda.

————. 2000. "It's Expensive to be Poor: Losses Suffered by People Saving in the Informal Sector." Kampala, Uganda.

Miracle, Marvin P. 1973a. "Economic Incentives for Loan Agents." In U.S. Agency for International Development, *Spring Review of Small Farmer Credit*. Washington, D.C.

————. 1973b. "Notes on Developing Small Farmer Credit Institutions in Third World Countries." In U.S. Agency for International Development, *Spring Review of Small Farmer Credit*. Washington, D.C.

Miracle, Marvin P., Diane S. Miracle, and Laurie Cohen. 1980. "Informal Savings Mobilization in Africa." *Economic Development and Cultural Change* 28 (4): 701–24.

Montgomery, Richard, D. Bhattacharya, and David Hulme. 1996. "Credit for the Poor in Bangladesh." In D. Hulme and P. Mosely, eds., *Finance against Poverty*. vol. 2. London: Routledge.

Moore, Frank J. 1953. "Moneylenders and Co-operators in India." *Economic Development and Cultural Change* 2 (2): 139–59.

Morduch, Jonathan. 1998a. "Does Microfinance Really Help the Poor? New Evidence from Flagship Programs in Bangladesh." Harvard University, Department of Economics and Harvard Institute for International Development, Cambridge, Mass., and Stanford University, Hoover Institution, Stanford, Calif.

————. 1998b. "The Grameen Bank: A Financial Reckoning." Stanford University, Hoover Institution, Stanford, Calif.

————. 1998c. "The Microfinance Schism." Princeton University, Princeton, N.J.

Mosley, Paul. 1996. "Metamorphosis from NGO to Commercial Bank: The Case of BancoSol in Bolivia." In D. Hulme and P. Mosley, eds., *Finance against Poverty*. vol. 2. London: Routledge.

Mosley, Paul, and Rudra Prasad Dahal. 1987. "Credit for the Rural Poor: A Comparison of Policy Experiments in Nepal and Bangladesh." *Manchester Papers on Development* 3 (2): 45–59.

Mugwanga, E. H. A. 1999. "Use and Impact of Savings Services for Poor People in Kenya." MicroSave-Africa, Kampala, Uganda.

Mundle, Sudipto. 1976. "The Bonded of Palamau." *Economic and Political Weekly* 11 (18): 653–56.

Mutesasira, Leonard. 1999. "Savings and Needs: An Infinite Variety." MicroSave-Africa, Kampala, Uganda.

Mutesasira, Leonard, and others. 1999. "Use and Impact of Savings Services among the Poor in Uganda." MicroSave-Africa, Kampala, Uganda.

Mutua, Albert Kimanthi. 1994. "The Juhudi Credit Scheme: From a Traditional Integrated Method to a Financial Systems Approach." In M. Otero and E. Rhyne, eds., *The New World of Microenterprise Finance: Building Healthy Financial Institutions for the Poor*. West Hartford, Conn.: Kumarian Press.

Neale, Walter C. 1969. "Land Is to Rule." In R. E. Frykenberg, ed., *Land Control and Social Structure in Indian History*. Madison: University of Wisconsin Press.

Negishi, Takashi. 1987. "Monopolistic Competition and General Equilibrium." In J. Eatwell, M. Milgate, and P. Newman, eds., *The New Palgrave: A Dictionary of Economics*. New York: Stockton Press.

Nisbet, Charles. 1967. "Interest Rates and Imperfect Competition in the Informal Credit Market of Rural Chile." *Economic Development and Cultural Change* 16 (1): 73–90.

Ohkawa, Kazushi, and Henry Rosovsky. 1965. "A Century of Japanese Economic Growth." In W. W. Lockwood, ed., *The State and Economic Enterprise in Japan: Essays on the Political Economy of Growth.* Princeton, N.J.: Princeton University Press.

Otero, María. 1994. "The Evolution of Non-Governmental Organizations toward Financial Intermediation." In M. Otero and E. Rhyne, eds., *The New World of Microenterprise Finance: Building Healthy Financial Institutions for the Poor.* West Hartford, Conn.: Kumarian Press.

———. 1997. "Latin America: ACCIÓN Speaks Louder Than Words." *UNESCO Courier* (January): 28–29.

———. 1998. "Types of Owners for Microfinance Institutions." In C. Churchill, ed., *Moving Microfinance Forward: Ownership, Competition and Control of Microfinance Institutions.* Washington, D.C.: MicroFinance Network.

Otero, María, and Elisabeth Rhyne, eds. 1994. *The New World of Microenterprise Finance: Building Healthy Financial Institutions for the Poor.* West Hartford, Conn.: Kumarian Press.

Park, Albert. 1998. "Rural Financial Market Development in China." World Bank, China Rural Vision Project, Washington, D.C.

Patrick, Hugh T. 1983. "Financial Development and Economic Growth in Developing Countries." In J. D. Von Pischke, D. W. Adams, and G. Donald, eds., *Rural Financial Markets in Developing Countries: Their Use and Abuse.* Baltimore, Md.: The Johns Hopkins University Press. Extracted from *Economic Development and Cultural Change* 14 (2): 174–89 (1966).

Patten, Richard H., and Jay K. Rosengard. 1991. *Progress with Profits: The Development of Rural Banking in Indonesia.* San Francisco, Calif.: International Center for Economic Growth and Harvard Institute for International Development.

Patten, Richard H., and Donald R. Snodgrass. 1987. "Monitoring and Evaluating KUPEDES (General Rural Credit) in Indonesia." HIID Development Discussion Paper 249. Harvard Institute for International Development, Cambridge, Mass.

Patten, Richard H., Jay K. Rosengard, and Don E. Johnston Jr. 1999. "The East Asian Crisis and Microfinance: The Experience of Bank Rakyat Indonesia through mid-July 1999." Harvard Institute for International Development, Cambridge, Mass.

Paxton, Julia. 1996. "Worldwide Inventory of Microfinance Institutions." World Bank, Sustainable Banking with the Poor project, Washington, D.C.

Penny, David H. 1983. "Farm Credit Policy in the Early Stages of Agricultural Development." In J. D. Von Pischke, D. W. Adams, and G. Donald, eds., *Rural Financial Markets in Developing Countries: Their Use and Abuse.* Baltimore, Md.: The Johns Hopkins University Press. Extracted from *Australian Journal of Agricultural Economics* 12 (1): 32–45 (1968).

Pingle, Urmila, and Christoph von Furer-Haimendorf. 1998. *Tribal Cohesion in the Godavari Valley.* Hyderabad, India: Booklinks Corporation.

Rahman, Atiq. 1992. "The Informal Financial Sector in Bangladesh: An Appraisal of Its Role in Development." *Development and Change* 23: 147–68.

Rao, G. Hanumantha. 1977. *Caste and Poverty: A Case Study of Scheduled Castes in a Delta Village.* Malikpuram, India: Savithri Publications.

Ray, Debraj, and Kunal Sengupta. 1989. "Interlinkages and the Pattern of Competition." In P. K. Bardhan, ed., *The Economic Theory of Agrarian Institutions.* Oxford: Clarendon Press.

Reserve Bank of India. 1954a. *All-India Rural Credit Survey. Volume 1: The Survey Report*. Bombay.

———. 1954b. *All-India Rural Credit Survey. Volume 2: The General Report*. Bombay.

———. 1954c. *All-India Rural Credit Survey. Volume 3: The Technical Report*. Bombay.

Rhyne, Elisabeth. 1998. "The Yin and Yang of Microfinance: Reaching the Poor and Sustainability." *MicroBanking Bulletin* 2: 6–8.

———. Forthcoming. *Mainstreaming Microfinance: How Lending to the Poor Began, Grew and Came of Age in Bolivia*. Bloomfield, Conn.: Kumarian Press.

Rhyne, Elisabeth, and Robert Peck Christen. 1999. *Microfinance Enters the Marketplace*. Washington D.C.: U.S. Agency for International Development.

Rhyne, Elisabeth, and María Otero. 1991. "A Financial Systems Approach to Microenterprise." GEMINI Working Paper 18. Development Alternatives, Bethesda, Md.

Rhyne, Elisabeth, and Richard Rosenberg. 1998. "A Donor's Guide to Supporting Microfinance Institutions." CGAP Occasional Paper. World Bank, Consultative Group to Assist the Poorest, Washington, D.C.

Rhyne, Elisabeth, and Linda S. Rotblatt. 1994. *What Makes Them Tick? Exploring the Anatomy of Major Microenterprise Finance Organizations*. Monograph 9. Somerville, Mass.: ACCIÓN International.

Riley, John. 1987. "Credit Rationing: A Further Remark." *American Economic Review* 77 (1): 224–27.

Robinson, Joan. 1933. *The Economics of Imperfect Competition*. London: Macmillan.

Robinson, Marguerite S. 1975. *Political Structure in a Changing Sinhalese Village*. Cambridge South Asian Studies 15. Cambridge: Cambridge University Press.

———. 1980. "Lightning Change: Planning for the Rural Poor in India." *South Asian Anthropologist* 1 (1): 35–44.

———. 1988. *Local Politics: The Law of the Fishes*. Delhi: Oxford University Press.

———. 1992a. "The Role of Savings in Local Financial Markets: The Indonesian Experience." GEMINI Working Paper 33. Development Alternatives, Bethesda, Md.

———. 1992b. "Rural Financial Intermediation: Lessons from Indonesia." HIID Development Discussion Paper 434. Harvard Institute for International Development, Cambridge, Mass.

———. 1994a. "Financial Intermediation at the Local Level: Lessons from Indonesia." HIID Development Discussion Paper 482. Harvard Institute for International Development, Cambridge, Mass.

———. 1994b. "Savings Mobilization and Microenterprise Finance: The Indonesian Experience." In M. Otero and E. Rhyne, eds., *The New World of Microenterprise Finance: Building Healthy Financial Institutions for the Poor*. West Hartford, Conn.: Kumarian Press.

———. 1995a. "Indonesia: The Role of Savings in Developing Sustainable Commercial Financing of Small and Micro-Enterprises." In E. A. Brugger and S. Rajapatirana, eds., *New Perspectives on Financing Small Businesses in Developing Countries*. San Francisco, Calif.: International Center for Economic Growth and Fundación para el Desarrollo Sostenible (FUNDES).

———. 1995b. "Leading the World in Sustainable Microfinance: The 25th Anniversary of BRI's Unit Desa System." Bank Rakyat Indonesia, Jakarta.

———. 1995c. "The Paradigm Shift in Microfinance: A Perspective from HIID." HIID Development Discussion Paper 510. Harvard Institute for International Development, Cambridge, Mass.

———. 1995d. "Where the Microfinance Revolution Began: The First 25 Years of the Bank Dagang Bali." GEMINI Working Paper 53. Development Alternatives, Bethesda, Md.

————. 1996. "Addressing Some Key Questions on Finance and Poverty." *Journal of International Development* 8 (2): 153–61.

————. 1997a. "Introducing Savings in Microcredit Institutions: When and How?" CGAP Focus Note 8. Consultative Group to Assist the Poorest, World Bank, Washington, D.C.

————. 1997b. "Microfinance in Indonesia." *UNESCO Courier* (January): 24–27.

————. 1997c. "Sustainable Microfinance." In Dwight H. Perkins, Richard Pagett, Michael Roemer, Donald R. Snodgrass, and Joseph J. Stern, eds., *Assisting Development in a Changing World: The Harvard Institute for International Development, 1980–1995.* Based in part on a contribution by Richard H. Patten. Cambridge, Mass.: Harvard Institute for International Development.

————. 1997d. "Sustainable Microfinance at the Bank Rakyat Indonesia: The Economic and Social Profits." Paper presented at a workshop on institutional commercial microfinance for the working poor, sponsored by Bank Rakyat Indonesia and the U.S. Agency for International Development, 12–13 June, Jakarta.

————. 1998a. "Microfinance: The Paradigm Shift from Credit Delivery to Sustainable Financial Intermediation." In Carl K. Eicher and John M. Staatz, eds., *Agricultural Development in the Third World.* 3d ed. Baltimore, Md.: The Johns Hopkins University Press. Reprinted with minor additions in Mwangi S Kimenyi, Robert C. Weiland, and J. D. Von Pischke, eds., 1998. *Strategic Issues in Microfinance.* Aldershot, England: Aldershot.

————. 1998b. "Sugianto, 1939–1998." *MicroBanking Bulletin* 2: 13–14.

Robinson, Marguerite S., and Donald R. Snodgrass. 1987. "The Role of Institutional Credit in Indonesia's Rice Intensification Program." HIID Development Discussion Paper 248. Harvard Institute for International Development, Cambridge, Mass.

Rock, Rachel. 1997. "Bolivia." In C. Churchill, ed., "The Regulation and Supervision of Microfinance Institutions: Case Studies." Occasional Paper 2. Microfinance Network., Washington, D.C.

Rock, Rachel, and María Otero, eds. 1997. *From Margin to Mainstream: The Regulation and Supervision of Microfinance.* Monograph 11. Somerville, Mass.: ACCIÓN International.

Roemer, Michael, and Christine Jones, eds. 1991. *Markets in Developing Countries: Parallel, Fragmented and Black.* San Francisco, Calif.: Institute for Contemporary Studies Press.

Rosenberg, Jerry M. 1993. *Dictionary of Banking.* New York: John Wiley & Sons.

Rosenberg, Richard. 1994. "Beyond Self-Sufficiency: Licensed Leverage and Microfinance Strategy." U.S. Agency for International Development, Washington, D.C.

————. 1996. "Microcredit Interest Rates." CGAP Occasional Paper 1. World Bank, Consultative Group to Assist the Poorest, Washington, D.C.

————. 1999. "A Note on Portfolio Quality Measurement in India's Regional Rural Banks (RRBs)." World Bank, Consultative Group to Assist the Poorest, Washington, D.C.

Rosovsky, Henry, and Kazushi Ohkawa. 1961. "Indigenous Components in the Modern Japanese Economy." *Economic Development and Cultural Change* 9 (3): 476–501.

Roth, Hans-Dieter. 1983. *Indian Moneylenders at Work: Case Studies of the Traditional Rural Credit Markets in Dhanbad District, Bihar.* New Delhi: Manohar.

Russell, S. 1985. "Middlemen and Moneylending: Personalized Trade and Credit in Upland Luzon, Philippines." Occasional Paper. University of the Philippines, School of Economics, Quezon City.

Rutherford, Stuart. 1995. *ASA: The Biography of an NGO.* Dhaka: Association for Social Advancement.

———. 1996. "A Critical Typology of Financial Services for the Poor." London: ActionAid and Oxfam.

———. 1998. "The Savings of the Poor: Improving Financial Services in Bangladesh." *Journal of International Development* 10 (1): 1–15.

———. 2000. *The Poor and Their Money.* New Delhi: Oxford University Press.

Rutherford, Stuart, and others. 1999. "Savings and the Poor: The Methods, Use, and Impact of Savings by the Poor of East Africa." MicroSave-Africa, Kampala, Uganda.

Sainath, Palagummi. 1996. *Everybody Loves a Good Drought: Stories from India's Poorest Districts.* New Delhi and New York: Penguin Books.

Schmidt, Reinhard, and C. P. Zeitinger. 1994. "Critical Issues in Small and Microbusiness Finance." Interdisziplinare Projekt Consult GmbH., Frankfurt, Germany.

———. 1996. "Prospects, Problems, and Potential of Credit-Granting NGOs." *Journal of International Development* 8 (2): 241–58.

Schmit, L. Th. 1991. *Rural Credit between Subsidy and Market: Adjustment of the Village Units of Bank Rakyat Indonesia in Sociological Perspective.* Leiden Development Series 11. Leiden: Leiden University.

Sen, Amartya K. 1999. *Development as Freedom.* New York: Knopf.

Schaefer-Kehnert, Walter, and J. D. Von Pischke. 1984. *Agricultural Credit Policy in Developing Countries.* World Bank Reprint Series 280. Washington, D.C.: World Bank.

Sharma, Miriam. 1978. *The Politics of Inequality: Competition and Control in an Indian Village.* Asian Studies at Hawaii 22. Honolulu, Hawaii: University Press of Hawaii.

Shipton, Parker. 1989. *Bitter Money: Cultural Economy and Some African Meanings of Forbidden Commodities.* Monograph 1. Washington, D.C.: American Anthropological Association.

———. 1991. "Time and Money in the Western Sahel: A Clash of Cultures in Gambian Rural Finance." In Michael Roemer and Christine Jones, eds., *Markets in Developing Countries: Parallel, Fragmented, and Black.* San Francisco: Institute for Contemporary Studies Press.

Siamwalla, Ammar, Chirmsak Pinthong, Mipon Poapongsakorn, Ploenpit Satsanguan, Prayong Nettayarak, Wanrak Mingmaneenakin, and Yuavares Tubpun. 1993. "The Thai Rural Credit System and Elements of a Theory: Public Subsidies, Private Information, and Segmented Markets." In K. Hoff, A. Braverman, and J. E. Stiglitz, eds., *The Economics of Rural Organization: Theory, Practice, and Policy.* New York: Oxford University Press.

Sideri, Sandro. 1984. "Savings Mobilization in Rural Areas and the Process of Economic Development." *Savings and Development* 8 (3): 207–16.

Singh, Karam. 1983. "Structure of Interest Rates on Consumption Loans in an Indian Village." In J. D. Von Pischke, D. W. Adams, and G. Donald, eds., *Rural Financial Markets in Developing Countries: Their Use and Abuse.* Baltimore, Md.: The Johns Hopkins University Press. Extracted from *Asian Economic Review* 10 (4): 471–75 (1968).

Snodgrass, Donald R., and Richard H. Patten. 1991. "Reform of Rural Credit in Indonesia: Inducing Bureaucracies to Behave Competitively." In D. H. Perkins and M. Roemer, eds., *Reforming Economic Systems in Developing Countries.* Cambridge, Mass.: Harvard Institute for International Development,

Spence, Michael. 1973. "Job Market Signalling." *Quarterly Journal of Economics* 87 (3): 355–74.

———. 1974. *Market Signalling.* Cambridge, Mass.: Harvard University Press.

Stiglitz, Joseph E. 1986. "The New Development Economics." *World Development* 14 (2): 257–65.

Stiglitz, Joseph E., and Andrew Weiss. 1981. "Credit Rationing in Markets with Imperfect Information." *American Economic Review* 71 (3): 393–410.

———. 1983. "Incentive Effects of Terminations: Applications to the Credit and Labor Markets." *American Economic Review* 73 (5): 912–27.

———. 1986. "Credit Rationing and Collateral." In J. Edwards, J. Franks, C. Mayer, and S. Schaefer, eds., *Recent Developments in Corporate Finance.* New York: Cambridge University Press.

———. 1987. "Credit Rationing: Reply." *American Economic Review* 77 (1): 228–31.

Sugianto. 1989. "KUPEDES and SIMPEDES." *Asia Pacific Rural Finance* (July–September): 12–14.

———. 1990a. "Development of Rural Agricultural Financial Policy and the Progress and Benefits of BRI's KUPEDES Program." Bank Rakyat Indonesia, Jakarta.

———. 1990b. "Transaction Costs at Small-Scale Banks below the Branch Level." Bank Rakyat Indonesia, Jakarta.

Sugianto, and Marguerite S. Robinson. 1998. "Sustainable Microfinance as Developed by the Bank Rakyat Indonesia." Bank Rakyat Indonesia, Jakarta.

Sugianto, Satriyo Purnomo, and Marguerite S. Robinson. 1993. *Bunga Rampai Pembiayaan Pertanian Pedesaan.* Jakarta: Institute Bankir Indonesia.

Sutoro, Ann Dunham, and Roes Haryanto. 1990. *KUPEDES Development Impact Survey.* Jakarta: Bank Rakyat Indonesia.

Thorner, Daniel. 1953. "Land Reforms in India: Some Speculations." In Daniel Thorner, ed., *The Shaping of Modern India.* Bombay: Allied Publishers.

Timberg, Thomas A., and C.V. Aiyar. 1984. "Informal Credit Markets in India." *Economic Development and Cultural Change* 33 (1): 43–59.

U Tun Wai. 1957. "Interest Rates outside the Organized Money Markets of Underdeveloped Countries." *International Monetary Fund Staff Papers* 6 (1): 80–142.

———. 1977. "A Revisit to Interest Rates outside the Organized Money Markets of Underdeveloped Countries." *Banca Nazionale del Lavoro Quarterly Review* 30 (122): 291–312.

———. 1980. "The Role of Unorganized Financial Markets in Economic Development and in the Formulation of Monetary Policy." *Savings and Development* 4 (4): 259–92.

———. 1992. "What Have We Learned About Informal Finance in Three Decades?" In D.W. Adams and D.A. Fitchett, eds., *Informal Finance in Low-Income Countries.* Boulder, Colo.: Westview Press.

Udry, Christopher. 1993. "Credit Markets in Northern Nigeria: Credit as Insurance in a Rural Economy." In K. Hoff, A. Braverman, and J. E. Stiglitz, eds., *The Economics of Rural Organization: Theory, Practice, and Policy.* New York: Oxford University Press.

UN (United Nations). 1962. "Measures for Mobilizing Domestic Saving for Productive Investment." *Economic Bulletin for Asia and the Far East* 12 (3): 1–26.

USAID (U.S. Agency for International Development). 1973. *Spring Review of Small Farmer Credit.* vols. 1–20. Washington, D.C.

U.S. Department of Labor. 1995. "Forced and Bonded Child Labor." Washington, D.C.

Varian, Hal R. 1989. *Monitoring Agents with Other Agents.* Working Paper 89-18. University of Michigan, Department of Economics, Center for Research on Economic and Social Theory, Ann Arbor.

Versluysen, Eugene. 1999. *Defying the Odds: Banking for the Poor.* West Hartford, Conn.: Kumarian Press.

Vogel, Robert C. 1979. "Subsidized Interest Rates and the Structure of Agricultural Credit in Developing Countries." In Bangladesh Bank, *Problems and Issues of Agricultural Credit and Rural Finance.* Dhaka.

———. 1981. "Rural Financial Market Performance: Implications of Low Delinquency Rates." *American Journal of Agricultural Economics* 63 (1): 58–65.

———. 1984a. "The Effect of Subsidized Agricultural Credit on Income Distribution in Costa Rica." In D. W. Adams, D. H. Graham, and J. D. Von Pischke, eds., *Undermining Rural Development with Cheap Credit*. Boulder, Colo.: Westview Press.

———. 1984b. "Savings Mobilization: The Forgotten Half of Rural Finance." In D. W. Adams, D. H. Graham, and J. D. Von Pischke, eds., *Undermining Rural Development with Cheap Credit*. Boulder, Colo.: Westview Press.

Von Pischke, J. D. 1978. "Towards an Operational Approach to Savings for Rural Developers." *Savings and Development* 2 (1): 3–55.

———. 1983a. "The Pitfalls of Specialized Farm Credit Institutions in Low-Income Countries." In J. D. Von Pischke, D. W. Adams, and G. Donald, eds., *Rural Financial Markets in Developing Countries: Their Use and Abuse*. Baltimore, Md.: The Johns Hopkins University Press.

———. 1983b. "Toward an Operational Approach to Savings for Rural Developers." In J. D. Von Pischke, D. W. Adams, and G. Donald, eds., *Rural Financial Markets in Developing Countries: Their Use and Abuse*. Baltimore, Md.: The Johns Hopkins University Press.

———. 1991. *Finance at the Frontier: Debt Capacity and the Role of Credit in the Private Economy*. Washington, D.C.: World Bank, Economic Development Institute.

———. 1998. "The Financial Systems Approach to Development Finance and Reflections on Its Implementation." Johns Hopkins University, Baltimore, Md.

Von Pischke, J. D., Dale W. Adams, and Gordon Donald, eds. 1983. *Rural Financial Markets in Developing Countries: Their Use and Abuse*. Baltimore, Md.: The Johns Hopkins University Press.

Vyas, N. N. 1980. *Bondage and Exploitation in Tribal India*. Jaipur, India: Rawat Publications.

Webster, Leila, and Peter Fidler. 1996. *The Informal Sector and Microfinance Institutions in West Africa*. Washington, D.C.: World Bank, Africa Industry and Energy Department and Private Sector Development Department.

Weiss, Dieter. 1998. *The Informal Sector in Metropolitan Areas of Developing Countries*. Berlin: Free University of Berlin, Institute of Economics and World Economics.

Wilmington, Martin W. 1983. "Aspects of Moneylending in Northern Sudan." In J. D. Von Pischke, D. W. Adams, and G. Donald, eds., *Rural Financial Markets in Developing Countries: Their Use and Abuse*. Baltimore, Md.: The Johns Hopkins University Press. Extracted from *Middle East Journal* 9: 139–46 (1955).

Wilson, Charles. 1980. "The Nature of Equilibrium in Markets with Adverse Selection." *Bell Journal of Economics* 11 (1): 108–30.

———. 1987. "Adverse Selection." In J. Eatwell, M. Milgate, and P. Newman, eds., *The New Palgrave: A Dictionary of Economics*. New York: Stockton Press, pp. 32–34.

WOCCU (World Council of Credit Unions). 1997. *WOCCU 1996 Statistical Report*. Madison: University of Wisconsin Press.

Women's World Banking. 1996. *Institution Building in Microfinance: Lessons from Funders and Practitioners*. New York: Women's World Banking and United Nations Development Programme.

World Bank. 1984a. *Agriculture Credit: Sector Policy Paper*. 2d ed. Washington, D.C.

———. 1984b. *Employment and Income Distribution in Indonesia*. A World Bank Country Study. Washington, D.C.

———. 1990. *World Development Report 1990: Poverty*. New York: Oxford University Press.

———. 1996a. "A Worldwide Inventory of Microfinance Institutions." World Bank, Sustainable Banking with the Poor project, Washington, D.C.

———. 1996b. "KUPEDES: Indonesia's Model Small Credit Program." *OED Précis 104.* Operations Evaluation Department, Washington, D.C.

———. 1996c. *World Development Report 1996: From Plan to Market.* New York: Oxford University Press.

———. 1997a. "An Inventory of Microfinance Institutions in East Asia and the Pacific." Sustainable Banking with the Poor project, Washington, D.C.

———. 1997b. "An Inventory of Microfinance Institutions in East, Central, and South Africa." Sustainable Banking with the Poor project, Washington, D.C.

———. 1997c. "An Inventory of Microfinance Institutions in Latin America and the Caribbean." Sustainable Banking with the Poor project, Washington, D.C.

———. 1997d. "An Inventory of Microfinance Institutions in South Asia." Sustainable Banking with the Poor project, Washington, D.C.

———. 1997e. "An Inventory of Microfinance Institutions in West Central Africa." Sustainable Banking with the Poor project, Washington, D.C.

———. 1997f. *World Development Indicators 1997.* CD-ROM. Washington, D.C.

———. 1997g. *World Development Report 1997: The State in a Changing World.* New York: Oxford University Press.

———. 2000. *World Development Report 1999/2000: Entering the 21st Century.* New York: Oxford University Press.

———. 2001. *World Development Report 2000/2001: Attacking Poverty.* New York: Oxford University Press.

World Bank News. 1996. "KUPEDES: Indonesia's Model Small Credit Program." From "KUPEDES: Indonesia's Model Small Credit Program" (*OED Precis 104,* World Bank, Operations Evaluation Department, Washington, D.C.).

Wright, Graham A. N. 1999a. "A Critical Review of Savings Services in Africa and Elsewhere." MicroSave-Africa, Kampala, Uganda.

———. 1999b. "Dropouts amongst Ugandan Micro-Finance Institutions." Centre for Microfinance: Kampala, Uganda.

———. 1999c. "Necessity as the Mother of Invention: How Poor People Protect Themselves Against Risk." MicroSave-Africa, Kampala, Uganda.

———. 2000. *Microfinance Systems: Designing Quality Financial Services for the Poor.* London and New York: Zed Books.

Wright, Graham A. N., and others. 1999. "Vulnerability, Risks, Assets and Empowerment—The Impact of Microfinance on Poverty Alleviation, Final Report." MicroSave-Africa and Uganda Women's Finance Trust, Kampala, Uganda.

Yaron, Jacob. 1992a. *Assessing Development Finance Institutions: A Public Interest Analysis.* World Bank Discussion Paper 174. Washington, D.C.

———. 1992b. *Successful Rural Finance Institutions.* World Bank Discussion Paper 150. Washington, D.C.

———. 1994. "What Makes Rural Financial Institutions Successful?" *The World Bank Research Observer* 9 (1): 49–70.

Yaron, Jacob, and McDonald Benjamin Jr. 1997. "Developing Rural Financial Markets." *Finance and Development* 34 (4): 40–43.

Yaron, Jacob, McDonald Benjamin Jr., and Stephanie Charitonenko. 1998. "Promoting Efficient Rural Financial Intermediation." *The World Bank Research Observer* 13 (2): 147–70.

Yaron, Jacob, McDonald Benjamin Jr., and Gerda L. Piprek. 1997. *Rural Finance: Issues, Design, and Best Practices.* ESD Monograph 14. Washington, D.C.: World Bank, Environmentally and Socially Sustainable Development Studies.

Yeats, William Butler. 1921. "The Second Coming." In *Michael Robartes and The Dancer.* Dundrum: Cuala Press.

Yotopoulos, Pan A., and Sagrario L. Floro. 1991. "Transaction Costs and Quantity Rationing in Informal Credit Markets: Philippine Agriculture." In M. Roemer and C. Jones, eds., *Markets in Developing Countries.* San Francisco, Calif.: Institute for Contemporary Studies Press.

Index

Bangladesh. *See also* Association for Social Advancement (ASA); Bangladesh Rural Advancement Committee (BRAC); Grameen Bank
    client ending domestic violence, 114–15
    client managing scarce resources, 107
    client saving for the future, 108–09
    informal credit market, 176, 219n4
    microfinance customers, 55
    microfinance providers, 88–89
    short- and medium-term interest rates, 205
Bangladesh Rural Advancement Committee (BRAC), 73, 89, 90
Bank Dagang Bali (BDB) (Indonesia), xxi, xxxvi, xxxvii, xl, xliv, 67, 232, 256, 270
    ceremonies savings accounts, 247
    client building income with savings, 112
    client saving for children's education, 116
    client using credit and savings products together, 109
    financial systems approach of, 52
    fixed deposit accounts, 259
    informal markets expertise of, 35
    loan funding by savings, 227
    loan policy, 74
    microcredit services, 53
    retirement savings accounts, 248
    savings services, 253, 254
    small loans and voluntary savings services, 28
    sustainability, 98n6
Bankin Raya Karara (BRK) (Niger), 56
Bank of Agriculture and Agricultural Cooperatives (BAAC) (Thailand), 254
Bank Rakyat Indonesia (BRI), xvii, xix, xxi–xxvii, xxxvii–xxxviii, xlii–xliv, 58–67, 104, 156, 201, 261, 264, 270, 272, 273, 274. *See also* BIMAS; KUPEDES; SIMASKOT; SIMPEDES
    Badan Kredit Desa (BKD) and, 66–67
    borrower transaction costs, 212–13
    client starting over using savings, 119
    collateral requirements, 165–66, 168n16, 213
    commercial approach to microfinance, 34, 44n24
    credit unions comparison with, 90–92
    customer examples, 14–16
    economic crisis and savings accounts in, 248
    effective interest rates, 202, 213–16, 222n42
    financial systems approach of, 22–23, 34, 44n24, 88
    fixed deposit accounts, 259
    gradually increasing loan sizes, 164
    Grameen Bank comparison with, 92–97
    high- and low-risk applicant differentiation, 153, 163
    imperfect information and, 162–66
    incentives offset limited liability, 164
    institutional sustainability, 93, 95, 96
    loans funded by savings, 94, 96, 227
    loan losses, 63–64
    loan methodology, 74
    loss ratios, 99n26

Mecca pilgrimages savings accounts, 247
microbanking (unit desa), 3, 8–9, 15–16, 66, 98–99n16, 99n18, 99n24, 231–32
microbanking (unit desa) development, 59–60
microfinance customers, 92
nongovernmental organizations (NGOs) comparison with, 88–89
outreach of, 47, 67, 165–66
performance, 1984–96, 61–64, 99n22
performance, 1996–99, 64–66
profitability, 67, 93–97
restructuring plans, 99n17
savings services, 92–94, 136, 228–29, 253–54, 267n21–22
startup subsidies for, 98n6
sustainability category, 57
transactions frequency study, 255–56
visiting delegations to, 99n27
BANRURAL (Mexico), 144
Bester, H., 156
BIMAS (Bimbingan Massal) (Indonesia), 59, 99n19, 106, 149n5
Black markets, 50
Bolivia. *See also* BancoSol; Fundación para la Promoción y Desarrollo de la Microempresa (PRODEM)
    client providing university education for children, 116
    collateral types in, 221n26
    informal financial brokers, 195
    informal lenders' interest rates, 209, 222n38
    microcredit client competition, 70, 218
    microfinance customers, 55
    microfinance revolution in, 28–29, 33, 34
    Social Emergency Fund, 67
Bonded labor, 17–18, 19. *See also* Attached labor; Moneylenders
    India, 178–79, 207–08, 219n9
Borrowers. *See also* Clients
    defaulting, 188
    food-deficit, 8, 9, 18–19, 20, 43n15
    high interest rates and, 32
    high-risk, 151
    loans to force default, 207–09, 221n36
    low-risk, 151, 153, 163–64
    training programs, 72–73
    transaction costs, 133, 146, 188, 210–13, 222n40–41
Bottomley, Anthony, 180, 194
Bouman, F. J. A., 13, 142, 180, 181–82, 191, 194, 216, 240, 249, 250
Braverman, Avishay, 51, 152, 156, 166n3, 175, 229
Brazil, agricultural credit subsidies in, 144
Buckley, Graeme, 200, 210
Business location security/insecurity, 11

Caisses Populaires d'Épargne et de Crédit (Niger), 227
Calmeadow, xliv, 67, 99n29
Capital
    dead, 233–34

Daley-Harris, Sam, 43n17

Dead capital, 233–34

"Dead mortgage" loans, 206

Debt bondage, 208

Debt farming, India, 178, 207–08, 219n8

Defaulting borrowers, 188
  loans to force, 207–09, 221n36

Default rates
  adverse selection/moral hazard and, 155–56
  informal moneylenders, 161
  political committees and, 145
  subsidized credit programs, 142–44, 149n6

Demand, microfinance, 6, 35–37
  BRI compared with other microfinance institutions, 85–97
  donor funding and, 11, 42n7
  estimates, 10–13, 42n5–6
  market research, 261
  for savings services, 106–07, 224, 225

Deposit accounts, definition of, 265n1

de Soto, Hernando, 233

Development Program Implementation Studies (DPIS) (Indonesia), xliii, 43n11

Dey, S. K., 158

Dichter, Thomas, 110

Disability, saving for, 248

Donald, Gordon, 142, 180

Donors
  benefits of sustainable microfinance institutions to, 264
  failure to recognize savings capacity, 249–50
  microfinance demand and, 11, 42n7
  subsidized credit delivery systems, 3, 7, 71–73, 147–48

Douglis, Carole, 123n6, 123n11

Dunn, Elizabeth, 123n3

Economically active poor. *See also* Borrowers; Clients; Poor people; Savings of the poor
  borrower training and, 73
  misconceptions about, 36
  scope of, 17, 18–19, 20–21
  voluntary savings services and, 30

Economics of Rural Organization, The (Hoff, Braverman, and Stiglitz), 51, 155, 175, 265n3

Ecuador, 118–19, 209

Education
  commercial microfinance and, 37
  of girls, 45n28
  nonformal, 11
  saving for, 116

Effective interest rates
  moneylenders, 14–15, 199–200, 221n32
  moneylenders compared with banks, 132–33, 202, 213–16, 222n42

Emergencies, saving for, 245–46

Ethiopian displaced family support with husband in jail, 118

Expanding/diversifying client enterprises/incomes, 105, 110–14
  building income opportunities with credit, 111–12
  building income opportunities with savings, 112
  developing/financing an enterprise, 111
  expanding income rapidly, 113–14
  gaining business experience, 112–13
  microloans for economically active poor, 110–11
  moneylenders and, 113

Exploitive credit practices, 178–79, 188. *See also* "Malicious," monopolistic moneylenders

Extreme poverty, 17–18, 20–21. *See also* Economically active poor; Poor people
  nonfinancial poverty alleviation tools, 21–22

Feder, Gershon, 176, 218–19n2

Finamérica (Colombia), 98n11. *See also* Corposol; Finansol

Finance at the Frontier (Von Pischke), 175, 180, 194, 199, 204, 216

Finance companies, 160

Financial markets, 49–52
  interactions, 50–51, 98n5
  types, 49–50

Financial savings methods, 135

Financial self-sufficiency, 58, 98n13

Financial Systems and Development (Germidis, Kessler, and Meghir), 175, 176–77, 179, 194, 199, 204, 219n3, 250–51

Financial systems approach, 2, 7, 43n16. *See also* Commercial microfinance
  benefits of, 44n25
  overview, 8
  poverty lending approach compared with, 22–27

Finansol (Colombia), 98n11. *See also* Corposol; Finamérica

Fitchett, Delbert, 181

Five-six loan terms, 16–17, 204, 221n31

Fixed deposit accounts, 258, 259, 267n23

Flat interest rates, 16, 42n10, 43n12, 203

Floro, Segrario L., 189, 192, 195, 196, 199, 204, 206

Flow credit, 187

Food-deficit borrowers, 8, 9, 18–19, 20, 43n15

Foreclosure, loan, 165, 168n19

Formal financial sector
  advice on microfinance to, 35–36
  developing countries, 49, 50–51
  failure to mobilize rural savings, 248–56
  government focus on, 12
  institutional outreach and, 57–58, 98n12
  microfinance demand, 11
  microfinance markets competition and, 134
  microfinance perception by, 34–35
  in rural credit markets, 162
  rural economy penetration, 175

Fundación Integral Campesino (Costa Rica), 57

Foundation for International Community Assistance (FINCA)
  Kyrgyz Republic, 120, 123n17
  Uganda, 111–12, 115–16, 123n11

microfinance revolution in, 28–29, 33–34

savings customers in, 253–54

short- and medium-term interest rates, 204–05

subsidized agricultural credit in, 149n5

voluntary savings in, 28

Inflation, 203, 209, 221n30, 222n37

Informal commercial moneylenders. *See* Moneylenders

Informal credit markets, 126, 130–34. *See also* Moneylenders

market interactions and, 131–32

noncommercial lenders in, 172, 173–74, 216

size of, 174–77, 219n3

Informal economy

developing countries, 49–51

inefficiency, 174

invisibility, 12, 42n8–9

microfinance demand, 11

misconceptions about competition with, 36

size of, 13

Informal Finance: Some Findings for Asia (Ghate and others), 176

Informal savings methods, 134–35, 234–44

advantages and disadvantages of various, 236–37

animals, 235, 238–39

cash, 235, 237

construction materials, 235, 241–42

deposits with informal savings collectors, 235, 242–44, 266n12

financial savings compared with, 244–48

gold, silver, jewelry, and the like, 235, 239

grain and cash crops, 235, 238, 266n10–11

grain and cash crops lent for profit, 235–36, 242

labor obligations, 235, 244

lending cash for profit, 235, 242

raw materials and finished goods, 235, 241

regular savings and credit associations (RESCAs), 235, 240–41

rotating savings and credit associations (ROSCAs), 235, 240–41

Information flows

international and regional, 36–37

in rural communities of developing countries, 157–60, 167n7, 167n9–10

Information gaps, microfinance, 35–36

Infrastructure, microfinance, 35

Institutional savings accounts, 263–64

Institutional sustainability, 28–35, 42n4, 55–58, 98n8–9, 256–62. *See also* Commercial microfinance

bank staff time use and, 146–47

levels and categories of, 56–57

loan products and, 146

paradigm, 73–85

political elite payoffs and, 144–46

preconditions for mobilizing savings, 256–58

prevention of, 142–47

transaction costs for borrowers and, 146

Institution building, commercial microfinance, 36

Integrated Rural Development Programme (IRDP) (India), 211, 222n40, 230, 266n8

Inter-American Investment Corporation, 209

Interest rates. *See also* Effective interest rates; Flat interest rates; Subsidized credit

Bank Rakyat Indonesia, 59

calculation methods, 16, 43n12, 201

client understanding of, 106

data characteristics, 197–98, 201, 221n28

debates about moneylender, 177–87, 219n5

in developing Asia, 201, 203–09, 221n29

loans to force borrower to default, 207–09, 221n36

long-term credit examples, 206–07

for microloans, 29–31, 32–33

moneylenders, 7, 9, 13–17, 42n11, 52, 196–210

moneylenders compared with commercial microfinance institutions, 7, 14–16

poverty lending and, 8

setting, 32–33

short- and medium-term credit examples, 204–05, 221n32–35

tiered, 258–60

very short-term credit examples, 203–04

International Monetary Fund (IMF), xxv

Internet microfinance discussion groups, 36

Investment opportunities, saving for, 245–47

Irregular income streams, saving for, 245–46

Java, village credit organizations, 57. *See also* Badan Kredit Desa (BKD)

Kenya

informal lenders' interest rates, 210

money, categories of among Luo people, 159

Rural Enterprise Programme (K-REP), xliv, 57, 73, 106–07, 113–14, 123n2, 148

Kindleberger, Charles P., xxxv

Korea, Rep. of, informal credit market, 176

KUPEDES (Kredit Umum Pedesaan), 14–15, 59–61, 63N64, 99n20, 254

collateral for, 165

development impact survey, 204–05

interest rates for, 64

noncollateralized small loans, 165

performance, 1984–96, 61–63; 1996–99; 64–66

short- and medium-term interest rates, 204–05

Kyrgyz Republic, 120

Lembaga Perkreditan Desa (LPD) of Bali (Indonesia), 57

Lending. *See* Credit services

Lewis, W. A., 140

Lieberman, Ira W., xvii–xix, xlvi

Limited liability, borrowers', 155, 167n6

Liquid savings accounts, interest-bearing, 258–59, 267n23
Live capital, 234, 265
"Live mortgage" loans, 206
Loan approval and disbursement, 80
Loan collection policies and procedures, 80
Loan funding, 96–97, 227, 232
Loan fungibility, 174, 218n2
Loan portfolio management, 81
Loan products, 80, 186–87, 211–12
    five-six terms, 16–17, 204, 221n31
    terms inappropriate for borrowers' needs, 146
Local finance theories, 125–37
London Labour and the London Poor (Mayhew), 18, 43n14, 196–97
Long, Millard, 196
Long-term investments, saving for, 247
Low-risk borrowers, 151–53, 163–64

Madura (Indonesia), village credit organizations, 57. *See also* Badan
    Kredit Desa (BKD)
Malawi
    Agricultural Credit Agency default rate, 144
    informal lenders' interest rates, 210
Malaysian informal credit market, 176
Malhotra, Mohini, 200, 206, 209, 221n26
"Malicious," monopolistic moneylenders, 178–80, 181, 184–85, 186, 219n6–7
    loans to force borrower to default, 207–09, 221n36
Managers, microfinance, 77–78
Mandatory savings, 7–8, 88, 93–94, 100n39
    Grameen Bank (Bangladesh), 92–94, 229
Mango orchard program, Adilabad, Andhra Pradesh, India, 39–40, 45n27–28
"Market for 'Lemons,' The" (Akerlof), 154
Market penetration techniques, 262
Market interest rates, 29–30
Market research, 258, 261
Maximizing the Outreach of Microenterprise Finance (Christen, Rhyne, and Vogel), 24, 42n4, 42n6
Mayhew, Henry, 18, 43n14, 196–97
McCourt, Frank, 167n10
McKinnon, Ronald, 222n44
Media in rural communities, 160
Mexico, 117–18, 144, 176, 209
Mibanco (Peru), 108, 148
MicroBanking Bulletin, The (MBB), xlvi, 33, 41n2, 58, 98n13
Microcredit Summit, 25–27, 43n17, 44n18
Microenterprises, characteristics of, 11–12
Microentrepreneurs, self-employed, 11
    skills and knowledge of, 12
Microfinance, 2, 3. *See also* Commercial microfinance; Credit unions; Demand, microfinance; Moneylenders; Non-governmental organizations (NGOs); Paradigms, microfinance
    definitions, 9–10, 41n3
    demand estimates, 10–13, 42n5

extreme poverty and, 22
financial systems compared with poverty lending, 22–27, 44n18
importance of, 37–41, 44n25
informal moneylenders and, 13–17
poor people's understanding of, 105–10
poverty alleviation toolbox in, 19–22
poverty and, 17–19
revolution in, 10
supply of services estimated, 9–13, 41n2
sustainable microfinance institutions and, 28–35, 42n4
Microfinance practitioner networks, 36
MicroRate, 70–71
MicroSave-Africa, 244, 261
Miracle, Marvin, 175
Mommartz, Rochus, 252
Moneylenders, 51–52, 167n13, 170–222
    BancoSol lending rates compared with, 165–66, 202, 213–15
    banks as competitors, 162
    borrowers' noninterest costs, 210–13
    BRI lending rates compared with, 15–16, 42n10, 165–66, 202, 213–15
    competition, 36, 216–18
    credit layering, 189, 192–93, 220n18, 220n22
    development perspectives on, 183–86
    expertise/scope of, 172–73
    funds availability, 189–90, 220n21
    information flows, 158, 161, 165–66
    interest rates, 7, 9, 13–17, 42n11, 196–210, 213–16, 221n32, 222n39, 222n42
    interest rates data characteristics, 197–98, 201, 221n28
    interest rates debates, 130–31, 177–87, 219n5
    interest rates examples, 199–201
    interest rates examples, Asia, 201, 203–09, 221n29
    interlinked transactions, 131–32, 188–89, 220n20
    leaving market, 220n19
    loan characteristics, 187–90
    loan terms, 16
    "malicious" monopolistic, 178–80, 181, 184–85, 186, 219n6–7
    market size, 174–77, 215, 222n43
    microfinance services, 28
    monopolistic competition model, 160–62, 182–86, 218n7, 220n17
    policy perspectives, 186–87
    products, 186–87
    risk information availability, 156
    scale of business, 190–93, 220–21n23–24
    transaction costs, 193–96
    "value for the people," 180–82, 185–86, 220n13, 220n15
    very short-term credit interest rates examples, 203–04
Money, categories of, 167n11
    Luo people, Kenya, 159

Profitability, 10
    Badan Kredit Desa (BKD), 67, 168n18
    BancoSol, 68–70
    Bank Rakyat Indonesia (BRI), 63–66, 95–96
    commercial credit and savings services, 29–31
    imperfect information paradigm and, 162–66
    of mobilizing poor people's savings, 251–56
Proshika (Bangladesh), 89, 90

Quality of life enhancement, 105, 114–17
    ending domestic violence, 114–15
    overcoming malnutrition, 115–16
    providing university educations for children, 116
    saving for children's education, 116

Rahman, Atiq, 219n4
Rating agencies, microfinance, 36, 54
Ratcliffe, Robin, 123n5, 123n9, 123n12–13, 123n15–16
Raw materials and finished goods as savings, 235, 241
Reddy, N.V. Raja, 45n27
Refugees, displaced, 18
Regional Rural Banks (RRBs) (India), 266n8
    borrower transaction costs, 211, 222n40–41
    fixed deposit accounts, 259
    political committees and loan defaults, 145
    savings services, 47, 227, 230
Regular savings and credit associations (RESCAs), 50, 98n3, 235, 240–41
Regulation. *See* Governments
Religious obligations, saving for, 247–48
Réseau des Caisses Populaires (RCP) (Burkina Faso), 254–55
Reserve Bank of India, 266n19
RESULTS International, 43–44n17
Rhyne, Elisabeth, 22–23, 24–25, 58, 218
Rischard, Jean-Francois, 41n2
Risks, moneylender, 193, 195–96, 219n12
Robinson, Joan, 182
Rosenberg, Richard, 30–33, 41n2, 58, 98n8, 201
Roth, Hans-Dieter, 207
Rotating savings and credit associations (ROSCAs), 29, 50, 160, 224, 235, 240–41
Rural communities of developing countries, information flows in, 157–60, 167n7, 167n9–10
Rural Credit Cooperatives (RCCs) (China), 145–46, 227, 250, 259, 266n9
    savings services, 47, 227, 230–31
Rural credit markets
    competition, 216–18, 222n44
    imperfect information paradigm and, 152–53, 160–62
Rural economies, misconceptions about, 36
Rural Financial Markets in Developing Countries (Von Pischke, Adams, and Donald), 180
Russell, S., 192

Rutherford, Stuart, 44n19, 44n26, 74–75, 107, 123n4, 200, 205, 237, 241, 243, 266n12

SafeSave (Bangladesh), 38–39, 44n26, 108–09, 123n4
Sainath, Palagummi, 178
Savings accounts, definition of, 265n1
Savings and Development, 249
Savings and credit associations, 160, 216, 224, 240–41
Savings collectors, 26, 44n19, 159, 224
    deposits with, 235, 242–44, 266n12
Savings of the poor, 126, 134–36, 249–56
    informal methods, 234–48
    preconditions for mobilizing by microfinance institutions, 256–58
    scale issues, 135–36
    supply-leading finance theory and, 140
    use of savings, 74–75
Savings services, institutional, 44n22, 99n21, 224–67. *See also* Informal savings methods; Voluntary savings
    access to, 38–39
    Bank Dagang Bali (BDB), 253–54
    Bank Rakyat Indonesia (BRI), 59–60, 64–65, 253–54
    beneficiaries of, 263–65
    comparison of BRI and Grameen Bank, 92–94
    credit services and, 29–31, 72, 109, 162, 264
    designing and pricing products, 258–60
    desirable characteristics of, 29
    extreme poverty and, 22
    financial viability of, 251–56
    formal sector failure to provide, 248–56
    informal savings compared with, 244–48
    institutions not permitting, 227, 228
    institutions successful in, but not in credit, 227, 229–31
    institutions successful in credit and, 227, 231–32
    institutions weak in, but successful in credit 227, 228–29, 266n6–7
    institutions weak in lending and, 227, 231
    interest rates, 254–55, 259–60
    market penetration techniques, 262
    mobilization patterns, 227–34, 266n5
    NGOs, 100n38, 227, 228
    operating principles, 81–82
    "penny economy" microfinance view, 248–51, 266n18
    pilot projects in, 261–62
    policy implications, 232–34
    poverty lending and, 7–8
    program sequencing, 260–62
    preconditions, 256–58
    transactions, frequency of, 255–56
Schmidt, Reinhard, on mobilizing savings, 251–56, 267n20
Self-confidence of poor people, 37, 39–41, 105, 121–22
Self-Employed Women's Association (SEWA) (India), 35, 52, 53
Semiformal financial institutions, 49–52